THE BYERLEY
TURK

By the same author

The Tippling Philosopher (2004)
Vagabond (1992)
Saddletramp (1989)

THE BYERLEY
TURK

Jeremy James

MERLIN UNWIN BOOKS

Published by:
Merlin Unwin Books
Palmers House
7 Corve Street
Ludlow
Shropshire SY8 1DB
U.K.

www.merlinunwin.co.uk

Designed and set in Sabon by Merlin Unwin Books
Printed in Great Britain by Jellyfish Print Solutions

ISBN 978 1 873674 98 7

CONTENTS

ACKNOWLEDGEMENTS

This book has been a long journey. On horse. In libraries. In Public Record Offices, museums, messes; in regimental headquarters. On battle sites. On foot. With friends. In academia. Across years. Information on the Byerley Turk and his owner has been hard to glean.

Little has come by whole page of revelation: most has been by way of excavation, minutely, line by line, a snatch here, a paragraph there, a word here, an anecdote somewhere else, a letter, a manuscript in another country: a story, sometimes, from a passing horseman; a chance encounter, someone with a document.

The quest has taken me overseas. On horse: by way of Turkey, Bulgaria, Serbia, Romania, Hungary, Austria, Germany, Belgium, France, our own English shores; and then Ireland – by car. Language has not been a slight interlude – particularly when the languages concerned were ancient: Ottoman records in Arabic script, in Ottoman Turkish. There was also Polish, German, Latin, and old court French.

Even English manuscripts are difficult to read and after days of poring over the things in the PRO in Kew, I threw my hands up while trying to read Villiers', Master of the Horse Accounts from the 17th century. They were beautiful, wonderfully decorative, presented in a hide scroll and I couldn't read a word.

Yet, as time went by, I became more proficient at reading manuscripts – I do not claim to be an historian.

The London Port books were a struggle and I don't envy anyone dipping into those: they were about a foot thick each, weighed a ton, I read every page and won a half a line.

Yet: it has been such a privilege to write this book: a privilege to sit in these libraries around Britain, in Europe, in Turkey. I am sure that professional academics regard it as a matter of course but I found turning the manuscript-gloved pages bewitching. Whether it was the Bodleian or York Minster, the sheer beauty of the calligraphy, particularly of Ottoman manuscripts, I found a joy beyond words. These things amazed me.

I also found the records moving, vivid to read: that lives had been lived and forfeited while the Byerley Turk, the horse, battled from one end of Europe to the other. How kingdoms fell, how tens of thousands of men, women, children and horses were lost.

I have a lot of people to thank for helping me: first of all CuChullaine and Basha O'Reilly of the Long Riders' Guild. Thank you for your continual support and for the extraordinary lengths to which you went to supply me with reference material, ancient books and manuscripts, parcelling me with literally hundredweights of valuable material from libraries all over the world. Your insights, encouragement, constant help, diurnal support, your close understanding of the complexities of the subject and how to get it down on paper were of inestimable value to me and I thank you from the bottom of my heart. You are good friends. You are extraordinary. Thank you too Kath Pinnervaria of Kentucky University Library for sourcing so many obscure titles: they were exquisite, complex to read but contained good, solid detail. Thanks too to the staff of the libraries, who were so kind and helpful everywhere I went: the Duke Humphries library of The Bodleian, Oxford; The British Library – all reading rooms – the staff at York Minster, the staff in Lyme Regis library, Northallerton Records Office, the three sweet girls who set by their studies in the public library in Beyazit, Istanbul and spent days rooting out information on ancient Turkish breeds of horse for me. Thank you.

Thanks to the staff and students of Bosphorus University library and of Istanbul University libraries. Also to the Jockey Club in Istanbul, for opening the doors of their collection of books. Thanks to Tony Sweeney, Ireland's premier racing correspondent, for his kindness, his astounding knowledge and for allowing the likes of a common horse coper such as me, to leaf through his books, not one of which were printed after 1720. Matthew Gammon and John Killen of the Linen Hall Library Belfast, bless you, the staff of the Public Records Office in both Kew and Public Records office in Belfast, you also. Thanks to the extraordinary, out-of-the-way-help I received in the National Library in Dublin and the Newspaper Library round the corner, who stuck around on a Saturday morning for me. Thank you very, very much. That's also to the staff on all the battle sites mentioned in this book: the presentation of information of these sites was superb.

Expertise is always admirable. My special thanks to Aisling MacMahon from the Battle of Boyne site, to Boyd Rankin for his exposition on gunnery, and to Lynne for her talk on the horses in the battle.

Wonderful. Thanks to Julie Cruise for your lucid description of the Battle of Aughrim and for supplying some oblique detail that I would have learned nowhere else. Thanks to Jan Watkins, my local librarian in Knighton for putting up with endless peculiar requests and my deepest thanks to Forrest Anderson for the early work on military research. Nigel Walker thank you for your help with the 17th Century Queen Dowager's regiment. Thank you Özlem Direk, Barbaros Bostan and Aziz Ozben for translations from Turkish. My thanks to Anne Peters in America for sending data on the Byerley Turk's offspring, and to Caroline Anne Baldock for a lot of information on both what it was like to sail in a wood square rigger, which I culled from her wonderful unpublished diary of her crossing of the Atlantic in the Golden Hinde. Thank you also Caroline, for all your help and advice on both thoroughbreds and the Turanian horse. Your wisdom and insights have been, to me, immeasurably kind and helpful. Thanks to you Louise Firouse in Iran for your help and depth of knowledge on the Turkomen and their horses. The whisky is on me, next time. Thank you also Robbie Campbell for the more esoteric approach: you were spot-on. I found the hard evidence. Thanks too to Mrs. K. Haralambos, whose excellent book *The Byerley Turk* published in 1989 I read with interest and takes up where my own work leaves off, in that it follows the tail male racing line of the Byerley Turk, whereas my own work deals with his history.

I owe a longstanding debt of gratitude to The International League for the Protection of Horses, for whom I worked for many years. With the ILPH I travelled the world as an equine nutritionist, which afforded me insights into world breeds and herbal medicines. Then finally I worked in a really tough field: to report on the transport of live horses for slaughter. And then I really learned. That was tough ground. Through it, quite apart from the main work we did, I gathered information on the breeds of horses cast into this trade and because I stood in the feed and watering stations watching them pass on, I was the one who had to collate it, and that was hell. Not because of the job. Because of the indiscriminatory way in which the Italian horsemeat consumer market is fed. It's a long story.

While writing this book, through the ILPH I found, obliquely, regimental information I needed to know. Their present Chief Executive, Brigadier John Smales, had links I discovered with the Byerley Turk in the 17th Century. Other names in their Council I encountered in my work – Maitland Carew, Fenwick, Villiers, Gilbey – there are plenty more. There was something else too. I became fascinated by the many paintings of the Byerley Turk. There are five of which I am aware. They were not easy to track down, so I went to the Council Members of the ILPH, made up from Britain's Great and Good, who ought to know. And they did. Colonel John

Sharples – thank you John for the trace to that painting and the place I suspected it might be: with your regiment, the descendants of Byerley's Carabiniers. The Royal Scots Greys. It was Colonel Byerley's show, with his great bay, not grey, between 1689-1690 that sent across the years an integrity, which Robert Byerley begun, and a name I shall never forget, nor forget to honour: a man with whom I had the greatest pleasure to work: Colonel George Stephen. My thanks also to Dr Douglas Munro, former Director of the ILPH and to Brigadier John Smales, the present Chief Executive.

Thanks to Milos Pavlovic, ex Chief Veterinary Officer in Serbia for the guided tour of Serbia and then the great fortress of Belgrade, upon which, the Byerley Turk once stood. Thank you Milos for details on the Sultan's daughter's holdings in the Balkans at the time and for the trouble you took on my behalf.

Thanks to all those people who put me and my horses up when I was riding much of the route described in this book, and to the Lipizzaner Museum in Vienna for information on the evacuation of Karster horses from Vienna in 1683.

I should like to thank Merlin and Karen Unwin for your unflinching support during the making of this book, for comprehending its dimension in the first place and for not throwing a fit when I was months late with the manuscript. It has been a real pleasure to work with you. Your rolling interest in the work and revelations the research kept on disclosing were of real value to me. Thanks to Jo Potter and Gillian Bissell in the Merlin Unwin office for what is bound to be a lot of work.

Helen Bradbury for your support, I offer my most profound gratitude. There were bleak moments: only you know: dark hours when I was struggling and didn't think I could do it. Your reassurance was vital then. You know as a writer yourself that a carefully delivered word of advice can turn pages of blank despair to prolific output.

Lastly, I have two old friends who made a lot of this journey with me. Not only did they cover the landscape physically, east to west, but when at home, they were my daily companions. Writing is a lonely task, but I was lucky: I had them. Two old horses, Gonzo and Karo who forced me to take them for daily walks up the hill when I would otherwise have become bound to my computer and made myself thoroughly ill. They are two old friends who forced me to attend to them, every day. In the long months this book took to write, they not only chivvied me to exercise but acted as models for me, causing me to include things I would otherwise have overlooked, and reminded me, every day, that this was a book about a horse: a horse set against his historical background. I have made it my business to try to stave off any drift to sentimentality. I have endeavoured to keep the horse as a horse, although I felt obliged to cut out the greater libidinous exercises of keeping a stallion, because had I have stuck to absolute detail in this regard this would have read like a horse porn story. Stallions, to those who have not handled them, make no attempt to disguise their energies and can be, and usually are, acutely embarrassing at exactly the wrong moment. I have not omitted it all: just the day-to-day diversions to which they are prone.

If I have failed in any of this or failed any of you, then I have no one else to blame but myself.

Jeremy James
July 2005

11

'Tis all a Chequer-board of Nights and Days,
Where Destiny with Men for Pieces plays:
Hither and Thither moves, and mates, and slays,
And one by one back in the Closet lays.

Rubáiyát of Omar Khayyám

PROLOGUE

Ahmed Paşa

The old horse was asleep. His head was down, his eyes were shut and his ears were drooping.

It was a little after five thirty in the afternoon. The sun was melting after a scorching day. The horse was exhausted, covered in flies and he wanted to go home.

He'd spent the day slogging round Çal dragging an iron-wheeled flatbed loaded with wood shuttering, cement, sand and breeze blocks and now it was time to quit.

And there he swayed in the shafts of his cart, fast asleep, with his filthy mane and stringy tail, with his big wormy belly and four plate-shod, unevenly cut feet.

His owner, Zoran, wanted 375,000 Turkish lira for him – about $400 – I could afford that. As I reached to pat the horse to confirm his price, he flattened his ears and flashed his long yellow teeth. When I tried to pick up his feet he took a wild hack at me. When I ran a hand across his back he shook it off. He was as mean an old horse as you can get but he had that indefinable something about him, I don't know what it is, maybe you know what it is. As the sun fell down amongst the hot tin shacks I thumbed the money into Zoran's hands and spreading his arms in a gesture of ownership passing, his horse, Ahmed Paşa, was mine.

And he wanted him out of his life right there and then. No question of one more night in his stable – no: it was now. Get him out! Take him away! Now!

Quite rightly, the horse refused. Why should he go anywhere with some pink misfit speaking no known tongue? No, to hell with him. It was time to rest.

It gave the locals plenty to scoff at as I wrestled him under his new saddle and saddlebags to the edge of the town. It gave them loads to cackle at as I struggled and pulled and tugged, got kicked and ducked his flaying front feet.

In the last embers of sunlight and despair I lashed a jersey round his head to blindfold him, to trick him, to whoops of derision from the stone-throwing, wrong-end-of-town-gang come to guffaw at the cowboy making his oh-so-cool lope into the sunset on his spanking new horse.

I kept the blindfold on until we were well clear of Çal and its lights, but before I took it off I turned him in circles to confound his direction. The knots popped undone, and the jersey dropped from his face.

It took a long time to earn his trust after that. And he made me crawl for it.

The Anatolian plateau of Turkey is beautiful: high and windblown, with pearl white houses and oyster-shell towns. It is silver-threaded by the wandering river Menderes with its waving banks of grey-green poplars, patchwork fields of attar roses and crank-handled olive trees. Stopping on a high bluff, Ahmed Paşa turned to gaze over this tableau – I was leading him on foot at the time. With his big dark eyes and ears pricked, he drank it all up, as though absorbing a landscape he knew he had more right to be in than I, to which he belonged and I didn't. He stared at it for about half an hour, in silence, then suffuse with the rhapsody, threw me a look, as if to say: 'See, peasant, what I am.' With a swish of his tail, he pushed past me and stepped magnificently up into the mountain.

The air, the high-charged air and strong spring grass did him good. The constant walking did him good. It did him a lot of good. He became a different horse: in front of my eyes, he metamorphosed from an acid old cart horse into a snorting, fully-blown stallion. Pride suddenly swelled inside him. Ancestry surged in his veins. His muscles bulged, he chest expanded, his neck crested, his big eyes glittered and he neighed at the top of his piercing voice at the high flying world we kept getting lost in. He missed nothing: not a single thing escaped his notice: not the foxes nor the swallows that buzzed us nor the eagles that wheeled and mewed above our heads, nor the tortoises that struggled, to his disbelief, slowly across his path.

And he became fit. He became very fit. His fitness removed patches of skin from the palms of my hands.

Without warning, he'd rip the reins from my hands, tuck his head between his knees and go broncoing off for a mile or two then jab to a sudden halt. Pouring with sweat, clinging onto the reins with skinned hands and yelling my head off we'd go hurtling away again, in another direction, where he'd flick me off his shoulder like a rag-doll.

And then I couldn't catch him.

He wouldn't gallop off or disappear out of sight. He'd stay just beyond arm's reach, swiping at grasses, swishing his tail, sighing and yawning, and edging away each time I lunged for or crept up on him. It was game he played for hours.

In those moments I confess to having dark thoughts. If I had had a gun I think I would have shot him. Certainly I felt like leaving him to the mercy of the flies and the sun, getting on a bus and cursing my rotten luck all the way home.

When I was wrung out, parched, drained and totally defeated, when I had had absolutely enough, had thrown my hands up and bawled out: 'Stuff you then!' and gone stalking off across the mountain to I know not where nor how since he had my saddle and saddlebags, passport and money – only then would he yield.

Wearily I'd climb back on. Then he'd take me plunging into chasms and over sheet rock and burst hot and lusty and sparkly-eyed into lost mountain villages as darkness plummeted in that electricity-less land.

After about a month he settled down. Then we spent heady hours gliding through groves of olives and through willy-nilly ransacked mausolea of that travertine stone you find in Turkey. Hoopoes swept up from the grass, sheep bells clonked in the valleys below; from far away came the bark of dogs lost to sight. We wandered in amongst the sarcophagi, jumped across fluted columns lying amongst weeds; we tiptoed beneath crumbling, triumphal arches standing nowhere in particular with no indication of who had put them there, when or why.

We shared everything together: cuts, bruises, torn skin, rope-burns, wind, rain, sun, flies, ticks and drank the clear, sweet water of springs, horse-troughs and sweep-wells we found along our way.

As we trekked through our solitary world, I became aware of something: a legacy that had been lost. We saw few horses and certainly saw none of quality. Yet hanging on stalls in street fairs and lying about in sheds and stables in the villages were clues and tell-tale signs that once, this landscape had been filled with horses. I found ancient saddles, riddled with rot and of a design you do not find in the west; I picked up rusty, old, intricately tooled Islamic float stirrups; ancient bridles, strange bits, filigreed and made of different metals. And village women were still plaiting horsehair ribbons and still making coarse wool grooming mittens.

One evening Ahmed Paşa took me slithering down a muddy pattika – little path – into a smoky village. It lay deep in a valley. There was no tarmac road, no track you could run a wheeled vehicle down. The houses were wooden and small. It felt forsaken, strange and other-worldly. I dismounted beside the village çaylevi (café) – there is always a village çaylevi. Two old men eyed me in silence.

The village mukhtar (the headman) offered me a palliasse in a room with a beaten earth floor for the night and Ahmed Paşa was led away to a stable where he was fed and watered.

When I went to visit him before turning in, I found the two old men muttering quietly to each other in the gloom beside him.

'Iyi akşamlar', they said: good evening. Turkish is a lovely, euphonic language. And then, 'At çok güzel', they said quietly: nice horse.

I was proud of that moment. 'Yes,' I replied, 'very strong. Thinks for himself.'

They bid me goodnight and turned to leave and one of them hovered and looked back. 'He's a Turkish horse,' he said.

'Yes,' I said. 'I bought him in Çal.'

He nodded. 'He's not pure,' he said.

'That makes two of us.'

'He has spirit,' he said.

I smiled. 'I have the scars to prove it.'

'That's right for that kind of horse,' he said, waved, bid me goodnight and left.

My ride round Turkey turned into a ride to England and I arrived many months later on a Criollo horse, and not on Ahmed Paşa.

His memory haunts me still: barely a day has gone by that I have not thought about him. He might have been the most brilliant horse in the world. He might have been the worst.

But what he had was something you don't find much in horses these days: he was his own master. I never owned Ahmed Paşa.

He suffered me to keep him.

He suffered me to feed and to water him, to go with him around Turkey and to ride him down to the sea.

It was he who owned me, and I knew it.

He was impossible in almost every way because he was packed with ego and passion and fire.

What coursed though his heart, red and hot, what made his sinew tremble, held his nostrils quivering, what pricked his ears, crested his neck and glittered in his big black eyes was blood and ancestry. Even years of apathy and chance breeding, diluted, sullied and muddied, could not alter that. His ancestry was there, ablaze, screaming and bursting with pride.

Over the years, I dug into Turkish history, overturned the libraries, blew the dust off the books and combed the shelves. I searched the universities in Europe and in Istanbul for glimpses of the horses of the Turks. They are almost impossible to find. It's as though history has tried to eradicate them utterly. But they were there: they were there.

Across those years my dreams were slowly filled with ghostly images of a wild-eyed, dark, proud, blood-spattered, fiery Turk stallion with his bow-wielding rider, in the smoke and fury of battle, lashing out, hacking, thrusting, biting, fighting, kicking – surviving.

This one, Ahmed Paşa, is for you.

Pureblood

– Men without horses are nothing.

Sparks fly from the fire into the darkness where they hang and glow in the scrub, red as pi-dogs' eyes. Above hovers a yellow moon.

– Men without horses are worse than nothing: they are the rayah, the cattle, the common herd.

A goatskin is fisted round the circle: lips smack against its brown leathery, sticky top as they gulp the koumiss, the fermented milk of the mare. Beyond in the darkness, the horses move, dust swirls, a whinny, a lost call, a wail. A stick is thrust into the flames. A circle of faces, mops of black hair, lamella armour, coarse silk, the spluttering sheep carcase spread-eagled on a web of sticks drips over the flames.

– The rayah huddle in squalor in their reeking gers and fear for their miserable lives. They hoard their precious rugs and cowrie shells. They gloat over them. They dig roots with their swollen hands. They hide their faces from the sun and the wind and they stare into the dirt. They stink of the filth of sheep and of camels, they crawl into their felts beneath the stars and do not know the glory of the night.

A hand arcs in the flickering flames: above, the stars shine in exquisite clarity, a spray of diamonds on black velvet.

– They know nothing of the purity of the hoof and the breath of our sacred horses.

A calloused finger points to the hooves shifting beyond the glow of the fire, and returns to rest on the curve of a compound bow. Hands remain glued to bows: small sinewy creations, strong and hard as the men who grip them. Their dark eyes flicker in the firelight, mesmerised by the fine hard face and the harsh voice of the charismatic in their midst, their leader.

– They lie in dark ignorance of the whispering steppe and the mighty, everlasting plains. Their feet know only the soil they are fettered to, like the dung of their animals and the shells of dead scorpions. They know not the white snow-clad mountains and the clear rivers of silvered fish. They clutch their infested bundles with their blackened fingers, and creep, in their rags, from this place to that place. They are vermin. We shall destroy them.

– We shall seize their women and shatter their possessions: we shall steal their sheep and drive away their camels. We shall kill their dogs, set ablaze their gers and lay waste everything they own even unto the last drop of their bile-coloured blood.

DESERT, EASTERN PERSIA, 1180

Nerini is a pretty little girl, fourteen years old and only daughter of Kemal Başkaya. Such a pretty name, Nerini, Ring-Around-The-Moon, she is a nomad, a wanderer, yo-yoing wool on a hand-held jenny out in the glare of the Kavirian sun.

With her hands set to her work, her eyes to her flock, her mind elsewhere, she hums a strange, terse little tune. She does not know that today she will weep and scream. She does not know that her father and brothers will be dispatched before her eyes; that her animals will be swept away and her home will be torn to pieces. She does not know.

In the scorching emptiness where she walks, her destiny flies toward her. She does not know that today in the bloodbath, in the fury of hoof, blood, dust and air, she will be wed.

How can this be? The desert is empty. She knows only her family, her camels, her sheep, her dogs and goats. She does not know any man.

The crunching her feet make on the dry, gravelly floor as she walks, appears immensely loud. The tune she hums seems loud. She can hear the grit under her feet; she can hear the sheep chewing and the dry clonk of their bells even though they are one hundred paces away. She sees the nazar boncugu, the Evil Eye, the blue beads about her animals' necks

20

twinkle in the sun. She hears the camels' great bellies rumbling.

Six months in the mountains, two on the plains, criss-crossing red Kizilijar, she throws stones at the long-eared foxes that slip amongst the sheep, dangerously close to the lambs. Wandering through the salt bush and tragacanth watching desert wheatears burst up from the low, brittle branches; setting traps in marmot holes and hurling pebbles at bustards, her tribe moves with the light.

As the sun beats the Kizilijar into a baking furnace, they drove their flocks north to the fire temples and towers of silence in the high Khorosan and the Mazandaran for the long, hot summer.

Life for her is spent in two parts: by day beneath the skies and by night beneath felt. The ger she inhabits with her family, is made of felt. It reeks of smoke and rancid sheep-fat. Her clothes reek of smoke and rancid sheep-fat. Her clothes are sticky with fat. Her golden hands, blemished with a striking mottled pink pigmentation on her fingers, are sticky with fat. Her deep auburn hair has never known water and is glossy and fine and surprisingly clean under her brightly coloured head scarf, edged with tiny cowrie shells. Her teeth are even and white.

Her tight, many-buttoned bodice is made of taffeta. Her heavy skirt is fashioned of coarse striped cotton, dyed red and green, held tight to the waist with plaited wool, black and white. She wears naal, fashioned from one single strip of camel hide, bound round and round to make strong, long-lasting sandals. The instep of her small feet and the backs of her hands are a hennaed gallery of whorls and wheels, four legged creatures, camels or goats or sheep or all three mixed into one fantastical beast, with stars and a crescent moon daubed on her golden skin.

She yo-yos the jenny, watching the two little crossed sticks that make it spin and gather the wool from her hand, this way and that way, yo-yoing, round and round and round. She senses her animals grazing quietly under the high, hot sun.

Something flickers on the edge of her vision.

The distance is changed: a small cloud of brown dust smudges the hot, blinding horizon. This cloud rises higher and higher so that in its mirage it seems to sink lower and lower into the polished desert floor. Gradually, the cloud stains the mercury in one long, amber lozenge. The girl stops her jenny spinning and narrows her brown eyes above her high, fine cheekbones.

She squints as the cloud strings out.

In miraculous symmetry it becomes longer and taller and taller and longer. A soft drumming, like the roll of distant thunder, gives it life. The sound increases.

The light in the girl's eyes intensifies. Moving her head from side to side, like an owl, she searches the strange rising lozenge and perceives, suddenly, within its far-off silver centre, flickering brown blobs and swiftly moving black tendrils. Her mouth opens, she blinks, then looks deeper. The jenny drops.

She shrieks a high sharp note, like an eagle.

She runs.

She runs in panic, and shrieks again.

Her sudden alarm, the volume of her high-pitched voice, causes her sleepy flock to flick up their heads in one movement. The dogs bark. The camels lope in confused direction: the fat-tailed sheep run clumsily after her.

The girl's speed has increased and now she is running flat out in her long, thick calico skirts. She runs with tremendous energy. Her head scarf falls but she does not turn to pick it up.

Ahead of her, a small gathering of gers huddle in a peaceful pall of communal smoke.

The canvas flap of one is thrown open. Two roughly dressed, short men, emerge. Narrowing their eyes they see the girl racing toward them, shrieking and pointing at the rising tower of dust.

A strange sound follows, like a whip that fails to crack, followed by a *thud*.

The sound occurs three times.

The first man to emerge from the ger, staggers back.

The whipping noise sounds again, followed by *thud, thud, thud*.

This first man falls, heavily, against the ger and slides to the ground. He stares in bewilderment at the three arrows protruding from his chest. The puzzlement on his face is matched by the other man's, who stares, stupidly, at the arrows. He holds out a hand and attempts to speak. *Thud, thud, thud.* Two arrows fly straight into his neck and one straight into his temple. Blooded grey clots splash onto the brown felt of the ger. He drops to the ground without a sound.

Horsemen appear, suddenly, in a storm of dust. It is as though they had been kneaded up, magically, from the floor of the desert in a vapour of horses and the djinn of the raw earth. Inexplicably they are in amongst the people and their felt homes. Lassoes seize the tops of the gers. The air is filled with screams. The girl darts in and out of the gers avoiding the horseman. The dust is thick. The horsemen are agile. She weaves between the gers fleeing from the knives, the arrows, the hooves.

A hand stretches out. The girl struggles as she feels her weight leave her feet.

She sees the brown side of a sweating horse. Her face is banged into a horse's rippling shoulder.

The grip upon the scruff of her neck is powerful. Her face is pulled through a horse's mane. The horse continues to rack. She is dragged bodily up across the pommel of a saddle. Her head fills with the sound of her own pounding heart, her own terror, the beating hooves, the shouts of a man. She chokes on the long hair of the horse's mane. Her face is pushed into the horse's neck. She flails her arms to free herself, and kicks but the grip is strong. Her legs are trapped by the horseman. She knows only the racking of the horse, the flying mane, the pounding hooves, the floor roaring past under her in a brown blur.

Powerless over the hands that pin her to the saddle and the horse's neck she sees the gers topple through her blinded wet eyes, through the dust and heads of horses, and bodies of passing horsemen. The gers yawn upward, exposing their rich, red interiors. Dowry boxes fly: precious cowrie shells are spilled on the desert floor. Men, her brothers, her father, fall. Another woman screams. She watches as her fat-tailed sheep are snatched off their feet and bound with leather thongs by dark men on racking horses. The camels are driven away. Her dogs are quilled with arrows.

Tribal rugs lie scattered on the ground. Trampled cooking pots glint in the sun.

The gers lie prone upon their sides, like the bodies of great dead whales, their lattice of bleached bones exposed.

More and more horsemen pass. The dust cloud thickens. The scent of horse strengthens. The sound rises.

Their numbers never seem to end. On and on they flow in a wall of brown dust.

Suddenly their numbers cease.

The great dust cloud recedes with the rumbling hooves and softens into the distance. The whirlwind has passed.

The desert floor is empty.

The dogs have gone. The camels have gone.

What was, is buried beneath the dust of the hooves of thousands and thousands of horses.

Only a hand-held jenny rocks in small eddies of hot air out in the glare of a Kavirian sun.

Dust descends.

Silence returns.

– 2 –

The Seyis

The seyis – a groom – is sitting in the deep shadow of a locust tree. The long, brown pods from the branches of the tree have dropped to the ground and lie empty, curled in contorted brittle shapes, like great, dried hoof parings. The big black seeds have gone, collected by villagers or chewed up by horses and sheep, the fractions remaining borne away by glossy, darting, black ants.

The seyis turns a short, straight stick in his hand. Holding it up to his right eye, he squeezes shut his left eye and squints along its length. Pinning it between his index fingers he studies it, revolving it, checking it for straightness. Balancing it on one finger, he tests its weight, then flexes it, minutely. Bending to pick up a handful of sand he slides the stick back and forth through it, polishing its white, drying surface and wonders idly into whose fleshy parts this hollow little cane, fletched and barbed, will, perchance, some dark hour, seek its way.

There is a light, hot breeze. It blows into his thin, grubby white cotton chemise and flutters his salvár, his baggy trousers. It curls around his thin neck, at the base of his white turban. It shimmers through the leaves of the great tree and they move, rhythmically above his head, cooling the ground beneath, where he sits. The place smells of horse: of leaves and dust and of horse.

His sinewy brown arms are darkened by the sun and his long slender fingers, blemished by a striking mottled pink pigmentation, are darkened by the sun and calloused, like the palms of his hands.

His face is striking. If the features on his face were considered individually they would be dismissed as unremarkable: as being plain even. His nose is long, his chin receding, his ears large although unlobed.

Yet when set together in the high cheek-boned structure of his face, in the carriage of his head and the cool, pure light that lingers in his eyes, they cast him with a visage of a reposed and remarkable beauty.

Having never known indulgence the skin is taut and covers his bones lightly. His eyes are large and very dark brown, almost black, and the skin surrounding them is wrinkled upward, as are the eyes of those who are accustomed to look out into the white hot glare of the sun.

The seyis is watching a mare. He is watching the mare and refining the stick and checking the far horizon, to which his eyes keep flickering, as though he senses, rather than sees, that something is coming.

The mare is grazing with the other mares. She knows he is watching her. He can tell she knows he is watching her. Even though he is some way from her, he knows she is looking at him, and she knows he is looking at her.

She is a Karaman mare. Her colour is blood bay, doru. The stallion was iron grey, demirkir, and a brute to handle. Undoubtedly he will have deposited all the fury a seyis can live without into the foal that the mare will deliver. The stallion spent most of his life on his hind legs, thrashing the air or a mare, squealing and galloping from one end of the Balkans to the other in long dusty pursuits of his prize. He was much admired for his speed and grace, if not for his manners.

Manners may be taught but they are also inherited and it is not without pained reflection that the seyis considers the other side of this equation: the mare. The lashing-tailed mare and her duplicity; her glaring black eyes and sudden lunges at his knees, her willingness to wheel her back end at him, stand on her forefeet and reveal the underside of her belly to the seyis or anyone else idiot enough to approach her. As flighty a virago to handle as ever set hoof on hard ground, she grazes out there in the sun, the picture of docility, yet the seyis knows full well that in her heart resides the will to kill. He cradles his chin in his hand: tonight is the night. The result is going to be a monster. Will the foal wallow in grief or rear in glory? Or will he just slide into the long, empty silence of yet another horse, forgotten in the ruthless processes of time?

The mare grazes. The flies buzz. The air rings with the sound of the cicadas and the creak of the heat of the plains.

The mares' coats shine in the sun. Their tails flick ceaselessly, they shake their heads and semaphore their ears: they scratch their knees with their muzzles, and kick at the big, iridescent-blue horseflies that pester them relentlessly.

Most of the grass is burned off. The mares pick at the hard dry stalks and move in under the trees in groups, into the shade and stand head to tail, stamping at the flies, waiting for the long heat of the day to pass. The seyis watches them.

He carries no book – no musical instrument. Only his half-crafted arrow. He sits in the shade and ponders the life of an Ottoman seyis, threadbare and lack-lustre, the days of his predecessors withered up like these stalks of dry grass, his world curtailed by government and regulation, by overlords and penury. He must lead the impotent life of the powerless under the roasting sun, husbanding horses for his bowl of çiorba and disc of unlevened bread.

He rises and walks under the trees, wanders through the moody mares, running his hands through their glossy manes and through their fine tails, skipping past their threatening hind strikes and he checks the horizon, gazing deeply into it, to the east, to the mountains beyond.

All day long the cicadas ring, the shadows of vultures and of eagles slip across the hot ground, bustards strut through the grasses striking at the big blue horseflies and at any insect or lizard that is disturbed by the mares.

The afternoon flattens into a dead level heat: the hours stop. Everything stills and ceases to move. No animals stand out in the scorching sun. Even the bustards have gone. Only the vultures and eagles wheel in the shimmering hyaline sky. The cicadas ring on even louder, their ringing now parched and sharp, giving the air a sense of acute aridity.

The mares doze, lower lips loose and drooling beneath the trees with their eyes closed. Such small breeze as there was has dropped. The air is heavy, and hot, stifling and still.

Flies buzz.

The roaring heat of the long afternoon creaks by.

Then, at last, as though a chain had been released, a gate opened, the sun cracks as it strikes the horizon. It dissolves into a crucible of gold and the great power of its face is abated.

Now the mares move out from under the trees and the seyis waits. He watches them graze and flick their tails at the evening flies as he has watched them graze and flick their tails at the evening flies every day. When the first star shines in the indigo sky, he whistles. At first the mares do not respond.

He whistles again and walks heavily away, toward the low, stone buildings, where the sweep well lies. He walks without turning. He walks

26

slowly. It is only when he reaches the sweep well, and swings the twin, great, long, wooden beams upward with a creak and as the wooden, iron-strapped bucket on the other end plunges deep into the well with a hollow sploosh, that the mares leave off their grazing and in a body, turn for the well, and head for the long stone trough into which the seyis is pouring sweet, cold water from the wooden bucket. He sings a watering song, a song that must never be sung unless horses are to be watered. To sing the watering song and not to water horses is to deceive them and to break their trust, for ever. For the horseman such as this, to break the trust of a horse is to invoke the wrath of the devil Iblis himself.

The mares drink. They drink deeply, steeping their muzzles up to their eyes, and lift their heads and the water runs from their chins, as they blow from their nostrils, their pink tongues held between their teeth; they savour its sweetness and the seyis watches with his dark eyes as they push and squeal and lash their tails and flatten their ears and make the timid ones wait. He does not hurry them, nor crack a whip, nor shout. When they are finished and have drunk enough, and ceased playing with the water they follow him through the village to the timar. In this place they will remain for the night, all except for one.

The doru mare: it was she who had told him that tonight would be her night. She had told him: it was a tiny gesture but he had not missed it. She had struck the beaten earth floor with a forefoot once, that morning. Her single strike marked the spot where she intended to deliver her mixed blessing, her little bundle of legs, teeth and razor hooves, that would probably emerge kicking, if not, biting – or both.

The seyis had spread a little oat straw and the mare had waited, and he knew why she was waiting and it was only when she was satisfied and left to join the other mares grazing in the sun that the seyis knew that this night she would deliver to him her foal, and that whatever manner of creature this foal was to be, that it would carry the blood of the Kipchak, Nogai, Oghuz, Petcheneg, Ferghana, Tekke and Turkoman horses and that no finer blood ever has or ever would course through the veins of a hot, sticky little foal, pushed out onto a beaten earth floor in a stone stable under a glittering Balkan sky. And that if the foal was to grow and kick his seyis half to death or blast his teeth out with his flaying front feet, his fury and breeding would promise him a career in the ranks of the sipahi, the most magnificent cavalry the world had ever fled from in terror, in the stables of His Imperial Highness Sultan Mehmed IV, somewhere beyond the growling mountains, to the east.

When grown, this foal, this horse must take his Tekke seyis with him, because he cannot make it on his own – neither he nor his seyis.

They need each other: a simple, bitter symbiosis: a value for a value. The seyis breeds the foal, gives him the bloodline, gives him life, rears him, trains him, schools him, does whatever must be done to him to make him out-dazzle the rest and then the foal, the horse must take his seyis to the power and the glory when the pay-back time comes. The seyis spins his half-made arrow between his fingers in the sunset and then clenching it in his fist, nods once: that's the deal. That's the deal.

The mare steps into the stable lashing her tail. She waits irritably for him to feed her: her saman, her chopped hay. As she eats he feels her great belly though she flattens her ears and curls her nostril and cow kicks with a hind. He runs a hand over her teats to feel the milk, to judge exactly when she will foal though she fails to stand still to let him do so.

The mare is fine, she is fit. Yet she is sharp. 'Yavaş –Yavaş ,' he says to her: 'softly, softly.' She glares and stamps her feet. Calm her down and up she rises. A queen cobra in a wicker basket. She's already weaving about and thumping the floor and whickering, blazing and snorting. All that can go wrong is about to go wrong. This is her first foaling, patience is the key. Is she frightened? In pain? Or just mad? The seyis longs for something simple and straight-forward – was there ever a chance this would be?

He leaves her, momentarily, to her temper. Entering a small room beside the stable, he props the little half-made arrow carefully in amongst three dozen completed arrows, of the same wood and length. Running his hands over them, his mind is distracted: a premonition? Something he dreamed, something held on the cusp of an arcane memory. There was a fire. What is it about this foal?

In the deepening distance, to the east, the thundering is slowly growing louder. Now the seyis puts up the shutters, barricades doors, orders the slaves to shut the other mares in, to dowse any oil lamps. Running his eyes along the roof of the stable, lines of apprehension corner his mouth. He goes round the building again checking shutters, checking doors and gazes off into the drumming eastern sky and shakes his head. 'Tonight of all nights! Mahş allah!' He spits, puts his hands on his hips, sighs and enters the stable of the savage doru mare.

***

The horse is life. The horse is a man's spirit, his soul, his wealth, his ally. The horse lives with man in the sun and the wind, in the snows and the rain. A horseman trusts his speed and his heart and feels the rhythm of his body and the wide world which he inhabits. He sees what his horse sees far, far away in the long great distance from which tonight, he may come.

Yet distance is as nothing to him: he may fly there like the wind; the wind his brother, the sky his sister, the sun and moon his mother and father. The snows and rivers and seas of grass are his cousins and his home.

The horsemen archers live by their horses. They live their brutal truth. There is no sentiment. There is lore. Horses are to be venerated.

Horses are to be revered.

Horses are sacred.

The horsemen archers live their instinct. Instinct is the horse, the herd: it is good, safe: nothing may attack a horse without the entire herd knowing. If an enemy stands in their path the herd will devour him: they are a unit. They are indivisible. There is one undisputed leader. With one undisputed leader, the herd obeys. The herd lives. It is opportunistic. It has no morality except that which preserves and proliferates the herd.

The horseman archers sweep through the wadis and valleys and mountains and high yayla, their summer pasture. They ford the rivers as though they were little streams. Nothing obscures their path. They snatch at the lilac grasses of the Zanján plateau and at night they stop and light fires and kill, roast and rip apart the fat-tailed sheep they have swept up on their racking horses. The herd moves with the food. Where the bounty is good, it will be reaped. A fit, fourteen year-old Tekke girl is good bounty.

It is better to be the consort of a conqueror than the concubine of the conquered.

Soon she will forget her family. Her sorrow will depart: her life will become filled with the moving world and its jewelled bounty. She will always be protected by her horseman archer husband. She will be protected by horses. She will help to make fires and to cook and to gather herbs. She will bear children and one day will have a son with the soul of a horse and a daughter who will yo-yo wool in the high yayla in Anatolia, as she watches over her flocks in a land owned by the horseman archers and she may hum tunes and sing songs in the knowledge of her absolute safety.

* * *

The stars glitter in exceptional brilliance above the black earth. The cicadas of the day are replaced by the frogs of the night. The air is filled with the belches of thousands of frogs and the high rasp of bats. A pair of little owls hoot in the judas trees.

Through the long evening hours the seyis has waited, checking the eastern sky, from which the drumming has now grown louder and the sky has been lit with blue and white flashes. Its air has become hot and sultry, and the stars have been disappearing into a black void.

A different sound emerges. It is preceded by a stillness, as though the earth itself were bracing to catch some impending cataclysm. Then it comes: it comes as a soft thudding. Soon, the thudding evens to a drumming, the drumming to a splashy roaring and the storm bursts over the stables with a blinding crack of light.

The mare in the stable tears at her tether. The seyis stands beside her as the rain hammers on the roof, against the shuttering, as it lashes into the yard and whips at the branches and the leaves of the trees. Once, a mare, in his memory, a beautiful mare, a gorgeous creature with a fine head, in a storm threw herself about on her tether and pulled the knot so tight she could not be released without a knife. In the storm and terror that mare had lashed and screamed, and then had broken free, but there was nowhere to go: the stable doors were shut.

The light reflects in the mare's eyes, and the seyis undoes her tether and sets her free in the stable. Throwing herself from wall to wall, she cries out and the seyis talks softly to her, reassuring her, smoothing away her fear. The wind buffets the trees, rattles the shutters, bangs the doors. The mare groans and arcs her back, paws at the spot she had pawed in the morning then lies down, abruptly. Thunder booms overhead: from somewhere a horse whinnies. The mare tries to rise but she is foaling. The seyis pushes her back down and leans on her neck: she must stay down. Bolts of lightning crack and shatter all round the timar: a slave calls out, then another. A light flickers in the stable. The seyis cries out. 'No oil lights! Do not light any oil lamps!' A slave calls back that it is too late. The flickering brightens: the lightning flashes, the storm rages. The mare heaves. Sweat runs down the seyis' face. He must keep the mare calm: he does not want to lose this foal. The thunder booms. The stable door bursts open: a terrified slave shouts: 'Ateş, Ateş' Fire! Fire!

The seyis turns to the slave: 'Fire?' and in the split second he loses his grip and the mare is on her feet. He lunges for the head collar rope but it's too late. The stable door shatters, the slave hits the mud and the mare gallops into the night. Off into the darkness she plunges, past the burning stables, past the old stone medrese, and the sweep well, out into the plateau and the locust trees in the storm and rain and crashes of lightning.

The Selchuks, the Oghuz, Turkomen and Kipchaks drive their animals into the new land. With them they seek the high pastures and the high yayla and make this their home. They drive their fat-tailed sheep, their camels, their neat brown cattle, their goats and donkeys and most of all their horses to this new green, khanate of the horsemen archers of the west.

The Selchuks build the holy city of Konya.

Upon the roads that lead from Konya they build cool caravanserai, with shade and locust trees and fountains. They build great mosques and medreses and write books and become learned and filled with wisdom.

They do not forget they are horsemen archers. They push west. They take more land. No-one can resist them.

The Sultanate of Rum becomes rich and powerful and strong.

It attracts the attention of a powerful Khan.

Genghis Khan sends more horseman archers that will change the face of the world.

At their head they carry their standard, a six horsetail sejan.

He destroys Rum. He destroys Rum and brings nothing in its place but his name, his six horsetail sejan and leaves the imprint of his warriors on all the faces and in the hearts of the people of all the lands he conquers.

More Turks come. Their leader is called Osman. He steeples his fingers. He must shape these men, his followers, into something higher than just a predatory herd. He picks up a book and reads.

The book is the Holy Qur'an.

He dreams a dream.

Osman's dream is of a tree. This tree has beautiful branches with many coloured flowers upon it. Beneath this tree are four ranges of mountains. These mountains are cloaked in great forests filled with the voices of nightingales. Gazelle walk free with their small bright does in these mountains and in these forests.

The mountains are the Atlas and the Taurus and the Balkans and the Kavkas.

In the valleys of the mountains are mosques made of pale, cut stone and slender minarets. There are villages with fountains and medreses and coloured birds sweeping through the branches of great cedars.

From the roots of this tree flow four rivers.

The Tigris, the Euphrates, the Nile and the Danube.

Upon these rivers float graceful wooden gulets and boats with lateen sails, with men fishing, their nets gleaming silver with their catch.

A strong wind draws the leaves of the tree upward. The leaves shape into the blades of swords which point angrily to the city of Constantinople.

Constantinople is a jewel.

It lies between two continents and two seas: it is a diamond lying between two emeralds and two sapphires.

- 3 -

The Foals

Ali-aga Izobegović sits on a low wall outside his house and moves his long white moustaches. With his right hand he slowly flips back and forth a rosary of amber beads, which alternately, he slips though his fingers one by one and counts methodically, repeating the Qur'anic suras beneath his breath. Shadows from the Corsican pines rake his face. His eyes are brown and hooded and are set deep in his face, and his face is a battered goatskin, old, worn and pock-marked, full of pouches and long deep lines.

Ali-aga Izobegović is a man who speaks without smiling.

'A smile,' he likes to say, 'is expensive.'

Dressed in a striped indigo and purple chapan gown reaching to his calves he wears on his head a cornflower-blue turban, round his slender belly beneath his chapan he wears a dark green sash with a wave-bladed dagger plugged in it. He is proud of this dagger, having cut it from the hand of a Christian mercenary who cut it from the hand of a Jerusalem sipahi in 1671. This knife has ancestry, power, and a story behind it. That it now lies tucked safely in his belt reminds those who meet Ali-aga Izobegović that he is not a man with whom they may trifle.

The timar, the land holding on which he lives, was conferred upon him by Ahmed Köprülü after he butchered a few dozen Christians from the back of his demirkir stallion at St. Gothard in 1672. His screaming horse and blood-covered yatagan, his sabre, found him admiration in the eyes of the Grand Vizier. So he won himself his timar. His timar forms part of the land of the Sultan's daughter. It has locust trees and oaks, ash and elms. Asphodels bloom amongst the rocks. There are lavender fields with humming-bird hawk-moths, and at night pockets of ground are lit by the pale green phosphorescence of glow worms. The pasture is filled with the

33

dry rasp of grasshoppers and is intricately tapestried with wild flowers. Swallowtail butterflies, peacocks and admirals play in the oleander. The slivova, the plum trees, ring to the sound of cicadas and the melodic bloop of golden orioles. The timar has three good wells, a stream and pasture running right across the Liskovac plateau down to the Porecka river.

Shaded by sweet scented, heavy-limbed Corsican pines, his house is low and whitewashed and has red tiled floors and enjoys the luxury of tooled bronze taps, from which cold spring water runs from one source and hot spring water from another.

Save for half a dozen surly slaves who occupy bare tallet lofts above the stables, Ali-aga Izobegović lives alone.

In the Candia campaigns he lost his two sons. He has only ever had one wife, who died six years before. Too old to go to war himself he has a Tekke seyis who breeds him his income, his raison d'être and his contribution to the Sultan for his right to the timar: his, earned in a few years of terror and an uncompromising style with horse and sword.

He regards the seyis in front of him, in his wet clothes, dark rings sacking his eyes. The groom is shivering.

'So?' Ali-aga asks softly, swinging his beads. Tekke seyises who lose quality foals are apt to be reminded by Ali-aga Izobegović of their shortcomings.

'I looked for them all night, Ağa, but could not find them – the foal or his mother. The slaves let the other mares out and they herded and galloped all the way to the river.'

'You went all the way to the river?' Ali-aga retains his position of ease upon the wall.

'To the far side, Ağa, all round the rocks, through the wood and back again. I searched all night.'

'What were the slaves doing?'

'Putting out the fire in the stables, Ağa.'

Ali-aga gazes away to the blue mountains beyond, his eyes pale like an angry cat's.

'The mare vanished: completely.'

Ali-aga Izobegović remains silent. Fury, he knows, is best delivered in a frozen wind, measured and merciless. 'Mercy,' he likes to say, 'is the preserve of God. Everything else is mine.' His pupils have tightened. If the mare and foal are lost this seyis' days are numbered. If not his hours.

'Then the mare turned up, as if by magic, by the locust trees, Ağa, not one hour ago.'

The old man throws his back his head. This, he had not anticipated. The seyis is almost as adroit at measured delivery as he. 'And the

34

foal?' he enquires politely. Ali-aga Izobegović is, they say, the politest butcher in the Balkans.

'The foal was nearby walking around sniffing leaves, as though being born of a gadding mother in a raging storm was the most normal thing.'

'Allah kerim,' Ali-aga says quietly snaking his eyes at the seyis, 'God is bountiful, is he not?' There is no smile.

'Evet – yes – Ağa. God is bountiful,' the seyis replies. His teeth are chattering. Whether from fear of his miserable life or from being cold and tired Ali-aga Izobegović cannot immediately decide though it diverts him anyway.

'Where did she give birth?'

The seyis shakes his head. 'It would not surprise me to learn that he had been born in the river and swum out, Ağa,'

'How so?' Ali-aga asks in a preoccupied way, now running the amber beads though his fingers.

'When it comes to the omens Ağa, this one has them all.'

The old man frowns. 'Oh?'

'Firstly Ağa, it was the date he was born: the 15th night of Shaban, in the 8th Month. The Night of Justification.'

'...when the Angel of Death inscribes his register...' Ali-aga says, sitting up.

'Just so, Ağa. That, the storm, and the fire.'

'Mahşallah!' Ali-aga Izobegović whistles softly. 'May his harness be forever damascened. We must find a fitting name for him.'

'There is only one name he can possibly have, Ağa,' the seyis offers cautiously.

It is not the place of seyises to name foals. The old man's eyes turn slowly to his, and then revolve away, to the blue of the mountains.

'It must follow the proper rule; beginning with the first letter of his father's name and then have one letter of his mother's,' he says, 'in her honour.'

The seyis speaks quickly. 'Yes, yes Ağa, it does. His father was called Ateş – Fire and his mother Zarif – Elegant. So...'

'So?'

'It can only be Azarax. Son of Fire.'

Ali-aga falls silent. The pines move. He whispers the name: Azarax. A Ghazi name. He should trust this seyis more. 'What colour is he?'

'He is doru, Ağa.'

'Like his mother, then.'

'With demirkir on one side.'

Ali-aga snaps his fingers. 'Ha! I had forgotten.'

The seyis looks at his feet. 'It is the omens, Ağa. Every one. Even unto the last.'

Ali-aga contemplates his seyis, his strange pink mottled fingers clasped in front of him, eyes to the ground, shivering. No, the seyis would not forget. He remembers everything. Everything to do with horses.

'The last?'

'He has the Whorl of the Spurs, Ağa.'

Ali-aga Izobegović throws his head back yet again and regards this seyis with his shrewd eyes. 'Upwards or downwards?'

'Upwards, Ağa.'

Ali-aga dismisses him with a flick of the wrist and watches him stumble off under the moving shadow of the pines. The Whorl of the Spurs: a rare whorl, and upwards. Safety in battle. He looks at the trees. The storm did them good: they look fresh today. It is good to have fine trees: as good as it is to breed good stock: good stallions with fine kismet. Azarax. Son of Fire. Stallions are pertinent to the soul: especially if you have to fight for your life from the back of one, which is no laughing matter.

***

The seyis shares the same breakfast as the foal. Holding a wooden bowl under the stamping mare's belly, he teases out her milk in warm frothy jets. Into this he dips pida, flat bread with honey and crams it dripping into his mouth. He hunkers down against a burned-out wall in the dewy morning sun.

Squinting into the light he watches the mare and her new foal browsing about under the shining leaves of the judas trees.

Taking a sudden interest, the foal's head rises and he steps lightly toward him on his supple young hooves. The seyis watches, forehead wrinkled, pida to his mouth. This creature is barely a day old and yet he shows no apprehension. Defiance is written all over his face, as if to say: what is this thing offending my view squatting rudely here?

The seyis checks the foal's approach with a raised hand, recalling with clarity the time he had been buckled at the loins by a well-aimed blow from a creature not a minute older than this. With a mouthful of pida and mare's milk he shouts: 'Ho!' and the foal stops. The seyis chews. This creature is definitely his mother's child and he knows his mother and her galaxy of charms. How one moment she pads about as benign as an octogenarian hadji, dewy-eyed, pliant, full of benevolence and smiling goodwill then within the bat of a bee's wing flattens her ears, levels her head and lashes out like a viper.

The seyis lays his hand on the foal's neck. His father has left his passion in him too. He was ever the one for the knee-cap strike. No, this one merits a little respect. Traits like that tend to hover in the spirit. The seyis holds the foal where he is and looks deep into the fierce, self-assured young eyes. 'You little monster, you.'

He chews on gazing at him, his Whorl of the Spurs, what an augury! Men are going to kill to own this creature. The storm, the fire, the Night of Justification – the seyis raises his eyebrows and dips the pida back into the milk.

The little foal's eyes are bold. Brazen. He holds the seyis' stare. It is there, the seyis perceives, the fire, the ego, the seething point of light: the soul. If it is the will of Allah that he has a destiny then it is the will of Allah that the seyis is charged to see him achieve it.

The thought detonates in his mind like a cannon blast. He stops chewing. His face straightens and he blinks, once; twice.

This foal, this ominous foal has been given to him and to no other seyis so that his destiny will be accomplished. The weight of the moment straightens his spine.

He looks again into the little creature's eyes: 'Mahşallah!' he breathes. Can it be? Or is he mistaken? Is this not all mere chance? A patterning of events that means, ultimately, nothing? He looks deeper. No: it is there, in his eye. Definitely. The presence. The fire. This foal will go far. He will take the seyis with him and the seyis must deliver him to his fate, wherever or however that may be. Of all the foals he has bred, there has never been one quite like this, not one who came with all the auguries, all the omens, all in one momentous birth. 'Where were you born, little Azarax?' he whispers. He envisions the forest of legs of the mares in the mud, the howling wind and lashing rain, in the roar of thunder, the crashing lightning, his mother on the ground for the ten seconds it took to produce him, then she rose and stood with the other mares, hovering close, intuitively protective, as this little, wet creature shook his head and blinked in the storm, and hearing her voice above the thunder, the soft whickering voice, struggled to his feet and took the first milk that impelled into him the power of life. Within ten minutes the mares would have cantered to the river to stand beneath the trees and he would have cantered with them – ten minutes old. 'Allahu akbar!' the seyis whispers, 'Allah kerim!'

He must school him as he never schooled a horse. He must train

37

him as no other horse has been trained; teach him all that he needs to outrun, to outsmart, to outwit, to outlive all that lies in his path. The pure symbiosis of man and horse, horse and man. Already they depend upon each other; the foal upon him and he upon the foal.

The seyis holds up the bowl to his lips and swallows the last of the milk.

He stands, lays his hand upon the foal's back and steels himself to honour his charge.

'Yes, little Azarax. I shall do what I am asked. I will lead you to your destiny – even though it is on some far-flung shore of this brutal world. But answer me this, Son of Fire. When you graze the lilac grasses on the plains of eternity, when your long shadow slopes across the rolling seas of time and everyone knows your name, will you remember mine?'

* * *

He might have had an auspicious birth; he might have the mark of the Whorl of the Spurs and the heavenly horses of the western steppe might gallop beside him in some parallel universe that is his spiritual home, he might have heard the withering cry of the spectre stallion who haunts the grave of the Khans of the East, or perhaps Raksh, that fabled horse, might protect his footfall: but he remains on this earth, a foal.

The seyis watches as he jabs along sometimes beside, sometimes behind and sometimes in front of his mother: sniffing plants, darting sideways from leaves that come skimming across the ground toward him. He watches him flee from stones, and leap sideways to avoid puddles all the time with his ears flickering; revealing at once his growing comprehension of the world and his ignorance of it. 'Azarax!' the seyis repeats again and again.

Having no other foals of his own age, Azarax treats the seyis as his plaything. After a week of this the seyis becomes unsettled by the way the foal treats him, questioning whether it is respectful or disdainful, whether he is taking advantage of him or enjoying the closeness of their company. Soon he begins to sense that subtly this little foal is running rings round him. One day he is friendly, the next he is not: he is distant, then not distant, he is typical of a horse. Yet he is not typical. The seyis finds himself thinking about him, watching him, watching what he does, following him around. Then suddenly the tables are turned and the foal watches the seyis, watches what he does and follows the seyis around. In these times the foal's eyes are disturbing, and the look he gives knowing and hard, like a judgemental though silent little god – who is in control here?

Over the days that follow, his training begins. The seyis rides Zarif, the mare, the foal's mother and the foal follows. Each subsequent day, he extends the distance, the foal, Azarax, always following, his strength increasing as he learns to extend himself and by the end of the second week, he gallops round and round his mother as they ride through the timar, down to the river.

At the river, the seyis chooses a shallow place to ford, and although the foal hesitates, when he sees his mother blithely crossing the water, he leaps in, picking his feet high out of the splashing water, little rainbows arcing round him, follows her to the far bank, and vaults out into the grasses and reeds on the far side, and shakes vigorously.

Every day they cross the river, going a little deeper each time, until one day the foal finds himself swimming behind his mother, and because his mother wades slowly through the water and the seyis calls him quietly and then rewards him when they have found the far bank by getting off the mare and rubbing the little foal's head and praising him for what he has just achieved, so the foal becomes confirmed in his lack of fear of water, or of jumping or slithering from river banks into it.

They pass through cool, shady woodland, past rocky outcrops, and stand high above long blue vistas, in the warm, buttery winds, and then walk slowly back through the creaking grasses and across the brittle ground to the timar.

Soon, the walks become trots, and canters, and gallops and plunges through water; they become hard climbs up steep, brashy hills, and long, gravelly slides down them.

After a few days, around the foal's neck the seyis fits the nazar boncugu, the blue bead, the Evil Eye to ward off the djinn, then slips a hemp headstall onto the foal's head. Within two days of having this headstall upon his head, the foal can be led. It is the first step to training: patiently to teach a foal to lead. It is not easy, for the foal cannot be pulled and will dig his feet in if any attempt is made to teach him to lead by dragging. The seyis will use neither whip nor stick for fear of setting up a system of response to pain, which is an evil route to follow. He teaches him to lead by encouragement and reward alone. Because there exists already an intuitive closeness, because the seyis' breath smells of the foal's mother from their shared breakfasts of her milk, the foal accepts him as an elision of his mother and learns to walk at his word, to stop at his word, to turn this way and that, at his word.

'Yavaş–yavaş, Azarax,' the seyis says, 'Yavaş–yavaş.'

After several weeks of riding the mare and having the foal follow, the seyis puts a sack across the colt's back, and ties it loosely. A few days later he ties it a little tighter and loads the sack with strange clanking objects. At first the colt starts when he hears these things clanking upon his back but because the seyis has not at any time betrayed nor destroyed his trust, the colt allows this to happen. It is a new game. Within one week, Azarax is carrying upon his back a peculiar assortment of goods: a kagan shield, a saucepan with stones in it, some rope and sticks and even, one day, a puppy. By this time he has found his strength and gallops on his own freely around the fields at top speed. He learns to corner fast and feel the power surging in his supple young limbs and in his growing, young body, he changes upon an instant, and steps out self-assuredly bearing a burden of a saucepan with stones in it, stuffed in a sack on his back and rope and bundles of cloth and sticks and a shield and on top a puppy and a seyis walking beside him holding all safely together and he is unalarmed.

* * *

The summer beats on the land and the ground becomes hard. Fissures appear. Sodom apples grow on the baked, bare earth. The leaves on the trees turn a dry green, the water in the wells drops. The stables have been rebuilt and the bow and quiver of arrows the seyis lost in the fire have been replaced by new ones.

And the seyis now has two colts to look after.

The second is a yağiz colt, whom Ali-aga Izobegović names Bora, The Wind. His father was called Bekçi, meaning The Lookout, and his mother Rüya, meaning Dream.

A strange shift in relations takes place as soon as Bora appears. He takes the place of the seyis in Azarax's affections. Now all Azarax's attention is devoted to Bora. He plays with him, runs at his side, nibbles his ears, bites his knees, stands close beside him and the seyis finds himself feeling an absurd pang of jealousy, but he knows that it must be so. Azarax is a colt, a horse and not some magical being with whom he shares some peculiar, unearthly communion. He is a horse and will make friends with horses. Even though the seyis is somehow elided with his mother he is also not her: he is not a horse: he is no more than an accident of the earth, a diversionary implement that amuses and distracts the foal from the long heat of the day and protects and comforts him in the dark hours of night. With horses, the seyis admits unhappily to himself, it was ever thus. You have one horse and you have a trusting ally who reveals to you the mysteries of his world and his oblique perceptions of yours. You have two and you have two horses who have retreated into their inscrutable society, who regard you as an irrelevant curiosity, their uncomprehending slave, and exclude you from the superior processes which they inhabit.

It is in full and complete knowledge of this, in its utter acceptance, comprehending that only upon their terms can he exert any form of control, that the seyis takes them in and out of rivers and up and down hills, through woods, past the rocks, up to the high view, then back to the timar.

He schools them to the best of his ability, as a pair. Each day he does something to accustom them to noise and to different sounds. He bangs a drum: he clangs metal; he shouts, he waves flags, lights fires, he releases small fire-crackers, which at first make Bora run and gad about, while Azarax remains indifferent to the sound which makes the seyis wonder if he is deaf. Yet he knows that he is not for the young colt pricks his ears when he hears the distant braying of a donkey and responds with a high pitched squeal, announcing not only the splendour of his own voice but the perfection of his hearing. No, the seyis explains to himself: it was the Night of Justification; the storm, the fire and his destiny. Often the seyis notices Azarax peering off far into the distance as though he perceived something out there waiting for him that one day, he would find. That something lay beyond the wildest dreams or imaginings of an insignificant Ottoman seyis, whose sole command, he knew, was to take him there, come hell, come hardship, come war.

Within weeks of their foaling, the two colts know the sound of pistol-shot: they know the sound of men shouting, are unafraid of banners being hoist in front of them: they know how to run beside a man, to answer his voice to a command, to be led by him: they pick up their feet when asked and know already how to stand still. The seyis has lobbed little sticks at them, and small smooth stones and first of all they allowed them to strike them because they could not see them coming. Soon they learn to look for them, and learn to skip out of their way so that after a few weeks of this, the seyis would throw a stone hard at them and they would both shift before it struck.

By the time they are six months old, they are confident: nothing alarms them. Smoke and fire and flames do not make them rear. Gunshot and powder explosions are everyday occurrences to them. They avoid sticks and stones if they are hurled at them. They have even been carrying saddles.

There is no such crudity in the life of a slightly-built Ottoman seyis as the need to break a horse.

There is only the skill to make one.

The janissaries strut with pride announcing their feats of bravery. They run up their sleeves and reveal their scars. They strip their shirts and show their muscled bodies. They carry only their weapons, their Bektaşi belief nurturing their souls. 'Allahu akbar!' they shout; God is Great! They do not fear the hair's breadth that separates heaven from hell. If they fall they shall land upon their feet at the Gates of Paradise. They swear an oath of allegiance to their Sultan, Vice-Regent of God Upon Earth, over a decorated tray upon which lies a bowl of salt, the Holy Qur'an and their yatağan, their scimitar, their sabre.

The sacred insignia of their regiment is the Kazan, a great copper cooking pot.

It is a symbol of the old days, of the horseman archers and the Steppe, it is their communal bowl. Islam is charged to feed the wayfaring man: the guest is invited to sit and eat. The Kazan offers hospitality and unity: come, sit, share with us. No-one is turned away. To sit next to a Kazan signals sanctuary. In battle, the orta, the regiment, rallies around it. To carry it is an honour. To tip it over is a sign of insurrection and mutiny. To lose it, a disaster.

***

Symbols are life to the janissaries, to the sipahi, the çebelu, the deli, the gönüllü, the kapikulu, the pirs, the paşas – to all men who risk their lives in war. Badges, belts, hats, buckles, colours of regiment – all have symbolic power. Omens are important to men who risk their lives in war. A good omen fills an army with zeal. Omens lend belief to an army. A clever leader interprets whatever he finds, as a good omen.

There are good and bad omens. A sneeze is an ill omen. Weather, is ominous. Rain can break the spirit of an army. Sunlight is a good omen. Clouds that darken the face of the sun can be interpreted as bad omens, where the outcome of battle is uncertain. Clouds that cross a crescent moon are a bad omen for a Turk, whose standard is the Crescent Moon. Wind is ominous. If wind blows away the turban of a leader, defeat is certain to follow. If rain falls upon an army that advances and keeps falling upon an army that advances, the omens are bad. If a Kazan is dropped or falls to the ground, that regiment is doomed.

Animals, birds, snakes, mice seen in grain, moths in candles, owls landing on tents, all are omens. The shadows of vultures falling across a man signal his death.

The Whorl of the Spurs on a doru stallion, is ominous.

The seyis watches the colts play and observes how their baby faces

42

are turning into the faces of two magnificent young horses. How their eyelashes have grown long and straight and beautiful and how their mouths are set in this serious expression and how now they have stopped quidding – the signal of obeisance between foal and adult horse. How they try to bite each others' knees and even his, should he stand too close. How one will suddenly take an unprovoked nip out of the other which always leads to an ear-back reprisal and a high pitched squeal and a stormy, dust flicking chase that ends with them both on their hind feet pawing at each others' heads and that's the time for the shout and the intervention of a Tekke seyis.

He watches them as they graze nose to nose and sees how loyal and united they have become and how when one lies prostrate out in the warmth of the sun, the other will be on its feet, standing guard. He laughs when they see something for the first time, how they gadded about when they saw a tortoise and threw their heads about shouting and squealing and tried to kick it and missed by yards. He watched them gaze at a viper that crossed their path, their big innocent eyes burning with excitement, and how then they had run around the spot where they saw it, trampling the ground and jumping about like deer. He notices as the games of youth become more serious, how they mature into two fine young colts, full of confidence and fun and slightly dangerous.

When they are a year old he weans them. Because they are confident, it is not difficult to achieve. Even their mothers are not discontented when they are weaned. The colts are strong and demanding, which has already begun to irritate the dams. When weaned they are left close to their mothers and not taken away immediately. Yet the day comes when the seyis begins the long walks with them, taking them further and further away from the security of their mothers. One day he takes the dams from the colts and the next day the colts from the dams and when the mares call, the colts reply and then he brings the foals back into their vision and he keeps doing this until their confidence has steadied, and the mares graze in the knowledge that although their foals are weaned they are also not far away. He keeps this up for weeks on end until he does not return the colts and the mares do not notice. In this time he puts a stirruped saddle upon the colts, leans across the saddles and finally, he mounts. He mounts first of all for a few minutes only, getting off without alarming the young horses. Making a fuss of them, he has them in his hand: they are intrigued by this experience: the seyis is light and when he is upon them he does not overbalance them. This is the most critical time of all for a young horse because if you get it right now it will always be right and the seyis knows this. If the young horse panics for one second the seyis does not confirm

43

him in his panic but slips off and smoothes away his fear. Then he will not mount that colt immediately, but the other one and when the first one sees him do this, he responds to it and so when the seyis mounts him again, he is unafraid. It becomes a game to them. It takes four days to make them to the saddle – perfectly to the saddle – and then he begins to school them. All the time he maintains their confidence and their trust because this is the bedrock of the art of the horseman: to break the trust of a horse, for a horseman of purity, is to invoke the curse of Iblis.

Ali-aga Izobegović has watched the development and training of these two young horses, unsmilingly. He has been sitting under the shadow of the judas trees, on the cut travertine by the medrese, where the water trickles lightly, running into a cool, stone trough. From here he has been able to see the colts do what their seyis has asked them to do, and he has pointed and shouted and got up and wandered over to the colts and stroked their downy coats. He has watched them grow and learn new skills: he has seen them being led with their mothers and now he sees them carrying their seyis upon their backs, as proud as he to do so.

One day he calls the seyis to his house.

Into his hands he counts out one hundred aspers. Thirty-six months have passed since Bora was foaled. Thirty-seven since Azarax first stood in a circle of wet mares in a raging Balkan storm.

He says quietly: 'The sançakbey has sent word.'

The seyis' brow furrows. Providence has struck without warning.

'Take them to the müsellem of the tayçi. Then to Istanbul, to the baş imrahor Soliman Chia, my friend. The beylerbey of Silistra is my family bey. You must go with him. There will be war.'

A knot tightens in the seyis' belly. The moment he longed for, the moment he feared. The squib of opportunity has been tossed, lit, at his feet. In one heartbeat his life has been flung into another direction and he has been offered no choice. 'Inshallah!' It is the Will of God. He looks into the face of Ali-aga Izobegović: blackberry eyes revealing nothing: this is a man who has lost all his comrades, his two sons and a wife and now is about to lose the only other human being for whom he ever cared, whose absolute skill has won his absolute admiration – but it reveals in his face, not a thing. Not a glimmer. If a smile is expensive, tears cannot be bought. Their value hovers beyond.

The seyis drops the saddles and loads heyber (saddlebags) onto the young horses' backs, lashes them down, straps his bow and quiver to his side and walks away with them and Ali-aga Izobegović watches them go. He watches the young horses leave with their seyis between them, walking down the long track away from his timar, where the distant mountains rise, a smoky cobalt blue, and where the ground they walk is hard and dry. He watches the dust curl from their feet, and as the figures sink lower and lower into the ground, the seyis' hand rises and the old man whispers: 'Güle-güle, my sons! Go laughing!' and he steps up onto the travertine by the medrese and watches until they dip from his sight. Then he sinks to his knees and sits down listening to the trickling water that runs into the stone trough by the medrese. He leans his head back against the cool travertine stone and slowly swings his amber beads in his right hand and repeats, softly, suras from the Holy Qur'an.

It is July 1681.

***

Nearly 300 years before, in 1389, the night before the battle on the Plain of the Blackbirds at Kosovo a great gale blows. It blows toward the army of Murad I, Sultan of the Turks. The dust rises in huge billowing clouds. Bustards that have been picking through the dry grasses now fly into the air with heavy, thudding wing beats. Flies buzz in the choking dust, which burns into the Turks' clothing, into their eyes, into their mouths, their ears, their hair. It smarts in the eyes of the horses. Murad's forces are smaller, the army he faces stronger, the dust clouds blinding.

Even with their thousands of knights and flying banners, with their loud trumpets and booming drums, even with their big black, serious horses and their silver-handled swords, even with the wind at their backs, the Serbs fear the glittering Ottoman sipahi before them.

The next morning the wind has dropped. The Omens have spoken for the Turks. Battle is joined.

Murad's sipahi horsemen destroy the flower of Serbian nobility; the Balkans fall.

Victory follows upon victory.

Even though Timur Lenk, Tamerlane and his archer horseman come to despoil and to plunder and even though Tamerlane humiliates Sultan Byazet I and drags him to Samarkand in a cage, the Ottoman Empire grows.

Armies wither before the invincible Turk. Cities crumble. The decisions their leaders make are right. It is as if they are touched by a divine spark. It is as if some special Hand selects for them the right leader, who makes the right decisions, as though some sacred wind blows for them and sets them on their diamond-studded way.

They become heirs of the Roman Empire, kings of Constantinople.

In 1453, Mehmet II The Conqueror levels the ancient unbreached walls of this ancient city with such shot as the world has never seen. Huge round stone balls each weighing 1200-1500lbs (545-680 kg) destroy it in hours: walls that have stood for centuries collapse before him. On 11th April, he sets his vast cannons to face the Kizil Elma. For 40 days the cannons speak across the Golden Horne.

The city falls and Mehmet rides in upon his Nogai charger and as he rides and gazes at the ruins he recites: – the spiders weave the curtains in the palace of the Caesars, the owl calls the watches in the towers of Afrasiab.

Constantinople is a shell: a ruined shell. And yet – it remains a diamond: a diamond between two emeralds and the two sapphires lying in his hand.

Mehmet is Sultan, Khan, Ghazi and Emperor.

He is Caesar. A Turk, a Muslim and a Byzantine.

He is Padishah, Imperial Sovereign, King of Kings. Margrave of the World.

***

The Holy Christian Church of the Holy Wisdom, Ayasofya in Constantinople, that has stood for a thousand years is turned upon his command into a Holy Mosque. The Crescent replaces the Cross.

On May 29th 1453 the holy Christian city of Constantinople is renamed. The name is taken from the Greek 'eis tin polin', meaning 'to the city'. Istanbul.

Bosnia, Herzegovina, Serbia, Albania and Morea (The Peloponnese) are won. Crimea becomes a vassal state, Persia is invaded, Algiers too becomes a vassal. Under the reign of Suleiman the Magnificent, Zaila, Barqa, Rhodes and Hungary all fall. Vienna is besieged for the first time. Bessarabia, Yemen, Cyprus are taken, as is Bahrain. The Turks conquer Tripolitania, Muscat and occupy ports in Eritrea, Somalia and Kenya. They take western Persia, Georgia and Abkhasia, Crete, Podolya and Ukraine. They become masters of Syria, the Levant, most of Egypt, and north Africa. The Mediterranean is their lake, the Red Sea is their lake, the western coast of Arabia is theirs and they hold the keys to Mecca and Medina.

The mountains of the Atlas and Taurus and Balkans and the

Kavkas are cloaked in great green forests and filled with the voices of the bul-bul. Çelan walk free with their small bright does.

In the valleys of the mountains are mosques made of pale, cut stone and slender minarets. There are villages with fountains and medreses and coloured birds sweeping through the branches of great cedars.

Upon the Tigris, the Euphrates, the Nile and the Danube lateened gullets sail, their nets silver with their catch.

- 4 -

Hard School

Two strapping young horses: swift in action, bright eyed, tails high, ears pricked, heads up, nostrils fluted and taut as bowstrings. At the minutest sound they stare wide-eyed into the direction from which the sound came, pushing together behind their surrogate mother, their seyis, whom they abandon to the invisible threat which approaches. And here he is, sweat pouring down his face, draining by degrees, struggling every step of the way, losing his voice from the constant chatter he has maintained since they left their home twelve long hours before.

Around them the limbs of trees claw upward into the racing sky; grey, lichen-covered rocks crouch like coiled monsters; streams seethe, the wind tosses the high heads of the forest and in the flickering gloom beneath, yellow-eyed wolves slink through the shadows in the dark and barren land that is north eastern Serbia. It is the summer of 1681.

They edge forward, jabbing their sharp young hooves into the ground, knees high, eyes blazing, then dig hooves in and stop abruptly. They refuse to move. They cry out with their high pitched voices and then cry out again and again when they hear strange, dismembered voices of other young horses calling back from far away: their own echoes.

They pull on their reins and bow their necks, they flute their nostrils and snort. They prance and throw up dust and become a monstrous pair to handle, even though they are still young and have no real stallion-power in their bodies.

The seyis has walked them through the night in order to exhaust them so that he might avoid the worst of this, a reaction he had foreseen. Yet still, even as day breaks and even after they have been walking all night, he finds himself wrestling with them.

As the day has worn on they have behaved in opposed ways: Azarax wishes to walk swiftly and Bora drags upon his lead rein. Azarax is full of energy while Bora stumbles along with his ears back. Abruptly, to no obvious signal, they swap roles: Bora becomes the lead and Azarax, the slouch. And now Azarax must be dragged as Bora high steps forward with his ears up, snorting and yelling at the limit of his lungs.

Stumbling between them, the seyis is stretched: one hand holds the rein of the horse he is this moment riding and the next walking; in the other clutches the rein of the horse he is leading – he is dragging.

Keeping a firm hold of both he knows only too well that it is an easy thing for these two young horses to rid themselves of their shackle and go galloping off.

It is a likely thing for a horse to do if he becomes suddenly alarmed or confronted by something he has not met before.

It is in the nature of horses to do so.

Horses in groups signal to each other if they suspect that something lies in their path. The horse playing the lead will over-exaggerate what he sees, which will transmit as a clear semaphore to the rest of the herd even if the rest of the herd in this case contains only one other horse and a seyis. The lead horse will become wary and snort and tense and jump at the tiniest sound. He will stop dead in his tracks and stare incredulously at stones, at tree stumps, at an unfamiliar object, even at a familiar one, leap sideways from a rustle in the bushes, suddenly gaze off at some phantom of his seething imaginings in the far-flung distance. He will huff and puff and be an appalling nuisance. Any horse, ridden or otherwise, that takes the role of lead will do this: which makes the lead horse always the hardest to ride.

The seyis is aware too that his own increased caution transmits itself intuitively to his horses, heightening their own bit-chewing, white-eyed reactions.

By mid-day, after a whole night's ride, he is exhausted. It has been a long, weary battle. For every second of it he has fought to keep these two, strong, frisky young animals calm and it has robbed him of all his strength. When it seemed as though they too had become weary, inexplicably a new wave of energy had coursed through their bodies, as some noise had creaked through the trees and excited them all over again. They had gone jabbing forward with little steps on the very brink of a full-blooded bolt, snorting and reeding, and once more he had had to hang on and keep talking, keep stroking their butterfly spirits smooth. By mid afternoon, the seyis was running on sheer mental energy alone.

On their way to the Müsellem's stables, the seyis and his two wild-eyed charges had stayed in remote villages, huddled in valleys some of which were like sheep that have lost their teeth, their age impossible to

49

tell. Some were so mean and small that they were scarcely fit for the white storks to build their ragged nests. Some had both Christian and Muslim inhabitants, with churches and mosques and a shared sense of settlement and of accepted co-existence. Others harboured a darkness, where the air was haunted by the ghosts of some atrocity, by an almost tangible violence that left it scarred and menacing. Hunched, round-shouldered men sloped through slanting shadows, past stacks of rotting wood and collapsed buildings and slid through half closed doors, where hands clutched daggers and dark fingers coiled round triggers and the stocks of long-barrelled muskets.

Law ceased at the periphery of the village. From there, anything might slip from behind a stone wall or swoop out of the night: madmen, cutthroats, runaway slaves, armed and dangerous, insane women driven to extremes by poverty might dash out in front of a passing horseman and cast in his path a child to exact from him the price of its blood.

**

For four days and nights they travel, crossing streams and rivers and brown landscapes, like three black ants crawling across a huge canvas with water-colour trees blobbed round the edges and then in amongst the trees, a slender tower, a minaret, another village. But they are not heading for that village: they are heading for the mountains to the east, way in the distance, a blush of mauve, like the bloom on a plum.

It takes two more days to cross the plateau. Then they strike upon a lake. On the lake's margin are two gypsy girls washing pans. The girls are pretty and dark with long black hair. They wear bright dresses with embroidery round the hems and they are barefoot. They are twins. As the seyis and his horses come sliding down the hill they watch him evenly as though every day a man came sliding down the hill with a couple of horses and then waded straight out into the lake. The girls watch as the horses funnel up the water and paw at it and splash the sweat under their bellies and round their necks. And they watch as the seyis slides off and drops in straight up to his waist and drinks beside the horses, drinks the water the girls are washing their saucepans in.

The lake isn't deep so they wade round in a big arc to the other side and the seyis unsaddles and lets the horses graze the young green fragmites.

Then it is his turn and he sits and watches the girls washing, watches them as they pick up their pans and watches as they stroll off to a hut by the lakeside and disappear within. A few minutes later a twist of smoke curls up, and he lies back in the hot afternoon as the horses graze.

And when the lake turns gold, they move on.

The day ends in a wall of fire as the heat drains out of the sun. A hush comes to the land and it stills. The only sounds are those of the horses' footsteps and the creak of the leather. Big poppies dot the crest of a ridge as they rise to its top, where they halt and look down. In the plain before them, pink in the dying sun, like a chunk of coral in ebbing tide, lie the Müsellem's stables.

They follow a flock of red, bell-clonking goats down to the stables as evening chases the light from the valleys. They pass another great creaking sweep-well and then his two horses begin to cry out and the voices of hundreds of horses in the valley below respond. Weaving on down through the half light the seyis and his two charges meet line upon line of horses trotting up through dense dust to the stables as the last embers of sunlight fade in the western sky.

The road is now filled with horses.

They have been assembled from timars and hiraşi all across the Balkans: from Bosnia, from Herzegovina, Serbia, Macedonia and from greater Rumelia itself. Behind them come dozens of men on horseback in a cloud of sunset-ochre like the remnant of some long-forgotten, glorious regiment riding high upon the backs of their red-eyed, blood-red horses. The horses, trotting, ears back, in absolute obedience, carried their dark-featured handlers, wearing their stained, threadbare, red corselets with silver bosses, men who had fought and survived many wars.

They walk past the seyis in a blizzard of dust without a glimmer of acknowledgement. They do not speak. They whip their animals up into the tayçi, past the two young stallions and out into the space beyond, where the young horses mill and call, like lost souls sent to slaughter at the decree of some distant and terrible god who cares not a jot for their manner of execution.

The hard, scarred men put up their tents without speaking a word, light fires and cook food and look at no-one.

The seyis rides to the stables and finds a place to tether his two horses driven into silence by the sight of so many others. A cart rattles past, drawn by a blocky Bulgaristan draft standing in his harness looking neither right nor left. Saman and barley is dropped and the cart rattles on. The seyis feeds his horses.

The evil eye falls upon them immediately.

Two tall Karaman thoroughbreds are worth their weight in rubies.

A Karaman stallion with the Whorl of the Spurs is a prize worth fighting for.

A small Tekke seyis armed with only a bow and quiver is rabbit to talon. An eye glints in firelight. A glance, a flash of light. The air prickles: a frisson: tension that was not there one hour ago is coiling tighter and tighter. The seyis blows out a breath. The palms of his hands have moistened. The flash of the eye again. He rolls out his bedding between his two horses and picks disinterestedly at the last of his rice wrapped in vinegared vine leaves. The eyes watch. A patch of heat stains the seyis' forehead.

Those men are not from the army, they are renegades, haunting the periphery of life, living by stealth, weighing the moment, poised for the opportunity to strike, to seize two quality horses and gallop off with them into the night.

Azarax and Bora stand quietly over their seyis. He lies back as the night folds in, as the lights from the fire die. He dare not close his eyes, yet sleep steals upon him and soon his body moulds onto the hard ground as his horses browse and chew their feed.

Intuition is a strong force.

Azarax wakes him in the blackest hour of night with a tiny reeding sound. The seyis' hand falls upon his bow. The horses stand completely still. The seyis cannot even hear them breathe. The night is utterly black. The shape that slips through the darkness moves closer. A foot crunches nearby. The speed of the strike is incredible. A sudden shimmer of light above him, the sound of a hoof on stone, a deep throated roar of a young stallion and a man screams out in pain. A metallic object falls to the ground. The seyis sees the outline of a horse rear against the sky, two flaying front hooves. Another man cries out. Feet hobble off into the darkness.

Silence returns.

Loyalty is uncompromising.

The seyis had not realised until this minute, its power. He reaches out and touches his horses' legs. Above him against the night sky he can make out the heads of two fine young stallions scenting their first victory, points of light burning in four dark eyes; ears pricked: invincible. A light wind plays with their manes. 'Mahşallah!' he breathes quietly, lying back in his bedding, his horses standing over him. 'Mahşallah!' he says again, and, placing a mottled hand under his head, he closes his eyes.

Stars peep from cloud and slide across the sky. Dawn brings the sound of a muezzin to the stables.

Nothing is said. The evil eye is closed. The seyis finds a dagger and throws it into the long grass.

The days pass. More and more horses come. A month later on 7th

September 1681, the Müsellem makes his selection. First the horses are divided by colour: reds – doru and yağiz to the east, kir – greys to the west, kara – blacks to the north, duns to the south, as old a tradition as the time the hooves of their thoroughbred ancestors thundered across the plains of Oxiana. Once in colour blocks, they are subdivided into type. Light horses for the çebelu, heavy for the toprakli sipahi, rangey horses for the deli regiments – the mad ones, as they call them. Then divided again: these are timarli sipahi: The People of the Six Units – sipahi, silahdar, ülüfeçi (left and right) and gurebas (left and right). The Aghas of the Bölüks: the Beys of Kethüda, the Pirs of Kethüda, the Başçavuşes and the Çavuşes.

The seyis' two horses have been selected to be toprakli, heavy cavalry mounts, gazetted to the Privy Stables, the Royal bodyguard. The toprakli are front line cavalry. Honours will befall them. The seyis' heart does not still in his chest.

They will go straight to the Imperial Palace in Istanbul. They are pure blood and only pure blood flows through the veins of the horses of the Sultan. They will be hassa sipahi mounts.

The hassa sipahi are cream; and cream, as they say, always rises.

***

On 27th July 1634, forty seven years before the seyis walked his horses to the stables of the Müsellem, a child was born to the wife of a timarli sipahi officer in the village of Merzifon, in Anatolia.

The child was named Mustafa. The sight of a sipahi father in his embroidered silks and chain mail, his conical brass helmet, his pistols and yatağan (sabre) with his gold chanfron mounted on his Germiyan stallion, with his gem-studded quiver filled with sharp-tipped arrows, caused the growing child to gaze in awe upon such an illustrious being.

On a diet of heroes and of glory, of Ghazis and honour, of daring and dash and the conquests of the greatest Ottoman of all, Suleiman the Magnificent – the child dined. Such nourishment is caviar to the soul; it causes a child to dream: it caused this child to dream of placing his feet in the footsteps of great men. To dream of stepping out of the footsteps of great men and treading those of his own: of shouldering great names aside to find a space for himself to strut in.

The offspring of a wealthy timarli sipahi officer occasions to meet men of influence. For an Empire that is fuelled by merit, the advances of a precocious child are not unwelcome. He may make his way in the Court of the Sultan, first as a page and then as a sipahi officer, a courtier, a beylerbey and at last, perhaps, the Grand Vizier himself. Many men of humble origin have risen to such vertiginous heights before: the Köprülü dynasty had; a triumvirate of Viziers, who wafted through the corridors of the Topkapi Palace in their silk embroidered, gold-threaded gowns. Their birth into Albanian slavery did not prevent them from commanding an Empire.

It is to the last and most distinguished of these Köprülü Viziers that the child Mustafa inveigles his interest and soon becomes his earnest assistant, running errands, between him and the Shadow of God Upon Earth, Sultan, Mehmed IV.

The Sultan Mehmed IV likes to hunt. So Mustafa panders to the Vice Regent of God and with him daubs his hands in the bowels of dismembered wild animals. He discovers hidden valleys full of wild fowl and of black bears and great wolves, of tusked boars and antlered deer. Into the slathering jaws of his huge baying hounds he drives them. He writes poems about how great a huntsman is this illustrious Sultan: none so fine had ever crossed leather upon a horse and killed so many animals in a single day in the history of all the world, as he.

And this causes a Sultan to cast about for ways in which he might reward such devotion.

He finds it in his sister, and awards this handsome young man her hand in marriage. Mustafa becomes the brother-in-law to the Sultan.

His position is advanced: his wealth assured: his opinion is sought. Yet still he serves with skill the Grand Vizier Ahmed Köprülü who is fast gluing together the pieces of Empire which the Sultan by his absence, is squandering.

When Ahmed Köprülü dies, Mustafa steps into his still-warm slippers.

Now he is forty-six years old, tall, dark, of regal bearing and is called Kara Mustafa. Black Mustafa.

He juts his beard, folds his hands across his big, ample belly and contemplates the turquoise Marmara Sea.

Kismet, destiny, is his.

Has he not upon his own account risen from obscurity to hold the highest office in the land? Is he not now related to the Ottoman dynasty? Where else must such kismet point him? His pride takes him toward his decanters of brandy and dreams: dreams he dare not speak. Men are pawns: they can be removed from opposition with the aid of nothing more than finely chopped hair and ground glass delivered in a simple cup of coffee: their land will be confiscated and added to his own.

He is a man of cunning, a man of conceit, of unquenchable desires: his wife must share him with his one thousand five hundred concubines, and another fifteen hundred slave girls. He is larger than life. His aspirations and dreams remain undiminished by the moderating influence of religion or experience. He is a man who acts in absolute terms without compromise and without patience.

***

In Novi Pazar, a small, dusty town in Rumelia, a green standard with a single crescent moon flutters above an elegant kiosk. The kiosk is decorated with gold and tiny glass windows which reflect the dazzle of the sun in hundreds of flickering little lights. Its roof is poised between function and high art being shaped eccentrically to emulate the curve of a fall of snow. Its doors are richly decorated, studded in brass and upon the lintel scripted in the jewelled calligraphy of the hand is 'Shadow and Spirit of God Amongst two Seas, Emperor and Sultan' – a copy of the inscription embossed above the Imperial Gate in Istanbul. On its wooden verandah with his legs apart stands a well comported man, the Sançak Bey – the regional administrator – with neatly trimmed moustache, jewelled yatağan, red turban decorated with an aigrette of pheasant and jay feathers and a blue satin cloak with ermine collar. In front of him, two hundred men on snorting, stamping horses have assembled in a dusty horde. Some from the Müsellem's stables and many more from timars and hiraşi from right across Rumelia and even from above the mouth of the Danube in the north west Black Sea.

The tughs, the horse-tail standards, are risen.

The horses they ride are descended from the Ghazis horses, cross-bred with local types, and now have become breeds of their own, particular to the area. These are solid horses, good for long missions and excellent for carrying weight. They have dense, short cannon bones and flat knees. They are spirited to handle and stamp the ground and snort and swish their tails and the stallions roar at the mares. The men assemble beneath different coloured standards and wear colours to match; they wear chain mail and two swords, a pair of pistols, a kagan shield, lance and çirit darts. Some carry bows and quivers filigreed in gold. They laugh and their eyes twinkle. Their long moustaches move when they grin, they spit and shout that they will show these soft town kapikulu what a provincial sipahi looks like and beat their backsides blue with the flat of a yatağan.

In the midst of assembled horses, and these big potent men, the seyis feels small and under-equipped, ill-armed with only his bow and quiver and small knife. He touches Azarax's flanks, and with Bora on a lead rein eases forward and stands stock still.

A drum roll chatters.

A horn rings out.

The men cease talking and shouting and pay attention to the portly Sançak Bey. When the drum ceases rolling the Sançak Bey holds up his portly arms and speaks.

'The Grand Vizier has called for his army!'

The men roar.

'The invincible army of the Turks!'

The air bursts with the impassioned voices of zeal.

'You will muster in Istanbul!'

The men roar again, shake their swords in the air and bang their shields.

'From all across the Empire thousands of men on thousands of horses will converge upon the city. And then you will march beneath the Holy Standard of the Prophet to Holy War!'

The timarli horsemen burst into a tremendous shout that rattles the glass in the windows of the kiosk and is heard all across the little town. They beat their fists on their chests and shout and wave their glistening helmets in the air. Horses rear and plunge and squeal and the men cry out: 'Allahu akbar!' God is great!

The Sançak Bey points to their leader, Ozay Dursun, a bear of a man riding a bear of a horse, both clad in lion skin; the horse – a stallion – rippling in as much muscle as his master; each an exact match one for the other, the man with massive biceps and the horse with bulging gaskin and stifle muscles, the hair cut in whorls and tattooed black; the two of them, unconquerable; the man, roughly shaved, handsome, laughing, rearing upon his huge plunging horse. The stallion tosses his head and his long mane flows in the air and he lands foursquare and solid upon his solid quarters and the seyis regards him with a stupefied expression. What chance has he in the ranks of men such as these?

Ozay Dursun shouts, the men cheer, the Sançak Bey hands the standard to a beautiful youth who carries it to the leader. Snatching it from his hands and holding it high in the air, Ozay Dursun waves it single handed above his head and shaking it in defiance of anyone who ventures an army against the Turks. The roar of 'Allahu akbar!' rakes the air. Dismissed in a single gesture by the Sançak Bey, the riders, released from any vestige of wishing to remain in their timars with their warm wives and smiling children, impelled by this raw man on his raw horse, swing behind the flowing standard above Ozay Dursun's head and lope magnificently down the long street of Novi Pazar shouting 'Allahu akbar!' in unison. The horsemen fold in behind in a dusty stream as the drums beat and the meterhane, the Turkish military band, squeals its high pipes through the rafters of the town.

They will head down through Bulgaristan but first must cross the Danube on the Silistra Ferry.

The Silistra Ferry, drawn across the slow moving, murky river by sweating slaves pulling ropes, whipped to their work by toothless task masters, extorting money in the service of the Sultan from any traveller, be he hadji, brigand, bandit, seyis, sipahi, janissary, paşa or peasant who wishes to cross the Danube, at Silistra. The Danube here is wide, its far bank disappearing behind veils of mist. Pay your aspers, be drawn across, the slaves in their rags will haul on the ropes, your horses may stand on the flat of the ferry – see how the ropes glide off, out of sight. Something huge plunges in the water. Out in the mist. Men draw their swords. The ropes creak, the slaves sweat, the fifteen horses on each ferry load chew their bits, whites cornering their eyes. Ferry loads of men have been hacked to death on arrival at the far side, the ropes have been severed and the ferry drifted away in the murky current to a demise that no-one ever knew. Arrows have flown suddenly through the mist. Fall off the ferry and drown. The Danube takes her toll. Fifteen aspers per man and horse. Come, pay, ride the Silistra ferry, watch the slaves sweat and pull.

***

Across the long hot Ludogorien plain they canter, past long lines of tired, swaying oxen drawing hundreds of laden wagons of grain, slogging their way to the menzilhane, the victualling stations that will supply the great army that is mustering in Istanbul.

They reach Varna, a crumbling citadel. Once, here, stood a palace of giants, and these huge, columns of stone supported a roof so high it was lost in cloud. The giants were slain in a terrific battle so long ago no-one even remembers its name.

They follow the cliffs beyond Varna to a beach and canter down to the sea. The horses thrash the water and men soak their bodies and their sweaty clothes as pods of dolphins dip and glide through the dark blue waters of the Euxine waves.

Fine blood draws men's hearts as swiftly as it draws their eyes. He is a man of low rank who rides close behind the seyis sitting upon his yağiz horse, Bora, leading the doru, Azarax as the column rides up from the tide. He is a Greek auxiliary, poorly mounted upon a ribby horse who hates him. Near this place the road divides on a corner beside rocks that fall to the sea. The day is hot, the cicadas ring out, seagulls call in the sky, the waves roll on the gravelly shore below. The column rounds the corner, the Greek spurs his unwilling grey, squeezes the yağiz horse to his left, pushes the seyis at the rock's edge, and lunges for the bridle.

In mid-flight the teeth of a doru horse close round his wrist. He is ripped from his saddle, spilled down a bank and now lies below, groaning on the rocks, lapped by the waves, right down on the sea shore.

Two karaman stallions trot off with their seyis, tails swinging, followed by a riderless grey now jogging sweetly along with his ears pricked and stirrups flapping. 'Mahş allah!' the seyis whispers. He does not look back. No, this seyis has learned the value of loyalty. He does not question it. An eye for an eye. Life is cheap. He pats his horses' necks. 'At çok güzel!' he chuckles. 'You brilliant creatures. It was him or me.' Twice, in less than a month.

***

Six days later, flush from the journey, faces rouged by wind and sun, this hard band of timarli sipahi stand in a rolling cloud of dust outside the northern gate of the walls of Theodosius, in Istanbul.

Istanbul, Crossroad of the World: one way west to Buda and Vienna. To the east runs the road to Herat, Samarkand and China. To the south Babylon and Zanzibar while the northern road leads to Kiev.

Here, in the polyglot, polychrome city of stones, with its myriad minarets and mosques of faience and gold, through the streets mingle turbanned Moors and muttering Jews, Zoroastrians, Christians and those ancient Turks from the east, the Ghazis, the mysterious Seven Sleepers, Necklace of God. Here lies Eyyub, Holy Man, Arm of the Prophet, Blessings be Upon Him.

Entering the city by the gate at the head of the Golden Horne, the seyis sitting on his doru stallion, gazes in awe at the stacked towers, the many mosques, the Greek churches and, there, the tomb of Eyyub himself. The column follows the edge of the blue water of the Golden Horne. The men peer across to the other side at the many lateen-sailed corsairs moored to the quay, with fishing nets cast up in the sun to dry. The air wafts with a powerful aroma of sea, sea weed and grilling fish. Men cry out to them; welcome to the bosom of Empire; feel its invincibility, feel its permanence, feel its power.

Ozay Dursun canters his big horse to the Davut Ağa Mosque, where he meets six mounted, uniformed men on horseback. One of the men, gloriously caparisoned in a huge white turban, cloak, bright red corselet with gold bosses, wearing a gem-studded yatağan, soft leather boots, barks orders. He is Soliman Chia, the baş imrahor, Master of the Horse.

The Veterans bow their heads.

Ozay Dursun commands the seyis and his two horses to one side, together with two timarli sipahi and their horses. He whistles once and the rest of the troop lope off behind him, past the Yeni Davut Ağa mosque and out along the low shore-line below the Topkapi where the Bosphorus and the Golden Horne join.

The baş imrahor gazes coolly at the three men and the four horses that have been selected for the Royal Stables, and satisfied with what he sees, signals for them to follow. They trot away from the seafront at Galata up the hill towards the Topkapi Palace.

It takes five minutes for them to reach the end of the At Meydan, where the seyis sees the entwined snakes heads in the distance and the column of Theodosius and of the Obelisk, and is dazzled by the cool magnificence of the Blue Mosque, such a building he has never beheld. And as they continue swiftly on their way to his left lies Ayasofya then to his right the baths of Roxeanne. In front stretches the Sea of Marmara, but his attention returns to his left and to the great minarets of Ayasofya, and before it the glittering kiosk in front of the Imperial Gate, with its gold filigree and dazzling white marble.

Guards stand aside and salute as the baş imrahor clatters straight through the Imperial Gate followed by the small troop of horse which pass quickly through the outer court, enter below the Gate of Felicity with its gilded canopy and magnificently clothed guards, and run straight down to the Privy Stables, where they are ordered to dismount.

The cool darkness of the stables greets them, and the horses are immediately allocated stalls. Balls of barley bound with sheep fat and blackstrap are placed in front of them and their riders are ordered to report to the baş imrahor.

Told to wait in turn, the seyis is last. Finally he is admitted and asked to give his name and state his timar holding number and place. He is then asked to sign, which he cannot do. He can neither read nor write.

The baş imrahor regards him without expression. 'You are the seyis of Ali-aga Izobegović.'

'Yes, Ağa.'

'You will call me baş imrahor Paşa.'

'Yes, baş imrahor Paşa.'

Soliman Chia sits back and inspects the creature standing in front of him. A typical seyis: small, frail, foreign. Balkan bred, despite the high cheeks bones: a Tartar or Tekke originally. A pretty boy. He carries a bow, no doubt with pretensions to use it. Unable to strike a target from ten paces, probably. No strength in his arms. He has no sword. Only the hand that holds a sword will ever aspire to a sceptre. He is rayah. Common cattle. He will flee at the sight of blood. The only thing he lacks to make him the perfect seyis is the poor-me stance, the red, watery-eyed stoop of the victim, the hard-done-by, living in penury, hand-wringing tearful seyis, forgetting he put himself there and has made no effort to step out of it. But wait. This one is not quite that ilk. He stands up straight and his eye is clear. The world has not weighed on him yet. It will.

Soliman Chia's eyes return to the piece of paper on the table. 'Did you breed the doru and the yağiz horses yourself?' His eyes rise and settle on the disfiguring pink pigmentation of the seyis' fingers. The seyis moves his hands behind his back.

He nods. 'Yes, baş imrahor Paşa, I bred both horses myself.'

Soliman Chia grunts once again. There is little point in saying they are exceptionally fine horses. He would deign it a compliment, rather than an observation. Nevertheless he seems intelligent. Too intelligent for a seyis. He lacks ambition: though he has something indefinable about him. Something close to his heart. Perhaps there is an ambition there, but what is it? To be the perfect seyis? Could be. Or something else? Something connected with his horses: they are in good order and are well balanced. Yes, it is connected with the horses: to produce the perfect horse? Mmm. Interesting. I shall have to watch this one.

'As common a pair of mules that ever clattered out of a Rumelian gutter,' he grunts dismissively sliding the blade of a small knife under a fingernail. The seyis does not move, nor alter his expression.

'There is strict discipline here. Any breach is punished immediately. If you work hard and keep your horses well schooled you will come to no harm. If you are lazy you will be punished. Do you understand?'

'I am not lazy and yes, baş imrahor Paşa, I understand.'

Soliman Chia raises his eyebrows: 'Not lazy? Excellent. I am pleased to hear it. Though it is I who shall decide whether you are lazy or not. Now go.'

He watches him leave. Fool: should have kept his mouth shut: he was beginning to wonder if he might have had something about him, the horses are after all, pure Karaman, the best that have been delivered from the provinces for a long time. They will go to the hassa sipahi. As for their breeder – the earth will claim him as it claims all seyises when the cannons begin to play.

- 5 -

Soliman Chia, Baş Imrahor

The sky is dark, the sea is black and only the smallest glimmerings of torches flicker on the water: so many hundreds of lights slipping across the narrow band of waves that divides Occident from Orient.

All night long a steady procession of draft animals and wagons have been droved to the water's edge on the far side of the city, and loaded onto the wide, low-gunwhaled boats that bear them by oar and sail across the straits to Levant, Bebek and Karaköy. All summer this steady stream of men and animals have been pouring into the city and passing through.

The planning has been meticulous: the tonnage of rations required for the men, hardtack, rice, mutton, clarified butter, bread, honey, and the wood that is required to light the stoves to bake the bread or boil the meat had been calculated to the last okka.

In the past fifteen days the traffic in men at arms and animals coming from Haydarpaşa, Uskudar and further up the Bosphorus at Beylerbeyi has increased; all kinds of people arrive dressed in all kinds of clothes: men in flowing thobes of sheer cotton with gold hemming, men from exotic military units in huge feathered hats, horse-hoof armour and conical brass helmets. Veiled women borne in curtained chaises, glide slowly through the streets upon the massive shoulders of muscled Nubian slaves. Fantastically caparisoned camels stroll like heroes beneath the canopies of the tall wooden buildings. Men in enormous multi-coloured turbans mix with ragged dervishes; men in kapakh hats ride small brown horses, tall Baluchis with blue eyes pass by on long slender horses with long slender faces; men with war axes, pistols, swords, scimitars and daggers push menacingly through the crowds. Tattooed men pass, men from the marches of the south, men from the Kavkas in high boots and carrying richly filigreed kindjal daggers.

Pale, heavily laden donkeys have come with long, dusty contingents from Syria; strange accents are heard, women hide behind doors.

Peculiar scents arrive with these people. Some walk past in an aroma of perfumes: jasmine, attar, myrrh. They carry rosaries which they turn over and over in their fingers. The timarli sipahi from Mesopotamia arrive on their ranks of grey horses with their dark muzzles and burning eyes. They high step and call out, flatten their ears and challenge other stallions; they swish their tails and curl their nostrils, the men upon their backs darkened by their long hot journeys across the Syrian sands, the Taurus mountains and the high windblown Anatolian plateau. The backs of their hands burned and peeling, they ride past in an aroma of horse sweat and cardomom.

Artisans fill the streets: loriners, cobblers, tailors, carpenters, gunsmiths, metal workers, dwarves, women with goitres, men with no limbs pushing themselves along in the dirt and the grime on calloused knuckles, their hands toughened like shoes. Dancing bears on leashes struggle along the harbours, conjurors, magicians and tricksters play to spontaneous audiences in corners of the city. Firebreathers, stilt walkers, jugglers, prostitutes with hennaed hands, hennaed hair and tattooed faces and merchants in fine silks, wearing slippers with silver thread walk in their midst. Money changers and scribes and cobblers, farriers and black-smiths, little Tekke girls yo-yoing wool on hand spinning jennies come across the water on the slave-sweating ferries. They come to provision the army. They come to profit from war.

***

Overawed by the sense of power, the layers of gold, the dazzling white marble, the glittering guards, the acres of blue tiles, the decorated columns, the gilded ceilings, the strutting janissaries, the fine coaches and glossy horses, the seyis leads his two Karaman stallions into the Privy Stables, holding them firmly, terrified of making some appalling gaffe. The other twenty-two seyises watch him, watch the horses and signal him to separate them, to put one in one stall at the end of the stable and one at the other. This, he knows, will not work. It will not work because these two horses have been brought up together and have always been stabled side-by-side, stood at each others shoulders. It will not work because they are already threatening the other horses, already establishing their own position in this place. The head seyis, a Persian with a scar cutting down through one eye, flattening the eyelid and staining the iris red, takes Bora's rein and attempts to lead him off and is met instantly by high-pitched squealing, rearing and a thrashing of forefeet. The seyis tries an appeal not to divide them but the Persian seyis pulls on the rein harder and Bora plunges. All the other horses have begun stamping their feet and squealing and so the Persian seyis relaxes the rein and hisses: 'Shut up or we shall have the baş imrahor in here and we shall all be flogged. What's the matter with this horse, isn't he schooled?'

'Do not divide them, not now. Put them together,' the seyis says firmly and he feels the eyes of the others on him, their resentment at his arrival, the stranger in their midst, him and his two fancy stallions which now means they will have to do extra work, to move the horses around just to accommodate some Balkan timarli sipahi's ill-trained Karamans. Nevertheless, the seyis gets his way and the horses are tethered beside one another and they settle.

Leaning on the stall end the other seyises question him: 'Who bred these screws, how old are they, what can they do?' The seyis remains quiet and says nothing. He works around them, grooming them, picking out their feet and ignoring the jibes and soon they break away and leave him alone. Instead, they stand beside their own horses, grooming and looking over their backs at him, throwing looks between one another.

It take a few days for the Karaman stallions to become accustomed to their new surroundings and in that time they bind more closely and are to be found, when taken from their stalls, standing head to head, whickering at each other, nipping at the skin on each other's shoulders and manes, grooming each other.

When taken out for the first time to the At Meydan, the Horse Guards, near the great Blue Mosque, men drift towards them through the dust and stand with their arms folded, stroking their long great beards and nodding: 'Karaman atik – Karaman horses,' they say, 'Güzeleştirmek – Beautiful.'

In the evening the seyis returns the stallions to the Palace Stables, where all work under the threat of punishment: 'Watch out for Soliman Chia, the baş imrahor,' one of the seyises hisses: 'He is a monster. If he catches your horses with a speck of dirt on them, you will be flogged. If your horse throws riders, he will be shot. If he bites, he will be shot. If those horses of yours kick, they will be shot.'

Beads of sweat break out on the seyis' forehead as he grooms his two horses, humming a terse little tune.

Day by day more and more columns of armed men march through the At

Meydan and into the Palace grounds. Day by day, horsemen arrive and canter through the At Meydan, and down to the Kagithane Meadows. Lines of cannon drawn by great white oxen lumber across the At Meydan and through the narrow streets to the Pera Barracks. Hundreds of wagon loads of cannon ball and barrels of gunpowder rumble past the stables. Men driving light traps loaded with muskets and yatağan sabres trot past the outer palace walls and cross the Golden Horne to the barracks beyond.

One day the baş imrahor orders all fifty-two Palace horses down to the Kagithane Meadows. The seyis is riding Azarax and leading Bora. The column of horses is halted at one end and on the middle line of the Kagithane Meadows. On either side, two lines of cannon have been drawn up, facing each other. The baş imrahor wishes to know which horses are properly schooled and which are not. The cannons will be fired, he shouts, and the column must walk through the barrage, through the smoke and roaring muzzles, the bursts of flame and the stench of burned wadding and saltpetre.

The cannons will fire blanks, he says reining his splendid bay horse. But sometimes blanks kill, he adds with a chuckle, enjoying the whitening faces of the grooms.

He then canters to the far end of the meadows and when he is positioned at the centre line, he holds up a hand, and the column, three hundred yards away, begins to move toward him. When they are quarter way down the meadows, the cannons open fire. The heat blasts, plumes of flame, and billowing smoke cause most of the horses to rear, dip their hind quarters, fight their riders, and gad off in the direction from which they came.

The firing continues booming and thundering, belching huge clouds of white smoke so that the whole meadow becomes enveloped and it is impossible to see if the column still moves or if it does not.

At the far end of the meadows, sitting on his horse, which has also reacted to the cannons, the baş imrahor watches and presently through the smoke and flying wadding a Tekke seyis emerges riding one Karaman and leading another. Though both horses are excited, and jog, they are in control. All the other horses have gone. The baş imrahor blinks and looks away.

**

In the Royal Privy Stables a lone figure in the darkness smoothes the glossy quarters of a muscled horse. The horse shifts to one side, turns his long neck to the man, and whickers, softly. Another horse whickers, and another. Chains rattle. A vigorous shudder tells the seyis that the milk-white horse is on his feet. He stands at the end of the line, in a single open stall. Unlike the other horses he is untethered.

The sound of feet hurrying down stone steps triggers whickering responses from the stables as ears are pricked and all the horses turn their heads to the door. Hurrying feet and the appearance of royal grooms, triggers a response from fifty-two fit stallions, standing in two rows of twenty-six, who squeal for their breakfast.

Soliman Chia, the baş imrahor, who has entered the stable by the big double south door, walks swiftly along the two lines of horses, his hard eye at once falling on the slightest hesitation in the movement of a horse. In his hand he bears as silver-topped horse-whip. The silver topped horse-whip is not for the horses. It is for the seyis whose horse is found lying down, indolent in his stall. The silver topped horse-whip is for the seyis whose horse does not ripple with muscle and who, at dawn, does not cry out for his feed: it is for the seyis whose horse has a loose shoe.

Opulently dressed in his royal blue satin salvár tucked into short leather boots, Soliman Chia wears a huge deep blue silk turban today. Over his pale blue silk chemise he dons his mark of office: a gold-threaded riding coat, embroidered with Turko-Ghazi horse motifs. A glittering yatağan hangs at his side. A silver filigreed kindjal, a Caucasian short-sword, is plugged into his wide maroon cummerbund.

He is a powerfully built man with big, brown, rheumy eyes. He has a hooked nose and dense, grey moustache. His jowls are rouged by the Cypriot wine that always accompanies his long, nightly vigils during which, in secret, he curses the Great New Ghazi Hope, the Orderer of New Worlds, the Advancer of New Kingdoms, the Expander of the Ottoman Empire: the Grand Vizier, Kara Mustafa – whom he loathes.

He regards his line of seyises standing between their horses with his slow blinking, slow moving, wine-stained eyes. The seyises do not move. They fear to move. They fear the baş imrahor. Soliman Chia has little patience for grooms who do not do what he thinks grooms should do. His punishments are devised to fit the crime. One day he found two seyises guilty of wasting barley: they had spilled some from a sack. To ensure their respect for barley for the future, he had two piles of 250 okka (half a ton) poured onto the floor of a building. These two men were then made to move it grain by grain across the courtyard to an empty building opposite. The one who was last to move his pile would be ganched – stripped to the loins, bound hand and foot and dropped three metres onto a single iron hook.

In horror of such punishment the two men threw themselves into their task.

At first the other seyises laughed, to watch these two men running from building to building, into the hard sunlight and then into deep shadow carrying one grain of barley. The two seyises even laughed themselves, finding it a humorous occupation to run with one grain of barley from this building to that. Their laughter had soon ceased when they witnessed the piles in the empty building rising so slowly, while they had already seemed to have run so far. After an hour there was only a small handful in each of their stacks. After two hours there was scarcely more. Already sweating, they had stitches and had to stop to catch their breath.

Then they ran on and on, in and out of the shadows with their grains of barley. By mid morning they had begun to despair as the piles of barley in the other building grew so minutely, while the great piles appeared barely to decrease at all. By the end of the first day both were in tears and begged for forgiveness on their knees. Soliman Chia ordered that every single grain be moved. After one and a half days only one fiftieth of each pile had been shifted. After two days the men's faces were torn with pain and both cried out for mercy: their cries could be heard by the other seyises, and even the horses stood with their ears back. Soon they could run no longer and stumbled and fell between the buildings carrying the grains of barley. Finally one man could carry no more and cried out that he would rather be ganched. He was dragged away. It took the men three days to recover: neither was ganched but they had learned to respect barley.

On another occasion, a seyis who failed to water the Sultan's horse was made, in the heat of summer, to carry water to every horse in the Kagithane meadows. He was gagged and forbidden to touch a drop himself. If he tried to drink, like a concubine who had offended the Sultan, he would be stitched into a sack with two cannon balls, taken out by boat and sunk into the Marmara Sea. After one day his mouth was raw from the gag and he was already staggering. By day two he could barely pick up the buckets. By the end of the third day he was crawling on his hands and knees in amongst the horses in the Kagithane meadows, deliriously. Never did he fail to water a horse again. The seyis who once beat and terrorised a horse was shut in a stable with an insane stallion. Two hours later he was removed. He had lost an ear, his right hand was crushed, his hair had been torn out and he was unable to walk. No seyis in the Royal Stables ever terrorised a horse when they saw what a horse could do when the tables were turned.

The seyises' respect for Soliman Chia was strong.

***

The stable floors in the Topkapi Palace are swept to a polish. The horses are curried until they glow. The horses' saddles, bridles and harness are tallowed to mirrors. Their hooves cut to perfection, shod with seven nails on plate shoes, oiled and polished. No loose hair grows around the horses' muzzles. No dirt is found on their coats. The seyis' clothes are spotless and the monastic lives they lead are lean, hard, singular and exemplary. Every day the horses are taken out for a game of çirit and exercise either to the Kagithane Meadows or to the At Meydan. Here the seyises prepare their charges for their hassa sipahi riders and watch as the games are played. Favourite riders emerge over the summer, for whose masculine attentions the amber-eyed daughters of the Ottoman court vie. They even make favourites of some of the horses. Favourites come and go. The At Meydan is strung with flags and round its edges, carpet sellers ply their trade. Chai-khanas sell tea and succulent sweets and the meterhane bands play music throughout the day and deep into the night as the horses gallop. The seagulls fly overhead and the leaves of the trees shade the veiled and richly jewelled women in their chaises, drawn by huge, domesticated oryxes.

Any horses found to be below standard are taken away and sent to other regiments. Different riders ride different horses and one day Envir Altinay Paşa, a ramrod six-footer with a square get-out-of-my-way chin and a Magyar moustache, looks straight through the seyis when he addresses him, as though he were lecturing the air behind.

'From where have these two come?' he intones in a weary voice as though the reply bored him already, his eyes fixed on the other side of the invisible seyis.

'From the timar of Ali-aga Izobegović, Paşa,' the seyis replies quietly, 'in the sançak of Bor, in Serbia.'

'Never heard of it. They are Karaman?'

'Yes, Paşa.'

'They are schooled to gunshot?'

'They are schooled to musket, pistol, sabre, lance, çirit darts and arrows, Paşa.'

'Saddle the doru.'

The seyis has seen this man play çirit and he is good. He is good also with a yatağan, slashing above the horses' ears and missing – which some do not – and galloping at a target with the lance and striking – where most had missed. He has fired musket and pistol between a horse's ears and has hit a small target at over a hundred paces. The seyis does not saddle the horse as quickly as he might. This man is going to like this horse. But is the horse going to like the man? A butterfly flutters in the seyis' belly as he looks into the horse's eye. The secret of the auguries of his birth is one that he has kept to himself. Knowledge of it would have singled him out and the seyis would have lost his charge immediately. He had not even told the baş imrahor. He dreaded Ali-aga Izobegović arriving in Istanbul one day and spilling the story. He would be punished for not telling the baş imrahor. The Whorl of the Spurs was problem enough and had been the first thing the baş imrahor had noticed. But it has not been remarked upon by Envir Altinay. If this man chooses this horse, he will ride him always.

Envir Altinay mounts Azarax and canters him slowly round the At Meydan. He rides well but the horse is not comfortable. He's moving his legs badly and is not up into the bit. He and the man are not suited. Round and round they go changing gaits but the horse is wooden and not responding fluidly. If the man hits him in the mouth like that again, Azarax will throw him. The seyis closes a fist. He can see it coming. He'll be shot! Abruptly the man turns him and canters back to the seyis. Slipping off in one movement he says: 'Saddle the yağiz.'

Something passes between the two horses in this instant. The seyis notices but Envir Altinay does not. The saddle is girthed up on Bora and Envir Altinay mounts. Bora treats him well. He canters stylishly. He crests his neck and flutes his nostrils. His big eyes glitter and he moves easily, with grace and high style. So that was it. When Envir Altinay returns he is patting the horse's neck and is smiling. The horse had chosen the man. Even before he rode him. The yağiz, Bora, will be his first battle horse; the doru, the Ghazi Azarax, his second.

The seyis stands with his mouth open. How – why did they decide that? You brilliant creatures.

***

Lanterns are lit swiftly though the stables.

Between each pair of stallions a seyis now stands, having groomed his two charges, swept with his bare hands any stable dirt from their faces and bodies and cleaned any left-over feed or dirt from their mangers. Water from the goatskin he carries has been tipped into a stone trough.

In the darkness the seyis feels the smooth touch of skin over sinew. He runs his hands across the fine bodies of his two fine horses, feeling the hard stifle and gaskin muscles, the muscle across their chests and the iron-hard tendon beneath their taut, fit and velvet silk coats. He runs his hands over the horses' backs knuckling their spine to the wither and sweeping away the tiny pieces of dust and saman that the horses have flicked up there in the night, swiping at mosquitoes.

Upon the command of the baş imrahor, the seyises run to the feed room, fetch balls of roasted barley bound with blackstrap and raw egg, hurry back to their stalls and give one to each of their horses.

The stallions stamp their feet and whicker and neigh.

It is good if the stallion is impatient for his food: it is good if he eats it with his long dark, glossy neck bent to his food, his eyes blazing. It is good to see his ears flat as he bites with his strong teeth into the barley balls. It is good to see the fan of sinew spread out across the semi-circle of his broad jaw, the nasal sinew fly up and his orbital fossa plunge and dip above the eye with every mouthful.

The horses eat greedily. They watch with their big dark eyes.

From the high minarets of Ayasofya and of the Blue Mosque, come the clear cries of the muezzin.

Now all the grooms except one, leave their horses eating. They do not hurry to the mosque. Gathering in the courtyard of the Privy Stables, under the great wall beneath the harness rooms, as sun scatters the sky and sea in gold, they lay out their prayer rugs and, facing south, pray. Then all is still.

It is 10th October, 1682.

- 6 -

Two hearts, Two minds, One will

Kara Mustafa is at prayer. He prays for his soul. He prays for his Sultan. He prays for his Sultan's soul. He prays that this day his destiny is to be fulfilled.

He will wear gold and diamonds, pin a pearl in the lobe of his right ear and cover his great frame in pale green silk as befits the son-in-law of the Sultan, the Grand Vizier of the Ottoman Empire. The silk will have floral stitching and his turban will be vast and of the whitest white. He will scent his beard. He will girdle his waist in sashes of embroidered Chinese silks, deep maroon, threaded with gold. At his side his emerald studded sword will hang. He shall mount his splendid, stamping black charger, imbued with the spirit and power of his equine Ghazi forebears. He shall ride magnificent at his magnificent Sultan's side. The Standard of the Holy Prophet will fly in the wind. The Six Horse-Tail Tughs, the standard of the Sultan at War, will cause even the camels to roar. Scar-faced levents with oiled bodies, shaven heads and great muscled backs will unscabbard their swords and stab the air and they will glitter in the sky. The golden-sinewed army which he will command in his Sultan's stead will bear him like a monarch in a chariot drawn by his celestial steeds to the Throne of Everlasting Glory.

The Holy Roman Emperor will grovel at his feet.

Beneath the fluttering Holy Standard, beneath the flying Crescent Moon will the waves of the army of the Turks burst forth, unstoppable, and his horses will dung the encausted tiles in the Nave of St Peter's in Rome.

Upon the banks of the Rhine the people shall stoop and prostrate themselves before him.

Losing some land in Podolya to some Poles means nothing. Losing a little more to the Russian Bear means nothing. Losing thousands of men to the sword means nothing and although, since he became Vizier, he has lost more land than Ahmed Köprülü, the Vizer before him gained, he will outdazzle him yet.

Leopold I is his neighbour. Leopold I resides in Vienna, his capital, in Austria.

Kara Mustafa will not address him as The Holy Roman Emperor.

There are not in this world two Emperors.

His Sultan is Emperor.

The Sultan springs from a line so illustrious that the Holy Roman Emperor appears, by comparison, to be sovereign over nothing more than darkness, filled with cold, misery and disease, inhabited by a ragbag of tiny men with red noses and women not fit to be concubines nor serve meals to the servants of cockroaches. His horses are ill-bred, his people feast upon pigflesh, vilely. They are oppressed by this brutal king, bound in religion to a humble Levantine hammered to a cross. Their souls will forever be condemned to the eternity of squalor and grime.

The time is come to bring them Light. By the sword.

* * *

Ottoman lands abut Austria, which lies beside Hungary and Hungary is an Ottoman possession. A dispute between Leopold I and an Ottoman vassal Count in Hungary by the name of Imre Thököli provides the spark to ignite Kara Mustafa's keg. Without the fog of subtlety to obfuscate his vision, Kara Mustafa sees, with absolute clarity, what must be done.

On 6th August 1682, from the Imperial Divan in the Topkapi Palace, the course of war is determined. The army will depart in October in two stages. The first stage, on the 10th October 1682, will be the exit of the Sultan and his Imperial Bodyguard from the Palace with all ceremony. The next stage, 19th October 1682, will be the exit of the Grand Vizier and the army with all ceremony. They will march to Adrianopole, Edirne, one-time capital of the early Ottomans. There they shall overwinter. In March they will advance in a body to Belgrade, where their Africa corps will join them.

With their 150,000 strong infantry and artillery and 77,000 sipahi they shall strike into the land of Leopold I. The Khan of the Tartars will support the sipahi with his freebooters on their massed horse and the Leopold I will rue the day he ever inhabited a throne that abuts the land of the Ottomans.

His Emissary, Caprara, currently resident in Istanbul, will be taken hostage, although accorded the privileges fitting to his station, and accompany the Ottoman army to his homeland, where he may then, at his leisure, witness it being blown asunder from end to end.

***

The seyis hurries back from his morning prayers to his horses. The city is bursting with sound: wheels grinding over stone, men shouting, animals calling, birds chattering, storks clapping their bills, seagulls cawing, the baş imrahor barking orders. His horses have to leave for Edirne today with the Sultan. Even this force is to be divided. The Sultan wishes to hunt. He anticipates being in Edirne in December. The Vizier anticipates being in Edirne in November. The Vizier is leaving after the Sultan. The Sultan is to go to Edirne by way of every forest in Rumelia. The decisions of Sultans and Viziers are beyond the reasoning of seyises. Seyises deal with each day as it comes. They must live day by day according to the Higher Will.

Insignificant seyises look after horses – at the whim of their masters. And Envir Altinay Paşa has now become the seyis' master.

Envir Altinay Paşa is a skilled horseman and he handles horse and weapons well. He is a whirlwind of a man with his strong arms and the flying darts, he is a lion with his white teeth and his roar, he is an acrobat and can bend down in the saddle and pick a dart up from the ground and hurl it again. He has been riding Bora every day and although the horse has responded well, he trots and canters and corners and gallops with his ears back. The man is competent: he holds the reins well and sits properly, he looks out over the horse's head and not into it, he is relaxed and his hips move in unison with the horse's muscles – he is a fine horseman: the men cheer and even the seyises and slaves shout and whistle, he can hurl a çirit dart further than anyone and has knocked opponents clean from their saddles with one well-aimed shot. He relies on his hands to do this and his legs to do that. Even the Sultan has changed elbows as he cradles his chin watching the games and he too, is a fine horseman.

But Envir Altinay Paşa neither notices nor knows how a man's inner instincts are minutely recorded by horses.

He does not know that the voice the horse hears is not the outer but the inner one. It is the inner voice to which a horse first responds and then to the outer. If these voices are at odds then the horse obeys at a level which is mechanical, and will work only mechanically. The horse will not be able to use his talents. He will not be able to fit his mind to the mind of the rider nor move his legs as finely as he is able.

Something stains Envir Altinay's heart that makes the horse hold his ears back. Envir Altinay might be a Paşa, he might go to the mosque and pray five times a day: he might give ten percent of his income to the poor and walk like a man with the heart of a bull and the bearing of a Ghazi knight – but the horse knows something about him which he does not reveal.

'Show me a horse and I will tell you about his master,' the seyis breathes: 'I'm glad Bora belongs to me.'

The seyis watches as Envir Altinay ends the game of çirit. He has won again. Now he flings the reins over the horse's head and drops from the saddle, slaps Bora hard on the neck, barks an order to the seyis and swaggers across the dusty, roaring, cheering, whistling ground, past the column of Theodosius and the obelisk, past the spiral snakes on the spina and flops on to the Bokhara rugs under the trees to drink apple chai and croon with the silk-draped, dark-eyed daughters of the Viziers and Paşas and their silvery laughter who have come to pull the hairs on his chest and drown in his eyes.

The seyis leads the black-sweated Bora back to the stables. The horse nips the sleeve of his chemise and holds it in his teeth. He knows his seyis knows and his seyis knows he knows. We do our best. If a man does not know, he does not know; there is little hope. The horse steps on, drops the seyis' sleeve and feels the mottled pink, reassuring fingers tighten on his neck under his mane.

A high pitched squeal from Azarax in the stables signifies one who knows. The seyis would recognise that voice anywhere. Out of the voices of thousands of horses, he can pick it out as easily as he would a needle glinting in the saman. Bora responds. The horses greet each other in the cool of the marbled interior with noses to knees and the flying front foot. Muzzle to muzzle, the crested neck, the whicker. Saddle off and a bucket of water across the back. The seyis smoothes the water and sweat off with the flat of his hand. The horse looks around as though he has entered the stable for the first time: the seyis smiles. 'Bora,' he says and splits a colossal water melon into quarters, a half for him and a half for Azarax and as tenderly as a mother for her newborn child, gazes on, squatting down beside them as they slobber and gulp and chew and drool, their eyes flat and calm in the unity of each other's company, their seyis who watches over them and the sweet, cool, pink flesh of the watermelon.

The flies buzz in the stables, the noise of the çirit games cease, and the afternoon slows. A slow sea breeze ruffles the leaves of the trees in the inner court and in the stable yard. The seagulls caw overhead and namagua doves coo softly in the branches.

Azarax stands peacefully in his stall, eyes glazed as though suspended from the normal run of life, not quite asleep, not quite awake. Bora sleeps the sleep of a horse, eyes half-open. The seyis kneads the horse's muscles and hums some strange, terse little tune.

He waits until he hears the echoing footsteps of the baş imrahor retreat down the white marble into the long, hot afternoon. Except for the horses, the stables are empty.

The seyis collects his bow and quiver. He makes a tiny sound which flicks the switch that restores Azarax to animation, watches him stretch and yawn, clench his jaw, and shake. The seyis puts a hand to the muzzle, Azarax's big brown eyes swing to meet his and the horse is ready. On goes the bridle. On goes the cantle-less saddle. Up vaults the seyis. An unspoken word to Bora and he and Azarax clip out of the stables into the lowering afternoon sun.

The seyis leaves the instruction to his horse. Azarax walks and then, in his own time, he racks. From racking he turns to quarter trot.

The seyis is alert, waiting. It is a game.

From quarter trot, the horse gathers to half then to full then to extended trot.

The seyis obeys the horse.

Suddenly the horse switches his gait, his head comes up, the seyis feels his big powerful hind quarters spring and feels the three-beat drum of a canter.

It is a slow, paced canter.

From paced canter he moves effortlessly into a slow gallop.

From slow gallop they go to half, three quarter, then full.

The horse gallops. Sand flies behind him.

His breath rises and falls with each stride.

There is magnificence in the rhythm. The pace is powerful and even. The wind buffets in the seyis' ears. The horse's ears are levelled with the wind. Wind billows the clothes of the seyis. His eyes stream with water. The speed is high.

Of his own volition, the horse hits the sand harder.

The horse can feel his own power. He loves to feel his own power. He loves to feel his own power with the seyis because the seyis loves to feel his power and shouts in the wind to the horse that he is a fine horse and very strong.

He shouts it again and again.

He feels incredibly free.

It is as though the world is spinning beneath their feet.

The horse and the seyis are a streak of light in a blur of flying walls and sea and sky.

The seyis is low in the saddle and now the horse pulls on even harder. His stride has lengthened and it is enormous.

They belong to the air.

They belong to the air with the pounding touch of the hoof on the face of the earth and the horse spins it faster still.

This horse is stretched right out.

He goes even faster.

His energy is coming from the sun and the wind and the sea and the rushing floor of the world as he flicks it beneath his flying hooves as though it were a weightless ball and now he goes faster still. And then when it is not possible and the seyis is screaming and his eyes are streaming, the horse goes even faster. The seyis releases the reins, draws his bow, turns at the hip and when the horse is stretched out to absolute maximum velocity, the seyis shoots three arrows into his last three hoof prints, the mark of the horseman archer.

Two hearts, two minds, one will.

The hassa sipahi Envir Altinay Paşa is a fine horseman. He is a very fine horseman.

But his groom is in another league.

- 7 -

Omens of the Wind

'Seventeen royal horses will be leaving today,' the strutting, red-faced baş imrahor barks, 'the others will remain.' Rings flash on his fingers as he rolls the whip in his hands.

The night before, in their dim, candle-lit tallet lofts above the horses the seyises had been whispering. Only seventeen horses will be going with the Sultan's bodyguard to Edirne tomorrow, they hissed through the gloom to each other, eyeing the door. Shhh! The Persian seyis tiptoed to the door, felt its cool hard surface against his ear, held out a hand, sshh... depressed the latch, grimaced, edged open the door, peered out: no-one there.

Only seventeen going to war? What about the rest? – in lower whispers.

Staying.

Who's going? Who stays? Shoulders shrug.

Think of it: adventure: war! War means spoil, spoil means gold, silver, jewels. Money – one campaign and you are rich. Never work again: go and live in Buda, Belgrade, Tirana, Adana. I know a seyis – Syrian – he left this very building with Ahmed Köprülü's horse for St Gothard in 1672. He won so much gold he had to hire ten mules to carry it. Where is he now? Albania: living on the sea in a great white house with an Egyptian wife and twenty slaves. How about that? You could even win a timar! Imagine? Land of your own!

'What? A seyis? Win a timar?' the old Armenian runs a thick tongue across brown teeth. 'No, I'll tell you what happens to seyises: they get tossed to the guns. Do you think they are going to waste their prize janissaries on the first onslaught? Do you? Seyises are seven to the asper. If you don't get thrown to the guns you wind up as cannon fodder and work your guts out just in time to get blown to pieces. Or else dig mines just in

76

time to get blown to pieces. That's what happens to seyises. Timars and gold. There's no way any seyis is going to wind up with a timar, forget it. It's the lucky ones who will be staying, believe me. Whoever goes will never return. End of story. And as for the horses – your precious horses? They'll be çiorba in a week – that's if they make the journey to Győr. Know how far Győr is? A thousand miles. How much barley is there going to be for your horses? Know how many horses are going? 77,000. Now just how much grazing do you think there is going to be when that lot have taken a mouthful each? Want my advice? Get on your knees and pray. Pray to stay. A winter in Edirne? Have you been there? In a tent? With 150,000 army cut-throats and 77,000 horses? If you don't get murdered you'll freeze to death.'

They had gone on whispering during the night: never mind about the old Armenian, he's a misery, he'll never leave, he wants to die here, but think! Better than waiting for the baş imrahor to find a way to murder you. If you stay they'll just ganch you or drop you in a sack into the sea. No: it's the only way. Adventure – loot – and a timar!

The gold-threaded horse motifs on the baş imrahor's magnificent coat gleam as he swaggers, whip behind his back, between the lines of seyises. His lips are puckered. He has made his selection – with a last minute change. He stops in front of the seyis standing between his yağiz and doru horses. The top of the seyis' head reaches his shoulder. The baş imrahor draws himself up to his full height, curls his lip and gazes down. The great man's eyes rove across the doru, Azarax, and fall on his marking, the Whorl of the Spurs.

'I suppose you think this horse is somehow charmed?' the baş imrahor growls at the seyis, 'with his Whorl of the Spurs?'

The baş imrahor breathes heavily, examining the inner man behind the blackberry eyes. The other seyises have held their breath in excited silence: nothing like seeing one of their own punished. What will it be this time? The whip of the baş imrahor moves to his side.

'No, baş imrahor Paşa.' The seyis' belly tightens. The whip stirs again. The baş imrahor hangs over him like a huge, potent incubus in a lead-foot nightmare. Tiny beads of sweat prickle on the seyis' upper lip. If the baş imrahor finds out that the seyis did not tell him about the auguries of this horse's foaling he will be flogged.

The baş imrahor breathes in massively, towering over him, ringed fingers turning the whip in his right hand, rheumy eyes staring into the seyis' face as the seyis stares into the blue silk chemise and the horse motifs. 'Are you hiding something from me, seyis?'

A patch of red brightens on the seyis' forehead. If he looks guilty it hardly matters. The baş imrahor assumes all seyises are always guilty.

'Is there something about this horse you are not telling me?'

The seyis reddens. If he lies he will be punished. If he does not lie he will be punished. A fly settles on his face. He blinks. It moves.

'Well?'

The seyis' mind has seized. He will be ganched. Blood drains from his face. The fly moves to the corner of his mouth. He swats it.

'Stop fiddling with your face!'

Does he speak? No.

The baş imrahor leans closer: 'You were galloping this doru horse along the beach three days ago, weren't you?'

The seyis' head lightens. He feels himself swaying. He sways toward the baş imrahor's ample belly. The big man pushes him back angrily. 'Stand still! You did not have permission to gallop a horse anywhere. You took the horse as though it was yours. You asked neither me nor Envir Altinay Paşa. You endangered the horse – he might have been stolen and then you shot arrows which could have gone into the horse's backside. What do you say?'

The seyis' mouth opens. Words elude him. The fly settles on his forehead.

'A week running up and down the beach with a saddle on your head might give time to reflect upon it – don't you think?'

The seyis nods. He swallows. Able to speak yet? No.

The great man glowers on. A twinkle lights in his foxy eyes. Is that a smile? In fact when he had watched this seyis on his horse he had thought the gallop extremely fine. The horse moved with form and balance and he had never seen an animal running with such gusto. The Parthian shots had been a master-stroke. Only a descendant of the horseman archers could have achieved that. That was not learned: that was hand-me-down, in-the-blood stuff. It was impressive to watch. The doru horse is magnificent, the yağiz too. They display a touching loyalty to each other and indeed to this seyis. He had noticed that when one horse was led away the other always called after it and waited with his ears pricked until he returned and then they met as though they had been parted for decades, so effusive were their greetings, in which their seyis also joined. They are a curious trio. Loyal to each other. All-proficient in what they do. This seyis keeps his own council. He works hard and he is as he said: not lazy. He knows good horseflesh, rides expertly and is clearly the horseman archer. He should be advanced. But to what, is the problem. He is not one to command. What is it about him? He is a loner, that's what it is. He would not wish to be Head Seyis, he would not know what to do. But he could select and breed horses from across the Empire – that, he could do. He wouldn't have to rely on anyone; but he doesn't have the grit to give orders. But give him a horse – yes, that's it. Still, no point telling him now. If he is shown the slightest whiff of favouritism all these other seyises will conspire against him. They are not intelligent: they are prone to petty jealousy and underhand retribution. No. If it seems that I pick on him, they will leave him alone. He's strong enough. Then at the right time, I'll make him Master of Breeding, and he will not let me down. Such a pity Envir Altinay chose the yağiz, he got the wrong one, the arrogant fool. The doru is the superior horse – he doesn't bear the Whorl of the Spurs for nothing. Something else about this horse though. Something this seyis is not telling me. Not sure what it is. Not a lie: just with-holding something. I'll find out. Such an immense pity the Sultan Mehmet himself had dismissed the doru in favour of the milk-white horse. The doru should stay of course. Blood like this is hard to come by.

The baş imrahor bends to the seyis' face and breathes heavily: 'You are the most despicable, the most miserable little seyis that ever disgraced these stables.'

The seyis finds a tiny voice: 'Yes baş imrahor Paşa.'

'One more foot out of place and you will find yourself on the iron hook as the feast of the vultures,' the baş imrahor breathes syllable by syllable, 'Do you follow?'

The seyis nods violently, sweat trickling down his face. A wave of nausea courses through him.

The big man sweeps past. 'You!' he says, stabbing his horse whip into the chest of the groom in the stall beside the seyis, 'You will take your two demirkir horses. One will be ridden by the Sultan's cousin Hamit Çankayar Paşa, and you will lead the other on the west flank. 'You!' he says, pointing to the man beside him, 'You will take your two Gemlik kir horses; one shall be ridden by Orhkan Paşa and you will lead the other in the west flank also. You!' he says to the next man, and the next and so on, until the horses had been allocated to their paşas and hassa sipahi officers to accompany the Sultan's bodyguard to Edirne.

'The rest of the horses will stay,' he announces when he reaches the end of the line. 'His Imperial Highness the Sultan Mehmed does not wish them to go to Győr.'

The seyis' eyes hit the stable floor. What? He's staying!

Whip at his side, the baş imrahor struts slowly back up through the lines of the grooms until he stands once more in front of the seyis. 'And you!' he says holding the silver boss of the whip beneath the seyis' chin: 'You will take both horses to war. Envir Altinay Paşa will ride the yağiz horse and you will lead the doru. And remember, one single mistake and you will be flogged. Do you understand?'

The seyis acknowledges inaudibly, nodding, sweating: his chest tight and temples beating.

'And that goes for the rest of you!' the great man roars.

The grooms do not move.

'Understand?'

'Evet! Baş Imrahor Paşa! Yes!' the grooms shout in unison.

'Five thousand state sipahi will form the Sultan's escort. Now move!'

***

Animated like stage puppets brought to life by the hands of their master, the seyises spring to their work.

Half an hour later sixteen horses are saddled and bridled. Their saddles are soft tooled leather, studded with emeralds, diamonds and rubies. Their shabracs are of green baize, trimmed with gold thread and bearing a gold embossed Crescent Moon. The reins are of red silk stitched over leather and inlaid with silver thread. The bits are deep ported, gold on copper.

Each groom leads two horses from the stables out into the sun in the Courtyard, below the Topkapi First Court. Here they stand in line, in absolute silence, their horses not moving a muscle.

The milk-white horse – the seventeenth horse – is saddled by the baş imrahor. The saddle is heavy with diamonds. The horse wears a thick martingale plugged with rubies and gold tassels. The saddle has a crupper of leather and gold and silver thread lined along its length with emeralds.

The horse is spotless.

Taking his bridle the baş imrahor sweeps him past the horses that remain in their stalls, out into the sudden brightness of the early morning sun. The air is full of the sound of seagulls.

Reining him straight past the sixteen horses in line, they fold in behind in section, the eight grooms leading their paired chargers across the courtyard and up the ramp. Before them, the double doors to the outer court swing open. The milk-white horse turns left with the baş imrahor. The rest of the horses are led out though the double doors into the Second Court. The gates close behind them with a solid clunk.

The baş imrahor leads the white horse under the Privy stable arch into the Inner Court.

A single drum beat rolls.

This is a very confident stallion, he is exquisite, he knows it and he is hard to hold. The baş imrahor's grip is firm. Passing the twelve columns from the arch on his right, he turns the horse left at the Çeşmesi marble fountain placed by Mehmed II in 1453. Leading him under the shadows of the great gilded canopy of the interior of the Gate of Peace, he turns him left again and walks slowly through the Inner Court.

On his left behind the columns lies the gold faience of the Dome, a great gilded window, of fabulous intricacy, shadowed behind a gallery of painted columns supporting a gilded ceiling of patterned stucco. Blue tiles glisten on the walls.

The courtyard is filled with dignitaries and militia men, janissary generals in their vast üsküf hats, crested by a spray of ostrich plumes of over three foot long a-piece. Here stands the Chief Armourer, with the Sultan's sabre in its velvet case: the Custodian of the Herons; Chief Keeper of the Nightingales; the Kislar Ağa, the Chief Black Eunuch; the leaders of kapikulu oçak and the sipahi; the treasury and armourers, the artillery corps, and transport unit, code breakers, sapper unit, pioneers, supply units leaders – every kind of leader who, having gathered at the Gate of Felicity, now part as the baş imrahor approaches with the dazzling white horse.

The drums roll louder and the pipes of the meterhane band pick up their strange Pythagorean skirl and the walls and columns echo to its eastern wail.

Under the great hood of the Gate of Felicity, across the white marble floor, plunging into shadow, the horse is led straight toward a sheet of white marble. Turning left again, he walks across more white marble on his newly shod hooves, each inlaid with verses of the Qur'an, each with eight brand-new tipped nails ensuring that the horse will not slip on the polished stone he now crosses.

The horse is led past the Library in the Enderum, where only the Sultan, his family and his favourites are permitted to enter.

The baş imrahor leads the horse past the Palace mosque and walks the last few steps to the Sultan's mounting block. A double inner door is opened by two black eunuchs, and two huge hounds come bounding out, barking, their feet hennaed and bellies rouged.

Behind them the Sultan strides, looking neither right nor left, goes to the mounting block, steps up and crosses the marble while his baş imrahor, the Horse Master, circles the horse. The baş imrahor brings the horse to the block and the Sultan mounts. Taking the reins, the Sultan, wearing pale yellow silk adorned with floral embroidery, nods once. On his head is a huge maroon and white turban with its aigrette of peacock feathers held in position with one enormous emerald clasp. With the slightest movement of his lower limbs, the Sultan urges the horse back along the way he just came. They glide past the palace mosque, past the library, and out of the Gate of Felicity, where a huge roar meets him and the Standard of the Holy Prophet is held high. The roar from the assembled dignitaries stirs not a flicker of a smile across his face, not even an indulgent, soft glance from God's Vice Regent Upon Earth, but instead the hard, supercilious, dismissive stare of a man who knows absolute authority, who holds absolute power and who is utterly corrupted by it.

The two bejewelled State camels stand by the Gate of Felicity, fantastically caparisoned with long, pleated gold swags and carrying tall, gem-encrusted litters, bearing the Clothes of The Prophet, His Sacred Seal and the Holy Qur'an. They then pace majestically and remarkably quickly through the Inner Court to the Gate of Peace.

Riding regally through the big court and followed by the grouped military commanders on foot, the Sultan reins his horse along the central path: the Dome lying on his right.

He rides straight through the open doors of the Gate of Peace.

On the other side, the Grand Vizier, Kara Mustafa, mounted on a magnificent black charger, waits. His horse's harness, like the Sultan's, is caked in gems and gold. Behind him his personal bodyguard, diversely cloaked in tiger skin, lion skin, leopard skin and bear skin fall into formation as he passes. The palace paşas and hassa sipahi are now mounted on their snorting, big, proud, glittering stallions with their grooms behind on foot, as ordered by the baş imrahor, dressed in tunics of gold thread and diamond belts, holding the reins of their second horses.

The baş imrahor swiftly mounts a bay and moves smoothly in front of the Sultan.

The beat of the drums increases and the skirl of pipes becomes louder.

The entire unit makes its way through the great iron doors and under the vaulted brick roof of the Imperial Gate into a cool sea breeze. In front of them, the Blue Mosque fills the horizon; its six slender minarets gleam pale against the blue of the sea in the morning sun.

A wild cheer is picked up by a huge crowd come to watch the incredible spectacle of the world's most richly-clad army marching off to war. The sheer glamour of what appears on horseflesh before them has never been matched in the west, not even by the Court of the Sun King himself, Louis XIV.

Past the Kiosk of the Imperial Gate, the formation now quickens its pace.

The great monolith of Ayasofya rises to their right.

Seagulls wheel and caw above this magnificent procession as the hoofbeats clatter over the cobbles and the crowds cheer and roar, rising to a crescendo as the Great Six Horsetail Tughs are held high in the arms of eighteen strong men.

Passing two fluted ashlar minarets and one of brick, reaching up through the sky high above the horsemen, they wheel right, past the Hammam of Roxeanne and its five columns. The horses' hooves beat the stone between Ayasofya and the Blue Mosque, lying either side, huge, peaceful and settled, emitting a sense of certainty, of power and undisputed stability.

From the left, from the At Meydan and from the right, from the Palace Grounds, five thousand sipahi horseman in their gleaming helmets and glittering swords, their shining stirrups, glossy horses, gleaming breastplates and greaves, fold in to the procession and trot lightly on their 16 hands-high Turk horses, divided by colour: whites, greys, blacks, duns, bays.

The sound now has increased.

The air is full of the clip-clopping of thousands of horses, of the jingle of harness, of swords buckled to belts clattering against long sabres tucked the length of the horses' sides; of rattling pistols, of carbines and of filigreed yatağan daggers thrust in coloured cummerbunds.

Past the Million Stone on the right, where once a triumphal arch stood, from which, in the Byzantine era, all distances were measured across the old Roman Empire, the procession trots swiftly up the hill, leaving the Firus Ağa Mosque, a small building of delicate symmetry behind its four perfect columns, on their left hand side.

Glimpsing the Bosphorus and Golden Horne on the right, blue and serene, the early morning sun rippling across it, the seyis casts a swift look to his right and wonders if he will ever live to see that sight again. On foot with Azarax, he jogs along in his gold thread tunic and diamond-studded belt which he, like all the other seyis' had had supplied by the state treasurer and had slipped on just before leaving the palace compound. He's proud to be leading this beautiful horse in this fantastic procession, while up ahead, through the trotting bodies of the riders and the horse's heads and ears and tails swishing he can see Bora who knows he can see him and keeps an eye back on him and he knows, and feels, that all is well.

On they thunder past the Medreses of the Köprülü and of Kara Mustafa, in the process of being built: pure, pale stone, a simple, elegant construction which he was never to see finished.

On their right they pass the Column of Constantine and the huge Beyazit Mosque and past that the entrance to the Grand Bazaar and the exquisite Nuruosamiye Mosque, standing beside a row of buildings of startling beauty.

Down the hill trots the magnificent procession, past the oleanders and junipers in great swathes of gardens, under the shade of the cedars, past the clean lines of another mosque of the genius of Sinan, whose simple tomb is set there, understated, his monuments standing in perfection and glory all over the city.

On their right the Aqueduct of Valens slips by, the Fatih Mosque with its schools and hospitals and libraries, and through the great Middle Way, as it was called in Roman times, now boarded with high, galleried buildings from which the cheering crowds drop thousands upon thousands of attar rose petals on the departing army.

The Sultan's hounds run, tongues lolling, at the heels of his horse as an exuberant military march is played by the meterhane bands lining the route, their great kettledrums booming and pipes shrilling with the same eastern wail that first made itself heard in the fastness of the Steppes, from whence these people came, with their quick Ghazi horses, many centuries before.

The last stretch takes them up the hill to the walls of Theodosius, high above them, bordering the limits of the city.

Trotting through the Gate of Edirne, the huge force spills out into the expanse beyond the city walls, where another city, a mobile city, has encamped itself and is slowly detaching, like blown litter.

A strong breeze picks up from the sea and blows grit and dust into the horsemen's eyes. The column moves on for a mile, then halts.

To their right the little Takkeçi Mosque is surrounded by a sea of camp followers, who will be making their way to Edirne, with the army. Every trader, tailor, pedlar, saddler, loriner, blacksmith, cattle drover, butcher, cook, crook, vagabond, juggler, tightrope walker, magician and pickpocket who fancies to profit from the pocket of the Sultan or the soldier is there.

Telling the Grand Vizier that he will see him in December, the Sultan breaks away with his hounds, the baş imrahor and huntsmen and heads north.

Kara Mustafa barks orders to the leader of the sipahi to make haste for Edirne. He will return to the Palace and in a week, bring the army.

Formalities are kept to a minimum to prevent the huge crowd of gypsies and strangers and merchants and carpet-sellers thronging this military corps and trying to ply their trade immediately.

A hassa sipahi officer trots smartly to the front of the division and heads off towards Edirne.

The column follows.

Kara Mustafa sits on his horse admiring the glittering Imperial bodyguard passing by.

The seyis keeps his eyes riveted to the dirt: it is not for the likes of lowly grooms to stare into the faces of the mighty.

* * *

One hundred miles to Edirne.

As a journey on horseback, what does this mean? Until you have done it, a hundred miles is meaningless. Fifty miles is meaningless. A hundred miles has no significance. Is this fifty miles of rock? Is this a hundred miles of swamp? Is it fifty miles of rivers to ford, scree to scramble across, cliffs to confound you? A hundred miles of forests so dense that pioneers must be sent first to clear them? Fifty miles of mud, of clay so thick it is impossible to walk in a straight line for more than the length of the body of a horse? A hundred, two hundred miles of hail and wind and rain, sleet and snow? The elements complicate distance: heat complicates it, cold complicates it, water complicates it. The effort trebles. The sweat runs, the wind chills, the soul cries out. Gender complicates travel. A mare is easy, but not when there are stallions. Stallions scream and shout and lunge and pull; they are aggressive and lash their tails, kick and squeal and roar. They pull towards the mares, they threaten each other. The mares buck at the stallions. They exhaust their riders. The stallions are so obsessed with the mares, they do not care where they put their feet. They flounder, reins cannot be held, shoes are ripped off, horses stumble, knees are cut, fractured, broken.

No. Distance on horseback is measured in time.

A pioneer corps of thirty thousand had set out two months earlier to clear and widen roads, repair bridges and build pontoons to span the shifting marshes but does this make the hundred miles shorter? It might make it easier, but the hills remain: the mountains do not move. The rivers still flow: the stallions remain stallions and mares remain mares. Distance by horse is measured in time.

It will take five or six days to reach Edirne. To reach Belgrade it will take many days, many weeks, several months, even though it is only six times the distance.

Distance on horseback is measured in miles only in hindsight. When you have travelled for one week, two weeks, ten weeks, a magical moment arrives: we have covered five hundred miles. A threshold has been crossed, a barrier broken. When five hundred miles is complete, a thousand is as nothing. It is three months away. If it rains, it is many months away. But once that figure is known: even though it is meaningless, then all else becomes just a matter of time. Then the end of today is the blue horizon way over there, where the edge of the plain meets the rim of the mountains. Where the tall grey castles huddle square in your path and when you reach them they wither before your eyes and become huge, craggy outcrops and beyond, a lake, with boats and men fishing, a village with trees and as you ride toward it, it flees, the lake is gone, the boats are gone, the village is gone, there are no trees, only more grey castles in the distance and beyond, another lake, with a village and trees. No, on horseback distance is the horizon, measured in time. Tonight I shall be there: in that hollow, I see it, on the horizon. The horse knows, follow the horse, leave him the rein, he knows, he will find it.

The road is marked by wells and wells are the life-blood of a journey with horses. These are domed wells, seen from afar, painted white. The water inside lies in a dark, clear pool where no weeds may grow. The well is like an igloo, with a channel running from one side, a stone trough and within the well there is always a wooden pail. You dismount, climb into the dome through a tiny entrance and in the stabbing, cold darkness, pail the cold, clear water into the stone trough where the horses are already bending their necks. These domed wells are as old as time itself and stretch from here right across Anatolia to the jagged hills of the Hindu Kush: they demark the Turkic mind, and lie nearly always, at ten thousand paces apart. In the mountains they lose their domes and become white walls with a trough, but in the plains, they are always domed. Find the wells, find the road.

It takes eight hours to ride to Çorlu from the walls of Istanbul.

***

A matched pair of Karaman stallions, the property of a paşa, or of the Sultan. A palace seyis with a diamond belt and gold tunic. The eye of a one-eyed, black-toothed ostler burns as the seyis brings his two snorting horses together. The one-eyed ostler spotted them immediately, followed them behind, hovered in the shadows, lingered in the twilight.

A day apart has upset the horses. They like to travel together. They have cried out for each other all day long. The seyis has been riding Azarax who has pulled him further and further toward the hassa sipahi, calling out for Bora who has responded urgently and the seyis has had to keep circling his horse to prevent him from riding in amongst the hassa sipahi, where he would undoubtedly have been hit either with the blunt side or the sharp side of a yatağan for his pains.

The men wish Azarax to keep back. Azarax wishes the seyis to go forward. The other seyis' have shouted at him. The hassa have scolded at him. The horses are strong.

Why am I a seyis? Why do I not become a carpenter? Why do I not live in a town and walk to this place and that place with my plane and make doors? And then when the long hours of day are passed, I may go home to my wife and she will hum a tune and stir the çiorba and I shall be content and happy and sleep in her arms. I am exhausted and now I must groom the fretting, sweating horses and feed them, find them a bed, clean the tack, tighten their shoes, keep them calm, smooth their souls, I must sing to them. If I were a carpenter I could go to my bed in my house.

The smallpox-scarred state treasurer with rapidly counting fingers comes to snatch back the diamond-studded belt and gold tunic. He sits and counts the diamonds as the seyis hums a tune to his chewing thoroughbreds. Praise be to Allah for horses: I am glad I am not a state treasurer counting the stupid diamonds, they are worthless. How can you speak to stones? Horses are beautiful, sacred and beautiful. I speak to them and they speak to me, they are my blood, my life, my soul.

The one-eyed, black-toothed ostler who had offered to feed Azarax and Bora is refused by the seyis. He prefers, he says politely, reminding himself of his erstwhile unsmiling but polite master, always, to feed his own horses.

Ostlers who offer to feed horses are not thorough: they do not check the barley for stones on which a horse may crack his teeth. They do not check saman to see if it has mould in it. They do not split maize to make it easier for a horse to eat and they hurry so that they can go off and do something else. They do not sit with the horses and wait.

No: the seyis will feed his horses himself, rather than hand them to the keeping of a man such as he who fondles his dagger as he speaks and rolls his one grainy eye, like a cyclops.

– This man is going to attack me, the seyis ponders as he rolls a stirrup leather. I know it. He will attack me when I sleep. But not tonight. He will try in Edirne. He does not know my sword walks to my right and my shield to my left; he will discover.

When he has fed his horses and sat with them, patiently, the ostler asks him to come to join their company: talk, tell them who he is, tell them about the Sultan, the stables, tell them lies, scandal, tell them about himself, his horses – yes tell them about his horses – anything.

What can he say to these people? He does not know anything about the Sultan. He has only ever seen him once. Stables? What can he say about stables? And lies? What lies? He does not know any lies. What is scandal? He does not know anything about it. And about himself? What is there to tell? Horses? What about them?

He sucks a stem of saman, turns to Azarax, and runs his hands down his legs checking for splints.

– I am glad I am not a carpenter working in a town going from this place to that place, talking, hoarding my possessions, breathing the smoke and not knowing the glory of the night. No, give me the stars and my horses. Give me the rolling seas of silver grass and the breath of a Karaman stallion. Give me Azarax, my sword, and Bora, my shield, and together we shall climb the broken paths through the fighting trees and claim the flying sky. We shall see the silver fish in the rivers and stare upon the white ranges of the mighty mountains beyond.

– I hear his teeth on the saman, hear him chew in unison with his brother-in-blood, Bora, they are my faithful companions, they protect me, I shall protect them to the end of my life I shall protect them and bring them to their destiny.

***

Sleep. To sleep in the company of horses is no light matter. Horses are restless bedfellows. They chew. They sigh and yawn, and stretch and scratch and chew and chew. They lie down abruptly. They get up and sigh and blow through their noses and shake and scratch and chew and chew. They lie down again suddenly and next are up on their feet: and scratch and shake and yawn and chew and chew and chew.

He sleeps through it all.

And as he sleeps his horses watch over him and pull at his blanket and ruffle his hair and still he sleeps. And if a one-eyed ostler finds it in his heart to slip through the shadows and strike, he will felled like a dry reed before his breath stirs the air in which an innocent Tekke seyis dreams.

***

Edirne rises out of the hard dry ground in a silhouette of spires, whose conical roofs twinkle in the sun. The town rises to meet them, pushing up out of the arid land with its many mosques and pale faience piercing the sky, its blue-tiled ivans shady, inviting and cool against the brown backcloth of the dry land all around.

The town is surrounded by hundreds and hundreds of ten-foot tall cylindrically capped ricks of straw and saman, piled neatly in rows, glowing in the sun. The seyises point and smile: see how efficient is our Empire: see how everything is prepared. Nothing has been missed: see the wells over there: even new ones have been dug. Look, there is water in great cisterns, cut out from the rock and huge artificial lakes – there must be fish. Hundreds of thousands of them. Everything is here: everything for an army. See the great wooden menzilhane buildings, full to the brim with barley! Look over there – near the mountains: thousands and thousands of cattle and sheep and camels and donkeys and horses and all these little girls yo-yoing wool in amongst them, they have seen us coming and they are waving. There are even shepherds up in the hills with great flocks of goats and of sheep. There are so many animals here it is not possible to count them and see, there are even more now already going up to Belgrade and beyond, even to Hungary. We shall not starve: our bellies will always be filled, even the bellies of our horses. Our Empire is the biggest and the richest: we are the best provisioned army in the world, no-one can match us.

A great many tribes people, herders and nomads, have arrived with water-buffalo and ox carts, bringing with them all kinds of spices and perfumes and scents, and strong aromatic herbs and vegetables and lentils, and dyes and clothing and music and dance. Overhead huge flocks of starlings gather and weave and wheel in the sky like vast shoals of fish spangling their iridescent colours against the hard white clouds. Fingers point upward. The omens! The omens! Hands clap, voices shout: 'Allah kerim! Allahu akbar!'

The Royal bodyguard splits at the town gates, the sipahi dividing into three units: those to camp outside for the winter; and those billeted within. The toprakli sipahi will be stabled in the town.

The seyis finds himself leading Azarax behind Bora, ridden by Envir Altinay Paşa through the town to a set of airy stables prepared for the horses. Feed is ready, water lies in stone troughs, the seyises will be quartered above the stables as in Istanbul.

Having left with the Sultan to go hunting as they left Istanbul, the baş imrahor is no longer present. As the seyis settles the horses he sighs. 'What a blessing the baş imrahor is not here terrorising me. The first short part of the journey is over. Now comes the long winter. Short days and snow. It is lucky for me I am not living in a squalid tent with three other seyises, snoring and weeping and arguing. It will be hard on the men and the animals camped around the city all winter. It will not be easy for them.'

As he stitches a broken thread on his saddle he looks up and sees a long shadow spilling in from the doorway. He guesses in a moment who it is. 'Oh no. He has come like a bad spirit to haunt me. He has come to ruin my peace, to destroy my life. He is the evil one: the Evil Eye. How did he get here? He must have ghosted along in my wake all day. How did I not see him? Why am I not alert? This army is my army but it is full of thieves and filled with edginess. I can sense it. There are eyes everywhere. No-one wears their purse where it may be seen. Wear the diamonds, plaster your horse in rubies and emeralds – they belong to the Sultan and he who steals from the Sultan will steal only once.'

The one-eyed ostler tries to catch the seyis' attention, gesticulating, whistling, hissing, but the seyis resolutely turns his back and stitches on. He pushes the needle and the waxed cotton into the little holes in the leather and pulls tight, musing, 'What does he want? I know what he wants; he plans to steal my horses. He wishes me to go here or there or somewhere, and when I am not looking he will steal the horses. People lose their heads for stealing horses. Seyises whose horses are stolen are ganched.' The seyis' face tightens.

The needle moves in and out of the leather. Iron pierces skin. He runs a hand across his forehead. Is he going to be able to finish this sewing? He has never seen anybody ganched. He does not want to see anybody ganched. He picks up the needle and thrusts it into the leather and pulls it out at the other side. Maybe he is going to be the one who is ganched. He is terrified of the baş imrahor. He hates people who steal horses. He hates living in such close proximity to people. He wishes to be alone. Just him and his horses – somewhere peaceful. In goes the needle. Ouch! Into his thumb. He winces. The pressures are rising. 'Why is life so complicated? The baş imrahor hates me, I don't know why. I am sure he is going to find an excuse to ganch me as soon as he comes back. He hates the horses, what's wrong with the horses? Nothing is wrong with the horses; they are better behaved than even the Sultan's horses and better looking, I know they are. Everywhere I look there are people wishing to steal them and now this horrible ostler and this dreadful place on our way to a war. I don't want to go to war, what for? What have the enemy done? I have never even seen a Hapsburger, never mind wished to kill one. I wish I was back in Ali-aga Izobegović's timar, but even he was mad. Why is everybody mad? The only sane ones are the horses.'

***

The ostler leaves and the seyis continues his stitching. 'This man frightens me. Him and his cyclops eye and dagger. He is going to try something, I know it. I daren't leave the horses alone, not for one second.'

The needle dips in and out of the leather.

'I need more cotton: where is the cotton?'

The seyis checks his sewing bag: there is no more cotton.

'How can I have left Istanbul with so little cotton? Why did I not check? Now I must go and buy cotton from the market. Why am I such a fool?'

He looks around for another seyis and asks him: 'Do you have any spare cotton?' Of course he does not have any spare cotton. And why should he give him cotton even if he did have any?

'I must go and buy some. Where is the ostler? If I go now and come back swiftly he will not have time to steal a horse. Not with the other seyises in here.'

The seyis checks once again for the ostler. Reassured he has gone, he rolls up his sewing bag, puts the leather down and looks around again. Now he must leave.

The sunlight outside is dazzling. It momentarily hurts his eyes. The street is busy. The town is crowded. It is a press of men and horses, men and donkeys, chickens in cages, everyone is shouting. Women in chadoors elbow their way through the crowd: the seyis asks one where he might find cotton. Dark eyes behind a chadoor reveal nothing: a hand stretches out, golden bracelets against golden skin, a finger points: 'There, across the street, bolts of cloth, boxes of buttons.' The seyis acknowledges: 'Teşekkür.' It takes him ten minutes to find the place.

The cotton he wants is strong multi-ply. There is no multi-ply cotton. He must buy single ply and make it himself, waxing it so that it remains taut. He keeps glancing back to the stables, which have now fallen from sight. The cotton seller is slow: the price is high. The seyis rushes. The deal is bad. He argues with the cotton seller: a row breaks out: this is taking too much time. The seyis pays one asper for white cotton worth half an asper. He pushes through the crowd back to the stables and when he enters Bora has gone. He reels to the wall and has to put a hand out to prevent himself from collapsing. He puts his hands to his head. His breath comes in short jabs. He shouts to the seyis at the other end of the stable: 'What happened to my horse? Where's he gone?' Shoulders shrug. The seyis dashes out once more into the sunlit crowd. Has anyone seen a man leading a horse? A hand gestures in front of him. Everyone is leading a horse: which one did he mean? The seyis rushes up and down the streets, jumping up and down trying to catch sight of a yağiz horse. He looks here, he looks there: down this alley, then that. He runs through the market and to the mosque. He runs out into the open plain, he looks everywhere. By the time he rushes, sweat-stained back to the stable, his face is taut, and white. He is shaking and retching. When he enters the stable Bora is back but now Azarax has gone. Once again he shouts at the other seyis. Once again shoulders shrug. How can they not have seen, what's the matter with these people? Once more he dashes out into the street. Wait, wait. Think, think. The way to find a horse is with a horse. Back into the stable he seizes Bora's lead rein and leads him out into the street, into the crowds and then Bora does as he anticipated: he squeals. Dozens of horses squeal back, but there was one voice in there he recognised, above all others, far off. So did Bora. He squeals again. This time a clear cry returns.

Both man and horse push through the crowds. Up a cobbled street, down another, to the left, left again. Bora calls, Azarax replies. Bora pulls him along swiftly. Allah be praised, this horse has some energy! Soon the seyis is standing outside a grubby dried wood door. He bangs on it and screams out: 'In the name of the Sultan open this door!' Azarax cries out from within, Bora responds from without. The seyis hammers with his fists. Door bolts slide and the big doors creak inward on rusty hinges. The one-eyed ostler peers out. Thrusting the door open fully the seyis pushes in angrily with Bora, who he suddenly realises, knows this place. There are ten horses in here: the two stallions, Azarax and Bora, and eight mares. The ostler smiles and opens his hands. Well, what could he do? He couldn't, just couldn't, pass up an opportunity like this, now could he? Not blood like that. See? he says, sweeping his hand in extravagant gesture. All these mares!

Unable to speak the seyis snatches Azarax rein and leads them both out, back the way they came. They trot along happily, heads high, nose to nose, muzzle to muzzle, squealing, thrashing, high-stepping. They are, after all, a pair of young stallions. The seyis' step lightens. The horses yell their conquests through the streets. The seyis throws his head back and the sun lights in his eyes. So: in eleven months' time there will be eight little Karamans in Edirne. What a beautiful city this is, what a fine day. Look at my stallions. Are they not the finest in the Ottoman Empire?

***

One day a shout comes. High up in the tower of the Adâlat pavilion a man points into the distance. Stall keepers and carpet vendors, butchers, candlestick makers – all rush out of the town to see. The seyis is in the mosque and the imam invites him up into the minaret, to the şerefe, the high gallery, to see.

The seyis follows the imam to the tiny door of the minaret. He follows as he goes up and up and round, and round, and round, and as he ascends it becomes darker and colder. Up and up, round and round, darker and darker and colder and colder until it is pitch black, and the seyis is now on his hands and knees feeling his way and it is extremely cold and utterly black and the seyis wonders if they will go on forever going up and up and up and round and round and round in the cold and the dark. He shivers and becomes frightened but then a little light appears and then a little more and suddenly the imam steps into a blinding white ray of sunshine.

It is good to step out onto the şerefe, even though he nearly faints from the height.

The imam points.

In the far distance are columns of smoke and a thin dark line is spreading across it. 'Mahşallah!' the imam breathes.

The line becomes wider and wider and wider until it fills the entire horizon. It glints and shines and spangles with flashes of light like a huge scaled animal writhing toward them. As it draws closer a peculiar sound draws closer with it: a humming, mumbling sound and then a deep, deep roar. On and on it draws, like a great black sluggish sea, a huge, slow wave, moving menacingly toward the town, looking as though it will ooze straight over it and bear it away.

The seyis' heart beats and he holds his hand to his mouth.

He is so overwhelmed he cannot speak.

It is terrifying and yet utterly spell-binding, he cannot stop watching it. Soon he picks out the colours: the great green flags waving, the standards, the different coloured standards of the regiments. Then the greens of 50,000 janissaries and the dervishes in white and the archers and the artillery reds and the great üsküf hats bobbing up and down. There are so many flags and standards it seems to be a great ocean of them. Then to one side, in a massive cloud of dust, comes a thundering. The thundering gets louder and louder and he can feel it vibrating even in the şerefe and he is sure the şerefe is going to collapse. Then the glinting swords and cuirasses of the horsemen break through the dust and never before has he beheld such a sight and it makes him reel.

He had been told that the army had 77,000 horsemen. There are 40,000 sipahis alone.

The massed horse make the ground shake. Slowly their voices can be distinguished from the strange roar of the army. Horses in the town cry back to them. The air is filled with the cries of thousands of horses. Thousands of Ghazi horses. The omens are excellent. Men cheer, hats are thrown in the air: the town bursts with joy and awe and with excitement and apprehension.

The army fills the entire horizon, side to side. It fills the ground between where the seyis stands in his minaret, right the way back to the far horizon. The cloud of dust is thick, and yet he can make out in the distance ox carts, and a huge armada of camels. A great high trail of dust shows Tartar horsemen arriving.

Weapons flash in the sun, drums boom, music plays, the sound of one hundred and fifty thousand soldiers talking together fills the sky with a roar.

The sound of 77,000 horses is beyond the description of a lowly seyis, even one who spends all his time with them.

This great army splits around the town and suddenly and imperceptibly, comes to a slow halt.

It is time again for the imam to call to prayer.

Four hours have slipped by.

***

The army remains in Edirne over winter. The Sultan returns from his hunting in December and he and his Grand Vizier draw up battle plans for the attack on Györ. Russian Ambassadors come and go. French Ambassadors come and go. The Austrian Ambassador, Caprara, stays.

The baş imrahor arrives.

The seyis works in deep shadow in the stables. He grooms his horses in the darkness. He does not speak. He hides in the tallet loft at night and does not go into the town. He collects the horse feed from the saman ricks before dawn. He scurries from one end of the stables to the other. He exercises the horses when everyone else is eating.

The baş imrahor seeks him out. All horses are to be schooled to the cannon. His will be the first to undergo the first blasts.

Mine? Why?

Seyises do not ask questions.

The cannons are lined upon either side of the waterlogged plain. Few of the men assembled in this place, let alone their horses, have ever heard or seen a cannon fired. 'Why is it you who has to take your horses first?' the Persian seyis had whispered in the darkness. – 'Because you walked through the cannon fire in the Kagithane Meadows and nobody else did. And besides, you are a seyis: it does not matter if your horse turns upside down and you are crushed beneath it. They will not risk their hassa sipahi or a silahdar on such an exercise. No, when the horses have finished killing us expendable seyises, then the sipahi will mount them. You, you will

94

be next – after this seyis. He will die first. Allah take care of your soul. Goodbye. You have looked for the last time upon my face. Go, go before you lose your nerve and run away screaming as they shoot you.'

The seyis rides Azarax behind the line of the guns, patting his neck. The horse is calm even though the seyis' belly is a knot.

The first blast is a powder blank, yet the noise is enormous, the cloud of smoke colossal. Azarax tosses his head, plunges forward for a few strides, then gaining his composure and with a swish of his tail, trots on. Steady boy, good boy. Another blast, then another. The horse keeps trotting all the way along the line of guns as each one fires. Good boy, good boy. He turns between the cannons. This is the tricky bit. Now the hot blasts come. Still blanks – wadding. Huge white clouds of smoke: the stench of saltpetre. The fury of the blasts is deafening, the impact shudders his body, the horse moves smoothly. Up to the end and down the middle. Cannons fire randomly from either side and the seyis trots his horse slowly through them, without rearing, without plunging, without bucking.

In the shadows the baş imrahor folds his arms and nods. He thought so. Put a competent man on a steady horse first and you will have a steady herd. Something about that seyis and that horse: why is that horse not afraid of cannons?

The seyis wheels the great horse at the head of the valley and then canters to the contingent. Five hundred horses fall in behind. Once again along the back of the cannons, slowly, at a walk. Boom! Boom! Boom! Clouds of smoke. The seyis leads them back to the head of the valley and rides on his own to the baş imrahor. They should not do any more today, he says. That is enough. If we frighten them, we are lost. We do the same tomorrow, then a little more each day.

There is a flicker of a smile. One day, one day, this seyis will be baş imrahor. He is good. He is very good. And that doru horse – he is incredible.

***

Edirne has suddenly become an enormous city. Articles are for sale that have never been for sale before. Huge quantities of animals are slaughtered every day to feed this vast contingent of men. Piles of offal are shovelled into enormous pits. Bones rot and stink in the sun. Vultures drop from the sky. Wolves and jackals and foxes drag intestines about. Hooded crows, in great flocks, land in these pits. Wolves and crows near a camp are bad omens.

The armada of tents lies enveloped in a constant pall of wood smoke. Vegetables are brought in by the hundreds of cart loads.

Thousands of camels bring in thousands and thousands of sacks of saman from the great ricks around the city, every day. Donkeys and oxen carry water and barley and mules tread round and round and round in circles rolling millstones to make dough for the sixty thousand loaves of bread that are baked every day.

There are thousands of acres of tents; thousands of fires; hundreds of tons of firewood; hundreds of thousands of pots and pans. Men drag their struggling lunches to fires, slit their throats, skin them and drop quartered chunks of fat-tailed Awassi sheep into boiling kazans. Cows and goats are driven to their dooms in their hundreds through the smoke every hour. And the seyis takes his horses for exercise and to find a snatch of grass for them, if he can.

Then it rains.

The floor of the camp becomes a seething bog. A filthy, cold, miserable, wet morass of soaking men losing their morale and tempers by degrees. As winter edges in, the nights become longer, the days shorter and food more difficult to find.

***

Stables have been erected for horses out of wood, canvas and felt but these leak. The saman becomes mouldy, the barley has stones in it and the wheat has ergot.

In the constant cold rain, pits of excrement overflow and the place begins to stink. Animals become sick and men become sick and it is necessary to divert the men somehow to keep their morale from collapsing.

Gypsies are commissioned to bring their instruments and play their music. Dark gypsy girls with their big brown eyes, wide hips and bursting bosoms shimmer-dance to the rapid chatter of the tambourines. Whirling, raven-headed Circassian girls dance the Gazavat and it makes men's hearts beat and they whoop and shout and sing, and the janissaries have to keep them in order. Jugglers juggle, stilt walkers entertain the troops, fire-breathers and dwarves and story tellers all take their turn to distract a few hours of the soldiers' lives on the central stage of the muddy camp floor.

Tartars play their newly invented balalaikas and sing sad songs of the Steppes and Siberia and then it snows.

The snow stops the mud but the tents are cold and the wind is bitter and the cows and buffaloes standing around in it, die of exposure.

The cannon schooling goes on. Each day the horses have been exposed to more noise, more smoke, louder explosions. These lessons have been expanded to embrace musket fire and pistol shot, and fuses running along the ground. Each day the janissaries and azap troops have been running target practice so that every day has been filled with the crackle of gunfire and cannon blasts, with explosions and fire. Horses have been schooled to gallop past lines of men waving burning flags, to jump through flames, to canter over firecrackers. This has continued every day except Cuma, Friday, the holy day, so that slowly but surely, all horses have become accustomed to the sounds of war and will not, when the time comes, gallop off at the first blast.

***

The snow becomes deeper and the camp becomes more and more quiet. The nights are marked by brutal frosts and in the mornings the horses' whiskers are white and their coats rimed in silver. What had been pockets of mud outside their shelter have turned into granite hard hoof-shaped holes, difficult for the horses to walk across. Snow falls, not in big soft flakes dropping gently out of a benign sky but in little ones, persistent little ones, bitter and at an angle, with a freezing wind. The roofs of the town and of the mosques and minarets lie under curling white blankets, rounding sharp edges and softening high walls. Branches of leafless trees are weighed down. Ice lies in dark slabs across the camp in the mornings, men and animals slither on its polished surface. Black horses look remarkably black against the intense white of the snow: their coats are long and shaggy and blow in the persistent easterly wind that chills a man to the bone if he stands in it.

Tears that form in the corners of his eyes freeze on the seyis' face and when he leads the horses, his feet and hands are so cold he ceases to feel them. There is no water to wash in. The river is frozen. In some places the snow has drifted so deeply it alters the shape of the landscape. It is difficult to find enough liquid water for the horses and the big amphorae that were kept for watering the animals have frozen solid and broken and ice now stands in shapely columns, hacked at by men who knock off lumps to melt in pans above the many fires that burn throughout the camp, filling the air with a constant pall of bitter woodsmoke.

Yet the food has to keep coming and the water and the barley for the horses – and the horses need five hundred tons a day. All the ricks of saman and straw are finished and now forage has to be brought from Rumelia and from the menzilhane and by boat up the river Meric to the city walls.

During the long miserable months from October to March that

the army remains at Edirne, camels, mules, donkeys and oxen carry or drag sixty thousand tons of barley to the camp for the horses alone.

Slowly the season changes. The snow melts. Migrating birds return. The sound of the namagua dove is heard once again. Bustards can be seen picking about in the distance. Golden orioles bloop melodically in the trees. Hoopoes sweep up from the greening ground. Eagles fly overhead, the vultures have come back, the stench returns.

The training is over. The baş imrahor orders the seyis to appear before him in his tent. 'You will ride behind the hassa sipahi on your doru horse when we leave.'

This is the position of an officer. The seyis blanches.

'You are hiding something about this doru horse, are you not, seyis?'

The seyis' face twitches. The baş imrahor knows. He has to reveal it now: if he does not, he will be punished. He will be punished anyway. His mouth dries. 'It is his augury, baş imrahor, Paşa.' It is a confession: confess and you die, remain silent and you die.

The great man interlocks his fat fingers across his belly and sits back. 'Why is he not afraid of the cannons?'

The sound of men moving animals emits from outside. Somewhere a cow bawls. A horse cries out. Men shout: 'Bring him here, no, not there, here!' The noises intrude, they seem normal, everyday noises, they help defuse this moment.

The great man is waiting. His eyebrows ascend his turbanned forehead. Well? The seyis shifts his weight and clears his throat. The donkeys bray. Now a dog barks incessantly. Someone is trying to catch a chicken: the sound is absurd, humorous. The seyis feels a terrifying urge to smile: to laugh, to break the pressure of this moment. The big man turns his head to one side, eyes fixed on the seyis. He is waiting.

'He was born in a storm, Paşa,' the seyis confesses, quietly, eyes on the ground. He can already hear the axe fall.

The big man rises to his feet. The sounds continue from outside. Now a heavily laden cart goes by drawn by groaning oxen.

Ha! Such a little thing. Yet how great. But why not say so? No: there's more.

'Is that all?'

A deflating look flattens the seyis' features: a condemned man stepping from the tumbril, hopelessly parting with his last remaining coin as he palms it to the executioner: what thoughts really go through the mind then? 'On the Night of Justification, Paşa.' It is barely a whisper.

So that's it. And the Whorl of the Spurs. A horse like this will leave his mark in history. Or this seyis will. Or both. What to do? What to do? Take the horse from the seyis? He should be the Sultan's horse.

'Does he have a name, this horse?'

'He is called Azarax, Paşa.'

'Azarax, Azarax? That's a Ghazi name. It means Son of Fire. His father was called Ateş, then.'

'Yes, Paşa.' then carefully: 'There was also a fire.'

The baş imrahor – horse master, headmaster, judge, jury – sits once more shaking his head. He turns a knife over and over in his fingers, tapping the table top. All the auguries. I should have him horse-whipped for not telling me.

'I shall decide what to do with you and your horse later.' And dismisses him.

'The great have frequently sprung from the humble. This seyis is a man apart. It is his destiny to lead that horse,' mused the bas imrahor. 'Not mine.' He reaches out and pours himself a fluted glass of Cypriot wine.

'Azarax,' he breathes.

*　*　*

Two days later the order comes to strike camp.

Striking camp for an army of nearly one hundred thousand is a long process. Tents must be taken down and packed with great care onto pack animals. An animal has to be loaded evenly. The slightest unevenness in a load will cause it to topple immediately. Cinches and surcingles cannot be pulled so tight as to prevent a load from sliding – it will cause galls and if an animal has galls it becomes useless and pack animals rendered useless by careless packing result in punishment for the handler. So animals are packed carefully.

All the paraphernalia of the camp must be swept up and taken along: the bricks for making ovens to bake the bread, the amphorae for water, the half-carcases of meat that have not yet been eaten, the great bags of barley and of rice, of beans and lentils and huge bags of horseshoes and rolls of leather and spare chain mail and cannons and powder and shot must be loaded onto carts drawn by the great Rumeli horses and by water buffalo.

Ten days later, on March 16th 1683, the Sultan steps toward a big, gilded coach drawn by eight grey horses. Its rich interior is gilded, the floor flat and covered in satin mattresses and silk pillows.

As he approaches, a sudden dust devil whips around him, lifts his turban from his head and dashes it to the ground.

A worse omen could not have struck.

- 8 -

The enemy of my enemy is my friend

Leopold I, by God's Grace King of Germany, Holy Roman Emperor Elect, King of Bohemia, Hungary, Croatia and Archduke of Austria, pulls his long upper lip.

He stands in the great gilded reception rooms of Vienna's Hofburg. Pimples of sweat have broken out on his forehead. Staring with a fixed myopic stare at His Master of the Stables Ferdinand Harrach, he shakes his hands suddenly in desperation.

'What should I do? What should I do?'

Ticking off his fingers with quaking hands, he counts: he has listened to his hofmeister and to the Marshal of the Court, Albert Zinzerdorf; he has listened to Königsegg, his Imperial Vice Chancellor, and to Schwarzenberg, President of the Imperial Council and to Christopher Abele and to John Jörger; he has listened to Montecuccoli, his military advisor; to Hudwig of Baden his President of War Council and to the Duke of Lorraine – whom Baden despises. And now to Ferdinand Harrach, His Master of the Stables. He paces the floor and pulls his lip and wrings his fingers and with his hectic stormy eyes, pleads again: 'What should I do? What should I do?'

Sighing deeply he slumps heavily against a polished wood windowsill and gazes through the glass at the Burgplatz opposite, as though seeking inspiration from it, from its stone, from the city, from the sky, from God.

In the gloomy light of a March morning the immense Burgplatz, with its twenty-four great windows and huge offset clock tower seems to offer some sort of solidity, some security. To its right lie Leopold's apartments; to its left the government offices and the Chancery. The spire of the glorious medieval chapel of the Hofkapelle rises behind. And all of it under threat! The security evaporates. And he will be blamed. Leopold's chin hits his chest.

He drops into a deep maroon-velvet chair, defeated. Once again, he stares at Ferdinand Harrach. Pointing out of the window he stutters: 'Do you realize how long those Karster horses have been stabled, over there, beyond that wall, in the Stallburg?'

Ferdinand Harrach puts his hand to his mouth and coughs politely. Of course he knows. He shifts his weight from one leg to the other.

'One hundred and eleven years,' announces Leopold. 'One one one. Does that signify anything? What does that mean? One one one? Is that some sort of sign? A code? Those horses were put there by the Emperor Maximilian in 1572: imagine that! What would happen to them if the Turks got here? Do they eat horses? No. But by heaven, the Tartars do: they ride them and plunder with them and live, sleep, drink their milk, travel and probably mate with them. Certainly they eat them! Imagine a horde of wild Tartars in their shaggy kapakh hats squatting cross-legged on the floor of the Stallburg tossing lumps of flesh into a blazing fire and gorging their way through a hundred and fifty white horses! That is what will happen. Think of something!'

The Master of the Stables looks away to the dark towers beyond.'And what about all the paintings and statues, the museum, the books and silver? All will be plundered! All gone! All ruined!'

Leopold rises to his feet and paces the polished floor. The gravity of the moment is acute and yet it seems improbable and hard to grasp. 'Ever since Suleiman the Magnificent laid siege to Vienna in 1541, we have dreaded eventualities such as this. And what have we done about it? What has the attitude been? If there is no emergency, there is no need. Well there is an emergency now: the Turkish army is on its way. Granted no-one knows where it is going – it might be headed, for all we know, to Krakow, but it is not likely. The information Caprara has managed to smuggle out has suggested differently. Yes they have said Györ, they want Györ, that is the price of peace, but with an army that size? How many men did he say? Estimates from one hundred and fifty to three hundred thousand men, to take Györ?'

He sits and gazes once again out of the window at the Burgplatz, contemplatively.

'And what manner of man is this Kara Mustafa?'

The Master of the Stables clears his throat: 'There is conflicting intelligence,' he says. 'An Englishman reported once that he was a good soldier and courtier and has a clear and active mind. Others say that he is vain and arrogant and flays Christians alive for his sport.'

The Emperor gulps. 'Well, we can dismiss what the Englishman has to say.' He tries not to think of the other.

'What about fortifications around the city? Are there any?'

'The fortifications are complex and firm enough. There are the outer ravelins and walls and the glacis and counterscarps and moats. It is all well designed and even the most stubborn of besiegers would find it hard to cross the open space of the glacis without meeting a hail of gunfire from the palisades within. There are earth banks and buttresses and stoneworks and all manner of things to repel anyone wild enough to try.

'And yet, the stone is getting on in years, it is crumbling in places. The city has become so crowded that people have built on the open glacis: the canal is fordable, the moat is not wide enough and worst of all, the city is surrounded by itself: its suburbs. The Turks could ride through five abreast in broad daylight for all the cover these fine villas and shops and avenues and gardens would give them. They could be knocking on the door within half an hour and nobody would have noticed them coming.'

Leopold throws his head back, closes his eyes and gasps: Dear God.

'Also, there is no real garrison here in Vienna, ever since the bubonic plague ravaged us four years ago. The City Guards – such as they were – have been badly hit; they were not well-housed and lived in poor quarters, and did not enjoy any of the advantages or privileges of men expected to face the cannons first.

'But, there are some positive points: for the last three years there have been some improvements. At least we have a sort of a standing army – somewhere – of which Christopher Abele assessed the cost to be two million florins per annum, which caused Your Royal Highness to ask him to check his arithmetic, if you recall, Sire. Christopher Abele is shrewd: he increased taxation because he was convinced that a Turkish invasion was imminent. It would happen. And it would happen, he anticipated, in 1683. He has suspected it for some time and, well, he appears to have been right. And George Rimpler, an excellent engineer, has been overseeing the rebuilding or strengthening of the fortresses of Györ and Komarom and, well, Vienna – he's a Saxon who has seen service against the Turks in Candia and against the French in the Rhineland. A good man. Count Ernest Rüdiger von Starhemberg has been appointed as Commandant in Vienna and colonel of the city guard – he's not popular, but sound. Very brave. And somehow, he has found the money and recruited men to fill 400,000 sand bags, 300,000 bundles of faggots for raising parapets, cut 250,000 pieces of lumber of various lengths for barricading – all of which is causing the forestry commissions to groan.'

Leopold listens in silence, his expression changing from deep despair to some shred of hope.

'Then the really desperate implementations are about to take place: we are going to pull down all the buildings on the glacis.'

'Do what?'

'Pull down all the buildings on the inner ramp which was supposed to have been left clear for defenders to shoot at attackers, should they manage to crack the outer fortifications: a kind of reverse fire screen. Well, it's covered in houses. Demolishing these will undoubtedly anger the people who live in them. And now – soon anyway – we shall begin demolishing the suburbs, much to the joy of the inhabitants who have spent the last hundred and forty years since the Turks last destroyed them, re-building.

'So, no, it will not be an easy task and yes, it is causing a lot of sleepless nights. Not everyone is gifted with the vision to perceive that staying alive is the matter-in-hand here.'

'Dear God!' sighs the Emperor, rubbing his eyes: 'What about help? From outside?'

'Well, Waldendorf has visited Mainz and Ehrenbreitstein and Cologne and Heidelberg and found them attentive and polite but – no. It's to do with Louis XIV, the King of France. They are certain that he will march on their land if they leave. He's – like that. So Martiniz has been sent off to Rome.'

'And?'

'And he has appealed to His Holiness Pope Innocent X1, and His Holiness appreciates the urgency. That the threat from the east is real. And though at first he thought to appease everyone, he now thinks differently.

'He suggests that you, Your Royal Highness, as Emperor, must send for aid personally.'

'To whom?'

'To every Christian King in Europe.'

The Holy Roman Emperor sends appeals to every corner of the Christian world, with the proviso that even if their Sacred Majesties, the Kings themselves, cannot promise armies then perhaps men will come of their own accord, from their various kingdoms? And who will come? Volunteers, mercenaries, deserters, adventurers and deadbeats and murderers and...

In the coffee shops of London the message is bruited about.

London is a long way from Vienna. There is fun to be had in England these days: horse racing and gambling, misbehaving and drinking coffee, drinking port, creating insurance companies and amassing large and impressive estates. Why, good old King Rowley - Charles himself - indulges in exactly these kinds of things and what is sauce for the goose... So why risk your life in some dangerous foreign campaign which doesn't concern England, tucked neatly behind the skirts of a wild surrounding sea, far away and nothing to do with the Turk?

There are, of course, always those who see life differently. One or two aristocrats or dreamers or loafers or adventurers who haunt the coffee shops of London or who sit about in their grand drawing rooms with nothing much to do. When they learn of this plea for help from the Holy Roman Emperor Elect, it all sounds quite appealing. The prospect of galloping about on horses, fighting Saracens, like the knights of old. A kind of new Crusade, to defeat the old enemies of Christianity. A summer in Vienna might prove an amusing distraction where there is little else to do but go racing or gamble, play cards or drink port or fumble in a haystack with a rustic wench or two. There are other considerations too: spoils; gold, booty. Horses! Turk horses.

So they throw saddlebags across the haunches of their horses, ride to Dover where horse transporter Philip Marchant will arrange for their passage across the Channel. They will land at Calais and see how the wine tastes straight from the vat. Suitably refreshed they will gallop to adventure and glory and once more, like Richard the Lionheart, fight the infidel of the Crescent Moon, once more, to the glory of the men of the Cross.

***

Jan III Sobieski, King of Poland, Grand Duke of Lithuania, Russia, Prussia, Masovia, Samogitia, Livonia, Kiev, Volhynia, Podolia, Podlachia, Smolensk, Severia and Chernigov, is married to the beautiful Maria Kazimiera de la Grange d'Arquien.

Maria Kazimiera de la Grange d'Arquien is French. As well as her native tongue she speaks Polish, Russian, German, English, Latin, Greek and even some Turkish. She is a down-to-earth Queen: learned, loyal and spirited.

One early June morning in 1683 she asks her warrior king husband two pertinent questions. Does not the security of Krakow depend upon the security of Vienna? Is it, she asks, not possible that if the Turks march on Vienna, and Vienna falls, that they would then march on Krakow?

- 9 -

Manoeuvres

Exposed and bare in the cold March morning, the Sultan's bald head shines grotesquely in the rain, whitened and bulbous like a withering puffball in a drenched September meadow. His dignity is affronted, he is transformed: bull-neck, snub nose, small eyes and thin lips reveal a pugnacious child in a man's skin. He touches his head and cries out.

The horses flatten their ears, they reverse into each other, sidestep into each other, curl their nostrils, lash out at each other, lash their tails, neigh, whinny, flash their dark eyes. They have seen something. All of them. What have they seen? Their riders wrestle with reins. 'Mahşallah! Mahşallah! Mahşallah!'

The Sultan's hounds yap wildly jumping up at the coach, clawing at its yellow body. A huntsman whips them to the ground.

A page boy runs after the rolling turban. Footsteps splash through puddles, a hand reaches down, the Sultan hesitates on the coach steps then disappears within as the page boy leaps onboard, bringing the offending muddied turban with him, its aigrette of peacock feathers limp. The coach door slams.

Curtains are snapped shut.

It is 16th March 1683. It is the Ides of March. The Sultan is Caesar. Through his veins courses the blood of the Caesars: he is the inheritor of Rome. Constantinople – Istanbul – is the new Rome. The will of Providence is moving. Against this all men are powerless: this Sultan, this Empire, this campaign.

The baş imrahor's eyes settle nervously on those of a Tekke

seyis sitting on a doru horse whom he had ordered to ride close behind the hassa. The seyis returns the look silently, directly, as his horse moves beneath him. In the rising wind and sudden rain the baş imrahor's eyes linger. What does this all signify? What is it about that horse?

The baş imrahor barks an order, as eight grey horses take the strain, and thirty-two hooves plunge into the wet road. The Sultan's coach jerks forward with a solid bang and the cortege sets off at a heavy trot, its spoked wheels flicking mud in an even spray all over the glittering hassa sipahi. Rainwater dashes the coach windows and pits the roof; it runs off the narrow guttering, down the bodywork.

Alongside, the horses of the sipahi jingle in mud-flying, soaking unison. Behind wallows the Grand Vizier's ornate coach, within it, Kara Mustafa, sitting on the maroon satin quilting, gazing myopically through thick rain-stained windows. It was not his but the Sultan's turban that fell. He is dry: his turban is dry. No-one sees the smile. Behind Kara Mustafa's coach a string of others pitch and rock in the mud, drawn by teams of floundering Rumelian draft horses. Ermine robed courtiers sit on splendid silk cushions in the state coaches. The smooth-skinned beauties of the harem, draped in furs and Anatolian wools huddle together for warmth, eyes closed, hating every living second of this lurching, cold, wet ride to the shores of purgatory in their silk-padded cell. Caprara and his Austrian ambassadorial staff ride hostage in a four-horse chaise at the rear, gazing out of the windows recording for posterity, the fantasy unfolding before their eyes. Black eunuchs on horseback and a grim deli detail ride high on steaming horses, tight to their coach doors.

No one speaks of the loss of the Sultan's turban. To speak of it is to invite the footfall of the janissary Ağa, to feel his cold chains drop about your arms, hear them rattle, scream as you are dragged though the camp feet first, smell the deep earth as you are tumbled into it, feel it as it pours on top of you, shovel by shovel, okka by okka until the light of day vanishes, hope is extinguished, sounds cease, breath ends. No-one speaks of the loss of the Sultan's turban. Yet the image builds and it builds darkly in their minds: it is revealed in their gestures, it hangs on their faces: it hovers on their lips.

Wade on through the mud, protect the Sultan, breathe not a word.

Sliding around on Azarax's wet saddle, the seyis splashes behind the hassa sipahi through the angled downpour following them, north-westward. Now he must trot forward, rain running down his face, blobbing his eyelashes, dripping off his nose, his chin. Trot this horse? Trot him? He will be galloping with the hassa sipahi right out ahead, leading the entire contingent. He must rein Azarax. Behind him, the hooves of hundreds of pack horses, ponies, mules and donkeys churn the mud. Men shout, whistle, crack bullwhips; a dog barks, an ox complains, the rain hammers down. Wooden axles creak and grind as gravel spills into their crude bearings.

The Sultan's vanguard wallows and groans toward the two low hills that mark the exit through the Kapikule pass from Turkey to Rumelia. If this was supposed to be a dazzling mirror-image of the display that had departed from Istanbul in October, it is little more than a mud-spattered parody of it.

The day is grey; the hills are dark; the mud is deep. How many more signs do they need to be convinced that Providence is moving against them? Men tense their jaws remembering the moments when the omens had made them flip the rein of their lives: the sight of an owl, the sound of a jay, the augury in the sky – the tailed star. They had not questioned what might have been but had swung immediately and deliberately off at a new tangent and arrived safely. Then they had breathed and given thanks, prayed in the Mosque, lowered their foreheads on the floor, and moved on. But now, that imperative has been ignored. Disaster is bound to follow. What will befall them? And who, when they arrive finally at their destination, will they face on the battlefield? Will it be the Imperial Hapsburg forces, renewed, remade, refreshed and in strength, with the sun burnishing their cuirasses and the wind ruffling their plumes, their banners flying, while they, the Turks arrive soaked and exhausted on wet horses, sleepless and hungry with rusty swords and unusable powder, their fate already determined? Have the scales been tipped at last?

Already the horses pulling the coaches are panting hard. They cannot sustain a trot in this mud. The baş imrahor barks another order and everything that has not already done so, slows to a walk. Yet still it is hard going on the horses. They strain in their harness. Breath billows from their pink nostrils. Soon the eight grey horses of the Sultan are brown with mud and have become shrouded in a moving wall of steam.

It takes four hours to pass through the two low hills.

Clouds hang low in the sky. The distant hills moan and rumble. Horses, in their clinging harness, jab along heavily, ears back. The wheels of the coach stick. The harem's coaches are slowing, the great gilded coach of the Vizier is slowing.

The seyis' doru horse pecks, dragging the rein out of his hands. He pulls toward the Sultan's wallowing coach, his powerful limbs gliding beneath him. The reins are slippery and slide through the seyis' fingers, whose back and shoulders are frozen, his turban sodden and slipping down over his forehead. Soon the horse is churning mud right behind the baş imrahor, falling back amongst the hassa sipahi. The seyis eases the horse on the bit, urging him to drop back, but Azarax pulls on. Soon he will be side by side with the baş imrahor, for which he can expect a whip across his face and a flogging later. The seyis circles to keep his distance, the baş imrahor reins his own horse to the right to mount a bank and step out of the mud at his feet. His horse loses its footing on the clay bank and slips to its knees. The baş imrahor pitches forward in his saddle like a child on the neck of its first pony, off balance and nowhere to go except down, headfirst. The seyis touches the left rein, Azarax bounds, a hand seizes the baş imrahor's elbow. The baş imrahor regains his saddle as his horse regains his footing. As he draws a forefoot, his horse pulls a shoe which twists and is left hanging by two nails.

Immediately the seyis drops from his doru and offers him up.

Standing between the two horses in the waterlogged road, holding up the procession, the seyis waits as the baş imrahor regards him stupidly with his bulging eyes. The seyis points to the twisted shoe and signals him to change horses. It is not the place of a seyis to give orders to the baş imrahor. The big man's face darkens but he follows his signal and swinging to his right, puts a hand on the doru horse's wither and heaves himself from his grey straight onto the doru's back. Seizing the rein he hisses: 'You will see me later.' The seyis is left holding the stricken grey as the baş imrahor trots off through the mud and catches up with the Royal coach under squealing protest from a doru stallion.

The seyis leads the grey through the mud to one side where, with difficulty, squatting in the mud with cold, greasy hands, he removes the buckled shoe. The column shuffles slowly past: dim eyes slide his way, then return, dismally to the dismal quagmire: it is the baş imrahor's horse that cast a shoe. Another ill omen has struck.

The shoe comes away in the seyis' hand. But should a seyis ride the baş imrahor's horse?

The other seyises avert their eyes and ride past, shunning him like a leper, as though his crime, whatever it was, were transmissible. It was his own fault. He should not have been where he was. He will be flogged. If they sympathise with him, they too will be flogged. He might even be ganched. What was he doing riding right beside the baş imrahor anyway?

The seyis struggles through the mud leading the horse, falling further and further behind, his mind crowding with grim images. He can already feel the ropes round his arms and his legs, and sense the whirl in the gut as he is dropped onto the hook. It was Azarax's fault: no, it is his fault for not having corrected this habit. The horse pulls, he knows he pulls, yet he has done nothing to stop him. It is his fault: he deserves to be ganched.

Soon he finds himself travelling with the baggage train a long way behind the Sultan's vanguard. His face is white, his hands are clammy, his mouth is dry, the rest of him is soaking. He feels the eyes of the ox drovers upon him. He can feel what pulses in their minds: this man is bound to die: we will watch.

If he attempts to catch their eyes they look down into the mud and trudge on. There is self preservation in silence. His hassa sipahi will have him flogged for certain for failing to attend him. His crime was to help the baş imrahor. What was he supposed to have done, let him fall? He keeps running over in his mind those words: 'You will see me later'. Did he say it as though he meant to have him punished very severely? However you looked at it, what he had done was a presumption and presumptions, to a superior, amount to a capital offence. He will die, for certain.

When he arrives in the camp with the baggage train the first man he seeks out is neither the baş imrahor nor his hassa master. He seeks out the nalbant, the blacksmith, and reshoes the baş imrahor's horse.

As the nalbant works the seyis gazes into the camp, through the tents, looking for his horses. But he must stay with the nalbant and this grey horse until he is reshod. He looks past the cows, the chocolate-coloured donkeys with their eighteen-inch ears, the mules, the horses, the oxen, the bullock carts, to the mountains beyond. He will run. Flee. But hide where? If he is caught he will be beheaded. If he stays he will be ganched. He wrings his hands and his face is torn. His belly is in turmoil: visions of his punishment, flogging, ganching, beheading, crowd his mind. The baş imrahor devises punishments to fit the crime: what will he think appropriate? When the horse is reshod, he cleans the mud off and grooms him to perfection in spite of the rain. Heart racing in his chest, stepping through the tents and smoking fires, he seeks out the baş imrahor's pavilion.

As he approaches he sees Azarax and Bora standing outside it, both still saddled and both eating saman quietly. Beside them stands a janissary guard with execution in his eyes. The guard steps into the pavilion, spits out a string of words and returns to his musket, held vertically between his feet. He grips the muzzle like an axeman who, blade down, waits for the order to swing. A moment later the pavilion flap is thrown open. The baş imrahor looms in silhouette in the light-filled interior. Hovering on the edge of the pavilion the seyis cannot see his face. He hears only the laboured breath, like an old bull. Moments slip by. The seyis swallows.

'Take the horse away and have him reshod,' the baş imrahor grunts at the janissary.

'It is already done, baş imrahor Paşa,' the seyis responds immediately.

The bull breathes.

'Who gave you orders to do that?' he snorts.

The seyis hesitates. 'I – no one, baş imrahor Paşa.'

The baş imrahor moves out of the pavilion into the darkness. 'Take my horse away and feed him,' he orders the janissary. The horse is led away. The seyis looks over to his doru horse, then returns his attention nervously to the baş imrahor, whose dark eyes flash. Azarax touches his leg with his nose once. The seyis makes a tiny sound.

'What was that?' the baş imrahor snaps.

The suddenness of the question makes the seyis jump as though fired on. He stammers: 'I was responding to the horse, baş imrahor Paş a.'

The big man regards the horse eating his saman quietly. Sweat has broken out on the seyis' forehead; he shivers.

'Responding? Responding to what?'

'He touched his cannon bone with a nostril, baş imrahor Paşa.'

He regards the seyis, and then his horse.

'So?'

'He was acknowledging me, Paşa. He was saying he recognises me, Paşa.'

The baş imrahor steps toward the seyis and regards his face in the dim light of the camp. The seyis believes what he has just said. The baş imrahor walks around him, more sensing than seeing him.

– There is an innocence about this seyis. And a purity. This is a man who never thinks evil thoughts. It is as though his mind is completely free of such things. This is a simple man with simple thoughts: simple needs, simple responses. He has no insights into the world of men. He has few relations with his fellow men, nor does he seek them. He does not need them. He is not the slave of life's emotions. His insights are all reserved for horses: he matches his horse. His horse is like him. It seems as if the horse is more alert than his seyis, as if the horse does all the thinking. It is the horse who transmits his thoughts to the seyis, who then acts on his behalf.

He pauses as he walks round the seyis and regards him in the half light: a muddy ragamuffin with a mind of glass: he can see straight into it. This seyis feeds his horse, he tends him, he walks, grooms him, he rides him yet he barely talks to him – he has no need to. He makes no fuss of him and yet between them there exists a tangible bond: he does not need to give the horse a command because the horse already knows.

The baş imrahor straightens his back.

'Why were you riding close behind me this morning?'

The seyis can barely speak 'I... don't know, baş imrahor Paşa.'

The baş imrahor holds up his hand. – I ordered him to, that's why. What made me ask him to ride with the hassa? Because a little of whatever it is about this seyis and this horse has rubbed off. It is ridiculous. But it is true. A glimmer of a smile flickers across the baş imrahor's face, a tinge of humanity rarely squandered on a seyis: 'Go and eat,' he says, 'and take your horses with you.'

He watches him disappear into the smoke with his horses, the doru in front, leading. As he floats away Envir Altinay, his hassa sipahi master, steps out from the light of the pavilion. 'I was planning to have him flogged.'

The baş imrahor throws him a sharp look. Pity this ridiculous, arrogant man. He does not even measure up to the ankles of the little man with his perfectly schooled horses.

Envir Altinay turns on his heel and walks off to the flamboyant pavilions of the hassa sipahi.

The baş imrahor pours himself a glass of wine and, leaning on a pole of his pavilion, gazes out over the torch-lit, smoky, camp.

What is all this about auguries and destiny? Is it not mere nonsense? And here's this entire military force hanging on to absurd signals and portents as though their very next breath depended upon whether they see a white cat, a white viper, a white eagle, a tailed star or a turban hurled to the ground from the head of their Sultan. We cannot escape them. Men and women gaze into the eyes of seers who say, it is written in your stars that if you do this or that, then this will happen. And it does. And if it does not they mock the seers and the seers say: ah, but you did not interpret me aright. I am susceptible to this myself. Even I, Soliman Chia, fifty three years old, baş imrahor to His Imperial Highness, Vice Regent of God on Earth. And here we are off to fight a war with a neighbour who has given us no offence. Why? To satisfy the evil ambitions of the biggest fool in the land of the Turks, Kara Mustafa, Grand Vizier, destroyer of Empires. A man without a whiff of the humility, the purity of that seyis. And what will happen to the seyis? They will make him work with the cannons and if he survives that, the mines, and he will not survive those. And his horse? If he lives, the Poles will capture him or the Hapsburgs or someone and ride him to heavens knows where for what purpose – who can tell? And I? Where shall I be? Shall I be with this illustrious force, in the foment of war, sword in hand, severing infidel heads, with the battle cry in my throat, screaming for victory for our Holy cause? No. I shall be at my Sultan's side, hunting on some sunlit Balkan hill as our Empire burns and collapses around us. And yet, that horse has crossed my path. Is there not a purpose in all things? Is my destiny linked with his? And who am I? I am the baş imrahor, am I not? I can have whatever horse I please.

* * *

Tempers fray, noses are broken, daggers are drawn. Horses kick out, oxen refuse to move, donkeys dig in their toes. The rain lashes down. Weapons rust: musket muzzles have to be constantly greased. Swords stick in their scabbards, leather bridles and saddles stiffen.

They arrive in Plovdid at eight o'clock at night on 8th April. The journey has taken twenty-four days from Edirne.

The army passes through Ihtiman and crosses the mountains north of Samokov and north of Vitosha. Had it been dry, they would have seen junipers, vetches and scabious, bluebells and goatsbeard, pyramid orchids, buttercups and yarrows, campions and ragged robins – an embroidery of colours, broken only by rocky outcrops. Linnets would have flown with the skylarks and the world would have sung above their heads in the glorious, sparkling melody of the meadows.

But in the cold April rain, Vitosha is in a winter all of its own. Down the long slither to its base, lies Sofia, in a bowl rimmed by mountains.

The men and animals are worn out. They are filthy. Clothing rots on backs. Feet are frozen, cut and septic. Shoes, made on the road from freshly-slaughtered hide, more of a burden than a help and scant protection from the cold and the wet, have fallen to pieces. The baggage carts are wallowing along behind.

The mighty Ottoman force arrives in Sofia on 17th April 1683.

Sixteen days later they reach the south side of the Danube and cross the river Sava. The army encamps at Zemun, a mile west of Belgrade. High above them on a great rocky outcrop at the confluence of the rivers Sava and Danube, stands the grim fortress of Belgrade, a castle in the sky.

It is 3rd May 1683. It is forty-nine days since they left Edirne. They have averaged just over six miles a day.

The Imperial horse of the Sultan's bodyguard and the main body of the toprakli sipahi form two columns. The hassa sipahi with each of their seyises stand in coloured parade formation, pennants fluttering on lances, plumes in helmets ruffling in the breeze rising from the Danube, standards flying on either side of the road leading up to Belgrade Fortress, which is at the heart of the capital of Serbia. And Serbia is the knot in the platinum ring that is the Ottoman Balkans: Albania, Montenegro, Macedonia, Kosovo, Bosnia and Serbia, a region edged by a turquoise sea and rolling tree-clad hills, of limestone gorges, of silver streams and clear wide rivers, of rich upland pastures and snowy mountain peaks. It was here that the seyis' horses were foaled, not one day's ride from the route the army took past Niş on the road north to Belgrade. Yet no waving crowds lined their path here: no toothless old men hobbled to doorways, leaned on sticks, rolled up their sleeves, showed their scars and waved and shouted: 'Güle-güle!' No pretty, smiling young girls with high cheek bones and jet black hair stood on tip toe throwing petals of attar roses on the handsome men and their magnificent horses as the proud army thundered by. No: here the roads were empty: shutters were closed. Memories of an age when the long-vanished nobility of Serbia and her long-gone knights had faced the Ottoman sipahi on the Plain of the Blackbirds at Kosovo lived on. The old men and their work-weary, bent-backed, thick-wristed old wives did not look out and cheer as the Ottoman army passed by. No, they had heard too many partisans scream, seen too many partisans burn, watched too many children disappear, felt the heavy heel of the boot of the overlord upon them to wish them good fortune. Only sullen looks accompanied this army north and a seyis upon a doru horse remained quiet. He did not stand in his stirrups and pat the neck of his doru horse and say: 'Over there lies the timar where this very horse was foaled! How proud Ali-aga Izobegović would be to see his stallion in the ranks of the hassa sipahi now!' No. There lies in the straight face the art of self-preservation. To smile was to invoke the cry of 'sympathiser!' Or 'partisan!' If the Turks didn't get you, the locals would.

Ali-aga Izobegović was correct. A smile is expensive.

**

The Grand Vizier's pavilions are pitched in the centre of the camp at Zemun surrounded by his chiefs of staff, the Lord Chancellor, Lord Treasurer and Master of Ceremonies. Near to these on an open piece of ground, beneath a canopy, is the Place of Justice, where the Vizier presides over punishments and executions.

To one side lies the treasury, in stacks of chests filled with coin and gold, guarded by sipahis. Next to these are the tents of the hassa paşas and their attendants who make up much of the fighting force of the army. At the rear are the sipahis with their horse-lines and their grooms.

**

Now the Africa Corps arrive. They have come from the Kavkas, from the eastern Empire, from Egypt, Libya and Tunisia: Arabs, Berbers, Bedu, Greeks, Armenians, Kurds, Caucasians, and more Christian renegades from the west; converts to Islam: 180,000 men with a grudge to bear, men with a mission more determined than the Bektaşi Muslims who are their comrades-in-arms. Men with a zeal to repay the injustices they have suffered, bitter men, men with hatred branded on their hearts.

With these new men appears a new restlessness, a new ruthlessness, a new opportunism, new exploitation, new entertainments, new excitement. A breath of a new African wind, a new Armenian wind, a new eastern wind, a new kind of aggression. They steal through the torch-lit camp at night and stalk through it by day. Their rules are different rules, their colours and scents and languages strange, their morals coded, their habits peculiar, their food spiced. They have come for one reason and one alone: to win. To win booty, to win gold, to win silver, crowns, women, glory, renown, timars, chariots, heads, horses – money. To win money – on horses.

They bring animals of all kinds. Leopards, lions, bears, boars, bulls, huge scarred camels, strange birds: peacocks, ostriches, enormous spurred cockerels, and great black rats. These animals are their entertainment: they are teased and baited, forced to dance, to walk over hot coals, whipped round rings, jumped through hoops and set one against each other in mortal combat: lion against lion, bull against bull, camel against camel, dog against dog, rat against rat, cockerel against cockerel, stallion against stallion. The wagers are high, the earnings deep. One Ethiop made so much gold he bought six mules and is now gone.

Says the Persian seyis with a timar in his eyes: 'Who will look for him? No-one. Even the janissary Aga places money. They say even the Sultan attends the bullfights. They say he placed a great bet and won and then stayed for the rest of the fights, until the last one, between the stallions, and this was the best. It was the longest, the most bloody. The stallions were like none I have ever seen. Some were torn to pieces. There was one who knew how to do it. He is a great victor. He is a black stallion from Dagestan: his blood is pure. His mane is long and his tail is fine. He shines like obsidian, and has muscles on his body as hard as rock. There is so much money on the stallion who beats him, it will take more than a hundred mules to carry it away. The scouts are looking for the one to beat him. The Sultan has ordered the baş imrahor even, to find a horse, but the baş imrahor says he will not. Trouble is coming.'

The seyis hurries back to Bora and Azarax who are tethered on long lines in the early May sunshine, enjoying the deep grazing along the banks of the Sava river. They graze contentedly, swishing their tails at flies, blowing at the strong Balkan ryegrasses. Their coats are glossy, their eyes are bright. They whicker when their seyis approaches, arch their necks and look up with their big deep eyes.

Three tall men stand nearby swinging amber beads. They speak in low tones, and acknowledge the seyis politely when he arrives though they do not approach. They watch as the horses step toward him with their big eyes shining. They hunker down in the grass and watch as the seyis un-tethers them and leads them back to the hassa sipahi lines and they follow at a distance. The seyis re-tethers them in places where they would not normally be tethered, then waits until these men are gone and takes them back along the river bank to another place, a place behind the aspen trees he has found, where they may graze in peace unobserved, and he remains with them. Night falls and he returns to the hassa sipahi lines and finds the lines filled with strange men in flowing robes and headdresses that cover their faces, leaving only slits for their eyes. When they see his Karaman stallions they stop, point and confer. They drift away in a cloud of sharp scent, talking quietly to one another, swinging their beads and looking right and left, and they fill the seyis with foreboding. In these nights the seyis sleeps between his tethered stallions and his bow and quiver lie by his hand.

And he hears the roar of bulls and of camels, the shouts of men, their brutal cheers, he hears the high pitched screams of stallions and his mind is troubled as he sees his own two young horses pull and tear on their tethers and stamp and cry out.

Rumours abound: a grey stallion was beaten immediately, a white one was destroyed as soon as he entered the arena. Two red stallions had their knees broken one after the other and still the nights are filled with the cries of horses and the roars of men.

The days crackle to the sound of musket fire and the boom of cannons and once again the seyis must train the horses to the guns. Artillery regiments fire at targets half a mile distant, the horses gallop past, the janissaries and new Africa troops fire their long-range muzzle loaders at the storks and crows and eagles and vultures. Mock cavalry charges with five thousand horses crash and thunder across the plain below Zemun and under the eye of the Fortress, stern and austere, standing high on the rock of Belgrade.

By night the Sultan and his Grand Vizier Kara Mustafa are entertained by leopards and lions, by wrestlers and jugglers. They sit beneath gorgeous canopies in the light of a thousand torches as oiled men heave onto one another's shoulders and balance while acrobats flip through the golden lights of the burning torches and men walk on high wires or stand on great leather balls and clowns clown and veiled girls sway in sensual unison to the skirl of the eastern pipe and evoke an ancient memory and stir an ancient spirit and awake in this vast army an energy that courses with a lust for blood.

Then come the animal fights, the bulls and the lions and the stallions.

One by one each stallion falls to the black victor, a Dagestani thoroughbred, the horse who carries in his veins the blood of the Kipchaks and the Nogai, black as night, quivering in muscle, red with blood, panting and proud and brutalised. The crowd want more. Next they wish to see this black horse beaten: he who has fuelled their nights with passion, he who has filled their pockets, he who they have loved because he is a winner, now because he has won so much, they wish to see him destroyed. The money runs each time on the new stallion but still the old one wins.

The Dagestani is ruthless and fast, he attacks immediately and there is no stallion that can resist him. Even when the odds increase and they put two stallions in to fight him, still he wins.

The seyis has not slept. He hears the horses screaming, hears the men roaring, the fires burning, the torches flaring, the passions seething. His own horses have become frantic, their muscles shake as they bend their heads to the sounds and the seyis casts about, hot in his blanket. Behind his closed eyes the bloodied images run: he lies on this side and sees a stallion fighting, he lies on that side and hears another whickering. A red stain marks his forehead, his lips whiten and flatten on his teeth, his nostrils flare like his horses, his hands are fists, his arms are knotted with tendon and muscle, his head shakes, blood pounds in his ears. Fools! Squandering the blood of sacred horses in such vile and cowardly ways! His eyes smack open: above him the fine heads of two young horses cry out for vengeance, for blood. They fight at their tethers and stamp and lash their tails.

Suddenly the seyis sweeps up from his blankets, runs away from the hassa lines and pushes through the crowds to the arena and for his first time sees the black Dagestani stallion in the ring: thick-necked, fast, bloodied, defiant, tossing his head. The horse jabs up and down in the torchlight surrounded by a wall of faces and wildly gesticulating arms. Then it canters, ears back, weaving backwards and forwards along the arena walls, snatching at this outheld hand, lashing at that, flashing his teeth like the caged and tormented beast he is. The dark eyes of the seyis narrow.

Show me a horse and I will tell you about his master.

Even from where he stands in the crowd of violent men palming money into one another's hands, he can hear this horse cry out. He can hear his pain and his fear and his hatred of these men. He can hear his loathing of the man who is his master and the cruelty that is inflicted on him. Not a day will go by when this stallion is not locked in some stable and taunted and goaded and whipped until he can bear it no longer and when his fury is at breaking point he is loosed into the ring to do his work. Yet the seyis sees him for what he is: a horse. A clever old horse. An old horse who has learned, somehow, to survive. The horse stops moving and looks up. Around him men are screaming and shouting.

The wagers increase. Two stallions!

The horse turns his head and pricks his ears, slowly: somewhere in this madness he hears the call of a single soul.

Two kir Bursa stallions are entered and split as they enter but the Dagestani does not attack them. He trots around the ring looking up into the faces of the men. A whip cracks. He canters. It cracks again. The Bursa stallions squeal. They do not know what to do. One flies at him, he parries, then kicks, lethally. Down goes a grey, shuddering, and strikes the ground hard in a cloud of dust, unmoving. The crowd roars. The other grey canters, terrorised, ears back. A whip cracks again.

Why the seyis finds himself running back to the hassa horse-lines with his mind made up, he cannot tell. Why he finds himself seizing a looped rope, untying his two Karaman stallions, and running back with them to the arena, he does not know. He pushes through the crowds and stands at the arena entrance with Azarax on his right and Bora on his left. He does not see the baş imrahor's eyes fall on him, nor see his hands grip the rail. He does not notice men stand up and the crowd cease roaring. He only hears an inner voice say to his horses: stay together, stay together, then feels his own fingers in Azarax's mane. Then his feet leave the ground and the faces around him blur in the high speed of a powerful horse.

***

Never had so much dust flown from the arena as it did that night, they said later. It flew higher and higher and the squeals from the stallions became louder and louder. Higher and higher the stakes ran as money poured from pocket to pocket.

The Bursa stallion was pulled out of the ring and then the black

Dagestani stallion's owner yelled and shouted but the Karamans worked as a unit, undivided, and kept the Dagestani running. Never had they seen such unity, the audience said later.

Round and round and round they chased, pinning the black stallion between them and then suddenly the black stallion was lassoed and in a triga of horse they galloped hard, straight at the spectators by the entrance who scattered like leaves and the three plunged into the darkness beyond the light of the torches. The sound of hooves receded into the distance as the men who lost their money shouted and swore and cursed, chased out into the night and cried for the blood of a Tekke seyis and his Karaman stallions.

Later that night the enraged owner of the black Dagestani strode to the horse lines with his dagger, but a big gönüllü warrior called Ozay Dursun seized him by the throat and spat a promise in his face he would never forget. One hour later twenty gönüllü horsemen rode into the arena and destroyed every last piece of it. And the owner of a Dagestani stallion now begs on the streets in rags; while a smart black stallion stands at a tether beside the horses of a Tekke seyis in the ranks of the hassa sipahi, in Zemun, Belgrade. The baş imrahor, Soliman Chia, folds his hands in his lap, closes his eyes and smiles.

20TH MAY 1683

The Sultan takes the salute. He has made Kara Mustafa, the Grand Vizier, Commander in Chief, and the army will now march north.

In the army that passes by, the seyis catches the eye of the baş imrahor for the last time, sitting on his grey, watching. The seyis feels his gaze upon him as he rides and as the column rises up the hill he looks back and sees him wheel his grey alongside the Sultan on his milk-white horse and across the distance something melts. And though he hears no outer voice he hears the inner, silent one, the one that speaks loudest of all: 'Güle-güle,' it says: 'Go laughing, my sons. Go laughing.'

***

The invincible Turkish army marches onwards. The sun bursts unexpectedly from behind the clouds and burns fiercely. The blue sky has a brilliant radiance as though some different energy has been impelled into it suddenly, since the departure of the Sultan, and his hunting retinue, the baş imrahor and the hounds, the huntsmen and the hunt horses – an unwanted nucleus, that had never merged with the army yet had become attached to it as they moved uncomfortably together, north to Belgrade. The deadweight is gone, the darkness lifted, the Sultan has departed.

Was the ill-omen not the Sultan himself?

The sun shines on Kara Mustafa. It was not his turban that fell. See how his army is transformed! See how the auguries of the sky sparkle upon him and his invincible force!

The air is clear, the land is flat. They pass into Bosnia.

Far to the left lies Djakovo, and to the right Vukovar, but the army marches onwards to Osijek, where it arrives on June 2nd 1683.

Here the river Drava tangles with the Danube in a swampy, disputed triangle, in amongst rotting goat-willow trees, sedges, moss, lichens and carcases of the long-dead. Whole armies have been lost in this place: the marshes lurk in a constant twilight. The air is composed of swamp water atomised into an eternal fog. Shapes glide silently through it.

The pioneers whom Kara Mustafa had sent ahead from Istanbul many months earlier are still repairing the long pontoon bridge that had first been built here by Suleiman the Magnificent, to cross this deadly swamp. No-one stays near this place at night. Strange sounds are heard. Spirits haunt it. Horses that stray into it are doomed. Clouds of midges hamper men's work by day. They bite the skin and leave a boil that takes a month to heal. The swamp accepts the great oak tree trunks the pioneers cut to make the pontoon and swallows them whole. It is almost impossible to find an oak great enough to withstand this quagmire. The pioneers have been working on the pontoon for five months. The army must wait until it is completed.

Kara Mustafa is not a man endowed with patience. He stamps on the end of the pontoon and curses. He rails at the men, sweating and frightened and covered in boils, to complete it. He does not care that some have fallen into the swamps and disappeared into its depths. He is not interested in those who were sucked under the mud with the oak trunks. He has the chief engineer flogged. He makes a decree. For every day longer it takes to build, he will have two pioneers cast into the swamps.

The pontoon is completed in twelve days.

Twenty four men die. Two bodies float to the surface and remain floating either side of the pontoon, faces upward, skin white, eye sockets empty: the enterprise's ghoulish, rotting attendants.

***

The first contingent to cross the pontoon on 19th June are azab troops. These foot-soldiers feel forward nervously with their toes and grip the rails with their hands, their eyes wide and white. They move in complete silence. Only when they reach the far side do they shout and wave. More men cross. Then some çebelu light cavalry on light Mesopotamian horses cross. Then the sipahi. The Grand Vizier mounts his horse and crosses. His coaches and harem rattle across the thick wood planks. The toprakli, the People of the Six Units, the deli, the silahdar, the janissaries, the forces from Africa, from Macedonia, from the Caucasus, the Arabs and their light horses, all pass. An everlasting line of men and horses steps onto the pontoon and the lines seem to go on and on and on. It took three days for them all to cross the pontoon.

On the far side, the brown mass of Siklos̆ Castle crouches on the horizon. It was near here, 142 years earlier, in 1541, that the Ottomans won a great victory against the Hungarians in the Battle of Mohacs. After this battle the Ottoman army had pushed north and seized the city of Buda. Kara Mustafa recalls this as he basks in the warm springs with his concubines and his army sweats in the hot plain.

The mood of an army is capricious. It blows with its fortunes. A fortnight earlier they had galloped in a blaze of sunshine and glory at the heels of their exalted Commander, but today their trust in him is blighted. The sight of grey carcases in the murky water haunt their dreams.

Kara Mustafa loves nothing except his destiny; he will sacrifice any man and anything for his private ambition and his private ambition outstrips even their generous saint Hadji Bektaşi. Even if the Holy men, the bearded hadjis and hodjas who travel with the army dare to warn him that God punishes the vainglorious, he will not heed. If they advise him to regard the consequences of what he does, he refuses to look.

And he is miserly. A high-handed leader, even if ruthless, will be accepted by an army if that high-handedness is accompanied by largesse and generosity from which men may snatch up winnings and booty and spoil. But Kara Mustafa grubs up the small coins. He begrudges even the ülüfe, the fodder ration money for the sipahi, making it tight on the men and tighter on the horses. He is niggardly in distributing bonuses. He does not hand out favours, he does not offer compliments: he orders punishments; he delights in executions, he likes to see men tortured. He enjoys other men's pain. He does not talk to his men, they are beneath him.

Already the crops are gathered in. The days become scorching. Bare feet cannot withstand the heat of the naked earth. The sky is a furnace. Dust is so dense that men cannot see one another though they ride alongside. The seyis covers his horse's nostrils and faces in a sheer veil. The other seyises watch and dismount and cover their horse's faces in sheer veils. The air is choking: men splutter and cough and gag for breath. Animals flounder in the dust, eyes become red and swollen. Soon the dung of thousands upon thousands of horses dries into a fine, green powder and this falls on the baggage train and even the oxen choke and cough and stop and wheeze, and their drivers curse and spit and cough.

The order is given for a change of marching hours.

The pack horses and immediate military baggage train will begin to travel at seven o'clock in the evening, the Paşas and Vizier after midnight. They will be accompanied by lights. And the light will be equal to the light of day. The Arabs from Aleppo and Damascus will provide it. These people are called Massalagibashee and the lights they bear are not torches, but bituminous lengths of oiled wood, which is burned in an iron brazier and held as a torch. These cast so much light that night becomes day.

For the army the days and nights become reversed as they cross the southern Puszta to Székesfehervar which they reach on June 25th 1683.

The journey from Edirne to Székesfehervar is 950 miles. It has taken them one hundred and two days to reach it.

Horses galloping into the army's midst in a storm of dust announce the arrival of Selim Ghirai, Khan of the Tartars, Khan of the Crimea. They have come with many horses true to the tradition of the Tartar. Every man has four horses: one to ride, one to carry booty, one for a spare and one for the woman he intends to whisk off her feet, or drag from her eviscerated husband, or pull from her screaming children, bundle across a saddle and gallop her back to his rancid-fat-smelling ger, a million hoofbeats away.

Huge red and green standards usurp half the sky above a lake of dusty gold.

Upon a great grey horse, Ibrahim, Paşa of Buda, approaches at a fast canter, pulls his horse upon its haunches in a cloud of dust, dismounts and greets Selim Ghirai, Khan of the Tartars.

***

Kara Mustafa summons Ibrahim of Buda and Selim Ghirai to a Council of War. He plans to by-pass the fortresses of Györ and Komarom and march straight on Vienna.

He says it so abruptly that these old warriors cry out. Not so! It is folly to leave enemy fortresses as strong as Györ behind, says Ibrahim of Buda. It is best, first of all, to secure the fortresses and then attack Vienna. Next year, maybe.

Selim Ghirai, the Khan of the Tartars, agrees. Györ is a gateway to Europe. It is not good to leave it so that the gate can be shut when you have passed through, lest you be nailed up in a trap.

The injudicious do not heed wise counsel. The intelligent advisor knows to turn wise counsel into a tale, so Ibrahim Paşa tells Kara Mustafa a story.

It is a story of a great Khan. One day this Khan called all his great warrior lords to his tent. On his tent floor lay a silk rug in the middle of which stood pile of gold. The Khan told his warrior lords that whosoever could gather the gold without walking on the rug could keep it. The lords were amused. Their Khan had set them a puzzle. So they looked and considered and walked round and round and thought deeply. Round and round they went, scratching their chins through their beards and gazing at the gold. All of them, that is, bar one. This one sat quietly, on his own, on the floor, beside the rug. When the others had stopped walking round and thinking and scratching their chins, not knowing how to get the gold without treading on the rug, he waited until they had become still. Then he leaned forward, took the edge of the rug and rolled it up. So he gathered the gold. This is what the Vizier must do: roll up the land and gather the gold.

The eyes of Selim Ghirai Khan twinkle. His great white moustaches move. He folds his strong brown arms and sits back. Ibrahim Paşa is his old and excellent friend for good reason.

Kara Mustafa's eyes flash.

Whoever disagrees with his plan is a fool.

Ibrahim Paşa sweeps from the tent.

Selim Ghirai follows. Out in the darkness beneath a spray of stars, against the sound of a million crickets, these two dignified old warriors have no need to speak.

In the Grand Vizier's tent no-one dares to speak.

- 10 -

And the Cannons Play

The piles of booty are mounting, the timars are nearly within their grasp. Jewels, gold, precious stones, silver, women – slaves. The seyises grin. Two more days and we shall be upon them! See how the horses are eager to be at war! Feel them gather beneath us! They are not afraid!

The Emperor Leopold in Vienna flies out of the Hofburg Palace door and bundles his pregnant wife aboard the waiting Royal Chaise. Six Karster horses' hooves cut into the patterned cobble stones. Off they clatter through the streets followed by three hundred mounted lifeguards, the coaches and phaetons of the grandees of the court.

Hurtling through the Rothenturm Gate, over the drawbridge, over the canal, the Royal entourage flees across the wooden bridges of the multi-streamed Danube, pushing their way through terrorized crowds, lashed and horsewhipped by the lifeguards.

The glitter, the glamour, the powdered faces and periwigs, the embroidered waistcoats and silks, the pomp, hauteur, the red-lined cloaks and silver fox stoles wrapped round the regal frames of Vienna's courtiers are whisked away The owners will have to drink champagne under other ceilings, to dance under other chandeliers in other gilded ballrooms, in some other city, some other country, while the people of Vienna, their people, are abandoned to the swords of the advancing Turk.

People fight over vehicles, carts, traps and lame old horses to flee the town, only to find themselves robbed outside the city gates by others doing the same. Some Viennese are robbed or cut to pieces by advancing Tartars on the road.

As 60,000 struggle to flee Vienna, others struggle to enter. Those who have already seen the Turks approaching have seen the Tartars too.

They have seen how swiftly they travel: they have seen the Turk horses, the glittering horsemen, their flashing sabres, their confident faces, the way they chased off the Austrian Imperial Cavalry.

Rumours abound. Nothing will stop the Turks but God himself. They need a miracle.

***

The seyis runs his hands along Azarax's neck and feels the hard muscles that spill downwards. Long distance travelling alters a horse. Azarax wishes to be further ahead, to see over the next horizon, climb the next mountain, scent the air, gaze across a new world. He becomes more alert, his mind widens, becomes sharper, more acute. Yet his wisdom also deepens, he becomes more malleable, more accepting. On the move he will eat food that he would not even have looked at, at home: on the move he accepts other horses that he would batter into a corner on his timar.

Yet though Azarax's mind becomes broader, so also he becomes more tightly fused to his companions: to Bora and his seyis. He calls for his seyis if he walks away. He recognises him from afar. He throws his head in the air and looks so far past his seyis when he walks toward him, that the seyis turns to see what he is looking. But he suspects it is a spectre in a world beyond, something from which men are excluded but which remains an intimate part of a horse's soul. Can he see, actually see, what the seyis cannot? Does the seyis have any part in this vision of the future? Or is he a mere instrument in its execution? And what part, in that destiny, does this journey play? To end at its beginning? To know a place for the first time? Or to step into another world and another age – for ever?

In the days and nights, the seyis has tended his horses. He has looked after them, seen to their every need, fed them, watered them, brought them fruit: figs, pomegranates, peaches and pears. He has put garlic in their barley balls and watched the horses rid themselves of worms because he knows the secret of the phases of the moon, and the timing of the medicine.

In all these matters he rejected the received wisdom and sought for his horse what he felt, intuitively, they required. He had watered them profusely when the other seyises said no, you must not water a hot horse. He had ignored advice, and now his horses carried muscle and weight, they did not look pinched nor parched, their tongues were not dry and their eyes had not shrunk into their skulls. Instead their eyes glistened, their bellies were filled with the seeds of fruit and green grass, they moved with the power of the barley and were not consumed by the worms.

At night, when Envir Altinay Paşa dismounted, his seyis was there to take Bora away, to bring him back to Azarax and then the stallions flayed their feet and lunged at each other's knees in mock fight and cried out as he made their feed which he changed as frequently as he could, knowing that a horse given a variety of feed is a horse that never flags, nor lacks strength. The best way to feed a horse, he said once to the Persian seyis who watched as he mixed dates with raw egg, barley, chopped figs, skinned pomegranates and sliced pears, is, he said, to give a horse the best feed. The Persian seyis had walked away shaking his head, thrown his horse barley and saman and wondered why his coat did not shine and his spirit did not burst through his skin with the radiance of an inner sun. He wondered why his horse did not pull at his sleeve as did the seyis' horse and stand over him as he slept, a stern and vigilant sentinel. He wondered why when his hassa rode him away and he collected him at night he threw up his head and flattened his ears and dragged his feet to return to the miserable comfort of his ignorant keeper.

Yet Azarax and Bora are no soft, gentle mewling little horses who nuzzle the hands of a passing stranger. They are not the gentle rocking little ponies who stand at a door waiting for attention. They are independent, haughty, egotistical, aggressive, powerful stallions. Every day they roar at mares. Every day the seyis wrestles with muscle and sinew that is all horse: all stallion, barely controllable. The seyis and his two stallions, all the three of them, reject the company of other men. It is their seyis the horses trust and all others are excluded. In mirror image, their seyis trusts only them, and in this regard the three of them emit a tangible air of isolation. For all the quiet and unassuming ways of their seyis there lies in his heart a disregard of his fellow man, a mistrust, and in his eye is cast the same inner detachment as that of his horses.

The gönüllü who ride by, glance at the quiet seyis on the doru Karaman and say: 'The horse is magnificent, yet look at the rider – he carries no weapons except a bow. He keeps his own counsel, he does not smile; he does not sit and laugh and drink raki, he stays with his horses and his horses stay with him. He has no armour, he has no sword, he has no shield. In the fire of cannons or in the mines in Vienna, he will die, he will die.' And they gallop off in a shroud of grey dust on their dapple-grey Germiyan stallions.

The fire reflects in the shining eyes of a leader of men; his teeth flash splendid and white in the darkness, his skin is ochre, taut from hours passed in the saddle. Ozay Dursun holds up his hand in the firelight and as the smoke curls around the gönüllü seated cross-legged around the fire, he says: 'I know who this seyis is. I have seen these mottled fingers before. Once, centuries ago, a young girl spun a hand-held jenny out in the harsh light of the Kavirian sun. With her were a dozen camels, some Awassi sheep, a rib-skinny dog or two. One day she saw a smudge on the horizon and ran in flight. She was snatched off her feet by the horsemen archers and galloped away and in the high yayla of Anatolia four hundred years ago her daughter gave birth to a son with the soul of a horse and an ancient knowledge. Tell me: does the carpenter bring an anvil to his work? Does the calligrapher bring an axe? Does the surgeon bring a shovel to his patients? Does the teacher bring a stone? The day will dawn when revealed to you will be what lies in the soul of a mottle-fingered seyis who rides on the back of a Karaman thoroughbred. He is fully armed: he has all he needs: a bow, a quiver of arrows and a fast horse. He will save your lives yet.'

* * *

The seyis gazes down at the racking shoulder and the flying ground beneath. The distance is a thick haze. Near him is the smell of horse, heat, sweat and the buzz of millions of flies. Harness jingles, hooves thunder, the air is dyed the colour of blood. Red eyes move in the gritty blizzard. Smiling eyes. One more day, two at most and a timar will be yours!

Up ahead a horse cries out and Azarax responds. A sudden light breeze blows a hole in the dust and the seyis peers through it into the long, fabulous army, with its standards flying. Behind him it stretches back to the fog of yesterday and the day before. 'Allah kerim!' he whispers, and turns his head from horizon to horizon to the standards and helmets, spears, swords and lances, glinting in the sun.

8TH JULY, 1683
The heads of the officers of the Imperial Hapsburg garrison of Mosonmagyaróvár roll at Kara Mustafa's feet. Kara Mustafa mounts his horse and canters on north. The horse is powerful, his strides are long, the dust flies behind him. His nostrils flare red, as he leads ten thousand toprakli sipahi thundering in glory behind. As the Ottoman army presses on, Christian garrisons collapse before it.

'See?' says the Persian seyis. 'The day is already upon us! We are a plague of locusts. We are the fire that sweeps the forest. We purge the land, we bring in our wake our sunlit world, and will deliver to these people blighted in their darkness, light. We have nothing to fear from them and less to learn. We come as a white hot blade to cut through their ice, nothing can stand in our path.

'On my timar I shall grow olives and cucumbers and there will be a river with fish and tall trees and fountains.'

In the Medieval castle town of Hainburg, the severed heads of the town's garrison are stacked in a pyramid outside Kara Mustafa's pavilions.

'See?' says the Persian seyis again. 'Our leader is like the mighty Tamerlane. He is Conqueror, Lord of all the Earth. His destiny is immutable. His power knows no bounds. Our judges are in heaven, they are not in this world. My timar will be so great that it will take a day to ride from one end to the other and I shall have Karaman horses, like yours. They will be tall, like yours, and beautiful and everyone will know that I, Hala Zoran, seyis to Hamit Çankaya of the toprakli hassa sipahi, won a timar at Vienna, for my brave fighting in July 1683.'

***

Kara Mustafa rides to the Lustschloss of Leopold, above Vienna, with its gilded ceilings, formal gardens, marble pillars, orchards, fountains and menagerie of wild animals. Here, Suleiman the Magnificent pitched his pavilions when he besieged Vienna 154 years previously. Will Kara Mustafa sleep soon in the grave of his hero? Or conquer where he failed?

On Saturday 14th July Kara Mustafa mounts his black horse and rides to St Ulrich above the city. By his side gallops the janissary Aga, the Beylerbey of Rumelia. The eastern quarter Kara Mustafa sends, in a flamboyant gesture, to the Beylerbey of Diyarbakır to destroy. He points to the western quarter, and offers it with a courteous bow to the Beylerbey of Aleppo. Commands are issued, and in minutes the cannons are run into line. Cannon beys swing them around and hundreds of bronze muzzles square to the ravelinned walls of Vienna.

The vast Ottoman army surrounds the city. Behind the burning suburbs and out in the fields beyond the city, in amongst the trees and in public grounds, white circles of canvas are laid out, men hammer pegs into the hard ground and 25,000 tents are conjured up, like mushrooms rising in a warm September night. 10,000 baggage wagons draw in amongst them, bullocks, horses, line upon line of camp followers, fill the city's peripheral horizon: smoke from thousands of fires coils up and darkens the sky.

Kara Mustafa gazes on. His written ultimatum is shot over the walls of the city by arrow: *Surrender, Be Spared; Leave with all your*

Possessions, or Be Put to the Sword.

Feldzeugmeister Count Ernst Rüdiger von Stahremberg, leader of the Viennese garrison, does not reply.

One hour slides by: two hours slide by.

At a little after three in the afternoon, on 14th July 1683, Kara Mustafa, Grand Vizier of the Ottoman Empire, spins the flying wheels of fate, slides his brown eyes to the artillery ortas and with a wry smile and a nod, bids their cannon play.

- 11 -

The Wiener Wald

All routes to the city are sealed: the water supply is cut. The road from Krems to Pressburg is in Ottoman hands: patrolled, blocked. Nothing can pass. Viennese stragglers who are found rattling along the road to Passau with carts loaded with furniture meet swift ends. Men sink to their knees on the hilt of yatağan. Fingers that closed round the necks of violins now curl round pickaxes: they will excavate mines under their own city. Their soft hands will blister: when they can dig no longer they will be decapitated and their heads set on spikes in view of their friends and relatives on the walls. And the women? Old ones are abandoned and left weeping over the corpses. As for the young ones: their expectation of life depends on their looks. Goods of any value disappear: rings, necklaces, jewellery, clothes, trinkets. Crucifixes are stamped into the ground.

The Tartars lay waste the countryside. Galloping through farmsteads on rock-hard Kabardin and Karabakh horses, they toss burning torches into hay ricks, barns, grain stores, feed stores and down into cellars. Into wells they drop lifeless bodies. By the time the cannons begin firing outside Vienna, the Tartars are already fifty miles ahead, in Melk. They ravage Auersperg and Purgstall. They have already burned Breitenbrunn by the Neusiedler See.

'I told you so,' says the Persian seyis winding his turban: 'It is happening. Already the Tartars have booty. I saw one with a big ugly red scar on his face go scorching by on a bay Karabakh and when he came back he had a Hapsburg girl kicking and squealing, slung across his saddle and he was whooping and shouting and went thundering past on his way to Allah knows where – not one hour ago! And his saddlebags were stuffed with gold cups and chalices from these Christian churches, it is marvellous! Within one week this city will be on its knees. I have heard there is more treasure in this city than Samarkand. When we storm it, I shall gallop along the streets like that Tartar and fill my saddlebags with gold and flash my sword in front of Kara Mustafa and he will stretch out his arm with his eyes blazing and shout: Look! How brave is this seyis! Reward him with a timar! And it will be mine, all mine. You will see. Over there. Do you see that place? It is called the Wiener Wald: I shall have a timar there. Beautiful!'

The seyis wipes the blood from both of Bora's shoulders. When he collected him from Envir Altinay Paş a he thought at first that the blood was the horse's. When he found it was not, he thought it was Envir Altinay's. Envir Altinay had thrown his yatağan to the seyis when he had handed over the horse and quipped, 'Clean that up!' The paş a looked at him smugly, waiting for the seyis to react, burdening him with an emotional response, as though a groom owed his master the obeisance of recognition for having killed whoever it was he had killed. Envir Altinay silently defied the seyis to beg him to reveal how many Hapsburgers he had butchered that day so he could notch them up, swell his ego. As if the seyis gave a damn. No, the blood was not Envir Altinay's.

'Tomorrow I shall take the doru,' Envir Altinay said, wiping his brow with the back of a thick, strong arm. The seyis' expression had not changed. He took both horse and sword, and walked away and although the paşa had shouted after him: 'Clean the sword first!' he ignored him and attended to the horse first.

He wipes the blood off Bora, feels his beating heart, wonders what images fill his mind: what sounds, what noises, what horror? The whites of the horse's eyes show as he looks back to where he has just been. He is black with sweat, and even Azarax meets him with unaccustomed quiet. The horse breathes rapidly for an hour, standing still as the seyis pours cold water over him, wipes the sweat off, cleans his legs and under his belly, checks him inch by inch for shrapnel or bullet wounds. The seyis' own heart had beaten irregularly, his hands shook as he searched the stallion's sides for the telltale spot that would kill him, slowly. These are the worst. A piece of shrapnel no bigger than a pinhead. If this had been found, the horse's ears would fix in a half-pricked position, his head would raise and the third eyelid would flutter across his eye and he would tip on the points of his hind hooves and spread his legs, his jaw would seize, the third eyelid would close and tressel-like, he would quiver and sweat; nothing could save him. He would die an appalling death, by degrees.

There is no wound. There is no shrapnel. The blood must have been the blood of the Hapsburgs. Bora is unmarked.

15TH JULY 1683: The hassa horse lines

A little after dawn, purple sky and quarter moon. It is day two of the siege. Adjutants of the Beylerbey of Adana and Sancakbey of Nicopolis and the serçeşme of the Seymen, call the toprakli to mount. Kettle drums start up: boom, boom, boom! Carefully the seyis slips the bridle up over Azarax's ears and slides the big deep ported copper and steel Ottoman bit into his mouth: this horse has a very soft, sensitive mouth. Bang that bit and the rider will be on the ground looking into the horse's belly – and probably at the receiving end of a flashing hind to the head to help him remember that this horse has a very soft mouth. The seyis smoothes Azarax's back, slips on the saddle and girths it. Envir Altinay vaults up. Tall, broad shouldered, superbly confident – that great chin, those defiant eyes – this is a man who has no comprehension of defeat. He winks once as he takes his kalkan shield from his seyis and the yatağan he has so carefully cleaned, sharpened and skimmed with a film of oil.

'We shall be back before the sun has passed the clock on the Hofburg – if it's still there!' He spins the horse: 'I'll bring you back a fat Karster – how would you like that?' The seyis wrinkles his nose. Envir Altinay laughs and gallops the horse to the troop heading jauntily out of the camp toward the Danube. There are rumours of the toprakli facing three regiments of dragoons led by a man called Schultz – as if they care. The seyis watches him go. Strangely, he is not worried for Azarax. Why is he not worried?

He returns to grooming Bora, hand in the horsehair mitten, musing: 'I am puzzled. Why am I so at peace about Azarax? Soon the janissary orderly will be along with his whip, ordering us to man the cannons, to dig the mines. Some hide: some run. They forget their horses. Save their own lives: live another day.'

The seyis attends to a life he values above his own. The grooming mitten runs across deep brown hair, softer than the down of a little bird. It is a moment of silence, like a prayer, to feel the skin of the horse, feel him relax under the pressure of the mitten, watch the shine, pick off flaky eruptions, melt into the horse's psyche as the horse melts into his. As the horse half-closes his eyes dreamily, his lower lip twitching minutely, the seyis hums a tune.

Suddenly, he hears a voice he knows. Above the cannons. A horse runs out from the hassa lines. Bora calls. Envir Altinay Paşa has returned on Azarax and drops straight off his back. 'I can't handle this horse. Saddle the yağiz. Hurry.'

It takes a few short minutes.

Too fast. The seyis watches helplessly as he canters off. Azarax snatches at his rein, screaming. He is a brute to hold and lifts the seyis off his feet. Bora glances back across his flanks: the seyis captures the look with horror. Envir Altinay would not allow such sentiment. Does he care? Did he even notice? The seyis' expression is distraught. That was not good, not good at all. Bora was expecting to stay. He has been deceived; his trust is broken. To break the trust of a horse is worse than a curse.

Envir Altinay rejoins the massed toprakli sipahi cantering away: black tails, black legs, black hooves biting the hard ground. The riders, with their shoulders back, sit deep in their saddles, taking the thrust of the horses' three beat strides. The dust rises, the sound escalates, more and more pour into the column and it grows and grows until the whole plain in front of the Ottoman lines is packed with them. 'Allahu akbar!' a voice shouts and is answered in deep throated unison, silencing the guns, silencing the firing from the city walls. The sight is awesome. Turning to their right the column canters behind the toprakli Crescent Moon standards, thundering straight out of the soul of the Steppe, the hearts of Genghis Khan, of Tamerlane, of Suleiman the Magnificent, Conqueror of the Two Seas and all the land from China to the soil on which they now amass. Lances flash in the sun, green standards fly, the harnesses glitter with gold, emeralds, tourmalines and topaz. The men are dazzling in their conical helmets and chain mail, vambraces and ankle plates. The horses are magnificent: heads up, eyes glinting, manes tossing, tails streaming, glossy-backed and quarters plunging, the sound of their thousands of hooves a deafening roar.

The azab, janissaries, engineers, gunners and auxiliaries stand up, wave, cheer, whistle. 'How would you like to face that lot?' a janissary officer shouts to a comrade. He shakes his head: 'Mahşallah!'

Was not there once a voice that shuddered through the cloud and thunder, the lightning and the hail and breathed that all men might hear: 'I have an army which I call the Turks and when I am wrathful towards a people I shall loose it upon them'?

The seyis watches Bora disappear into the dust. Envir Altinay is a powerful horseman: it would take half a dozen swordsmen coming at him at once to bring him down.

But what will become of the horse?

***

Glory goes to those who were born into glory. The rayah, the common cattle, are born into grime and in the grime they will rot. Not for them the splendour and the sapphires, the trophies and triumphs. They must toil in the dirt and the heat and when they are blown to pieces in the trenches and in the mines, no-one will mourn them. There are others queuing to take their place.

Stripped to his waist in the artillery batteries, the seyis struggles with the heavy iron shot for the cannon beys. His physique is meant for the saddle: he is not a creature of the sod, of burden. Deadweight exhausts him. No hand reaches down to help when he drops the shot. No sympathy extends as he struggles with his sweating hands to grasp it. He is kicked and told to move, to do his work or be flogged. He carries the shot straight-armed, stiff legged, leaning back, face red and contorted, veins pounding. He rolls the barrels of powder and is deafened by the roar of the guns, by the flashes from their muzzles, is blinded by the backfire from the touchholes when he gets too close, has his foot crushed when a cannon recoils and he has not cleared the gun. His face is blackened with powder. His mind is on his yağiz horse and Envir Altinay; and he looks up to see if the sun has crossed the Hofburg. He works like a troll in a dungeon, with boiling metals and sweating bodies, the stench of burning cloth and cordite, the constant roar and the bullets that fly over his head.

By midday he muscles are already spent. How, he wonders are his horses? Do they feel as he does? Do they have water? They must be hungry. Has some sipahi taken Azarax and lost him in a barrage of musket fire? He looks up. The ground before the batteries shimmers in the braising summer sun: a blinding light. What of the people in the city receiving all this terror? And their horses. What about the horses? A shell explodes nearby, blasting him off his feet. He slams his head against an artillery wheel. Someone pulls him to his feet and points: there is a barrel of water to which he staggers. A wooden cup hangs from a string. He takes it, dips it into the warm, dirty water and drinks. Water runs down his chest: he pours it over his head. Someone shouts at him to work: the shot needs carrying. As he turns he catches a glimpse of two hassa janissary officers sitting in the shade of a pavilion blithely playing backgammon as the cannons roar and shells explode around them. The rayah are born into grime and in the grime they may rot.

Sunset: end of a gunnery shift: a turbanned hadji stands in front of the seyis and mouths words. He points to the distance. The seyis shakes his head and pushes past: he does not hear him, cannot hear him. The heat of the day sears the bloodied earth as he limps through the destruction. He finds a space to sit on a crumbling wall: holds his crushed foot, blackening to an evil bruise. His chin puckers: sweat runs down his face. The world has capsized. It rings. There is no other sound except the ringing.

He stumbles back toward the city of tents.

Sixty to seventy thousand timarli sipahi horses are tethered in amongst this vast city of canvas. Unlike other cavalries, the sipahi horses are not tethered in lines: they remain with their owners, and their owners have come from all across the Empire: from Rumelia, from Wallachia, Bosnia, Serbia, Anatolia, Marash, Shashrzur, Luristan, Mesopotamia, Armenia, Kurdistan, Syria.

The timarli sipahi horses stand beside the tents, like their ancestor's horses stood beside them at night. The timarli sipahi groom them, feed them, saddle them, armour them, gallop them off to fight and return them, wringing with sweat, foamed white across their chests, black across their necks, to the tent. Everything happens at the tent: the sipahi eat and sleep and rest and clean their muskets, sharpen their swords and boast about their horses' pedigree, the Ghazi pedigree: the Turko-Ferghana, the Chagatai, Kipchak, Petcheneg, Oghuz – real horses, golden horses – from which their own horses had sprung many centuries past. They are Turk horses and Turks are superior: bigger, faster. Turk riders and their horses are one. They are not divisible. Many put felts on their horses – like their ancestors. The felts are thick and brown and keep their coats fine, keep the glare of the sun off and the horses trim. The sipahi spread manure beneath these horses, into soft beds, and what remains is thrown onto fires which provides heat for cooking and keeps away the flies.

The hassa sipahi horses are tethered under canvas near the hassa sipahi tents, reds and yellows and green with their hassa insignia emblazoned on them: Sura from the Holy Koran is encrypted into intricate designs and embroidered onto the white canvas, with the regimental orta crest flying from a pennant at the apex.

Horses are taken out to join the attack singly, ten at a time, a hundred at a time or all of them at once but never the same number return. Sometimes none of them return and their stalls are left empty and the horses that were standing next to them cry out for them late into the night and into the next long, hot day.

Black vultures wheel in the broken sky; their shadows flicker across the canvas, across the horses and the hassa, across the azab troops and the janissaries in the trenches and the men look up and pray for the intercession of their Bektaşi hadji – their saint.

* * *

Everything is burned: charred roof joists, angled in an exuvia of gutted geometry, the corpses of shattered homes: charred plants, charred grass, charred furniture. That was once an elegant chair now lying upside down, bottomless, three legged and half burned. These suburbs, desolated suburbs: there was happiness here, before the Ottomans came. The seyis stumbles on, swatting flies from his face, his lips. His arms ache, his back aches, his legs are weary. He dreams of simple food: rice. Just rice: plain white rice. His eyes are heavy, his face stings from phosphorus burns. To sleep, just for an hour, to sleep, in some peaceful place. To know once more – keyif – the delight of the moment: silence, some repose, horses by a river, beneath trees in a silent land where there are no guns, no wars, no wounds, no flies.

He hurries with his bruised foot to the canvas. He longs to see his Azarax: to look into eyes he comprehends. He has missed his company all day. What did the old Armenian seyis say? A timar? A seyis win a timar? No, seyises are blown to pieces or buried in the mines. And what of this brave fighting? Where? All the seyises work at the cannons and already three have been blown to pieces and this is the first full day. But I am alive. I am alive.

And the horses? What have I brought them to? Can this be their destiny, this place? Why did I bring them here? I should have stayed in Istanbul. I should have run away with them instead of riding to the müsellem. I should have sneaked away from the army when we passed Ali-aga Izobegović's timar. What use is this war? How can this be the right place to be? How can this be a place of destiny? It is nothing more than a place of destruction. I have brought the horses to a place of destruction.

He rubs his eyes with the heels of his palms. He half-runs, half-hobbles on.

A sudden foul waft makes him retch: inexplicably, a dismembered human torso is lying under the canvas amongst the horses. How did it get there? It is black with flies. The seyis reels and runs along the tethers with his hand to his mouth to the place he left Azarax tethered.

Where Azarax is not tethered.

He looks once. Blinks. And looks again. The earth saps the blood from his body in one dull, hideous vortex.

He bends and vomits.

His precarious hold on his two horses now strikes him: that which he feared most has been visited upon him.

'My horse! My horse!' he cries out. 'Who has taken my horse?' He struggles along yelling at the other seyises. No-one knows: a horse is just a horse unless he is yours. The seyis runs in and out under the canvas, checking the tethers and the open ground. His doru must have been taken by one of the hassa sipahi who'd lost his own. Oh God, let it not be so! Which orta has he gone to, where? Which hassa sipahi?

His face is white. His strength has abandoned him. Stopping to catch his breath he bends and a doru horse flashes across his vision. He dare not look up. Self-deception is the most pernicious deception of all. Did he imagine what he saw? He looks up in the dying light of day.

That unmistakable shape. With monstrous casualness Azarax browses about in amongst some destroyed farm buildings two hundred yards away, swishing his tail, stamping at the flies. The seyis retches again. When he stands upright he is shaking: a wave of emotion plugs his throat. He struggles towards the horse, hand on his chest. As they meet, the horse touches his knee with his nose and whickers, softly. The seyis collapses on the ground.

The horse nuzzles through seeded thistles, nettle roots, and dried-up dandelions and watches him from the corner of his eye, a soft look, with eyes that reflect light as no others the seyis has ever known. Some horses' eyes seem to absorb light, take it in and not cast any back out, but this horse, this strangely aloof creature, with his calmness and savagery all rolled into one fabulously diverse character, will lay his ears flat, lash out with a hoof or bare his teeth – yet be so tender. Sometimes he is like his mother: touch me, if you dare. Yet he can pick up a minute particle with immense delicacy, he can gallop through cannon fire, he will obey his seyis as he obeys the draw of his own soul. Those eyes burn with a ferocity and a purpose that no other horse's eyes can hold, and yet now, the expression cast by the way he holds his eye is one brokered between defiance and utter bewilderment. A heartbreaking look: of violated innocence.

The horse browses. The even crunch of his teeth, the swish of his tail, the soft brownness of his coat, the flickering ears, contrive to haul the seyis back from the abyss. He holds out a hand. Emotion, exhaustion and relief wash over him. Above the seyis, the setting sun is deep crimson. Yet a lark is singing. At the very end of the day. Above the distant cannons and guns and shouting, above the meterhane band banging out its music and janissary guards yelling orders, the seyis hears the lark and slowly his face wreathes with a smile, the smile becomes a chuckle, the chuckle a laugh and the laugh becomes uncontrolled. He laughs, writhing about, holding his belly – hysterical. Too much. What is this feeling that washes over him? Relief? Fear? Pain? What? This little bird sings. Thanks be to the Prophet, Blessings be upon Him, for this little bird and for my horse. Oh Allah, the Compassionate, the Merciful, help us.

The laughter ceases.

Taking his trailing lead rein the seyis rises and moves Azarax toward another abandoned farmstead, another scratch of grazing, and as he crosses the higher ground he sees the toprakli return to camp. A pathetic, ragged remnant of the force that had left that morning. Their colours are gone, the standards destroyed.

He winces.

They limp in pathetically.

Do more toprakli join, from behind? No.

His head feels light and dry.

Is this the complete, returning force? Yes.

How many are there?

Two hundred, three hundred.

How many left this morning?

Eight thousand.

Does a big hassa sipahi paşa on a yağiz horse canter back to the hassa lines?

***

That night Azarax cries out.

The stall beside him is empty. He turns his dark face to the direction in which Bora left that morning and cries. His great body shakes as he calls and as the night passes, his calls become more urgent. All night he calls, yet no yağiz horse responds. The seyis stands with him listening to his cries. The darkness beyond is filled with the boom of cannons and the ripple of musket fire, the shouts of men, the tragic whickering of injured horses but not the sound of the voice for which he and his horse listen. What hope is there? The seyis runs into the darkness twenty times but always when he returns his face is a mask. The glands in his neck are swollen. His eyes are red. His nose runs. His head is still ringing from the cannons. He stands beside his doru horse as he calls and calls.

Exhaustion overcomes the seyis and he climbs into the bunk he made between his two horses. He turns over and over and over. He sits up suddenly and listens. Then lies down. When it comes at last it is a sleep, of a troubled kind.

Sleep.

A hand is laid upon his forehead. The fingers are mottled. There is a voice, a female voice. A voice he has not heard since he was a child: a voice that hums some strange, terse little tune. He sees a hand-held jenny, spinning, spinning. Something glances across the edge of his senses. Something stepped lightly: it was a hoof: he heard it. Is he asleep? Is he

137

awake? There are lilac grasses and sight of a land he knows in his heart, where a yağiz horse gallops toward him. 'Bora!' He gallops through the butterflies and the grasses and opens his mouth as if to cry out but there is no sound. By a pebbly river he sees the yağiz horse again. He watches as he bends his head to graze. He is safe. Is he safe? Where is Bora?

Bora, I can feel the touch of your skin, the softness of your coat, softer than the down of a little bird. The fineness of your mane. How your tail is different from Azarax's, more dense and yet as fine. Your ears were longer, are longer, your face curved more, your eyes full of trust. You bit my ear once. It was my fault. I remember many things about you, Bora, even though Azarax was there at the time, but now I seem only to remember you. I remember the lake and gypsy girls, how you waded out into the water, and when we finally left that night, the lake was golden. I remember the red goats and their bells and the Müsellem's stables lying below in the valley. Bora!

I believed Azarax's destiny was also your destiny too, Bora. I do not believe it now. It was a djinn sent to deceive me. You trusted me when I handed you to Envir Altinay Paşa. I saw something in your eye when you had to go with him the next day and the day after. And when Envir Altinay Paşa came back for you and swapped Azarax for you, I know you realised I loved Azarax more than I loved you, I know it. I saw it.

If there is a Heaven of Horses, you will wait for me and you will bar me. You will say: this seyis is no good. He led me to my death.

And where will destiny lead me? Where? I have taken the wrong turn and my horses are paying the price. Where is Bora?

The jenny spins and spins. The voice hums on. 'He is beside the river,' she says softly, 'He is with me.' The mottled fingers move from the seyis' forehead and lips touch it.

A horse nuzzles his hair. Hot breath in his face. He sleeps breathing in the breath of a stallion, who breathes the breath of his seyis.

***

The cannons roar, the mines explode. The seyis lugs round shot, up and down the gritty slopes, while bullets fly over his head.

Who cares about another dead horse: what about the men? Are they not your friends? Did not the Kurdish seyis and the Arab seyises get killed only yesterday?

A bullet comes so close the seyis actually feels the air screech in its wake. It terrifies him. One inch closer and he would have had his brains blown out.

Now there are only two of you left. Even the Persian seyis is dead: he was buried alive when we detonated the mine – they don't bother to warn them, you know. Just lay the fuses and bang! There is no time to worry about seyises in mines. He had dreamed of winning a timar, the fool. Which seyis ever gets a timar?

Number twelve cannon blows up, killing its entire crew, showering the seyis and his crew with hot intestines and shattered limbs and bones. He abandons his work and runs across the firing lines and throws himself in the canal even though faeces are floating on its surface.

Damn your remaining horse, no, you will work in the mines. Any sipahi now will take your doru horse. His days are numbered, if not his hours. Horses are killed in battle, did you not realise? If he lasts another day he will be lucky. Get in there and dig.

**

The brutal, bloody weeks pass. The siege rumbles on. The seyis labours in the mines beneath Vienna's walls. Azarax is taken out on mission after mission by sipahi horsemen whom the seyis neither sees nor knows. Nor is he aware what time they ride the horse back or if Azarax returns on his own.

But at night he finds him standing at his tether, patiently waiting, saddle on his back, sweating, hungry – but alive. Even before he is within sight, he knows when the seyis is approaching and calls out and the seyis calls back, and hurries to him. The seyis finds what he can, shares with Azarax what food he can find – and sometimes it is a lot and he brings fruit and lentils, barley and maize – then sleeps beside him and listens as the horse lies down, listens to his restless spirit and wonders what fills his thoughts. Day after day this continues and the seyis dreads the moment when he will return and not hear Azarax's voice. He knows that when this happens he will have failed and that whatever fate threw in his path, whatever auguries were set for him, he has failed to bring the horse to his destiny.

Yet a greater destiny unfolds:

2ND SEPTEMBER 1683. A ravelin falls into Turkish hands.

4TH SEPTEMBER 1683. A huge explosion rocks Vienna. A wide breech is made in the wall and through the dust the janissaries rush, firing pistols and carbines and bearing the horsetail standards. That night, distress rockets are fired from the town. The Turks are jubilant.

6TH SEPTEMBER 1683. Part of the Löbel is destroyed and long slabs of wall crack and slide into collapse. Vienna is falling. A few more days and it will bear a new name: the Ottoman city of Viyana.

8TH SEPTEMBER 1683. Rockets are seen outside Vienna in the direction of the Kahlenberg. A relieving Christian army is approaching.

10TH SEPTEMBER 1683. Rumours in the Turkish camp are rife: a huge Polish force will attack the next day.

11TH SEPTEMBER 1683. A force of 200,000 troops of the Imperial Force advances along the Danube toward the Ottoman lines. The huge Polish cavalry under King Jan Sobieski is drawn up above the Wiener Wald and is set to attack the next day.

Kara Mustafa orders all his troops to remain awake all night. He orders non-combatants, engineers, seyises, slaves and captured Christians to continue mining, in the belief that if he can explode the mines under the walls, the walls will collapse, and in the breach, his troops will storm. Vienna is within his grasp: it will fall at any hour.

On the night of the 11th September 1683, the seyis sleeps astoundingly well, even though the camp has been ordered to remain awake. Earlier he had gone out to what remained of the hassa horse lines, then some perverse chemistry in his body had made him fall soundly asleep the minute he was told that all men had been ordered to remain awake.

He woke with a start a little before dawn on 12th September. The pre-dawn light is beautiful: an aubergine sky studded with diamonds.

Azarax gazes down upon him, his eyes glossy as the sky, reflecting the stars in tiny prisms of light, diamonds all of his own. He regards his groom with immense curiosity, ears pricked, sniffing cautiously as though the man had just emerged from a chrysalis. The seyis looks around, stretches, and rubs his eyes. He tips his pillow of saman and barley into the trough in front of the horse, watches and waits.

This is as good a day to die as any. Today, the fate of this army, this siege, this city, this seyis, this horse, is to be determined. 'Why do I feel so unconcerned?' he wonders, and stretches again. 'This day I will die and I do not care. I have slept exceedingly well. So has my horse.' And he pats him as a novice would pat a shaggy pony after his first canter.

They are both surprisingly refreshed.

'What will fate deliver today? Is this my last dawn? Is this brilliant halo of light emerging in the east the last sun I shall see? Why am I so unafraid?

'Insh'allah. It is not in my hands. What will be will be. I need have no fear.'

As the first rays of the sun flail the hard blue, cloudless eastern sky, the seyis tightens the horse's girth. The horse's sipahi rider today is armed with a yatağan and pistols. He is a young lad.

The seyis holds the doru horse's stirrup and waits for him to mount.

The hassa sipahi rider tosses the reins across the horse's neck, the seyis pushes down on the stirrup on the opposite side and then when the lad is mounted, he looks up at him. He's very young, at most twenty years old. He has black rings under his eyes. His hands are shaking. He can barely hold the reins. His face is white and his knuckles are drained.

The seyis tries to smile. 'This horse's name is...'

'I don't wish to know his name,' the lad retorts.

The seyis' belly tightens. 'Have you been in many engagements?' he asks delicately.

The question is left hanging in the air. The seyis looks away, along the horse lines. This is a fast, high mettle horse and he takes a lot of handling. Azarax will not know how to deal with a nervous rider. He will hesitate. And while this frozen-with-fear sipahi flounders about not knowing what to do, Azarax will be a stationary target and will be shot from under him.

The seyis leans toward the horse who dips his head and eyes him archly as if to ask: Why? Why this boy, not you? The seyis puts a hand on Azarax's neck as the young hassa sipahi bangs the horse's flanks. The horse turns and flies out of the seyis' hand. He canters off, folding in with the other sipahi as they spill out from the horse lines.

The seyis cries out. The horse canters on. The seyis draws in a breath and holds it. The horse disappears straight into section, becoming lost in the herd, in the regiment, in the swirling dust and massed body of the sipahi.

The seyis runs for a few yards and then stops. He stands, watching him go, arms limp by his side. The horse has been swallowed up in a mass of haunches, necks and heads, in twinkling armour and fluttering standards.

The swiftness of Azarax's departure and the abrupt dismissal of his groom, leaves the seyis breathless.

There is no-one to understand, to sympathise. This is war. It's only a horse – so what?

Then he is standing numbly beside his bunk, in the scent of the horse, the heaps of dung, the half-eaten saman. He reaches for his bow and quiver. This, his bow, is the pivot of his skill: its fulcrum: its axis. And what relevance does it have now?

He runs a hand over the tops of the arrows: there are forty-five of them, packed tightly, yet the minute one is taken out they loosen and can be extracted easily. He turns the bone, wood and sinew bow over and over in his hands. It took him a year to fashion this bow. First he had to find the water buffalo with identical horns, then wait for her to be served up in the heat of a fire before he took her horns and cut them down the centre and so shaped the beginnings of this bow. He bound the wood and horn together with glue made from the buffalo's boiled hooves, then lashed it with her sinew and polished it with her tallow. For weeks he had honed and planed and balanced it so that when it lay in his hand it felt as though it was supposed to be there, as though it were part of him, an extension of his eye, arm, hand, shoulder. The arrows he fletched with goose feather, each made with the feather from one wing, so that the arrow would curl either right or left. Each flight he stained with a black stripe so that when the arrow flew it appeared to corkscrew and when it found its mark, there lay his signature.

He picks up the bow, points one end in the ground, curls his leg round it, depresses the top and strings the silk cord to its toggles. It is a thing of beauty. Raising it to his shoulder he pulls the string. The movement is fluid and comes to him with great ease. He can feel the muscles ripple across his back: his archer's muscles.

What is he going to do with a bow in the mines?

What is he? A groom: just a groom. Rayah. Common cattle. Sent for slaughter at the whim of a lunatic in a battle that is already lost.

The janissary with the whip appears, whipping whoever still lives and is not on horseback, to the mines. Crack! Crack! goes the whip. Hey! You!

The seyis places his bow back on what was his bed. Someone may find it: take it. Keep it as a souvenir. Throw it on a fire. Does it matter? Without a horse it is useless anyway and his horse has just been galloped off to the vultures by an incompetent.

The city of tents passes him by.

Shots ring out from the Wiener Wald. The ground moves beneath his feet as he nears the mine entrances. He doesn't even bother to notice a stream of men pouring down the Wiener Wald, how his own cavalry is mustering. He doesn't bother to watch the great janissary ortas taking up positions, nor see Ibrahim of Buda with his great fluttering green standards ride past at the head of 23,000 horse.

He doesn't feel the ground vibrate under his feet nor hear the great thundering of hooves and the swirling dust as the horses go by. He does not hear the shouts all round him nor the bullets that whistle past his ears. He does not see the Ghazi gönüllü go by with Ozay Dursun at their head. Today they will gallop headlong into the Polish cavalry and they will take many lives. They will also lose theirs. But this does not matter to the gönüllü. When they die they die with their comrades and they will gallop their ghazi horses in the fields of Paradise. They gallop past in a blaze of colour but the seyis does not see them.

- 12 -

The Poles

In the heat-charged, airless twilight, hacking at a wall of black earth with a worn-out pickaxe, the seyis is pushed roughly aside by sappers rolling kegs of gunpowder. They disappear further into the tomb-like darkness. He glances around at the men slaving in this bleak hole: is this really happening? It's a dream: a nightmare. He will wake soon. No-one speaks. A janissary cracks a whip. 'Dig, you bastards!' he roars and flays a Christian's back, bringing him to the ground. The seyis bends and taking the man's arm, helps him to his feet. Snatching back his arm, the Christian returns to the hard earth wall with his bare hands. As the seyis swings his pickaxe, he watches for fire running on the ground: no-one in here is going to tell anyone when the fuses are lit.

A chunk of overhead earth slumps in front of the seyis and the Christian, exposing a large section of unsupported roof. The seyis' voice ratchets up as he shouts for timber supports. Lengths of cordwood arrive and he and the Christian raise them into position sharing the work between them, sweating in the semi-light, hammering the base into place and pinning planking into the cordwood tops as they crowbar them upright. The Christian does not speak but pinchbars the wood and shovels earth with his hands into worn-out baskets slung across the back of a blue Bosnian mountain pony.

The pony is led out by another terrified Christian, who shouts as he leaves the mine and keeps shouting. The seyis' brow furrows. Why is he shouting? What is happening? A shot rings out. The pony canters back into the mine. The janissary pulls another Christian from the earth wall and pushes him to the pony. 'You!' he roars. The man takes the pony and does the same: he shouts as he exits the mine and keeps shouting. Another shot rings out. The pony canters back in, panniers flapping, sides heaving.

There is no escape from this mine. To stay is to be blown up, to leave is to be shot.

By one o'clock the Wiener Wald foreground is a blaze of colour: massed pancerni on massed horse. Infantry fan out on either side, their standards held high above them, glints of sunlight on musket muzzles, on sabres. More Imperial horsemen plunge out of the shadows of the trees into the bright sunlight: sparkling cuirasses, polished helmets, panther skins and winged plumes at their backs. The sipahi hesitate. The Poles are even mounted on oriental horses: they wear lamellar armour; those that wear chain mail wear it like a Turk. The animal skins – the panther skin, leopard skin and tiger skins – are like the deli horsemen or the gönüllü; they even carry kalkan shields.

At the head of this contingent, resplendent royal choragiews – ensigns – flutter: the yellow and red of Prince Jakob and the crimson and blue of the Polish King, Jan Sobieski. Mounted on a dun Turk stallion, harness sparkling with gold filigree and precious stones, the King is royally dressed in oriental style. On his head is the kalpak with plume, pinned with precious stones; he wears dark blue silk and in his hand he wields the great bulawa sword. Beside him is his son Prince Jakob, equally resplendent. Around them in tight formation are the winged hussars with the Crown escutcheon, in their leopard and tiger skin pelts, polished armour and gleaming breastplates. They are arraigned like a chessboard, with Sienawski's heavy reiters on the left, hussars in front with sabre and carbine and the pancerni Cossacks in rank at every hundred paces.

The King halts this contingent. Orders are barked. The horses, snorting and high-stepping are already moving; the King wheels his horse and in a steady slow canter, the huge unit gradually picks up speed.

With a roar of 'Jezus Maria, ratuj!' the choragiew of Crown Hussars, the eliery, the crack storm cavalry under the Command of Zygmund Zbierzchowski, lower their 19- foot pennon-tipped lances. The wind begins to sing and squeal in the feathers of the winged hussars. Faster and faster the horses' hooves beat into the ground until the lances are level and the unit bursts into a full thundering gallop.

The sounds of shattering lances cracks over the field as they burst straight through the first and second lines of Ibrahim Paşa's sipahis.

On a single command, the eiliery return, having lost a third of their men and horse, including the Starost of Halicz, the top of whose head was sliced off in one stroke.

Further charges are made, and the Poles fall. The Turks are succeeding.

The sipahi mount a counter attack. The Poles retreat behind German infantry lines.

A riderless, mahogany blood-bay Karaman stallion canters freely

145

across the battlefield in the sights of a German infantryman's musket. 'Leave him!' an officer shouts. 'Booty, lad, booty!' The lad keeps the bead on the horse as he canters out of sight. 'Damn,' he breathes.

Hot, black air; smell of tar, cordite and the bitter scent of powder. A flash – a lit fuse? Something sparked down there. Mines explode for no reason – everyone knows: they just explode. Some go with a blinding explosion, some in a fireball. Some cave in when the fuses go. You don't hear a thing, they say: you're just buried alive. You are trapped and who's going to dig you out? How many mines are there here? Ten: twelve: fifteen. Some so close together that if one explodes, the one beside it goes too. The seyis swings his pickaxe. No air in this place: suffocating. He keeps thoughts of his horse from his mind. Can't think about him. Not at all. He never expected a parting like that. Brutally short. Yet there was something else. He bites at a blister on his palm. That was it: the horse was calm. What does that mean? It means he was alright, that's what it means. The boy riding him was a disaster: he'll be dead in less than a minute. And then Azarax? Will he live? The seyis swings the pick, once, twice. Sweat runs off his nose, into his eyes, down his back, his chest, his arms. His hands are soaking and blistered. The place stinks. No, the horse was calm. He will be alright. Never mind about me, as long as the horse is alright.

Another flash explodes from deep in the mine, and then shouts erupt: 'Get out! Get out!' Suddenly a length of cordwood splinters and the roof explodes. Hurled onto the floor of the mine by the weight of earth, the seyis responds instinctively to the thump of a hoof on stone. Grasping a running strap dangling from a leather tug, he is dragged from the mine by powerful, short legs while the rocks and earth pour down black behind him and the voices of men are silenced for ever in its throttling depths. Those legs drag him on and on over the splintered cordwood and stones and earth. A burst of sunlight. He looks up into the sweating flanks and big, dust rimed eyes of the Bosnian pony.

He lies still, coughing. The pony stands, panting, covered in earth. Musket fire crackles above his head: men have been blasted clean out of the mine next to the one in which he was working. The landscape has changed: a big earth bank has been flung up. They can't see him from the city walls: no gunfire: he has a chance. His ribs ache.

He has to move now or they'll force him back in the mine. The pony, the pony! Crouching beside the pony, holding his mane, he counts: 'One, two, three... now!' and it runs. It runs along the trenches, jumping bodies and fallen debris, it weaves its way through the labyrinth and the seyis runs behind crouched, knowing that the pony will have remembered the lay-out better than he and where he might run into a dead end, the pony won't. The pony runs fast and the seyis just manages to keep track of it by its disappearing tail and then it runs up a ramp and with a victorious whinny breaks out into the old burned-out suburbs, a section protected from gunshot from the city walls. Now the seyis grabs the pony's forelock and leads it weaving through broken stonework in the direction of the city of tents and he stops and ruffles its woolly head. 'Teşekkür!' he whispers in a furry ear, 'Thank you!', then slaps it on its backside and hisses 'Heydi! Away you go!' and watches as it canters off through the shattered trees and collapsed walls, as it jumps the furniture and curtains and crockery that have been blown out through the streets, until it is lost from sight.

* * *

Discoloured fingers with mottled pink pigmentation rise on the gritty surface of a shattered stone wall. Behind them, a sweating, soil-covered face; high cheek bones and brown eyes. From his vantage-point, the seyis watches Ibrahim of Buda's sipahis about half a mile to his left, to the south east. Ibrahim is wheeling his horse away, galloping off with a huge body of horsemen. What is he doing? He's abandoning the field!

Behind them, the men under the Hapsburg Commander, the Duke of Lorraine, advance. Ottoman guns fall into their hands. The deli and gönüllü attack from the south.

Riderless horses mill around in the middle of the battlefield, confused, disoriented, standing in the line of fire, some suddenly thrown sideways by roundshot and musket fire. Many lie still, in a tangle of men horses, lances, swords, pennants, standards, carbines.

Peering into the lines of horse retreating with Ibrahim of Buda, the seyis searches for sight of Azarax but can identify nothing: the dust is thick, smoke blows across the field, the hollow whirr of roundshot flies through the air. It is impossible to make out which side is winning. Yet as he watches he sees that the main thrust of the fighting is concentrated toward Kara Mustafa's pavilions.

Running in a crouched position, the seyis reaches the perimeter walls of the suburbs. He finds himself curiously relaxed.

Discharges of smoke blow across the open ground between the suburbs and the tents. The decision is now: live or die! All he has to do is make a fast jinking run to the tents over there: two hundred yards. What's he waiting for?

It is a blur. The hard blue sky; the smoke; the ricocheting shot at his feet. The distant cries of men, the sound of hooves: but he does not look round.

His run is all forwards. He swerves, tumbles, takes advantage of pits, of stone walls, of shattered tree trunks. The ground whirrs under his feet: his breath, his heart, pound in his ears. The tents appear to jog up and down, looming closer as he rolls onto his side suddenly, gets up, swerves again and is in amongst the canvas. 'Mahşallah!' He keeps running until he sees the tattered remnants of the hassa lines.

It is a surreal spectacle, like a ship, becalmed in this raging sea. The sea of tents is a desert: it is as though the occupants had all been snatched up leaving their food half-eaten, their belongings scattered about. And this ship, abandoned. Any sign of the horse? None. Just his dung. The seyis squeezes his eyes shut. Now what? He falls onto his bunk bathed in sweat. His hand settles on the bow he had left there that morning and he lets out his breath.

He rolls onto his back and gazes up into the flapping, filthy, holed tent canvas: the pole and the stained canvas. It is strangely peaceful and he closes his eyes. Oh for a moment's rest. One minute, two, ten: he needs it, to slow the heartbeat. A noise comes from outside. Hooves. A horse in amongst the tents! Can't be. Suddenly he is fully awake again. Quiver over his shoulder, bow in hand and arrow fitted, he's out among the tents, moving like a hunter. The rump of a bay horse vanishes behind a tent about thirty yards away. There are others. One appears close by. A sipahi horse. Riderless: saddled, blood-spattered and riderless. Perfect! No, wait. Crouching, he runs through the tents – and there he is.

The seyis straightens up and blinks. A double-take.

Twenty yards away, standing beside a nondescript sipahi tent, picking at what remains of some sipahi horse's breakfast, is Azarax. Not possible! Is it a dream? Look again. No – he is still there. Saddle, bridle. Sweat – yes. Wounds? No! Azarax greets the seyis once again with such blistering nonchalance the seyis finds himself speechless. 'Mahşallah,' he breathes, over and over. Why did he come here and not to his tether as he always did? Or did he? I don't know what he does in the day, while I am in the mines. It is at night I find him standing at his tether. Maybe this is what he does every day? Maybe he takes some poor unsuspecting sipahi out for a mile or two, throws him and comes galloping back home to finish off every horse's breakfast each day? Is this what you do, Azarax? The sweat on him suggests he has been galloping. But what about the lad? Did you throw him, Azarax? Did you? Or was he shot? Hacked off your back? Is there any blood? No blood. You threw him, didn't you? You threw him and then came back here to finish off every horse's breakfast! I don't know what to think. I am delighted! This is brilliant but it is not anyone's idea of gallantry. But what is that to you? You are alive! Poor hassa lad: he will be safer on his feet, he should not have been on horseback anyway. Water, you need water.

The seyis searches frantically for the goatskin and a wooden bucket. He watches the horse drink, pink tongue between his teeth. Azarax looks into the distance and sighs loudly, as though all of this were a massive bore, beneath him, an absurd game which soon he must rejoin; only this time with a true horseman on his back. The battle roars. The seyis can't stop touching him. Azarax moves forward. That light flickers across his eye. Pushing his muzzle close to the seyis, he blows softly, a distinct gesture which seems to say: I'm fine. The seyis touches the soft nostrils. The big eyes swing to him: something immensely delicate passes. Azarax nuzzles the back of the seyis' hand, then raising his head, shakes vigorously. Snorts. Scratches his nose against his knee and yawns hugely. This is a horse fit for war.

The seyis nods. Mind made up? 'Evet!' he says – yes! His foot is already in the stirrup. In perfect control, at forty-five miles an hour, a streak of blood-coloured mahogany bay thunders into battle.

***

The horseman archer was the most effective attacking force that ever roared into battle. The accuracy he demonstrated with his bow, as his horse responded to his every movement, afforded him an efficiency unchallenged even by carbine-carrying cavalry. The speed at which he travelled and the manoeuvres his horse could undertake made the horseman archer an almost impossible target to hit, save for obliterating him with grapeshot, which was only effective at close range. A single, highly skilled horseman archer was the most deadly soldier of his day.

The seyis carries forty-five arrows. His hands work with his eye and he does not have to think. The hands move up with the bow, the bow length dips, the silk touches his face, his eye and the feather are joined, and the wind and the distance become a part of the subtle process calculated by hands, eye and feather. Then the bow length dips a little more, the sinews tighten and relax and he breathes out as the arrow flies and the bow takes itself up and the target is struck. The beauty is in the strike: but before the arrow has struck the bow dips again, the eye and the hand move, the silk touches the face, and eye, feather and the bow are one with the hand and his breath releases as the arrow flies and the horse flies beneath him. The movement is fluid and swift.

He does not even watch as his victims fall, arms outspread, tumbling backward, so sure is his aim. The horse jinks, and the seyis, not holding the rein, moves with him: two minds, two hearts, one will. His horse swings out to one side but keeps galloping. The pancerni attention is held on the horsemen in front: they cannot see the seyis through the dust, until it is too late.

Galloping hard he cuts out to the left of the pancerni who are now closing fast on the gönüllü. Pistol shots ring out behind. The horse cuts directly in front of the pancerni, and Azarax is suddenly riderless. Then from the gönüllü comes a cheer as they see their seyis hanging onto the side of the horse, then swinging upright and, thud! thud! thud! Three pancerni cavalrymen drop their lances, slump forward into their horse's manes and slide, falling under their horses' hooves. Azarax comes to a breathy halt, the seyis is now out of range of the pancerni and will not close with them. Pistol and musket shots continue to ring out as he rides round the mass of men and horses and continues the work of a horseman archer.

Kara Mustafa is flanked by the sipahi and silahdar, and the pancerni cannot break through. The fighting is intense. A horn sounds and in a single movement the pancerni Cossacks withdraw. Behind them artillery and infantry have advanced and rake the Turkish horsemen with musket-fire and cannon.

The seyis keeps Azarax to one side and now wallops his neck and whoops with joy. The heart of the horse and the heart of the man beat as one. Then as though gliding on air he moves toward the advancing pancerni, jinking and changing leg, and the seyis' arrows once again fly. Not one arrow is wasted. Teasing a group of pancerni Cossacks towards him, to challenge him with their lances and sabres, he draws them into the yatağan of the waiting gönüllü.

The hot-heads who take his bait do not return. The main Polish unit regroups, the cannons cease firing and in one huge push they charge again, but the sipahi and silahdar and gönüllü are stubborn. Driving them by sheer weight of numbers up against the river Wein, the pancerni position alters. The seyis sees Ozay Dursun battling three pancerni at once and spots a lancer coming straight at him. The combined velocity of the seyis' arrow and the speed of his horse flips the lancer straight over backwards and thud! thud! thud! Ozay Dursun slashes his yatağan at three men already dying.

More and more Imperial cavalry pour into the fight; the Turks are now being driven further and further back. Kara Mustafa retreats to The Holy Standard and orders that all Christian captives have their throats cut.

Selim Ghirai Khan now fighting at the last moment shouts: 'The King is amongst us!' Sobieski has appeared on his dun horse, in the midst of the bloodshed, and his appearance finally breaks the Turkish stand.

Weapons drop, men run, horses are spurred. Pursued by the Imperial cavalry, Turks are hacked to pieces as they flee. Jinking in and out of the charging pancerni horsemen the seyis looks for his comrades and once again sees Ozay Dursun outnumbered, so he responds with horn, wood, silk and goose-feather fletching. Ozay spins his horse as his opponents fall from their saddles. Even from where he sits on Azarax's back some fifty yards away, the seyis sees Ozay's nod. The recognition of true warrior to true warrior: the split-second mark of battlefield comradeship. You look after me and I shall look after you. We are brothers. We shall outlive this day, you and I.

Kara Mustafa makes one last stand as the Polish cavalry closes, before seizing the Holy Standard and his private treasure and fleeing through the rear of his own pavilion, grabbing the first horse he sees. Clutching his stolen jewels beneath an arm, he gallops away from his defeat, screaming.

- 13 -

Triumph and Disaster

12TH SEPTEMBER 1683, 7.30 in the evening

A face reflects beneath the dust as a hand sweeps across the polished surface of a harpsichord which lies marooned in a shattered room in Singerstrasse.

Through this room, bar-shot had whipped at immense velocity; its vortex had ripped curtains from rails, sent sheet music spiralling into the air, scattered feather cushions, blasted paintings from walls, shattered mirrors. An inlaid grandfather clock had somersaulted across the room. Glass and china had disintegrated, books were tossed from shelves to floor: the room destroyed in one single volley. Yet the harpsichord remained unscathed.

The hand transfers the dust to breeches, which, two months earlier, the owner had complained were too tight; that his jackets no longer fitted; that he had gout and huffed and puffed as he climbed the stairs. That the harpsichord needed replacing, that he needed another house, finer furniture, another wife.

But this means nothing now.

A low sun sinks in the western sky. The man's wife sweeps plaster shards off a ruined chair and sits. Two teenagers, a boy and a girl, stand beside her watching the man, in silence.

Gently, the man lifts the harpsichord lid and stares at the keys. His expression is blank: as though he does not comprehend what he is looking at. An uncertain smile flickers across his features. Poising his hands over the keys, he hesitates, then closing his eyes he spreads his fingers and releases that first touch, that first crotchet, that first quaver, that first minim, that first bar, pain. Pain, whose dark shape has hung over him and his family for two months; pain, that has stalked their lives through the house, in the streets of Vienna, by day and by night. Pain: fear, hunger, thirst. He has lain sweating in bed in the long hours of night, kept awake by the constant barrage of cannon and musket shot, alert to the tiniest sound, waiting to hear feet running in the street, for axes to cleaving wood, for screams, shouts, footsteps rushing up the stairwell to consume his world, his family's world, in terror, blood and fire; and now, as his fingers touch the keys in the first notes, the threat of terror lifts. As the music quickens and lengthens, the pain drains out over the cascading keys as the music ascends, majestically, exuding its power to soothe, to heal. The man's face tightens with emotions long held back.

Hand grasps hand and eye meets eye, as smiles and tears wreathe faces and the keys of the harpsichord pluck the strings and the music glides in long flowing melodies. Flexed fingers feel their fluid proficiency and are reborn with a new vigour, as neighbours and strangers stop in the darkening street outside and listen to a sound that had been silenced. They dance and laugh and sing – even though the suburbs and the land beyond the city and much of the city itself lies in ruins: they are free.

* * *

The magnificent King! Hero, colonel and commander of the most exquisite cavalry the west has ever launched: Jan Sobieski, Grand Duke of Lithuania, Russia, Prussia, Masovia, Samogitia, Livonia, Kiev, Volhynia, Podolia, Podlachia, Smolensk, Severia and Chernigov, King of Poland, rips off his cuirass, hurls it to the ground and collapses on a silk divan in the cool of Kara Mustafa's pavilions. Exhausted, soaked with sweat, he needs a moment's peace. He needs a moment alone to grasp the enormity of what has just taken place. He closes his eyes and furrows his brow and then rolls off the divan onto his knees. He nearly forgot.

On entering this pavilion earlier he had found that one of Kara Mustafa's servants had not fled, but had remained, and when the lad saw King Jan Sobieski, he had prostrated himself and called him Conqueror. Now, as Sobieski climbs back off his knees and rolls once again onto the silks he understands what the lad had meant. The word he had used was fatih. It was the term used for Mehmed II when he seized Constantinople, when he replaced the Cross with the Crescent. And now Sobieski has set in motion the same thing, only in reverse. He has replaced the Crescent with the Cross.

He has beaten the unbeatable Turk.

His pancerni have sent the Turks from the walls of the city of Vienna and put the sipahi to flight. It is impossible to grasp. Hundreds

153

of years of supremacy overturned in one day. He has led his men to glory, glory that will crown him saviour, the greatest King of all, he who fearlessly faced the Goliath, the giant, the oppressor, Babylon, Jezebel, Satan in their midst – he and his winged hussars. History will not forget this day. He closes his eyes: my God. He runs his hands down his sweating face. Blue eyes open.

There is more.

There is booty!

Gold, coin, precious jewels and – a larder. Wine, brandy, smoked meats, vegetables, fruit and oils, honey, bread, coffee.

One of his quartermasters comes panting in to the pavilion to report that they have found turpentine, sheepskins, linen, wool, ropes, tools, oil, saltpetre, pitch, nails, horse shoes, muskets, halberds, scythes, hand-grenades, fuses, mining equipment and kitchenware. Dozens of camels; and the Turks have fled abandoning their entire stock of field cannon.

Sobieski raises his eyebrows and spread his hands. What is there to be said? On his knees once more, his palms meet in prayer, emotion snatching at his throat: 'Omnipotens Deus, pro his et universis docis tuis, agimus Tibi gratias...'

Euphoria is a powerful tonic: it keeps his eyes open. What else lies about? Hands on knees, he pushes up. What's this? Water: cold water in an amphora in a gilded filigree box. Beautiful. In here? A bath. And here, look, a fountain – in a tent! And cats and rabbits, parakeets and, strangely, a decapitated ostrich.

Hands behind his back, he wanders through the many rooms of the pavilion finding each one more extraordinary than the last: decorations, tassles, silks, cushions, exotic clothes and gilded slippers, sweet white wines and scented candles – is this really the command post of a Field Marshal? Sobieski gazes around, amazed. No wonder Kara Mustafa lost. And he expected his army to live in the squalor of those stinking tents, horses at their sides, in the flies and dung, while he lived – like this!

As he picks through the boxes and lifts the lids of the Ottoman chests, and sips Kara Mustafa's excellent wine, the measure of his victory becomes clear.

The clouds part and all is revealed in gorgeous panoply, like mist lifting from a shrouded valley exposing beneath in yellow sunlight a golden stream, a brilliant rainbow, pale grass and shining green trees. And there, at the valley's head, above the waving crowds, the flags and cheers, the music, the banners and standards, is his Crown of Triumph. Victor. Conqueror. King. Tomorrow he will ride resplendent, plumed and laurel-wreathed into Vienna at the head of his magnificent cavalry and the devil with protocol: after all, when the fighting was to be done, where was Leopold I, Holy Roman Emperor?

***

Enormity of victory is balanced only by scale of defeat. What is victory? To win a battle? To chase off an enemy? To hold the high ground? To kill more? Lose less? To say that today this is ours that was theirs yesterday? To win back? Remove a threat? To restore peace? To return laughter, freedom, happiness to the oppressed?

If victory is all these things, then what is defeat? How is it to be measured? Upon whose terms? By which standard? Is a defeat the surrender of land? To give up today what you will seize again tomorrow? To retreat? Retrench? Regroup? Rearm? Or is it total loss, wholesale? Absolute? When artillery is lost, men are lost, hope is lost, souls are lost, land is lost, horses are lost, ambition snuffed out?

Absolute victory is mirrored by absolute defeat, when the victor trots one way and the vanquished gallops the other; when all the world knows that today, in this place, one army resolutely destroyed another and there now exists between them a polarity of absolute jubilation and utter despair.

On the eve of battle the night before, the Ottoman camp followers – the wrestlers, jugglers, acrobats, snake charmers, blacksmiths, leather workers and sword sharpeners – had pulled the pegs on their tents, as though some intelligence had been whispered to them that had not been whispered to the army. They had loaded their tent canvas, their carpets, rugs, boxes and what food they had left, onto heavy four-wheel carts drawn by pale hump-necked oxen. These big, stately cattle had their cloven hooves shod with half-plate shoes to the fore. Their horns were decorated with silver-tips from which hung red, blue and yellow tassles. Their pale bodies were dyed with henna, patterned with hieroglyphs and symbols peculiar to the tribes who owned and handled them. The big oxen cudded quietly, were good natured and docile and pulled their loads ponderously but without complaint. They had melted into the dusty horizon without haste, winding away quietly into the burned orange evening with the camp followers ambling along in their salvár kamises and sandals, whittling sticks or playing pipes or beating small drums, drifting away unhurriedly with the air of a people who, having found themselves at the end of a fair, knew that it was time to move on, even though their hosts had begged them to stay, if only for their company's sake. They walked away, the sun burnishing their smooth skins, the young men tall and athletic, carrying only musical instruments and long canes and the army's morale had departed with them. It had drifted off with the calm oxen and the brightly coloured camp followers across the meadows and through the ochre trees and out into the golden plain, leaving its corporeal form in the shape of tired and frightened soldiers, gazing on, distraught and in divided heart. During the night hundreds of them had thrown down their muskets and run. They had deserted their companions, their posts, their sentry duties and fled to the pale oxen and their gentle handlers. Kara Mustafa had ordered their immediate execution as he had ordered the execution of all the camp followers, yet no-one had acted upon it.

During the battle, Ibrahim of Buda had further undermined the will of those who remained to fight when he galloped away from Kara Mustafa's pavilion with 8,000 men. And when Selim Ghiray had seen Sobieski close to Kara Mustafa's centre he too had bolted with his Tartars. It had been a double betrayal, reliant upon Kara Mustafa's defeat and death.

But he had survived. Kara Mustafa did not die.

He had fought with a yatag̃an to the back of his pavilion and finding his horse already gone, dragged a toprakli officer from his and galloped off through the tents, stumbling over the guy ropes, trampling his own men, whipping them out of his way, killing whoever stood in it.

Cannonades had burst into the massed troops of man and horse, and the kapikulu sipahi had fallen by the hundred, nothing could save them. When those that survived saw that Kara Mustafa too had fled, they followed, routed, scattering their weapons behind them.

During that final battle, the seyis had felt strangely exhilarated, free and invulnerable and Azarax had responded, as though enjoying the retribution for Bora's death. When a pancerni Cossack had come close enough to seize his bridle and hack at the swordless seyis, the horse had reared and thrashed his forefeet, laid his ears back and, wild-eyed, had savagely sunk his teeth into the pancerni, crushing his shoulder, ripping him from his saddle and hurling him to the ground in one movement.

The seyis had gazed on amazed and cried out for joy, still shooting his arrows. But by now the whole Ottoman army was shifting like a shoal of fish and as one great grey body had swung to the east and was now pouring through the tents and out through the trees that lay beyond the burned-out suburbs. They had kept going without looking back, raked by musket and canister shot as they ran, shells exploding in their midst in splashes of red dust, splintering bone and shattering limbs. Then he too had galloped away, toward the Danube to avoid the musket fire and cannon before cutting right in a gap in the tents. He galloped parallel to the huge numbers of men and horses fleeing in a disorderly jumble, in a dense cloud of dust, the thunder of hooves, the shouts and screams, the jingling of bits and bridles, the clanking of arms and the crackle of muskets and the foul, ever-present stench of dysentery, sulphur and saltpetre.

The feeling of exhilaration had not left him. When another pancerni Cossack galloped at him waving a glinting curved hussaria szabla screaming a Siberian oath and mounted on a white horse with its nostrils flared, ears back, mane flying and eyes blazing, the seyis had casually aimed and placed a black and white arrow straight through the man's skull, sending him somersaulting over the back of his horse stone dead. The seyis then calmly loped away, counting the last of the arrows in his quiver, as though he had just hit a melon for target practice, and it meant nothing to him.

The pancerni and Imperial dragoons harassed the retreating Ottoman army until the sun turned the land to the colour of blood and then they stopped, wheeled their horses and returned to Vienna. The Turks had continued in headlong flight, deep into the night, silhouetted against the orange sky like an army of brown ghouls, ragged and confused, limping, defeated and dishonoured.

Regiment was no longer distinguishable from regiment, men had even run the wrong way, some had taken their chances in the Danube and leapt from high rocks and been washed away with the current.

Exhausted, they hobbled, staggered and stumbled on into the darkness. The sky before them was pitch black, yet the sky behind them was lit by new explosions: not the explosions of cannonades or of mines. They were fireworks.

Vienna was celebrating.

***

Kara Mustafa weeps out loud: huge tears roll down his face: his great sobs can be heard all across the plains as, in his great turban, flowing green silk and bloodied robes he laments and weeps. Huge sobs wring from the very depths of his soul. But the tears that drip into his beard are not tears of sorrow for his defeated army: these are not tears which beg for the forgiveness of his once-proud toprakli and kapikulu and janissaries, or of the people and homes and lives he has destroyed.

These are tears of bitterness and fury – tears of a man who played dice with the devil and lost.

These are the tears of a gambler who threw his hand again and again and, warned to stop, would not. Who sneered at the devil and shook the dice and the devil grinned and played on – but the game was already over.

Kara Mustafa weeps out loud and refuses to pay the price he is asked: for the devil has claimed his soul. He will not surrender it. The avenging angel has signed his name in his register and will deliver him to his fate: Takdirat! Evil destiny!

Stones will be their pillows, the earth their bed; their companions, scorpions and ants. And who will tend the horses? How will they tend their horses in the night? The horses will neigh and turn their necks and roll their dark eyes and then, in the darkness as men moan and weep and cry out for food and water, the horses will run back to what has been their home: they will gallop back to Vienna.

The night swallows the defeated army. For hour upon hour they stumble beneath a hard, starlit sky as Kara Mustafa screams and weeps and slashes his sword and lashes out at the men who founder in his way. Nothing now can stand between him and the bloodbath that is to follow. Every man in his way will pay with his life.

His first victim will be Ibrahim of Buda. His next, Selim Ghiray, Khan of the Tartars. He will execute every paşa close to the Sultan, their servants, slaves and what remains of their seyises.

***

When the Ottoman army is driven from the walls of Vienna on 12th September 1683, it releases a wave of destruction upon the Ottoman Empire. Mohacs will be lost, Buda will be lost, Belgrade will be lost, the Balkans will be lost, Rumelia and Morea – the Peloponnese. Ottoman forces will be driven back to the very gates of their ancient Empire. Their horses will be lost, their Karamans and Germiyans, Anatolian, Ayvacik Midillan, Canik, Çukurova, Gemlik, Kapadokya, Katamonu, Rumeli and Uzunyayla – all lost, taken and assimilated into western horse blood, bringing height and speed to the horses of their enemies, losing advantage for the people who bred them.

The last two bitter months of October and November see the final destruction of the toprakli sipahi at the battle of Parkany, after which those pitiful few that remain alive from the army of 150,000 men, disperse to winter quarters.

Unable to face his Sultan and tell him that of his original force only 10,000 remain alive, Kara Mustafa takes refuge in the fortress of Belgrade, Serbia.

It is December, 1683.

- 14 -

Peace and War

The seyis had waited on the Leitha riverbank after the rout of the Ottoman army, unaware of Kara Mustafa's order that anyone connected with the Sultan be put to the sword. Kara Mustafa could not afford to allow news of the destruction of his army to reach the Sultan's ears.

As the sun rose, the seyis had been grooming his horse with the flat of his hand, picking mud and dried blood from Azarax's coat with his finger-nails. Both the horse's and the seyis' bellies had been rumbling and though the seyis had noticed other men eating something, he had had no food himself. Azarax had been wading through the reed on the river bank, browsing for greenery, but so had every other horse and now the lot had been stripped. They'd even eaten the river weed. Hungry and with no reason to stay, the seyis saddled and mounted his horse in the dewy morning sun. Men who had fought all the previous day, who had fled the previous evening until fatigue had forced them to dismount and lie on the hard earth in the darkness, were coughing and few had slept. All were anxious to be gone for fear of a dawn attack by the Poles or Hapsburgs, which they could not possibly withstand, not without fresh reinforcements, which were unlikely to come since the fortress of Györ stood between them and the safety of Buda.

As the seyis was passing slowly along the edge of the stirring Ottoman camp, a group of his fellow horsemen had come cantering fast through the morning haze and surrounded him. They were heavily armed, big men on big horses, some badly bruised and recently wounded. None of them smiled and seemed uncertain for a fleeting moment that they had found the right man. Azarax had spun in the midst of the horsemen and the seyis had had trouble holding him, since this was a horse that liked a way out, and if he didn't see one, was apt to make one for himself. One of the men barked a question: 'You, seyis! Do you know Soliman Chia, the baş imrahor?' For a moment the seyis hesitated: what kind of a question was this? 'Well?' the man shouted as his horse stamped and tossed his head. 'Do you or don't you?' The seyis looked from face to face as Azarax pulled and threw himself about beneath him.

'Answer!'

Hesitating for a second longer, 'Yes,' the seyis suddenly confessed, wondering what he had let himself in for: 'I know the baş imrahor.' He had a bad habit of telling the truth, which had got him into trouble more often than a pack of lies.

'Come with us.'

They had formed an escort around the seyis, so he and his horse had no choice. The small squadron cantered away without another word.

Moving quickly from under the still-dark trees, their bits and harness jingling, the clanking of their swords and kalkan shields muffled in the leaves, they had left behind the massed bodies of men rousing from their uncomfortable and exhausted night. 'Deserters!' the stirring men hissed.

The riders ignored them.

Another group of men on horseback joined the silent group, two of whom cantered alongside the seyis as if to confirm his identity: 'Yes, that's him,' they said and the unit grew to twenty-seven men on horse, including the seyis.

After two miles, the company slowed to a trot, then a walk, and took a detour off the main road, through some rocks away from the river and away from the direction which the main army was bound to follow: the road to Györ and on to Buda.

They walked for a further mile then racked and once more broke into a slow canter and now they covered great distances.

Still no word had been spoken. But the seyis took some comfort from the fact that he had not been disarmed: he still carried his bow, and though not spoken to, was treated with respect, as if these men knew something about him, which he himself did not know.

He was unable to read how Azarax was reacting to this, but he had a forward-looking manner, pricked ears and an eagerness to be going wherever it was these people were leading him.

By midday they saw a twist of smoke rising in a tall plume directly ahead of them and within twenty minutes, they reached a big circle of canvas-hooded carts and heavily-laden, four-wheel wagons. Pale hump-necked oxen with their decorated horns grazed on short tethers nearby.

The group were Ottoman camp-followers who eyed the approaching force casually, lying about in shadows beneath the carts, sucking stems of grass or sitting on the laden wagons. When one of the riders dismounted and approached on foot, a smile crossed the face of a thick-set, hairy-chested man, who struggled to his feet from beside a wagon. He waved a fat hand in the air and shouted loudly: 'Hoş geldiniz, arkadaş! – Welcome, my friend.'

The unit dismounted in a body and moved into the camp's circle of wagons. Following suit the seyis landed lightly on his feet. He recognised these faces – they were familiar to many seyises back in Vienna: these people had not only entertained the troops with their music and acrobatics, their wrestling and juggling and songs and dances but had brought food for their horses, saman and barley, and they were well stocked with it now.

Their calm faces were a welcome relief after witnessing for weeks the anguish and grief that tore at the faces of soldiers and miners and seyises back in Vienna. Here were people smiling again, and approaching with armfuls of hay and sacks of barley.

They handed the men peksimet, hard tack, gave them chai and sweetmeats, sat them down as the young people held, fed and watered their horses. The horses fell on the food with blazing eyes and flat ears.

Still no-one spoke to the seyis and still he asked no questions, yet fingers pointed to him and the camp followers nodded: 'Yes, it is him,' he overheard them say: 'He is the one.'

'I recognise his horse.'

'He is a royal seyis. From the royal stables. That is one of the Sultan's horses.' 'He is the man. With the doru horse: the Karaman stallion.'

By three o'clock the unit remounted. There was no ceremony: no long goodbye, just dust, hooves, reins, hard faces and the sun descending behind them as they headed east, eating up their shadows flying out in front of them.

* * *

By nightfall the horses were walking stiff-legged, ears back and heavy footed. They had ridden past the Neusiedler See, across the riverine plain between the hills to the north and south.

Towers of smoke climbed lazily in the eastern sky: 'Two hours more,' said a man in a leopardskin.

Two hours. The seyis accepted his fate. He looked down beyond his horse's shoulder at the little black and green beetles that scurried across his path, watched the brown-headed shrikes that flew down suddenly from nowhere into the dry bushes, and popped from branch to branch, then flew off again. He felt the sudden little differences of vibration in the air;

how the horse's ears responded to them, flickering a semaphore response to their subtle influences; felt the different temperatures that weaved through the air, sometime cool, sometimes warm, here a sudden balmy waft and here a piece of dead air, lifeless and still. He leant forward on his creaking saddle on the gritty inclines, alert to the horse's muscles bunching as he trotted uphill: this horse always trotted uphill, a good athletic horse always will trot uphill but never down. He mused at how the pace of the journey was controlled by the horses, how they stopped suddenly in a group and scented and how one suddenly looked away to one side. The seyis knew that she had smelled water and that her rider, if he was good, would respond. He was good, and gave the horse her head and soon all of them were standing round a domed well, glowing in the evening sun, and the men and their horses drank while the seyis hummed the watering song by the side of his blood-red stallion, sipping up the crystal water. From above came the voices of the hooded crows, over there a fox slipped through scrub, there were animal tracks everywhere: foxes, badgers, cats and of course horses. They moved on.

The seyis watched the swing of the legs of the horse in front, watched its tendons flex, its fetlock joint ease the weight of the horse over it, watched as the horse flicked its tail at flies, noticed a tick on the horse's inside hind leg and made a mental note to singe it off later. He saw the horse look back across its flanks past its rider's legs, aware of the seyis' eyes upon him, then turned back and carried on walking into the deepening sky and the dust in front. The seyis listened to the rhythm of the horses' hooves, all synchronised one moment then broken the next. How constant the sound was, even with a big group of horses moving at the same speed: there was always a split second when their nearside fore-hooves would strike the ground at the same time and then it would be gone, but it would happen again.

The hard floor of the plain was bare: thin spikes of dried grass pushed through it, to one side lay a burned-out village, behind them Mosonmagyaróvár, with its piles of rotting heads and somewhere ahead, lay Györ.

A little over two hours, thought the seyis later as the green standards of Ibrahim of Buda hung over their heads. Ibrahim's camp was well-provisioned, the men looked well-fed, their horses were in good condition.

The unit dismounted and a lad showed the seyis to a line of stalls, like a stable, where there was a place for Azarax between a Karster and a bullock. 'Where did the Karster come from?' he asked the lad. 'On the road between Linz and Vienna,' the lad replied. 'He belongs to a Tartar now. He shot an arrow through the guardsman who was riding him, took the horse, the man's boots, his money, some gold stuff from his uniform, slit the man's throat for good measure and, well,' he says, slapping its neck, 'here's his horse.'

Once Azarax was settled, the seyis was pointed to a tent nearby, so close that his horse knew where he was, could see him. Someone has calculated this nicely, the seyis thought. There's bedding. And better still, water. The lad held a silver jug and poured cold water from its slender spout as the seyis washed, amazed, in silence. When did someone ever do this for a seyis? It was usually he who held the jug. The lad treated him with immense courtesy. In one hour, the lad said, he will call for him. Now he may rest.

What was the meaning of rest to this seyis? Rest to this seyis was to be with his horse, so to his horse he returned: to stand beside him as he ate, watch over him as he drank, watch as he held the sweet water in his mouth and watch how his ears twitched when he swallowed. Rest to this seyis was to wipe the sweat off Axarax, to smooth his coat, check his legs, look at his feet, check if the shoes were tight, search for cuts and bruises; find the horse with the tick and singe it off with a burning ember, return to his own horse – and try to grasp what had just taken place. A lifetime seemed to have gone hurtling by in these last two days: or was it all one long day? He couldn't remember. Change had always come like a storm into his life. Since he had known this horse, his life had been flipped on its head and each time destiny had pointed in a new direction, they had cantered towards it, galloped, slithered and this time fought.

He ran his mottled fingers through the horse's mane. You are my brother. Your will is my will. Where you go, I go. What befalls you, befalls me. If there is honour, it is yours. Why was I fortunate enough to be chosen to be your seyis? Why?

The lad returned. The hour has passed in a moment.

'Follow me.'

✻✻✻

The fire reflects in the twin images of their shining eyes, already lit with an inner, burning zeal. Their teeth flash splendid and white in the darkness, the mens' skin is ochre, tautened by hours passed in their saddles as they glided across the sunlit plains beneath a white hot sky. Sparks fly from the fire into the darkness where they hang and glow in the scrub, red as pi-dogs' eyes. Above hovers a yellow moon.

– Men without horses are nothing.

A stick is thrust into the flames and the fire brightens to reveal the circle of faces, the mops of black hair, the lamella armour, coarse silk chemises, the spluttering sheep carcase spread-eagled on a web of sticks dripping fat onto the flames.

A goatskin is fisted round the circle: lips smack against its brown leathery, sticky top as the men gulp the koumiss, the fermented milk of the mare. Beyond the fire, in the darkness, the horses move, dust swirls and a horse whinnies – a lost call, a wail.

– They huddle in squalor in their reeking towns and fear for their miserable lives. They hoard their precious belongings. They clutch their ill gotten coins in their pale, soft hands. The carry their papers from here to here. They hide their faces from the sun and the wind and they stare into the pavements. They stink of the streets and of the filth of each other. They crawl into their linen sheets beneath their roofs and do not know the glory of the night.

A hand arcs in the flickering flames, expanding words in dramatic gesture. Above, the stars shine with exquisite clarity, a spray of diamonds on black velvet.

– They know nothing of the purity of the hoof and the breath of our sacred horses.

A dark finger points to the hooves out beyond the glow of the fire, and returns to the scalpel edge of a bone-handled yatağan. Hands remained glued to swords, their dark eyes flickering in the firelight, mesmerised by the fine hard face and gravelly voice of Ozay Dursun in their midst, their leader.

He looks up.

The seyis stands on the edge of the firelit circle and Ozay Dursun bids him enter. Those seated make space.

'This is the man,' Ozay Dursun says. 'Come, sit by me.'

* * *

The warmth of the fire, the koumiss, the food, the journey, the battle, the mines and the nightmares conspire to hang heavily on the seyis' eyelids. His head topples to one side, his mouth opens and he slumps to his left. Ozay Dursun pulls him upright, hands him more koumiss and urges him to eat more although his belly is already packed with food.

The night deepens. Men tell stories, their faces alive in the firelight, bright-eyed and filled with excitement. The seyis sleeps, leaning against Ozay Dursun.

Sometime in the course of that night he is pulled to his feet. His worn cotton chemise is stripped off his back and the seyis wakes from his stupor terrified he is about to be flogged and struggles to break free. Strong arms hold him and although he shouts, a chemise of dark blue silk is pulled over his head. His filthy turban is tossed onto the fire and a new, deep maroon turban replaces it. His rag-like salvár joins his turban in the flames and he is pushed into a new salvár of coarse cotton and raw silk, tightened to the calf and padded to the seat. He is given silk socks and soft leather boots. Around his neck Ozay Dursun hangs a gold chain with a Qur'anic inscription which Ozay kisses. The chapan slipped over the seyis' small frame is red with black stripes, made of heavy silk, split up the back, with loose shoulders and pinched at the waist: an archer's coat.

'You swear upon this Holy Qur'an and this flask of salt, by your bow and quiver, that you will honour this code: to stay the lives of the innocent and to fight those who oppose truth and right.'

'I swear.'

'That you will abjure evil in all its manifestations and make war upon those who wrongly profess the knowledge of Allah.'

'I swear.'

'That you will cause no harm to unarmed men or women or children.'

'I swear.'

'That you will ride with the gönüllü as their archer in battle and in times of peace live in peace and breathe not a word of your oath.'

'I swear.'

'That you will refrain from theft and from fraud or untruth or from an intemperate life.'

'I swear.'

'That you will follow the teachings of our dervish Gül Baba and defend his Holy tomb in our holy city of Buda against the infidel.'

'I swear.'

'That you will uphold our traditions and live by our chivalric code.'

'I swear.'

'Welcome to the brotherhood of the Ghazi.'

Ozay Dursun pats the seyis' shoulder. 'You already have a Ghazi horse.' The men laugh richly, deeply. They had been in that battle: they had seen those arrows fly. Their lives had been spared because of this small seyis and his Ghazi horse. Oh they knew, they knew all about him, even those who had not met him: they had heard. The head of their order in Istanbul had told them that among the seyises of the Sultan was a Ghazi horseman archer.

'Who is the head of your order in Istanbul?' asks the seyis.
'Our order. You know him.'
'I know him?'
'Of course you know him.'
The seyis searches Ozay Dursun's eyes. 'Do I?'
'The baş imrahor. Soliman Chia.'
The seyis' eyes widen.
'That you know the baş imrahor and that he knows you, makes you a target,' Ozay Dursun smiles. 'If you had remained with the army, you would be dead by now – on the orders of Kara Mustafa. Anyone with connections to the Sultan, who could carry news of this defeat back to the Sultan, is already a dead man.'

* * *

Ibrahim of Buda was executed by Kara Mustafa in the days that followed, as were all Paşas with blood-ties or with courtly associations. Murdered alongside them were their servants, their seyises and anyone else with the slightest knowledge of the workings of the Ottoman Court. Selim Ghiray, Khan of the Tartars was hunted down, and any Tartar believed to have known him personally was killed also.

In Istanbul, the baş imrahor awaited news of the great campaign of 1683 which he was certain would have failed, since he and only he had been aware all along of Kara Mustafa's incompetence. At last news of his defeat arrived, though not until late that November and it came from a surprising source. It came from a woman, the Sultan's daughter, whose land in Serbia adjoined the timar of Ali-aga Izobegović. She had been Ibrahim of Buda's wife and had been helped to escape Kara Mustafa's night of the long knives by a group of Ghazi horsemen who said they had been protected in the sword fight that followed by a deadly archer mounted on a fast doru horse.

As the baş imrahor held the rapidly-scrawled parchment in his hand, his chin fell against his chest. Allah kerim! Kara Mustafa's demise is sealed. This appalling man, this wrecker of civilization, this bloated destroyer, is to meet his rightful fate. Praise be to Allah that the Ghazis remain! He sighed deeply, pinched the bridge of his nose between thumb and forefinger, and sighed again. He gazed out of his window overlooking the Marmara Sea. 'There is only one man on a horse of that colour who could have acted like that. I sensed it in that seyis when first I saw him. One day he will take my place. After all, only a Ghazi can ever be baş imrahor. And since that man is also the finest horseman ever to set foot outside the Balkans, then it follows he must take my place. But not yet; he has more to learn. More battles to fight. And then his destiny is to be baş imrahor, though I am the only one who knows it.'

He sweeps up the letter and walks swiftly through the corridors to the Sultan.

The same day the High Chamberlain sets off for Belgrade on horseback accompanied by a small retinue of horseman and the state executioner, a deaf mute with a silk bow string.

On the orders of the Sultan, Kara Mustafa is strangled. He lifts his own beard and fits the bowstring to his own neck. He dies where he falls. It is Christmas Day 1683.

6TH JANUARY 1684

Two horsemen plunge hock-high through powdery snow. The sky is hard blue, the birches are leafless. The streams run beneath frozen mantles. The breath of the horses billows in the air around them. Plumes of steam issue from the nostrils of the horses whose coats have thickened and lengthened as the winter has deepened. 'Your doru horse is changing colour,' Ozay Dursun had remarked. 'He is darker.'

As Azarax has matured, his conformation has changed; he has become less angular, more rounded; is bigger, taller, thicker set. His character too has become more defined, more contained. His movements now are less those of a young horse, less sharp; they are more considered, more graceful. He swings his head and neck like a great swan, bent at the poll, looking forward with great dark eyes. And his eyes now assume a penetrative quality when he looks at a man, as though he sees through him, as though he can read what is written inside. It makes those who notice frown and look away, as if accused of some crime. Azarax's eyes hold a disturbing power.

And as his body grows, so his mind distils, and he becomes a calmer, quieter companion. Yet those who mistake this apparent docility for meekness rapidly learn otherwise. This horse is a stallion: he might seem placid, but one wrong move and back go the ears, the teeth flash and there in front of them stands a big, uncompromising beast who would strike out and maim – and then sigh and resume his breakfast as though nothing had happened. No: he has quiet dignity, but this horse is his mother's child, he is his father Ateş' offspring: he is Azarax, Son of Fire.

The two horses plunge through the snow side by side, Ozay

Dursun's horse Malik is deeper through the chest, heavier in the quarter, a Ghazi breed of old, a Germiyan, black-legged and big-hoofed, independent animal. He reflects the character of his rider: self-sufficient, strong, level-headed. He is also a stallion – a difficult combination – two powerful, lascivious stallions, who would have killed each other had it not been for the comradeship of their riders. A friendship forged in battle: my life belongs to you.

They head south. In front of them, news of the Ottoman defeat at Vienna has run like a hare.

A defeat is a defeat. Who wishes to have defeated soldiers loitering in their houses? Do they not bring bad luck? Are they not part of this disgraced army? Are they deserters? Are they cowards? Are they the ones who ran?

Last night the seyis and Ozay Dursun found themselves shivering in a dilapidated building feeding their horses scraps of mouldy fodder while they went hungry themselves and the wood they struggled to light refused to burn.

Tonight it is another village: men arriving on horseback in a village as night falls require two things: a bellyful and bed – for horse and man. Such nights, when these requirements are met, are a treasure. A fire in the face of the frost, fed horses, stabled horses, warm fingers, warm feet, food. A bed, dry clothes.

It is the villagers who decide: what manner of men are these that approach? What is their essence? Before they can even see their faces, this intelligence is already known: it is perceived from afar, from the way they ride, from they way they approach, the way they hold their reins. It comes from the horses: do they toss their heads? Are their tongues bleeding? Are they sweating?

The two stallions stamp into the village as though they own the place. This is correct. The horses call out. This is also correct. Their head carriage is haughty, their ears are pricked. This too is correct. The men's faces are smooth; something lingers in their eyes. It is clear from the way they hold themselves; they have pride, these men.

'You may stay with me: I have two places in my stable. I am a poor man but I have a fire and food. Your horses will not go hungry. Come, enter.'

Inside there is a stench of sweat, of the human body. Winter dirt, woodsmoke, filth. A fire with a kazan on it. Home. One room. The horses just fit in the stables: move the cows, the sheep, the donkey, the chickens.

'There is saman, barley. Do they wish hot barley?'

'Mahşallah! Of course they wish hot barley.'

'With eggs?'

'You are a hadji.'

'Welcome, my home is small: you bring it everlasting light. Sit, eat. I too have been in the snow.'

They blow the steam off the apple chai and sit in silence. Watching eyes piece together the story: two yatağan, two şinşir sabres, a kalkan shield, vambraces and lamellar armour, a bronze conical helmet and heavy silk clothes. And the smaller one: he carries a bow of great beauty and a quiver of arrows. They possess between them a spirit of calm, like austere dervishes: dervishes, not bandits.

Children stare at their burnished faces in the firelight, young men ask questions but the guests sit, hands now cupped round the hot çiorba, revealing nothing. They speak instead of the width of the plains, of the white-topped mountains, they speak of the rivers full of fish and their sacred horses. They tell them of the glory of the night, the beauty of the stars, and the wide, wild world they inhabit.

They tell the children stories of heroic horses.

In the morning the two horsemen mount and give their thanks. They offer money but it is pushed back into their hands. You are the travellers: my home is your home. Little children reach out to touch their horses, the riders bend down and touch their little heads: 'Allah boğişlasin,' they say, 'God bless you,' and lope away down the-never-to-return road.

Who were those men? What were they?

It is only several days after they have left that the poor man finds a piece of gold in his sack of barley.

What is given is returned: this is Islam.

They were Ghazi.

***

Across the white plains, past frozen wells, and on through the wide empty world, the two horsemen ride their horses, day after day, until the blue light of evening strikes the eastern sky and Azarax stops dead in his tracks.

Up goes his head and he calls.

They stand upon a high bluff. Sitting back in his saddle, the seyis points. Azarax calls: again and again. His great body shakes as he cries out, his high pitched squeal answered only by the moaning wind and the crashing waters of the Porecka river.

Down the hill the horsemen slither and they canter up a long white track until pine and judas trees break into view, rimed in snow, while beyond lies a line of low white buildings. A light flickers in the darkness.

A voice calls out.

A hand reaches up, the light shining in its owner's eyes. He is aged, but he is the same: the same fit old frame, the same goatskin-battered face, the same wave-bladed dagger, the same cross-me-and-I'll-kill-you eyes. The seyis bursts out laughing.

Never before had it happened. No-one before or after saw what the seyis and Ozay Dursun saw that night.

They saw Ali-aga Izobegović smile.

* * *

Passing straight through the stable door, as if he had emerged from it not an hour before, Azarax turns right and lets out an indignant squeal and lays his ears flat on seeing that his stall is now occupied by a cudding water-buffalo, to whom he takes immediate and violent exception, thrashing out with a forelimb and threatening with his teeth. A potential full-blooded stallion-attack is hurriedly averted by one of Ali-aga Izobegović's slaves, who chivvies the terrorised water-buffalo by lamplight to the far end of the stable where it turns, gulping, gazing back through the half-light at the mad thing that has just entered. And while another slave cleans up the mess it had been contentedly and sleepily living in all this time, Azarax weaves about on his rein, squealing and snorting and disturbing all the other animals in the building and in the others beyond. It is only after a good hour's hard industry by the slaves that he accepts his former stall and high steps into it, haughtily, sniffing, lashing his tail and whickering angrily. As if to say this ill-mannered squatter, this filthy old water-buffalo has caused such appalling insult; and he throws her threatening glances with his great, flashing black eyes.

Ozay's horse, Malik, is found a place under less arduous terms beneath the same roof and then all are speedily bedded, fed, watered and curried to a high standard before their handlers might reasonably expect to leave, feed, water and bed themselves.

'And what of the yağiz horse, the beautiful one? The mischievous one you named Bora?'

The seyis shakes his head.

No more questions. Ali-aga Izobegović too has fought in battle.

It is a time for rest: for quiet, for calm. To grow tomatoes and courgettes, to grow onions and feel the earth run between the fingers. To go to the little village and even, perhaps, to search for a wife.

Winter passes.

Sitting beneath the locust trees, the seyis turns a short, straight stick in his hand. Holding it up to his right eye, he squeezes shut his left eye and squints along its length. Pinning it between his index fingers he studies it, revolving it, checking it for straightness. Balancing it on one finger, he tests its weight, then flexes it, minutely. Bending to pick up a handful of sand, he slides the stick back and forth through it, polishing its white, drying surface. There is a light, hot breeze. It blows into his sheer, pale silk chemise and flutters his raw silk salvár. It curls around his thin neck, at the base of his fine maroon turban. It shimmers through the leaves of the great tree and they move, rhythmically, above his head, cooling the ground beneath, where he sits. The place smells of horse: of leaves and dust and of horse.

The mares' coats shine in the sun. Their tails flick ceaselessly, they shake their heads and semaphore their ears: they scratch their knees with their muzzles, and kick at the big, iridescent-blue horseflies that pester them relentlessly. The seyis walks under the trees, wanders through the moody mares, running his hands through their glossy manes and through their fine tails, skipping past their threatening hindquarters and checks the horizon, gazing deeply into it, to the east, to the mountains beyond.

All day long the cicadas ring, the shadows of vultures and of eagles slip across the hot ground, bustards strut through the grasses striking at the big blue horseflies and the lizards disturbed by the mares.

The afternoon flattens into a dead level heat: the hours stop. No animals stand out in the scorching sun. Even the bustards have gone. Only the vultures and eagles remain, wheeling in the shimmering hyaline sky. The cicadas sing on even louder, their ringing now parched and sharp, giving the air a sense of acute aridity.

The mares drink at the sweep well. The seyis sings the watering song, watches them steep their faces into the water and hold their pink tongues in their teeth as the clear water drips from their chins. Allahu akbar! They are beautiful mares.

The seyis rides his fine stallion up into the plain and down to the river and leaves the route to the horse who knows every step. The horse stops on the bluff and looks out and calls. He stops by the rocks and cries out a name that only his seyis knows, since the name he calls is written on the seyis' heart as it is written upon the heart of the horse. Azarax does not stop calling. Each day he cries out and waits for the voice to return. He takes his seyis to the high bluff and looks over the plain, over the pebbled Porecka river into the distance. Out there, somewhere, he can see something. And though the seyis follows the direction of his horse's gaze, as he had looked a thousand times, he cannot see what it is his horse sees.

The two Ghazi horsemen bask under a Balkan sun. Ozay now has a wife. The days of summer are long and sleepy. And then, in the quartering of the moon, in the dipping of the sun and the fall of autumn leaves, another winter arrives. Followed by another summer, and another winter and then, a spirit moves.

***

There lives in the soul of a fighting man a glowing ember that will not die. A glowing ember that recalls how it felt to walk away from the battle, alive. To march away, singing and victorious. A glowing ember that, each time someone speaks of war, glows more brightly; and when men swap stories of battle, it burns ever more brilliantly. So that when news of another war reaches the seyis' ears, the ember bursts into flame and he feels again the urge that courses through his body and races to his head. It fills him with blind courage.

It whispers in his ear as he hoes his garden: One more time: just one more time.

He hears it as he runs his hand through his stallion's mane and sends a curry comb across his flanks: Once more; just once more.

It comes to him as he sits in the cool of his house and breaks the pida, the flatbread, bites into a tomato that bursts all over his chin and sees, out in the glaring sun, another warrior, beckoning: Come: feel it again, just one more time. 'Then,' it whispers, 'you can hang up the sword; put away the bow, live in peace on your timariot. Grow old; tell tales. In the certain knowledge of having lived out your destiny; in the certain knowledge of having done your duty to your Sultan, your land, your God, your horse. Upon your Ghazi oath.

Just one more time.

Then he will know for sure on that last day, that it is all over; then he can look into the eyes of his proud blood-stained stallion, run his hand down his sweat-soaked neck, see the veins pulse beneath the skin on his face, hear the horse's breath short and sharp in his throat, see the tenseness in his ears and the red in his eyes; and know that it is over, really over this time. And on that last day he can turn away, pick a path across the discarded muskets and overturned cannons, through the shattered wagons, over the still bodies and listen to that eerie silence that follows great violence; look through the forest of broken swords and arrows and twisted muskets; and leave.

Then he can wade into the streams, wash his face in their cool, living water beneath the shadow of willows, wait for his horse to drink, watch him paw the shivering mica in the stream's bed, release him from his saddle, let him roll in the current, leave him be, allow him to be a horse, wait for him, throw water over his great frame, enjoy him as he grazes the fragmites reed, let him shout at the air and snort and huff and whicker across the woods to a mare out of sight, watch him shake off the water in a momentary, brilliant rainbow. When he is done, he can tack up and move on. Go home.

* * *

Azarax is now eight years old. He is in his prime. He has had two and a half years in the Balkans; two and a half years divided between Ali-aga Izobegović's timar near Bor and military duties. A year of reporting to Belgrade Fortress, a year of standing guard: of pacing the perimeter, walking along the low banks of the Danube beneath the Fortress, looking up into its height, listening to the starlings mobbing in the aspens, watching the swallows flying under the battlements then sweeping up under the eaves of the red tile roofs, watching ducks glide down and land in long vees on the River Sava as the sturgeon splash in the water beside them.

The seyis trots down the long high road of Belgrade that runs into its Fortress.

Fingers point: you see this man? Once he was just a seyis. Now he is a gönüllü. He is a warrior. Still they call him 'the seyis'. Watch him. Learn. They say he is a dervish. No one can ride his horse, except this man. If another man tries to ride this horse, he will be killed. This horse cannot be injured. He cannot be harmed. They say he sacred: he has doru on one side and demirkir on the other; he must be sacred.

Show us! they cry. Show us how to shoot a gourd hanging from a rope strung between two long poles fifty feet off the ground.

The seyis canters smoothly to the top end of the Belgrade Fortress and wheels the horse to face the run beneath the gourd. He does not inter-fere with his horse, nor spur him – he had no spurs anyway – nor does he kick nor urge him forward. The horse moves of his own volition and the seyis lets him flow. As the horse rises, his first strides are short, then his pace lengthens, hooves biting hard into the ground. The seyis rides fluidly in his cantleless saddle and as they approach the high rope from which the gourd is suspended, the horse releases himself into his floating stride and the seyis' head empties. He becomes part of the flow of his horse, the rhythm of his stride, he feels the wind and the beat of his hooves on the hard ground. He even closes his eyes, the better to feel the power of the horse and the way in which his own body responds, moving with him, in tune. Then, as though triggered by some power outside his body, his hands raise the bow and he feels the feather on his cheek and the horse's quarters rising up and down like the sea. The seyis' aim is not disturbed, as though the horse knows that the rhythm he is creating is part of the man and his actions. The seyis lies back and relaxes onto Azarax's quarters and feels his shoulders lying across their moving width. Then the wind and the sound of hooves, the brilliance of the sky and the sharp breaths of the horse cause his thumb to squeeze on the arrow as into his vision flashes the dark silhouette of the gourd, for a spilt second, and in that flash the arrow is released with his breath. The arrow's flight takes it on a curve that bends away from the horse and by the time the seyis is upright in the saddle, the gourd is lying shattered on the ground behind him.

The seyis trots his horse along the high centre road through Belgrade Fortress, as the roars of the crowd die down behind him, and he cuts right down to the River Sava. As he rides, the people murmur: there is not a gönüllü, nor janissary, nor azap, nor sipahi who does not respect this man. He is a Ghazi, a Turk of old, living amongst us. His horse has the best stable in Belgrade Fortress and his rider lives beside him, as if they are one being, this man and this horse. That is how it should be. Men and horses are one. Men without horses are nothing.

Two days later, the seyis is sitting with Ozay Dursun. And Ozay Dursun has become larger. His face has thickened, his eyes twinkle, his smile is wide. He looks even stronger than he did before. His pretty wife sits beside him, shelling peas.

Silence falls between the men. The seyis doodles an abstract pattern in the dust with an arrow: his mottled pink fingers appear vivid in the cool shade of the locust trees under which they sit. A buttery breeze blows the sleeves of his blue silk chemise.

'The Christian forces have left for Buda,' the seyis says quietly.

Ozay's face straightens. Buda is a Holy Ottoman city. It is where Gül Baba is buried.

'Three weeks and they will be at its gates.'

Ozay's nod is almost imperceptible.

'The Duke of Lorraine: but no Poles. There are Germans, French, Spaniards. Volunteers.'

Ozay looks at him steadily: 'And our forces?'

'Istanbul janissaries; Rumelians, a contingent from Aleppo and Damascus, Quoerifat Volunteers; sipahis from Bosffia, Syria and Silistra – and our people, coming under the new Vizier.'

'How many do they have?'

'A hundred thousand.'

'And we?'

'Half that number.'

Ozay looks at him coolly.

'We'll let them besiege us for a month or so, wear them down. Buda is well provisioned.'

'So we'll be even.'

'Then in July, we move in. Counter-attack the beseiging Christians in August. They'll be worn out.'

Ozay nods, and follows the seyis' stare out into the sun: 'One more time then,' he says quietly.

'And my Ghazi oath to honour. One more time.'

It is 14th May 1686.

- 15 -

The Fall of Buda

A streak of grey horse with a man standing upright in his stirrups, chapan-tails flying behind him and frantically waving an arm, comes galloping down the long dusty track to Ali-aga Izobegović's timar.

Ali-aga Izobegović, Ozay Dursun and the seyis are standing quietly beside the medrese at the time, by the fountain, near the judas trees. The stallions Azarax and Malik are the subjects of their discussion.

'It is the Armenian in him,' Ali-aga had been saying, pointing to Malik, Ozay Dursun's Germiyan, before anyone had noticed the man flapping his arms about on the grey horse: 'The mountains have excellent pasture and rich grasses. They bred these horses big to the bone and sent them down the ages to us in this way. Whereas the Karaman horse, Azarax, is lighter of bone. But like the Germiyan, he came from the Steppe many centuries ago, with men like this seyis, the horseman archers. They came from the Kipchak north to the Oghuz east, they mixed with the horses of the Petchenegs and the Chagatai and came thundering across the Kavir desert, to the high yayla. They had been west before of course, many centuries earlier. They took Rome from the Romans under Atilla and even then they brought their thoroughbreds, though men forget. They are our ancestors; we originate in the east. Men speak our language from here to the gates of the Tien Shan in China. And our horses? They came with our ancestors and from nowhere else. They were our horses: and we bred them big and fast. Turks. Pure Turks. When they came here they inter-bred the old Germiyan and Turkomen, the Ferghana, Nogai and Oghuz with the Kapadocians, Armenians, Kurds and Anatolians and gave us the Karaman, like this one,' Ali-aga says, slapping the horse's thick neck. 'Tall, fast horses, with bone and wither, flat knees and wide forehead, a brilliant eye, broad back and high intelligence. Horses of spirit and fire, of ego and pride, with hard blue feet and flashing teeth who are afraid of nothing, are their own masters and respect only those who respect them. Yes, this horse is a Turk! Cross him and he will kill you!'

The stallions both see the approaching man on the grey horse first. Up flash their heads. Azarax takes a step forward, and deep from each chest comes the rumble of enquiry, a deep whicker. Who is this?

The approaching horseman reins his sweating grey in a flurry of dust. He slides off in one easy movement, bows deeply, asks politely for Ali-aga Izobegović and offers at arm's length, a scroll.

Ali-aga Izobegović calls out for slaves to tend the man's horse, unsaddle it, take it to the shade, rest it, then give it water and feed and see that the courier is given refreshments immediately.

The seyis, Ozay Dursun, Azarax and Malik watch Ali-aga as he carefully unravels the blue silk cord that binds the scroll. He asks the courier from whence he has come.

'From Istanbul, Ağa,' he responds reverently (this man is a freed slave, Ali-aga perceives, judging from the manner of his residual obeisance) 'From the Privy Stables.'

'It has taken you many days?'

'It has taken me eight days, Ağa.'

'Eight days? That is quick! On this horse?'

'No, Ağa. I used the Sultan's post horses, changing every twenty five miles, covering about seventy five miles a day.'

Ali-aga Izobegović nods: 'It is an excellent system, brought to us by Genghis Khan. Well done. What is your name, my friend?'

'Genghis Çarlağan, Ağa.'

Ali-aga looks at him with his bead-brown eyes, then returns his attention to the scroll. Strange how sometimes a name is plucked out of the air and there, standing before you, is its bearer. Ozay Dursun puts a fist to his mouth and clears his throat. He catches the seyis' eye.

A co-incidence is an omen.

Ali-aga Izobegović reads the scroll with pursed lips. Neither his eyes nor his face reveal a flicker of what this letter contains. Having read it once, he turns away to the medrese, reads it again then rolls it carefully in his brown liver-spotted hands and says to the seyis: 'Come with me.'

What is destiny when it speaks with two voices? Which is the Greater Will? How can a man know? There must surely be only one correct way? The seyis had felt a wave of anguish rise in his chest even in this calm house when Ali-aga told him what the letter contained. It was not an order, he said. It was a request. But what a request! Never had he heard such a thing. He called Ozay Dursun in and repeated what the letter had said.

It had come from the baş imrahor himself. He had asked Ali-aga Izobegović to release his seyis to go to Istanbul to work as his right-hand man. That is to say, not as a seyis, but as a man with status. The letter had stipulated that there was no urgency.

Such a request was not to be ignored. It was a position of absolute honour.

The seyis stared at his feet. His face had whitened. His hands shook and he felt sick. He didn't know how to react. The faces of these two men radiated with delight but delight was not what the seyis felt inside. He did not wish to return to Istanbul. He did not like towns or cities. He was afraid of the baş imrahor. But now he was no longer just a seyis, he was a gönüllü and a Ghazi to boot. He had sworn a vow to uphold the Ghazi tradition and part of that vow was to protect the holy city of Buda and the tomb of Gül Baba. He would not feel right in his heart if he abandoned his oath in pursuit of personal benefit, if he abandoned his duty in the face of the Hapsburg Army which was this moment marching on Buda.

He said nothing. He looked out of the window.

Ali-aga Izobegović had swung his beads. 'Your destiny has been laid out before you,' he said softly. 'You must go.'

'What an honour!' Ozay said with instant sincerity, held out his hand, and the seyis had taken it, as Ozay congratulated him over and over again, and his eyes and his voice were level, without jealousy. He was delighted.

***

Sitting on his horse in the scorching sun of the plains of Buda, smelling the sulphur and the saltpetre stench of the guns, listening to the roar of cannon, hearing men shouting, breathing once again the sticky-sweet, retching scent of decomposing bodies, the decision made by the seyis had come to haunt him. From the day he had received the call to Istanbul to this, he had felt ill.

Firstly, there was the horse. Was he not given charge of this horse that he might bring him to his destiny? Did he not swear that he would do exactly that? It seems his destiny had been to return the horse to Istanbul where he would be the Sultan's mount. What could be finer than that? What higher honour was there? Why would anyone not want their horse to be the Sultan's horse? The seyis looks down. Why? I'll tell you why. Because the Sultan gets through a horse a month hunting, that's why. He rides horses until they are finished, utterly spent, with blood running from their nostrils and lungs ruptured, leaves them staggering to the ground, unable to get up. The brute just kicks them, gets another and does precisely the same again. Azarax's destiny was not to wind up like that: no. Not for any Sultan. And there was another reason. The seyis did not believe that the horse's destiny lay in Istanbul. It was as if some invisible leash were pulling him away from Istanbul, away from all that he had known. Yet, was it possible that he was deceiving himself? Was he tricking his own soul?

Buda is grey. The green flags and the Crescent Moon move sluggishly above it. The tables have turned since Vienna. Now it is the Turks who are within the walls, the Christians who are the besiegers. Great sections of wall have collapsed. Ragged Imperial standards have been pitched in piles of rubble, claiming yards of advance, at the cost of hundreds of lives.

The Imperial trenches run from one corner of Buda castle walls away to lines of palisading, yard upon yard of fences stakes, where the artillery lines are drawn up. It is not possible to see their number.

The Christian lines have that same, grey-brown appearance as the Turkish trenches in Vienna. Beyond the guns are the horses.

Behind the palisading, where the main body of the force is drawn up, helmets glisten, breastplates sparkle. The hot August sunlight makes this army twinkle against the dull earth. Horses canter across well-trodden spaces between row upon row of tents, creamy white against the taupe background.

The toprakli have drawn up at a distance of half a mile from the Hapsburg Imperial camp, on a shallow incline.

The seyis shifts in his saddle and watches lines of Imperial infantrymen march in columns to the trenches: others spill out from the trenches, and drink from water barrels placed nearby. There is an unreal quality to the scene below: a strange lull in the action. Nothing seems to be happening. From time to time, puffs of smoke emit from muskets, ripples of gunfire from the walls.

A cheer breaks out from the town itself – from Buda – and Ottoman flags wave from the city walls as the besieged Turks see their relief force in all its glittering glory, standing, impassive, impressive, with its many thousands of different standards held high, cool and detached from the miniature scene at its feet.

179

The journey had been hell. The new Grand Vizier was not a man of swift decisions. He advanced slowly, as though trying to drag out this campaign to relieve Buda. The new regiments he brought with him were from Syria, Quoerifat and Damascus. They were Anatolian sipahi, not used to Rumelian conditions. They were disorderly, their horses small. They were not well disciplined. Sections of horse had bolted again and again and had to be brought back by veteran Turks on Turk horses. None of the Syrian horses were schooled to the cannon.

And Ozay Dursun had changed. He had been uncommunicative: distant. The ride north from the timar which was home to him and the seyis had been conducted in silence, as though he had decided to cut his old companions from his presence entirely. He could not believe that the seyis had turned down the opportunity of going to Istanbul. It was an insult: it was stupid. 'Why? Just tell me why?' he had asked. He believed the seyis had denied his destiny and would now pay for it. And so would all who fought with him. He had ignored the signals and a man ignores the signals at his peril. The signals are clear and are sent to mark your way. The coincidence of the name Genghis was the first sign. Immediately it had happened. Immediately. He had been shown what to do and he had not done it. They had argued. Ghazi oath or no, he was flying in the face of the baş imrahor who was head of the order. The baş imrahor would not have asked if he thought it was wrong.

The seyis had banged his fist on a table. It was to do with Azarax! Something about Buda. He did not know what it was, or why it was, but the seyis was sure he had to go to Buda. He had once made a promise to this horse and he was not going back on it. He was certain in his heart that the horse's destiny was not connected with Istanbul. 'And wherever the horse goes, I go. What befalls him, befalls me,' said the seyis. 'He is my brother.'

'Ho! And what am I?' Ozay had snarled. 'And what if,' he had growled between his teeth, 'your destiny and your horse's are no longer linked? Perhaps you have already done what you needed to do. Perhaps someone else can take the horse to Buda! Even I could. And you go to your destiny, which is in Istanbul. For certain.'

The seyis had refused to listen.

***

Sweat breaks out on his forehead. He looks along the lines. Ironic, he thinks, that he is in exactly the reverse position from three years earlier. Then they were the besiegers, the Hapsburgs the besieged.

Imperial standards hanging loose in the dead flat heat of the day are a grim shadow in his memory. The white cross on a black background: the white cross on a blue background: the double-headed eagle against the pale blue: the Brandenburg black and white stripes: the red eagle against the blue and white stripes: the black double-headed eagle against yellow, bordered with gold and black: the white cross with the red fork streamers. He sees Ozay running his eyes across them. Ozay does not speak. The horses gaze down and across into the Christian camp, motionless, their ears pricked.

The seyis leans forward and ruffles Azarax's forelock between his ears. It's a good omen that the horses are standing so still. He looks at Ozay.

'It will be alright,' the seyis says, affecting unconcern, 'the horses are still.'

Ozay ignores him.

'We are blessed,' the seyis says, gazing out over the Bavarians in the foreground and the rest of the Christian forces scattered to their left and to the banks of the Danube beyond: 'We shall relieve Buda. Or we shall be in Paradise.' And he pats his horse's neck, as though it meant nothing.

The horses stir beneath them. Puffs of smoke from muskets in the Imperial camp sputter as infantrymen take hopelessly out-of-range pot-shots at the Ottoman force. The toprakli respond with belly laughs. Three janissaries step forward with long range muskets. A moment passes as they prime and load their big powerful weapons. Their faces are bright, they are marksmen with a skill. These men are not going to miss. With barrels resting on the shoulders of comrades, they aim. The long-barrelled muskets crackle sharply one after the other in the still, hot air. Crack! Crack! Crack! Two Imperial infantry men fall in the Christian camp at a range of four hundred yards. The Turks cheer wildly. A small point, but what a point! The toprakli howl with delight, break off and canter away from the brow of the hill. Spirits are roused as swiftly as they are dashed. Ozay's face lights up. Now is the time.

'Ozay,' the seyis tries, 'I know what you think. But I am allowed to think too. I believe that I am doing the right thing. In my heart. I can say no more.'

Ozay Dursun still does not meet his eye.

'Soon we shall be out there, in battle. You and I,' the seyis continues: 'I shall protect you with my bow and I know you will protect me with your sword. There is not in this army, nor in the army of the Christians, a man who can match you. You are the finest swordsmen here.

181

I know it. You know it. Soon, these people will know it.' And he offers his hand.

Ozay hesitates. His lips tighten. Can he do this? He regards the seyis' proffered hand and sighs. He owes his life to this man. He might well do so again.

'There was a promise we made together.' the seyis adds, 'Remember? We said, one more time: just one more time. We shall survive this. You'll see. Then we shall go to Istanbul. Both of us.'

Ozay looks down past his horse's shoulder. They should not be fighting between themselves. Not now. The man means what he says. He always means what he says. Perhaps they will survive this: they are, after all, a formidable pair. He hesitates, then grasps the seyis' hand: 'You better damned well stay behind me then, you and your bow, because if you ever get in front of me they'll hack you to pieces and if ever I get behind you they will blow me to bits.' Hands shake: strong grip: eye to eye.

The incredible brutality with which Ozay met the first line of Count Budian's Hussars stunned even the seyis. Six went down in as many seconds, two lost their heads entirely. The Turks had been surprised that the Christians had readily dispatched a force to meet them, and hussars at that; and the Christians had been taken aback at the speed and ferocity with which the Turks had responded. Supported by a dozen gönüllü, the toprakli flayed into them, cutting a swath straight through, leaving a broad line of blood-splashed uniforms and red and blue hats behind them. Though the Christian forces threw in more men, they were chopped to pieces and retreated immediately.

Limping back to their lines, the hussars spoke of one Turk in particular, protected by a deadly archer with black and white arrows: white to the fletching and three black stripes. The swordsman was a big man on a bay horse and he went though their midst like a thing possessed wielding twin scimitars. No-one had ever seen his like before. Men fell from their horses like butchered hens and when they started to retreat he shook his bloodied sabres in the air and spat. He and his archer were said to have dispatched at least sixty-five hussars in less than half an hour. Then they rode back to their ranks on matched horses, as though they had just won some child's game of pitch and toss.

'Tomorrow, look out for them,' said an Imperial officer. 'Those two: the swordsman and the archer. They are marked men. Make sure you get them. There's money on it.'

The seyis had slackened his girth as they loped back and as soon as they arrived at the Ottoman camp he vaulted to the ground, slid off the saddle and threw a goatskin of cold water straight across Azarax's back and did the same for Malik, Ozay's horse.

'You do this always,' Ozay had says.

The seyis smiles. He always does it when the horses need it. Not in winter – they don't need it in winter. No horse in his care ever had a sore back.

Ozay pulls off his helmet. The energy he had put into swinging those yatağan had lost him several pounds in sweat. His face, arms and chest are spattered in blood. He sits heavily on an ammunition box, puts his helmet on the ground, rests his elbows on his knees, closes his eyes, holds his head in his hands and breathes deeply. He is shaking. No matter how experienced a swordsman a man is, when fighting for his life from the back of a stallion, he always returns shaking. Courage comes from confronting fear. He looks up at Malik whose back the seyis is kneading with his fingers. Ozay rises slowly and pats the horse. The seyis nods – no words are needed. Ozay needs to rest: he needs peace, silence. Haunting images of the eyes of the men he has just killed are not so lightly dispelled.

The seyis, on the other hand, is not afflicted in the same way; nor is he tired. He is barely sweating. What he has been doing is staying out of the way and indulging in what some might call a sport: galloping about on a jinking horse, aiming his arrows at stationary or moving targets. It is not he who has had to look into the eyes of his victims, seen their guts spill out, as blue as watch-springs over their horse's withers, felt the shatter of bone and thud of sinew under the swingeing weight of a steel blade. He has not seen their arms severed, their faces gashed open, their necks sliced through and heads hinged off to one side, their blood flying into the eyes of their killer. He hasn't even watched them drop from their horses. The split-second after one arrow has been discharged, the next target has been selected, a new arrow fitted to the nock, and he is ready to shoot again. There is no musketeer who can react at this speed. A man with a musket or a pistol is a dead man. The only man he needs to fear is another horseman archer and the Imperial troops have no archers. He is, on this field, on this fast, responsive horse, top predator.

He runs the water over Malik's back and washes off the Hapsburg blood. Wringing out a cloth he wipes the horse's face. Malik is panting, nostrils fully expanded, veins prominent on his face, covered in sweat. He has a head like a chess piece, this horse: a classic head. Malik.

Ozay had not bred Malik. He had bought him. He had been careful about the timing, since it is bad luck, as every Muslim knows, to buy a horse on a Thursday, the 6th day of the week. He had bought him on the first day of the week, a Saturday, from a hirași, a stud in Konya, eastern Anatolia, in 1679. He had been six years old at the time, making him five years older than Azarax. Ozay had ridden him across Anatolia to Rumelia, where he had family, and there he had schooled the horse himself, and Malik was a well-schooled horse. Since Ozay was a big man, he needed a big horse and Malik fitted the bill, being well-made, strong and intelligent, but not quick in the same way as Azarax. Malik was clever enough; he did not need to be told what to do, and he had learned to feel Ozay's wishes, intuitively – and he needed to, since in battle, neither Ozay nor the seyis held their horses' reins. Ozay tied the reins long and dropped them on the pommel of the saddle and as he went hacking through the enemy, Malik would push and steer by the feel of Ozay's weight and by vocal commands alone.

But even though Malik always fought right in the bitter centre, and was stalwart, what he lacked was the aggressive edge that Azarax enjoyed in abundance. Despite his brutal career, and the appalling terror to which he was constantly exposed, Malik was a very gentle horse. When it came to feed time he would never push or lay his ears flat, or lash out with a fore-foot, as Azarax was apt to do. Malik would stand quietly, patiently, with his top lip hanging over his bottom lip and his soft nostrils would bounce as his feed approached and when it was put in his trough or at his feet, he would bend his great neck slowly, and eat slowly and purpose-fully as though he had never tasted anything so wonderful, even though sometimes his feed was nothing but scraps of dry stover. He would always clean his trough to the last tiny shard and then he would eat his saman, picking at it delicately with his great rubbery lips. It amazed the seyis to see him once select one tiny piece from in amongst the pile and savour it as though it were the essence of ambrosia delivered especially for him, from the Pantheon of the God of All Horses.

As the seyis wipes Malik's face and cleans the corners of his eyes and curries his soft coat, he knows that although this is the horse of a splendid Ghazi horseman, is a Ghazi horse himself and is fine in many respects, he is in fact, a soft old creature. Though he is big and mascu-line, knows how to throw threatening looks and can roar and squeal and be terrifying, he is docile at heart. He did not wish to come to Buda. He wished to stay at the timar and graze quietly by the river. He preferred to stand under the locust trees out of the heat of the sun. He had had enough of wars. He was different from Azarax. Azarax seemed to thrive on conflict. Azarax became brighter, his reactions sharper, he watched everything as though it were a huge game and he was enjoying its humour in some arch way, at the expense of the men around him.

Yet Malik: he was nothing more than a great, gentle giant, with big soft eyes and unhurried ways.

He had Kipchak in him: for sure. The seyis could spot it easily by the texture of his coat: unlike Azarax's whose coat was short, like a lion, the individual hairs on Malik's coat were fractionally longer than Azarax's. He was more of a winter than a summer horse. That was his Kipchak background. He could be bossy and stubborn and it was an unwise man who stood close to him when he was throwing himself about because to be caught by Malik when he was acting the stallion was to find yourself without a brain; but still he was not aggressive by nature and sometimes the seyis noticed that even in the thick of the fighting he would act as though he was apologising for his master's behaviour.

He had big knees and big feet – all of different sizes – and anyone who was unlucky enough to find his sandalled foot beneath one of Malik's would be unlikely to forget the experience for the rest of his life. But, if a man was shrewd enough to stay his distance, he would swiftly recognise that Malik was an exceptional horse, of presence and of real quality. Yet this horse, Malik, would have been perfectly happy to have drawn a wagon round on Ali-aga Izobegović's timar for the rest of his life so long as every Cuma, every Friday, he could go and graze down by the river and stand under the locust trees, out of the sun.

His eyes were a lighter brown than those of Azarax. His lozenge-shaped pupils were cobalt blue and the offside eye, his right eye, had a white splash in it, where the lens was fractured, where once he must have been struck by a çirit dart, or a stone, or sword which gave him a blind spot. In the way that horses do, Azarax had responded to this blind spot and filled the gap, he became the eyes of Malik, in the way that a blind horse will always be led by a sighted one. A blind horse will stick close to him, grazing muzzle to muzzle, standing side by side, sleeping side by side and will never leave the sighted horse. He will be his life-long companion.

The seyis had seen it on the battlefield. When a horse was suddenly blinded and was left standing alone on the field after the battle, his cries would be answered by a loose horse who would go to him and lead him and be his guide and would not be separated from him. Likewise Azarax fulfilled the role of guide horse for Malik and always kept to his nearside, his left side, either when level or behind him, so that he could see. He would not stand on Malik's blind side, where Malik could not see: it was Malik's sighted side he needed to be on, in exactly the reverse way to a man.

The seyis ran his fingers through his black mane and looked into the cobalt blue eye. Malik was fourteen years old now. He had aged suddenly. Grey hairs had sprouted on his forehead and round his muzzle. He was getting too old for these wars. His joints had begun to click when he walked and he was no longer so quick on his feet. He was adroit – no mistake – he could still turn and whip around with amazing agility for such a large horse, but he was not as fast as he once he had been. He could not keep up with Azarax, and with his blind-spot, if the seyis and Azarax ever got on the wrong side and in front of him, he would be lost.

He counted on Azarax, and the seyis, Azarax and Ozay knew it.

* * *

That night, in the light of the fire, the seyis sits with the men and listens to them talk. Abdul Rahman is Paşa of Buda these days. An old man; like old Ibrahim Paşa of Buda before him; whom Kara Mustafa had executed. Abdi Paşa, as they call the new Paşa, is a devout man. He governs a strong, well-victualled city and round the tomb of Gül Baba it is well known that a ring of heavily-armed janissaries stand, night and day. Buda is rich: people from all around have taken their belongings there because they know it is impregnable. Though the Christians once owned Buda, they will never have it back. They cannot be allowed to have it back: it is the key to the Ottoman Empire. If Buda falls, everything will fall, as far as Istanbul itself. So it will not fall. Abdi Paşa has been bringing in gunpowder – he can even make his own – and he has cannons and muskets and archers and janissaries and azap troops.

He has the best men and the Hapsburgs cannot beat him. Soon those that surround Buda will run short of rations. They will break. The sun will beat down and scorch them. There is no fodder because the land is burned up. There is nothing to eat. There are no birds and not so much as a green leaf for the horses. The Christians will sweat in their thick worsted uniforms, and on their hands and knees creep into the trenches and Abdi Paşa will rain upon them grenades and arrows and lances and musket shot, and inch by inch they will die and rot under the heat of an Ottoman sky. They will lose their will to conquer as they die in their ones, twos, tens, by the hundred and by the thousand. Their horses will cry out for food. The men will cry out with dried throats for water. The river Danube is foul. They cannot drink it. They will die if they drink from the river. They will crawl back to Vienna. Tomorrow we will crush them.

* * *

'The attack planned for 14th August on the Allied lines by janissaries supported by sipahi, was commanded by the Paşa of Bossfia, a man of no previous field experience.

186

'The Paşa of Bossfia led 4,000 Syrian sipahi directly at enemy lines. The Syrian sipahi are used to meeting Persians on horseback but they have no experience of Western Christian forces. The Paşa of Bossfia found himself confronting an undisciplined body of men on horse, not dressed in uniform, but variously, like civilians. The sight of this disorderly group caused the Paşa to pause his cantering contingent, bringing them to an abrupt halt, because he believed this was a troop of merchants with nothing to do with the battle. Upon seeing the sipahi line apparently unwilling to attack, the Christians galloped at them on massed horse with immense ferocity. The sipahi were immediately taken at a disadvantage, forced to bear the brunt of a full charge, some with lance, some without, then behind these came a new wave of attack, later identified as the Dragoons of Lord Taafe, an Irishman. In their midst was the son of the King of England, James Fitzjames, although not a prince, since he was conceived from one of the King's concubines as we learned later from a Christian prisoner whom we have since executed. This James Fitzjames, no more than fifteen or sixteen years old, was very able and willing to attack a mounted sipahi on his own terms. Naturally enough he was offered little resistance by the sipahi, since they did not have in their number a son of one of the Sultan's concubines to match his standing. He could not be expected to meet an ordinary timarli sipahi and even though there were hassa sipahi, they were not of the Sultan's blood and could not therefore meet him either. Therefore he and his immediate party caused much bloodshed.

'In this morning's action, we lost 3,000 of our best janissaries. Fifty sipahi were taken prisoner along with their horses, 58 standards were lost and eight pieces of cannon. The Paşa of Bossfia himself was killed. The engagement was a disaster.'

This account is reported to the Grand Vizier within earshot of the seyis and Ozay Dursun who are sitting beneath the awning of the toprakli orta tent awaiting their orders. They hold their heads in their hands incredulously. How could such a thing have been allowed to take place? How could the Grand Vizier have entrusted a major military encounter to an Anatolian Paşa? Why had he not sent the Beylerbey of Silistra? Or of Rumelia? Ozay throws his head back and closes his eyes.

If only they had a General half as good as Lorraine. You know what they say about good men and bad generals? Good men die first.

The two men continue listening.

The Vizier now makes plans to send men directly into Buda to bolster its forces, since it is obvious that the besieging Christian forces will continue mining and burrowing under the walls, just as the Turks had done at Vienna, until the walls collapse, then they will throw their forces against the city and hold off attacks from the outside at the same time.

Ozay hurls a pebble. 'Fool!' he hisses through gritted teeth. 'If Kara Mustafa had followed the principle of having a well-organised army – one that was prepared – he would now be sitting in the Hofburg in Vienna drinking brandy with his twenty thousand concubines and you and I would have timars on the Wienwald.'

The Grand Vizier continues: he offers extra money – twenty aspers a day – to any man who can get into Buda. There. That should encourage them.

Ozay's chin hits his chest.

'Whatever happened to the Great Cause?' he groans. 'The Ghazi? The Holy Warriors?'

'Well,' the seyis tries, 'We still have the Beylerbey of Silistra. He's been through what we have been through.'

Ozay nods, yes, true. Then throws his head back and closes his eyes again. 'I wonder how many – or how few – aspers he has been offered?'

'We'll live through this,' the seyis ventures. 'I don't know how but I know we will. It's Azarax – he is calm.'

'Then why is it I can hear the stones rattling on the lid of my coffin?' Ozay says, as he gets up and stalks away.

29TH AUGUST 1686. Dawn.

As soon as a black thread can be distinguished from a white one, the muezzin calls from the high şerefe of a minaret in Buda. His voice rings out all over the plain beneath the town and over the Turkish and Christian camp alike. The call breaks the stillness of the early morning and sings out as melodically as it has sung out each morning over the past 144 years, in Buda. It is a song of peace and blessing and there are those within the Christian camp who lie awake and listen to its melody and hum its song involuntarily as they make their way to matins or to mass. When the muezzin ceases, and the activity of both camps has begun, fires relit and bread baked, praying men stand in the Imperial camp and sing Christian hymns and the plain of Buda becomes a contesting medley of early morning religious devotion.

Men and horses are mustered.

The Turks had begun to move early and this has alerted the Christian forces. As soon as the first linnets begin singing high in the sky above them and before the vultures begin wheeling on the thermals and before the great heat of day begins to draw the sweat from men's bodies, the seyis sponges the two horses from one end to the other. In a pitcher of water the night before he had dropped lavender oil that he had brought with him, pressed from the mauve, richly scented lavender fields on Ali-aga Izobegović's timar. An emulsion of lavender oil and water on a horse's coat gives it polish and keeps the flies down. Men have lost their lives because of flies. The inopportune settling of a fly in a horse's eye or ear can make the horse shake his head just as his rider is about to parry the thrust of a sabre and this can cost him his life. The seyis had been diligent, particularly with Malik since he would be in the densest part of the fighting. The seyis had carefully wiped the emulsion under the horse's eyes and down his face along his mid-line and over his shoulders and quarters.

Malik had stood perfectly still, like a child told to go somewhere he did not wish to go: toes turned inward, head down, a plea to be let off: let me off today. Let me graze around these few bushes here today. Just today...

The seyis moves Malik's forelock behind his ear: 'A little more time,' he says, 'and it will all be over. For all of us: you will see. Be attentive, Malik. Do not let your mind wander today of all days, Malik, and you can go back to the timar and graze by the river under the trees.'

The seyis puts on his saddle and girths it up. Malik yields to the strain of the girth. His eyes are glazed. Is he hungry? No. Thirsty? No. Tired? – tired of all this? Yes. He has had enough. And what else is wrong? Ozay. Ozay has lost heart and Malik has picked up on it. Why has he lost heart? Is it because the seyis refused to return to Istanbul? Partly. But there was something else, something Ozay had said: he said the spirit of the Ghazi is not here. Gül Baba is not here.

Yet Azarax is alert: his ears are pricked and he is stamping about. Five years makes a lot of difference to the way a man or horse will think. Azarax has not had an easy time of it: plenty of shots have been ranged toward him: many a swordsman has come hurtling at him. He has been fortunate to have a seyis who meets them long before they meet him. And there have been times when the battle has surrounded them both but somehow he and the seyis had kept cool heads and remained alive.

When Malik looks at Azarax, it is in the way an older man looks at a younger one: you are younger than me, you must watch over me. I cannot move so quickly these days. Keep your eyes open for me: my eyesight is not what it was. I am older now: I have been in too many battles and my luck may be running out. Stay close.

Ozay mounts.

He and Malik are the same. Ozay too, is older. He too becomes tired more quickly.

And what if there comes a moment when you have to choose between your friend and your horse? Then, seyis, what then?

The thought spills into the seyis' mind like a poison.

The seyis frowns. What is this voice? Where did it come from?

Today you must make this choice. Who will you choose?

The seyis blots this toxic voice out of his mind.

What of oaths and destinies now? At the last moment one must die. Who will it be: Ozay or your horse?

Are my thoughts transparent? Why is Ozay looking at me like that?

The seyis tries a smile but Ozay is not smiling.

The seyis mounts and Azarax rears. It is the first time he has ever reared when the seyis has mounted. And it is the first time the seyis ever strikes him, hard with the flat of his hand on his neck. The horse is confused and throws himself about. The seyis steadies him, angrily.

And all the time Ozay and Malik watch, calmly, with dust-reddened eyes.

Are you going to watch over us today, seyis, you and your horse? Or will you abandon us in the last moment?

'Keep behind,' Ozay says: 'Remember? Behind. To our offside, because of Malik's eye.'

Never before has he mentioned Malik's eye.

By nine o'clock the columns are mounted. Saddle leather creaks. Horses snort, paw the ground. Some are already black with sweat; the day is already hot and dusty. No-one speaks in the Ottoman ranks.

At nine-thirty sharp the sipahi trot fast out of the camp, their standards fluttering over their heads.

The Syrian horses have picked up on the tension from the sipahi and they rear, and squeal and canter off sideways and have to be brought back into line with angry shouts from their riders. They raise their brown heads and their dark, soft nostrils dilate and expand as they blow the flutes down their nasal cavities: veins on their faces stand out as they toss their heads.

The column trots off swiftly then breaks into a light canter down and away from the camp as the power of the sunlight intensifies. Dust rises in huge clouds about them, a rider can barely see the man beside him. The flies are already busy and now spiral in clusters above the horses' and riders' heads in irritating black swarms.

190

On the hills opposite, the standards of the Imperial cavalry rise up toward them.

The sipahi halt. Their dust cloud rolls past them and flows down into the shallow valley at their feet.

The seyis studies the Imperial line: Azarax will not stand still. He thrashes from side to side, stamps his feet and throws himself about. This is a bad omen. The seyis' face has whitened. Maybe it is his turn to die today? And the horse knows it? The seyis' mouth dries and he steadies the horse, this time without hitting him. That was a mistake, a big mistake: he should have known better then to pick a fight with a horse. Pick a fight with a horse and you will lose, always. Steady, Azarax, steady.

The forces opposite are big: the Christians look big: their horses look big: big and determined: these are the Horse Regiments of the Generals Mercy, Houfler and Neuberg.

The orders from the Grand Vizier to the 3,000 Ottoman horsemen of the relieving force, have been simple. Get into Buda. The reward has shot up to a hundred aspers. Ozay had cracked a caustic joke about the price of Paradise lying somewhere between twenty and a hundred aspers but no-one had laughed. Getting into the city meant passing the Imperial cavalry, all its infantry, all its cannon. And cannon means explosive round-shot, grapeshot and chain-shot. It is a deadly gauntlet. The mission is sheer suicide, a waste of lives. But already the men are chanting: 'Bismillâhirrah manirrahim..La Illaha, Allahu akbar...'

Suddenly, the seyis has a bad feeling about this place. He has made the wrong decision: of course he should have gone to Istanbul. What does he think he is doing? If he had decided to go to Istanbul, Ozay would have gone with him and so would Malik. It was why Ozay had been so delighted when the news came. He did not wish to come to Buda. Ozay had sensed it, even then. Both he and Malik. What has the seyis done? What on earth made him think he should ignore the wishes of the baş imrahor? Will ever such an offer come again? Never! He has been a fool. You wronged your own soul and now you will suffer the nipping frosts.

Bora!

Look at Malik: he's chewing his bit and the whites of his eyes are showing. Stay behind, the seyis says over and over in his mind: protect, protect.

*＊＊

As soon as the last line of Ottoman horse meet the top of the hill, the meterhane band from the camp below strikes up with a loud boom from

191

the kettledrums. The high-pitched pipes pitch in. The kettledrums boom louder, orta drums take up the rat-at-tat-tat, then the big base pipes skirl across the columns, rows and rows of men on horses: stallions to the fore, mares to the rear.

Two notes from a ram's horn are blown, high and low – a right flank horn. The sipahis break the line and begin their downhill descent toward Buda and the waiting Imperial horse.

A thousand janissary infantry with long range muskets suddenly release a volley with an ear-splitting crackle. It strikes its mark, and a wave of front-line Imperial horsemen drop from their saddles and the sipahi thunder across them obliquely. They aim to draw the Imperial horse out, then hit them with archers.

The seyis gallops alongside Ozay but all the time Azarax keeps pulling out to one side to get ahead: the horses in front of him are far too slow. He could pass all of these with ease. Stay back, Azarax, stay back. It takes all his strength to control this horse today. Malik is galloping awkwardly: his legs aren't in rhythm, the seyis can tell he's not breathing with each stride but outside the stride: he's losing breath. 'Stay behind me, damn you!' Ozay shouts angrily, 'Behind!'

They gallop across the Imperial forces at an angle, the ground vibrating with thousands of hooves. A great cloud rises, the standards and horses becoming enveloped in the dust and men are coughing and horses snorting, their eyes blinded. Row upon row of Ottoman horse surge down into the valley, and in the confusion, the seyis loses sight of Ozay amongst the huge numbers of horses. The dust is now too dense to see through and he does not know if Malik is in front or behind.

The sound of a bugle: an Imperial bugle.

Where are they? In the dust it is not possible to see two yards. They are galloping blind. The ground changes and the seyis suddenly finds they are on an incline: that's better. Azarax pulls on powerfully, outstripping the horses all round him.

For a brief instant the seyis bursts out of the dust to find himself facing a huge wave of Imperial cavalry heading downhill toward them, the Christians leaning back into their cantles to balance the thrust of their downward-sloping horses, exposing their riders' bellies.

Perfect!

Thud!Thud!Thud!

Down they go – it's child's play.

The sipahi, toprakli and gönüllü burst out of the dust a moment later. The whole sipahi column swings to the left and gallops uphill, the most advantageous position for horse and rider, to meet the Imperial horse.

The first swathe of Imperial horsemen hit the hard stony ground beneath their horses' sliding feet.

The seyis strains to see Ozay and spots the flashing twin yatağan. Cutting straight through his own lines, he gallops behind him and, to let him know he's there, sends an arrow past his ear straight into the eye of the Houfler hussar he's battling on his right. The man flips straight over the back of his horse as if struck by a vast invisible fist.

Once again, in absolute awe, the seyis watches Ozay plunge directly into the massed horse behind the first wave, his yatağan drawn. Any pistol ranged against him or his horse, any lance or sword raised by an Imperial cavalryman, is answered by the unerring accuracy of a water-buffalo and locust-wood bow and an arrow with black and white fletching.

The sipahi thunder up and on, screaming at the top of their voices, line upon line of them: toprakli sipahi, timarli sipahi, hassa sipahi, kapikulu sipahi, deli, gönüllü, Istanbul toprakli, çebelu light and silahdar.

At the head of St Paul's Valley, before the crest of the hill, the seyis loses sight of Ozay again and follows the wave of sipahi wheeling toward the hot, mud springs on the edge of the Danube that would give them access to the town.

Suddenly a battery of cannon fire opens up on their left. The hot blast burns the seyis' face even where he is, galloping to the right of the sipahi. Lines of men and horse fall out of view. The air is red with flying blood. The seyis reins Azarax: there's no way that Malik could cover ground this fast. He must be behind him. Circling Azarax, the seyis stands in his stirrups, searching. Where are they?

Massed sipahi, toprakli and gönüllü horse gallop toward the walls of Buda.

There they are!

They are a long way ahead. How did they get there?

Now on his own and exposed on open ground, the seyis yells at Azarax who digs his hooves in and they become a burning streak of blood-red bay. Two Houfler hussars gallop to meet him with couched lance. The first man flies off his horse with an arrow through his forehead and the next falls from his twisted rearing horse as Azarax goes straight at him and gallops beneath the rearing horse's flying front hooves.

No-one is going to get out of this alive: no-one. They will all die. Soon, they will be in Paradise. Ahead he sees Ozay and Malik and at that instant, everything slows, becomes dreamlike and other-worldly. The seyis feels curiously detached as though observing himself from outside his own body. A strange peace surrounds him. He feels the movement of the horse but all sound has gone. It is as if he and Azarax are floating through these screaming men and galloping horses, through the dust and cannon fire, the flames, the stink of sulphur, the bitter saltpetre. He sees Imperial musketeers drop to one knee, level their muskets at him and fire. He notices the detail: the puffs of smoke from the pan, then from the end of the barrel, the recoil of the rifle. He hears the ball zip through the air, inches from his face, feels Azarax take a checking stride, evading danger. They cannot kill me. They cannot kill my horse.

The seyis' body works with supreme skill. His legs grip Azarax, who jinks from side to side, ears flat, eyes blazing, kicking, thrashing out, biting, the engine of the seyis, his indestructible ally, forging forward, always forward, blood-spattered, rearing, whinnying, neighing, fighting, fighting. The seyis' arms move of their own volition: his head swims; his fingers find the arrows and fit nock to bowstring: the feathers touch his cheek, the thumb pinches, the horse moves but the arrow is steady and with barely a sound, it's gone. Another dragoon, another Imperial cavalryman, another volunteer, another Bavarian, another Spaniard, Croat, Irishman, Englishman, Hungarian is flicked backward over the rear of his horse and before he hits the ground the seyis has taken another and another. Still the seyis follows Ozay and still he shoots his arrows that are now dwindling in his quiver. A gönüllü on his left brings him back to his senses with a loud shout 'Haydi! haydi! haydi! – Go! go! go!'

They are right beneath the walls of Buda. He had not realised they were so close. They have made it! The seyis was not even aware that they were heading for it. He was following Ozay and Malik. And Malik, he knows, can see them.

Musket shot rakes down from the town battlements. Not one hundred yards away are the Iron gates to the southern end of the city. 'Make for the gates!' someone shouts.

The great Iron Gates yawn open. A line of janissary musketeers fan out and open fire to cover their approach. Ozay wheels Malik towards the iron gates and the seyis. 'Haydi! haydi! haydi!' shouts Ozay. The seyis sees the open gates and spins to his right.

He is now in front of Ozay and in Malik's blind-spot.

Malik cries out because he cannot see his companion. Perversely, because Azarax can see him, Azarax does not respond. Malik neighs again. Fifteen other horses, gönüllü, sipahi and toprakli plunge behind Ozay, their riders hacking with yatağan, hurling çirit darts and shooting arrows. Azarax is still out of his vision on his blind side. Malik neighs and loses momentum. Ozay has to fight him to keep him going forward. The seyis shouts: 'Come on Malik! Malik!' It is not far to the Iron Gate.

Ozay urges his horse on. 'Come on Malik!' the seyis screams, his voice frantic: 'Come on!' In slow-motion, Malik's big dark knees pump his weight forward on big heavy feet. He is exhausted. His chest is white with sweat, his nostrils flared red, his eyes wide; he is crowded in, half-blind, terrified and confused. He has lost his guide. 'Haydi! haydi! haydi!' Ozay commands. The seyis spins Azarax, shooting arrows past Ozay at the Hapsburg infantry to his right. He has only two arrows left. Never use your last two arrows. This he knows. It is branded on his heart. 'Come on Malik! Twenty yards more! Come on!' The seyis pulls the second-to-last arrow from his quiver. Never shoot your last two arrows because you will need them for the last two shots. They always come together. He raises the arrow nock to the bowstring.

'Get inside!' Ozay shouts.

The seyis spots the musket levelled at Ozay and shoots. It pins the man's upper arm to the stock of his gun, and the shot goes wide. Malik flounders, he's losing ground fast. Where there were fifteen horses closing on the gates of Buda, now there are only six. The roar of gunfire is deafening. The air is filled with smoke. Bullets ricochet off the walls and graze the stony ground.

'Come on Malik!' The horse just hasn't got the speed: he's flagging.

'Get in!' the Buda janissaries shout from within the city walls, 'we're closing the gates!'

Still the seyis hesitates. He spots the two Suabian musketeers with huge, heavy-duty castle muskets. One of the castle muskets is ranged at him and the other at Ozay. He has one arrow.

'Get inside!' shouts Ozay.

Ten yards, five, four... 'Malik, come on! Not far!' He's seen Azarax. He's going to make it! 'Come on Malik!' The seyis aims his bow, swinging between the Suabian aiming at Ozay and the other at him: which one? Which one?

The seyis turns in his saddle at the Suabian whose gun is aimed at Azarax: he feels thumb and forefinger release. Away goes the arrow and he watches it pin the man's forearm into his right eye. In the same instant the other Suabian fires. Malik cries out.

The seyis bursts through the iron gates with shot ricocheting off iron, off the ground and the walls. Four horses thunder in behind him. The janissary musketeers keep blasting at the pursuing Imperial horse and infantry, and they haul the great doors shut, squeezing them to the centre and sliding the bolts with a heavy metallic thump.

Inside Buda, his eyes stinging with sweat and head ringing, the seyis immediately spins Azarax. The other four horsemen are leaning over their horses' necks, sweat and blood running from their faces. The horses are gulping for breath, thrashing around, pouring with sweat.

Malik is not amongst them.

The seyis leaps from his horse, runs to the locked gates and pounds on them with his fists: 'There's one more to come!' he shouts. 'Ozay! Ozay!' He struggles to undo the metal counterweight bolts, looks for holes in the metalwork to look through.

'Open the gates, there's another to come!'

The gunfire crackles and booms outside.

The seyis slumps against the doors. He had heard that last neigh. If a blind horse loses his guide in a tight spot for even a fraction of a second, he will stop and call.

The seyis sinks to his knees against the metal doors.

2ND SEPTEMBER 1686

Five men entering a besieged city do not alter the course of a war.

The terms of the surrender of Buda to the Hapsburg forces, as dictated by Baron Creutz, a Lieutenant Colonel in Baden's regiment, were onerous to Abdi Paşa. No man, said Abdi Paşa, could live with the shame. We fight to the last man.

The Standards of the Holy Prophet are raised.

* * *

It began in the morning. A huge section of city wall had been undermined and collapsed. The city is exposed. It is only now a matter of time – and blood.

German voices, Spanish, Viennese, English, French, Dutch: men shouting orders in German, others shouting what they think is the inter-pretation. Onto them all falls a hail of stones, arrows, spikes, metal shards, exploding shot. Over their heads, above the city walls, come the screams: grape shot explodes in the air and terrorized men cry out as munitions explode on the rocks and piles of excavations. Men run through the swirling dust and flying debris into the Imperial trenches, to a collapsed section of wall, where they struggle to hold their footing on stones made slippery by blood. Swarms of blue-bottles erupt from the bloated bodies of men who had fallen there days and weeks before, and who now fill the air with clouds of a heavy, putrid, scent. Bitter hand-to-hand fighting is now closing the gap between the wounded, the maimed, the suddenly limbless, the dying, and the dead.

The storm of men rushing at the wall has now become a mighty wave and those that surge from the rear with swords and pistols are met in combat by vigorous Ottoman defenders swinging war-axes.

Hands push from behind the sweating wall of thick worsted coats and fight on through the day in to the dead, flat, fly-ridden heat of afternoon sunshine and dust. Men with twisted mouths and mad eyes swing sabres wildly at any face or limb or body that is dressed in a different uniform, while fencing off the blows that rain back. When a man feels his sabre judder against bone in the body of the man in front of him, he retracts his blade as swiftly as he can, for he is instantly engaged by another. If a man is seen to be powerful, two will engage him, and the effort to remain alive is doubled. Arms and hands are weary from swinging weapons but they cannot stop: to stop, to drop one's guard, is to be split from head to foot. Every last effort is now directed towards the collapse of the opponents' nerve, muscle and sinew.

The Christian commanders send more and more screaming, sweating, wild-eyed men at the flashing yatağan and şinşir. They beat and hack and slice until the Turkish line wavers.

Sabre in hand, Abdi Paşa cries out 'Allah!' as he too is sabred on his city walls.

The main gates of Buda are sprung. German, French, Dutch, Spanish troops and volunteers pour through the cobbled streets pursuing Rumelian, Anatolian, Syrian, Serbian and Bosnian Turk soldiers. Whoever stands in their path dies: old men, old women, young women, children or injured soldiers.

Feet pound up and down the streets of Buda. Women and children scream as pistols are fired. Men scream. Men look into the Buda stables then turn their attention back to human targets.

The sounds of slaughter and mayhem continue for two hours until the sound of fighting dies away.

Then come the calls for peace.

'Mercy!' men plead, 'Mercy!' Shots ring out.

Darkness has now fallen. The stable doors beside the south gate burst open. A young man in civilian clothes steps into the doorway. He is silhouetted against the light of fires flickering behind him. He is wearing a wide-brimmed beaver hat with a feather and long coat, corselet and great cuffs. He carries a sword in one hand and a pistol in the other. He calls to a colleague who appears with a lantern.

When the lantern is held up, with the shadows is revealed a man in amongst the tethered horses.

The young man with the beaver hat calls out again. A third man appears, and in broken Turkish asks who is hiding? A pistol is cocked.

The crouching man within hesitates, squinting through the darkness, past the horse's glossy quarters, into the faces lit by the upheld, swinging lantern.

He steps into its light.

What does he think he is doing?

He is looking after the horses, the man says. He is a groom.

- 16 -

The Never-to-Return Road

When the world capsizes there are the horses, always the horses. They will stand and listen and fill that void which the human presence cannot touch. When there is no other soul with whom to share your fears, your hopes, your dreams and your guilt, there are always the horses. The seyis buries his face in Azarax's mane. All the brave show of life is but a wind blowing through a veil. How long will he hear Ozay's voice, see his eyes? How long will the vision of Malik, sweating and terrified, galloping toward him through the smoke and flying bullets, the dust and blood, haunt him? How many times must he feel the tension of the bowstring, feel the arrow fly that saved his own skin? Like a coward he had left his friend to die. He is no Ghazi. He never was a Ghazi. He is a seyis, rayah, common cattle, born into grime and in grime he shall die. He will not go to the tomb of Gül Baba; he is not worthy of it. The soft muzzle of a horse touches his hand. Allah Kerim!

How long does it take to forgive? Can a man forgive himself? Must the pain he feels inside last a lifetime? Will he ever be free? Must he pay for what he has done in some other life? Or are some acts beyond redemption? Must a man resign himself to live with guilt? Knowing in his heart that once, when he was brought to the test, in the heat of the moment, he was unequal to it. The seyis looks into the dark eyes of his horse: does Azarax see grief in this eye? What does he see in Azarax's eye? A reflection of his own. He turns away. Horses have the power to make you search your own soul.

From the outside, the stable at the southern gate of Buda appeared an ordinary building, made of roughly-cut stone. Above the stable entrance, carved into a single slab of limestone was an inscription cut in highly decorative Arabic cipher, which the seyis had been unable to read.

'Take your horses in there!' a janissary had shouted, pointing to the big oak doors and mechanically, the seyis had obeyed along with the four other sipahi horsemen who had thundered through the smoke and gunfire into Buda with him.

The contrast with the world which they had just left behind could not have been more acute. A sweet scent of horses emitted from the building as they entered. The stable had been so removed from what lay outside that it was like walking into a mosque, with its peace and profound calm.

When he had roared in through the gates and slid off Azarax's back and screamed, Azarax too had called out. The seyis had yelled out for Ozay, hammering his fists on the iron gates and Azarax had neighed in his high-pitched, rising and falling squeal, again and again. It was only when the seyis had stopped shouting, ceased hammering on the gates and slid to his knees that the horse had stopped.

The seyis did not know how long he had stayed at the gate, on his knees. Nor how long Azarax had stood over him.

He recalled dimly the janissary's voice: the outstretched finger, the wild eyes; the inscription over the door. He recalled how, before entering the stable, he had taken his bow, wrapped it round his leg, bent it backwards against the grain, snapped it, and hurled the beautiful broken pieces onto the cobbles outside the stable door.

Within, it was refreshingly cool and dark and though barely conscious of it, the seyis led Azarax down its length. It was only the next day that he saw that it was a beautiful stable, of great antiquity and style. Like so many stables of the east, it was divided into stalls, the cast-iron stall-ends decorated with wrought-iron finials with moulded horses' heads, plated in gold. Six huge lamps were suspended from the white, fan-vaulted ceiling, made of wrought-iron, tall and intricately filigreed. The floors were wood cob, that is to say, hexagonal wooden blocks laid on end and fitted symmetrically together, then polished, providing a quiet surface for shod horses to walk on, always unslippery because of the interlocking of the joints. The walls were white and the windows arcaded with limestone mullions and shuttered on the inside. Two lines of horses stood back-to-back and the horses were tethered to brass rings. Their beds were of beaten earth, and covered with a deep layer of Danubian river sand. The stalls were big and the tethers long enough for the horses to lie down and roll. The feed troughs were of white Morean marble and the water troughs beside them, of granite.

Mechanically, the seyis unsaddled, washed and fed Azarax, then fed and watered the other horses, and he remained in the stable for the rest of the day. He was alone, except for the horses. Although the firing and shooting and sound of guns and screaming continued outside, within the stable, there was a surreal calm. In the night he crawled onto the saman bags, and thrashed from side to side, turning over and over in his mind what had happened, what he had done. He slept fitfully but the presence of the horses wove a calm into his soul and in the morning he woke to the sound he loved best in the whole world: the sound of horses whickering for their breakfast.

Curiously, no other seyis appeared: no labourer, no-one to see to the horses – so the seyis assumed the role and set about the work as though he had been a seyis in the Buda stables all his life. He doled out barley, having bitten into it first to ensure its quality and that it was not bullet-hard, since one or two of the sixteen horses in the stable were by no means young. Holding the little grains in his hand he pushed a finger into them and rolled them in his palm: barley, beautiful barley. Golden barley. The quality was so high he could crush a grain between forefinger and thumbnail and feel its floury essence, put it to his tongue and taste its sugars. Barley: queen of feed. He dribbled the grains through his hand into Azarax's marble trough and watched him eat.

A tiny, birdlike old man with bright eyes and a small face had entered the stables a few hours later dragging a clattering, wood-wheeled, box trolley. He had a hooked nose, like a beak, his chin and cheeks were covered in white down, and his eyebrows were a gingery white. He was dressed in a grubby white salvár kamise and a grubby white turban. Standing no more than four feet high, he was like a wily old hen that had escaped the fox and the oven over the course of a long life and now anticipated living for ever. He had a shrill voice and fierce avian eyes. If he removed his turban it would be certain he had a wattle of the brightest red. He brought peksimet and ayran – hard tack and liquid yoghurt – in his box trolley, explaining with many gestures of his short arms that Abdi Paşa had given orders that food was to be taken to all combatants – and the civilians – in the southern part of the city. There were many like him, the old man said. 'Eat!' he demanded emphatically, pointing at the peksimet and ayran. Though the seyis had refused, the old man climbed up and sat on a stone buttress beside him until, in order to get rid of the old fellow, the seyis had relented and eaten. Then the old man had stabbed a forefinger into his narrow pigeon chest and shouted: 'Dervish! Dervish!' and breathed deeply, inhaling the sweet scent of horses, 'Mahşallah!' he whispered. And as he spoke he looked deeply into the seyis' eyes and stripped the layers off and, oh, he could see inside, he could walk into those eyes. He had looked into those kind of eyes before: inconsolable eyes, filled with remorse, grief. This seyis had not answered his kismet when it came to call, had he?

'Ah, I see: you were supposed to go to Istanbul and now you are here, in Buda. You are living on someone else's time, my friend.'

The old dervish follows the seyis' flickering glance.

'This horse: I see, I see. His time. Let him be: it is his life: not yours. And now you have a penance to do. You no longer care what becomes of you, do you? You soul is out there, amongst the tangled remains of a friend, a horse, a standard, a flag and a sword? Is that correct? But look at what is happening in here – the horses are eating!'

Clapping his hands on his knees, the old dervish chuckles. 'Did you see the inscription above the door, when you entered this hallowed place?'

The seyis' head bows, like a puppet whose strings have been cut. One nod; chin on his chest. He frowns: did he see it? Some vague recollection hangs in his mind.

The old dervish leans forward: 'Ah yes,' he says, with his bird's eyes twinkling. A yellow finger nail points on the end of a crooked finger: 'You saw it, but did you have eyes to see what it said?'

The seyis' chin puckers.

The old dervish was from a long line of crafty old scallywags who have probed the broken souls of seyises like this one, who cannot read.

'It is addressed to horses,' he adds, cryptically.

The seyis slides his eyes at him, then swings back and continues grooming.

The dervish gazes round the glossy rumps, heads in the feed troughs: 'Listen to them chewing!' he says, and laughs, joyously. 'Shall I tell you what the inscription means?'

The seyis looks up: If you must.

'It means what it says: *Every grain of barley given thee shall purchase indulgence for the sinner. All the treasures of this earth lie between thine eyes.* That's what it says.'

Then he points. 'What are they eating? Whose hand put it there? You are not required to carry another man's burden. Did you realise that? So few people do. Go laughing, my son!'

He jumps from the stone buttress and trundles out through the stable doors with his trolley, warbling some crazy dervish song. 'The wisdom of the idiots!' he shouts as he closes the stable doors behind him: 'Listen to the horses!'

* * *

202

Three days had passed since the seyis had ridden into Buda. For three days of fighting the city had managed to shore up its breached defences.

But finally, it could hold on no longer. The seyis heard the final struggle, but nothing on earth, nor in his heart, would induce him to go and stand on the battlements and fight. He remained with the horses, in the stable. What befell him now, befell him. If the Hapsburgs were to come screaming down the streets, burst into the stable and blow him to pieces in a volley of lead shot, then that is what would happen.

And as the cannons boomed and guns fired, as men shouted, bugles sounded, sabre clashed with yatağan and scimitar, smoke filled the city and men fought for their lives beyond the stable walls, the seyis shovelled dung off the river sand, polished the gold finials, fed barley to his sacred horses, chewed his peksimet, drank his ayran and slept.

And now, on the evening of 2nd September 1686, a heavy calibre flintlock pistol in the hand of a nervous young Christian is trained on him, and he feels not an inch of fear.

What will be, will be.

'Move!' the young man orders waving the pistol muzzle, left hand stretched out as though to counterbalance the dead weight of his pistol. The seyis moves to the centre of the stable, between the two lines of horses. He feels like yawning.

'Anyone else in here?'

The seyis shrugs his shoulders. He doesn't understand this language.

The young man eyes him carefully. 'Search him!' A couple of soldiers in red worsted step forward: one grabs the seyis by the arms and the other checks him for weapons. They fling him to the ground.

'Take him out and hang him with the others!'

The seyis is seized, arms pulled behind his back and he is frog-marched to the door.

'No: wait.' Up goes the pistol again. The seyis is held by the soldiers beside the door. 'Check over there!' Hurling the seyis on the ground again, with drawn swords and bayonets plugged into the ends of their muskets, they stab at saman sacks, overturn piles of straw, rip open cupboard doors. The seyis remains where he is without expression, watching them calmly. They've spotted the gold leaf horse-head finials: they will be gone in an hour: all of them. One of the soldiers tries to hammer one off with the butt of his musket: the young man – the officer – yells at him to stop. 'Get out. Get out all of you. Not you,' – to the seyis.

One of the soldiers hesitates; sneers and the young man ranges his pistol at him and says: 'Now!' Then he pulls another pistol from his belt and cocks the hammer. The soldiers do as they are ordered. As soon as they have gone, the young man lowers the pistols, carefully releases the hammers and tucks them into his belt. Moving swiftly from one horse to the other in his black worsted coat with its great cumbersome cuffs and his high boots, his broad-brimmed beaver hat and stained waistcoat, he takes stock of what he has stumbled upon.

'Holy Mary Mother of God!' he breathes, as well a man might, who has just entered a gilded stable which houses the most magnificent horses in the world.

The seyis does not know if he is to live or die. He does not know if the only thing he cares for is about to be wrenched from his grasp. In a fit of remorse three days ago he had smashed the only weapon he had and now he wants it back. He hates these people. They are his enemy, they are infidel. He despises them because they killed his friend, they had killed Bora; they kill, despoil, and steal. They live in darkness. Smoke fills the streets, timber crackles beneath flames, while bands of vicious thugs roam the city, despoiling, breaking, ruining, stealing. Women scream, children scream: pistols shots ring out. Mosques are torched and minarets fall. Nothing is spared.

The seyis rises steadily to his feet. Kill these people. They are the enemy.

A golden youth steps into the stable.

The seyis has never seen such a being before.

He steps through the stable door and a glow steps in with him. That, and a coterie of sycophants, who wash up in his wake: an entourage of older men, grey and not so glorious, caparisoned in hugely exotic hats with feathers. Profusions of curled hair tumble from under their hats, spilling out across their chests and halfway down their backs. They have gilt frogging on their coats, enormous cuffs and facings, they wear high leather boots and thick worsted even in the dead heat of a plain in middle Europe. They are overheated: they look it. They are Gentlemen, as if the seyis cares.

The golden youth is a lad of sixteen years old or so. He has long blonde hair, his eyes are large and china blue. He is self-assured: mature beyond his years, a little smug perhaps. There is an interpreter who addresses the seyis: 'Who owns these horses?' A moment's hesitation.

'The toprakli sipahi,' the seyis stutters. Say anything.

'Not the Sultan?'

'The toprakli sipahi and the Sultan.' Say anything at all.

'And you? Who are you?'

'I am the seyis.'

That was firm. The men glance at each other. The what? If there was a hint of defiance or disrespect in whatever it was he had said, the swine should hang, immediately. He is the what?

'The groom.'

'Hang him!'

'No wait. Look at these horses. Can our grooms do this?'

The seyis suddenly fields his own question: 'These people – are they Hapsburgers?'

'No,' the interpreter replies, shocked by the impertinence.

'The young one, with the golden hair. Who is he?'

'It is not for you to ask.'

'Is he a Hapsburger?' the seyis asks, remembering hearing about the son of the King of England's concubine.

'No.'

'He is the son of the King's concubine.'

Taking one step forward, the interpreter strikes him hard across the face with the back of his hand and sends him to the floor again. Blood runs from the corner of the seyis' mouth. He lies still, on the wood cobs.

'What did he say?' James Fitzjames asks.

'He insulted you, sir.'

James Fitzjames steps forward and grasps the interpreter's raised arm before he strikes again. He looks into the seyis' face. 'What did he say?' he enquires, politely.

'He asked who you were, sir.' The interpreter decided to be diplomatic.

'It's a fair question. Tell him I am the son of the King of England.'

The interpreter does as he is told. The seyis stands, hands at his side. He is a Ghazi. It is time to die now? These people are his enemies. Why did he come to Buda? What did he promise his horse? Had he not been given the charge?

The seyis bows. 'Paşa,' he says. And stays bowed.

'What did he say?'

'He called you Lord, sir'.

The seyis rises and stands upright.

'That's more like it,' says the golden youth, James Fitzjames. 'When you first came into the stable, Mr Vaudrey, was this man armed?'

'No sir,' replies Edward Vaudrey. 'If he had been, we would have hanged him immediately. We nearly hanged him anyway.'

James Fitzjames regards the seyis through narrowed eyes: 'So as the battle was roaring,' he says, strutting, hands behind his back. 'As his brothers were being blown to pieces and his country was slipping from beneath his feet, he was calmly grooming horses?'

'It would appear.'

James Fitzjames chuckles lightly. 'Good grief. He is no soldier. Not much of a patriot either, I should add.'

He walks along the cob wood and runs his eyes over the horses on either side. 'I like very much the two dun horses,' he says pointing. 'I fancy I shall give them as a present to her Majesty the Queen. What say you Edward?'

'Indeed, sir.'

'Which would you like?'

'I shall take that dark bay,' he says, pointing to Azarax. 'He will do me handsomely. He's perfect for the Queen Dowager's Cuirassiers. They only accept dark bays, and what is he, if he is not a dark bay? And perhaps I shall take another too: this one,' he says pointing to a brown horse nearby.

'And my Lord Cutts: will you take one?'

The burly Irish peer in their midst steps forward. He is a big man with a florid complexion, bright eyes and a deeply lined face as though he bore all the world's burdens upon his shoulders. There's something soft about his eyes, something forgiving, the eyes of a man who once had had to beg for mercy and had received it and had not forgotten. 'These horses,' he says in quiet admiration, 'are of a breed I have never seen before. Indeed not one of these horses is of a type I know. Yet they are magnificent, are they not? Regard the length of the neck, the long ear, the set of the eye. Look at the gaskin on these horses: and the stifle. See how fine are their manes and tails. How high they stand. Never have I beheld such creatures and of such quality.'

'And what say you gentlemen,' James Fitzjames asks, in a manner that is already decided, 'That we take this groom with us? After all, he appears to know these horses and we do not. And besides, we are going to need another pair of hands at least.'

'Is that wise, sir?' the young Edward Vaudrey counters carefully. 'After all, we know that some horses got into the town the other day: how do we know he was not riding one of them?'

'Does he look like a soldier?'

Eyes swing to the seyis: no-one knows how to respond to that one.

'Are any of these horses injured?' James Fitzjames continues.

'None of them, sir.'

'Then I would venture to suggest that none of them has been

outside this stable or involved in any fighting. I doubt very much that any horse came through that barrage without being cut or marked; what say you, my Lord Cutts?'

'True. But let us make some conditions.'

'Very well,' says James Fitzjames, 'If this man does anything that appears slightly suspicious, we hang him instantly.'

'Hear, hear,' says Edward Vaudrey. 'If he in any way proves not to be the groom he says he is: in the slightest degree, then up goes the rope.'

'Agreed gentlemen?'

Lord Cutts purses his lips.

***

One day later and the stable is filled with saddlebags, saddles, swords, coats, gold plates, silver chalices – the catch of a conquered city – and the party of conquerors busy with their living plunder, the horses, the spoils of war. The seyis watches unmoved. Had the tables been turned, he knew his own people would be no different. The dice of destiny has rolled. This, he comprehends, in amazed satisfaction, is why he had come to Buda! A thrill courses through his body. Azarax's destiny now lies outside the seyis' control. Or does it? He looks up. How is the horse? How is he reacting?

He's been standing about in a stable with nothing to do for two and half days and that is about as much as a horse like this can stick without going insane. He looks wonderful: big and glossy, full of life and brilliant eyed, he's been nuzzling the seyis' arm over the past two days, as if to congratulate him upon their safe delivery to this next episode of their hazardous adventure. The seyis had rubbed Azarax's nostrils and ruffled his mane: 'You are my brother: I have brought you here – or did you bring me? We are spared: we are alive. Allah kerim!'

James Fitzjames appears with a grey horse he'd seized earlier. Lord Cutts had his duns; Thomas Bellasis, Sir Oliver St George, the wounded Lord Savile, Lord Mountjoy, Lord Forbes, Christian Lily, John Bradyll, Tom Bourke, and other men with names the seyis never managed to learn, were mounted on a varying group of horses, which had been captured from the Ottoman lines. But none were as fine as those discovered in the stable by the southern gate.

The seyis thrusts a foot into a stirrup and swings up on a horse. Just any horse. At least it is a horse. He had imagined he might be walking.

These men are all in high spirits. They won, didn't they? Jubilate Deo! The conquerors are returning with their booty! They will ride the high road to Vienna, Ratisbon, make their way to the Spanish Netherlands, then back to England. This will be a journey to remember.

The seyis sits patiently on his brown horse, deaf to the foreign language around him. It is the first time that he has stepped out of the stable since he and Azarax had entered on the evening of that fateful day. He looks up the cobbled street that rises to the east of the town: hanged men are suspended from gibbets and from walls on long ropes, they hang from windows, from balustrades, from anywhere there is a place to hang a body from.

His belly whirls. Mahşallah! He looks away. His eyes fall on the iron gate: what lies outside is the body of his friend and Malik. He cannot look there either. He looks at Azarax, gazing up the street, probably intrigued by the dangling corpses, trying to make out what they are.

The party is mounted, saddlebags filled, coats thrown over horse's manes; hooves clatter on the cobbles: voices sing out. They are on their way home: this little band of brothers. This band of volunteers who came to fight for the Hapsburg cause against the infidel Turk, now to return in triumph. Is there a friendly face here? Yes. Lord Cutts. He looks at the seyis and smiles. So he has a heart. The seyis looks down. Who is a seyis to look into the eyes of a Paşa, foreign or otherwise?

Edward Vaudrey is mounted on Azarax: the seyis regards him coolly: a young man, younger than the seyis, in his mid-twenties. Nice looking in an English way, medium height, neither fat nor thin, straight face with grey eyes: lithe, agile, competent with a sword no doubt and obviously not afraid of cocking a pistol. He brooked no nonsense from those soldiers. But what's he like with a horse? By the way he is perched on Azarax, he has a lifetime's worth to learn but Azarax isn't going to give him that. Look at this horse, scratching his nose on his knee, yawning, shaking, flickering his third eyelid: does this resemble a creature full of apprehension? No, of course not: like all horses he's an excellent judge. It's Vaudrey who ought to be apprehensive, thinks the seyis, with a flicker of a smile. He moves in his saddle and awaits with interest what is to take place in the very near future, trying meanwhile not to visualise what he thinks, since this is the squib that ignites the horse's mind. Visualise something and you might as well have screamed the horse a direct order in his own language. The seyis imagines Vaudrey at the horse's feet. He suppresses a grin, looks down at the reins in his hands and focuses his mind on the immediate reality.

He is leaving: he and Azarax. Their lives lie in the hands of their Maker. Insh'allah: it is the Will of God. Who is a seyis to gainsay it? On the contrary: he embraces it.

He looks up, breathes deeply. I am alive: Azarax is alive. We are doing what we should be doing. He pats his horse's neck, catches a look from Azarax's eye – he knows too. Of course he knows. He's known all along. Walk on!

The party clatters up the long incline to the west gate, past the corpses on the gibbets and hanging from the walls, past bodies still lying in the street, past the charred timbers and broken windows, past the collapsed minarets and a burned-out mosque, past knots of drunken soldiers staggering around the streets, past the hunched and huddled shapes of the defeated staring, hollow-eyed and in silence as they ride by.

A last look back: a hodja once told the seyis never to look back but it is best sometimes to know what is left behind. Goodbye war, goodbye memories. Goodbye everything. Goodbye nightmares. Goodbye Ali-aga Izobegović and the baş imrahor. Goodbye the Porecka River, the timar, the slaves, the stink of saltpetre. Goodbye Empires and Ghazis, ganching and gönüllü. Goodbye to you all. Welcome to the new road. I hope there will be no war, no bows, no arrows. No swords or çirit darts, muskets or cannons. The interpreter had told the seyis he had overheard Edward Vaudrey say that Azarax was going to be an army horse. Or if not, sold as a race horse.

'A race horse?' the seyis had snorted in disbelief. A race horse? Why, racing horses is what children do! It is what villagers do on Cuma with work horses! No one in his right mind would dream of racing horses of this quality. The man had said that these English considered it to be the Sport of Kings. The seyis had almost choked at the thought. He had heard these people lived in a benighted world. Did they not know that the sport of kings was to hunt with hawks on horseback? That was the Sport of Kings.

The west gate lies open. Below, beyond lies the Hapsburg camp through which they will pass before reaching the plain.

The party rattles through. Christians cheer from the battlements, hands wave, men whistle. Even the seyis feels it – like a conquering hero – and yet here he is with a group of long-haired Englishmen on twenty Turkish horses, heading for a place he has never heard of, by way of Vienna, a place to which he never wished to return.

Such are the bewildering vagaries of fate. The dance of life upon the tomb of death.

From Ottoman Hills to English Shores

Six heavily-armed Imperial outriders mounted on Karster horses flank the party as it clatters through the western gate. Banks of debris have been cleared to cut a way through the fallen rubble and masonry. The remains of the strapped-iron and wooden gates blasted to pieces by cannon shot flap loosely on iron hinges. The arch remains, surprisingly undamaged, as though the Imperial gunners had done their best to avoid destroying its architectural grace. In fact the reason had been more straightforward: a collapsed arch would have blocked the gateway and they needed it clear for the final storming. Sweeping under it, the horsemen now break out into what had been open country. Once, this road had been lined with walnut and plane trees, running all the way to the Raab river. Some remain. Near the city, none remain – merely the carcases of trees: blackened stumps, riddled with shot, major branches hacked off to supply fuel for the many fires still burning in the Imperial camp. A smell of burning flesh wafts across the plain.

On either side of the gate lie collapsed walls, timber shoring, shattered carts, decomposing bodies of men and horses, eyeless heads rotting on poles; squabbling crows fighting over entrails, slinking pi-dogs. The huge Imperial camp is shrouded in a pall of smoke. Bandaged men limp from one tent to another: injured horses stand three-legged and still under a smoky sky. In the distance on the brow of the far hill to the south-east, lie burned-out Ottoman tents, standards pricking the ground, angled around the charred frames of sipahi pavilions.

The seyis takes all this in. They had been right. When Buda falls, it all falls. Is there an Ottoman army anymore? Is there an Ottoman Empire anymore? Or have these Christian armies pressed on down to Belgrade? To the timar? Beyond? To Istanbul? 'And if I escape, to where?'

The seyis trots along on his new horse. He is younger than Azarax, never been out of the city judging by the way he's looking at everything, as though seeing for the first time. Does this young horse assume that the world was ever thus? Rotting carcases, burning ground, fired camps and blasted trees? Perhaps he is right. Even the seyis is inured to it: there was a time when he could not have looked on all this with equanimity. But now, it's as if his eyes have been covered by scales through which all senses are filtered and he no longer feels pity. All these men riding together are the same: their eyes do not reflect the horror that lies about them; instead they trot through it without emotion, cold to the loss this has all meant, the tears that must be shed.

The seyis' attention is elsewhere: being a horseman, he notices horsemen. These men ride to the bit and spur. With their legs they push the horse on and with their hands they pull him back. They treat these horses like mechanical contraptions and these horses are not going to stand for it.

The seyis winces as Edward Vaudrey hits Azarax in the mouth with the bit.

'How's the new horse, Mr Vaudrey?' shouts James Fitzjames, struggling with his grey as though he were trying to land a bear in a fishing net.

'Splendid! Splendid,' says Vaudrey, bumping up and down in his saddle, horse's head in the air, its mouth agape.

They trot though Christian camps, darkened faces looking up at them: powder blackened and shifty eyed: sunken cheeked, sallow men who sit in groups stirring pots, gloating over little heaps of spoil: silver coffee pots, silks, gold plates, jewelled daggers. Their uniforms are ripped and filthy. Their boots are holed: they have dark shadows under their eyes, they are bruised and many of them have facial cuts. They are a hideous spectacle. Creatures of the clay. These are men who kill for a living. And they are the victors.

Down through the camp they ride and out into the hot plain. They are paşas with feathers in their hats but they know nothing of horses.

East meets west on an equine spine. Superior horsemanship will out. The blood of superior horses will out. The seyis grits his teeth. These people think the horses are automatons: hit them here and they will do this, bang them there and they will do that. But their brutal methods undermine their ability to control them. High mettled horses will suffer no fools. Azarax rears upwards and Edward Vaudrey tumbles down across his back and lands behind the horse's hindquarters in an ugly, dusty sprawl. James Fitzjames explodes in mocking laughter. The seyis bites his lip.

The days have passed but the riding has not improved. Mr Vaudrey has found himself at his horse's feet more often than he expected. Unable to explain the horse's natural instinct to be at the head of the procession and to lead, the seyis could only sit back and watch as Vaudrey and Azarax battled against each other in a contest of wills. When Vaudrey failed to give the horse his head, then the horse would rear: when Vaudrey used the bit as a means of applying pain, the horse would throw him. When he used spurs to engage his hind quarters, the horse would buck. It was, for the seyis, who had never used spurs in all his life, a painful sight; for Vaudrey a humiliating experience; and for the horse, abuse.

In the evenings after a day's ride, the seyis would collect the horse from Vaudrey and smooth away his anger. Then Azarax would cast him a look, profound and grave, keeping an eye on him anxiously as though to ask: Why? Why are you letting him do this to me?

The seyis approached the interpreter one evening, to convey what he could to Vaudrey, to say, simply, that the horse wished to lead: to be at the head of the column, and that no amount of spurring him or hitting him in the mouth with the bit, whipping him or causing him pain would alter that. That the only way forward for this young man was to change himself: it was Vaudrey who had to yield to the horse, and not expect the horse to yield to him. Then the horse would accommodate him and he would find no finer animal to ride. The seyis walked away, hoping that some of what he said would make sense and that Edward Vaudrey would find himself on the following morning approaching the horse without bile in his heart.

Would an interpreter dare convey such a thing, from the mouth of a lowly seyis?

When the party stopped to rest in the heat of one September afternoon, Lord Cutts screwed up his harsh blue eyes, and observed the seyis leading the horses away from the group, tethering them beneath trees out of the glare of the sun and the biting flies. He observed the seyis as he went out of his way to find them water, and snatches of grazing. He observed as he fussed over them, removing ticks and the hippobosca flies. The seyis rubbed leaves into scratches and showed a dedication to their needs that did not pass Lord Cutts' notice, as he'd sit, sucking a stem of grass, watching. He watched the seyis' diligence, how each horse received his attention, how they all felt the touch of his hand upon them, felt the hay whisps run across their backs and as Lord Cutts sat and watched he realised a singular thing.

Here was this man, this foreigner, this groom, this prisoner, who spoke not a word of their language, gave these horses a confidence that they would received today what they had received yesterday – and more, if he could find it. The seyis' own world may have been plunged into darkness on every side, all he knew had been wrested from his grasp, but there resided in him a quiet resignation to his fate. Lord Cutts also noted that there was one horse here who received the best of his devotions. And as he watched the seyis run his hands down that horse's face and talk to him, softly, in the cicada-ringing afternoon, he pondered that the horse who meets with a good master will be the happier of the two.

Within a week, Vaudrey had given up riding Azarax and had swapped him for the brown horse.

Order was at once restored, and now, the burly noble smiled as they approached Vienna. Riding right out in front was the Turkish groom on his big bay stallion, as though he commanded this motley gang of aristocrats and adventurers. High stepping along the road, his horse scented the air as the spires of the town and the tall Hofburg rose in their sight.

As their journey across the hot plain continued, and as the barriers broke down, as kindnesses were exchanged between master and servant, respect flowed from servant to master and the group gradually took to their hearts the seyis in their midst, and treated him as one of their own. He rode in their company and was a very competent groom. He kept the horses in excellent condition, he had impeccable manners, was quiet and graceful, got on with his work, was useful and good natured, unassuming and, all things considered, was thoroughly English, despite being a Turk.

Then he did something that really shocked them.

On their arrival in Vienna, which they had entered like conquering heroes, with much doffing of hats and bowing, (though no one in Vienna had the first clue who they were or why this strange aggregation of English and Irishmen with a Turk in their midst should be behaving in such a grandiloquent manner) they had been magnificently wined and dined by the Emperor, and then presented upon their departure, with an Ottoman bow and quiver of arrows as a souvenir. The bow had been found in the pavilion of Kara Mustafa, and they were assured of its quality, being fashioned of bone, sinew and highly polished wood. A keepsake: a memento of the battle against the Turk.

It was however, unstrung, and on leaving Vienna they joked that the reason Leopold had given it to them was because no-one knew how to string it. Nevertheless, it remained an object of interest and of beauty.

They tried to string it themselves and failed, so the bowstring hung limply between its toggles.

'Why not ask Seyis to do it? Perhaps he knows,' Edward Vaudrey had ventured after they had all failed. They had adopted the name Seyis, having left their interpreter in Vienna, and had lacked the presence of mind to ask what the word 'seyis' meant.

Accordingly, the seyis was summoned and he was presented with the bow.

Not knowing quite how to handle the moment, the seyis had hesitated. Gestures indicated that the English Paşas wished to see it strung. So the seyis took the bow, put one end on the ground, wrapped his right leg round it, depressed it, pushed back with his calf and flicked it inside out, so it now looked like a bow. He then strung the silk to the toggles.

He handed it back to James Fitzjames.

'Upon my soul!' breathed Lord Cutts.

Though the company tried shooting arrows, they all failed to strike a target but the occasion which made them wonder about the wisdom of having the thing at all took place late one afternoon, on the road from Linz to Ratisbon. They had sighted a deer and had taken pot shots with muskets and missed. The deer had remained within vision but out-of-range. The seyis at the time had been riding Azarax since, although Edward Vaudrey had professed to be fond of the horse, he had also become weary of finding himself at its feet more often than not and had swapped for the more docile brown horse which the seyis had been riding. They got along with each other far better. Feeling more confident of his position with his travelling companions, the seyis had trotted up to James Fitzjames who was carrying the bow, begged it off him along with a single arrow, aimed towards the deer and from over a hundred yards brought it straight down.

Cantering to it he reached from the saddle and swept it bodily up onto the pommel a feat none of the company could possibly manage, then glided back to the party as though this was the most ordinary thing that could be done.

They had all stopped in their tracks.

'Ye Gods!' Lord Cutts said quietly, puffing out his cheeks and blowing.

'Are you thinking what I am thinking?' Christian Lily said to Jacob Richards as the seyis handed the bow back to James Fitzjames and offered him the deer.

'I know who this fellow is,' says Edward Vaudrey with narrowed eyes: 'He was the one we were all trying to kill, from the minute he and that deadly swordsman arrived in Buda.'

'Can't be!'

'It is.'

'How so?'

'That horse must have got into the city. We heard that four or five made it. He must have been one.'

'Not possible.'

'Certain of it.'

'What do we do?'

'Hang him?'

'Don't be absurd,' snorts James Fitzjames 'There isn't a mark on that horse. He's never been in a campaign. Of course it's not him. Good God, what's the matter with you? That horse was milling around in a stable in Buda when we found him, wasn't he? The man we were after was a different beast altogether: a ruthless, single-minded, adroit murderer, who spared no-one in his sights. He's hardly going to be this little groom jogging along so placidly in our midst now. The man we were after had a face like a criminal, he was covered in battle scars and was as fit as an athlete. I mean look at this fellow! Does he look like a hardened warrior? Does he? No, he does not. He looks what he is, a groom who is handy with a bow and arrow, and that is all. And there isn't a mark on him either. You're not going to tell me that he and that horse got into Buda through all that cannon shot and musket-fire without so much as a scratch, are you?' And he hands the bow back to the seyis along with the quiver, which the seyis accepts brightly.

'Something I have learned about these Turks,' continues the young James Fitzjames, 'They have a highly developed sense of honour. We brought this man along to help, and he has. He's looked after these horses every night and not once has he complained nor asked for a groat of pay.' James Fitzjames reaches in his pockets, nods to the groom, pulls out a gold crown, sends it fluttering through the air and the seyis is quick to catch it. 'He'll make a damn sight better friend than he will an enemy. Come on,' he adds, 'Ratisbon is ahead!'

RATISBON. 2nd October 1686

Ratisbon. A wall along the Danube, with towers and spires and low red pantile roofs. A small town, with two bridges across the river and leafy suburbs, doves and thrushes, swans on the water and coots striding the watery margins. The party enters the town, emerging from the fading green leaves of the oaks and willows, aspens and ash.

Ratisbon lies a little under half-way from Buda to the English

Channel. James Fitzjames, the Lords Cutts, Mountjoy, Forbes, Savile and their friends, stand on the bridge on their tall horses as they enter the city. Below them, in the water, they look down on the long craft that had brought them out on this adventure the previous May. On that outward journey they had sailed on the Rhine to Strasbourg, then ridden to pick up the Danube at Ulm and sailed from there downstream to Ratisbon.

It is a longer return journey by horse, and far more taxing. Yet these are men in high spirits and here again is a town where they find themselves welcomed as victors. Even the seyis is treated as victor, and though at night the party is entertained in lavish style by the city fathers, the seyis remains with the horses. It is not his business to celebrate war. Better for him, finer for him, to attend the quiet horses, to stand in their midst, listen to the fireworks crackle and sparkle above the city, hear the happy laughter and boisterous singing, the smashing glasses, the whoops and whistles, the music, the speeches; then turn a blind eye and a deaf ear, and be with his horse.

***

In the quiet of the stables Azarax stands still, dozing. A melancholy fills the air and the seyis runs a hand down the horse's face. The stable is dark but for a dim yellow glow coming from an oil lamp hanging on a wall somewhere beyond. Other horses move in the stable, yet the atmosphere within is calm and somehow, very fragile: 'Do you remember the first time we walked on a long journey together, from Bor to the müsellem's stables, on the way to Silistra, Azarax?' He curls a twist of the horse's mane round a finger. A moment slips by before he speaks again: 'How you and Bora held your ears so tightly pricked forward like four big leaves flickering in a breeze, picking up every sound?' He releases the curl and runs a hand down the length of the long, smooth neck: 'Do you remember how restless you both were for the first few nights when we slept out under the stars? How you got up and lay down and stood side by side, the pair of you, and stared into the night? Then you reeded and whickered and stamped your feet, and woke me and I had to watch with you? Was it a bear? Was it a thief? How I never lit a fire because we did not wish to be seen? How we travelled as discreetly as we could, finding ways off the roads and footpaths that felt dangerous, even though we had not even seen them before. How we relied on our senses to detect what lay ahead? If something felt wrong, then we would take another way, a longer way, and we never knew what it was that we had avoided, but knew that it was right to have done so. Life is like that: it is important to observe all the signals, listen with your

216

heart. Your heart and my heart are the same, Azarax. We share the same soul, this I know. I am incomplete without you. What will happen when we reach England? Where will we go? Will we stay together?' The seyis' eyes are very intense and the yellow light flashes across them:

'I do not know what lies ahead; we have only each other. I have you and you have me. And we have survived so far. Am I leading you or are you now leading me, Azarax? Here. Eat. This is barley. For every grain of barley... Do you remember Bora, Azarax? And Malik? They haunt my dreams. I see them every night. I hear their voices. I watch every night as Bora canters away with Envir Altinay Paşa and the toprakli at Vienna. The standards, the fluttering green standards, the glint of the lances and yatağans, their helmets shining in the sun and their kalkan shields bouncing on their backs; the thunder of hooves. And Malik. How he fought: how his big knees plunged through the dust and smoke and gunfire. He tried so hard to catch up with us, every sinew in his body was wrenched: I could see the veins in his face, the sweat across his shoulder; he was watching you and cried out. He was so close. What happened, Azarax? It was my fault. I am guilty. If there is a heaven of horses, Malik will stand at the gates with Bora and say: this seyis is no good, he sent us to our deaths. Do not allow him in this place.

'So. Sleep. Can I sleep here? I shall lie at your feet as I have always done. Look over me Azarax and I shall look over you. Allah kerim. You are my keyif. Iyi geceler. Allah rahatlık versin, Azarax.'

***

As they travel on, the party of paşas and their Turkish horses and the seyis stay sometimes in fine houses and sometimes along the river banks. They sleep beneath the stars and doze flat out in the middle of the day. They travel twenty miles or so a day, riding for two hours, then stopping to graze, riding on for two more, then stopping for food for themselves. In the afternoon, they ride for two hours, stop to graze and then ride until they find somewhere to stay for the night and that is when the horses become agitated. Every night is different. Every place has different feed, and for the horses it means either stables, usually dotted all over a town or village, or else they are tethered out on grassland, brought oats or barley and sometimes even the hard durum wheat that grows in Europe, which, unlike soft wheat, may safely be fed to horses.

Some days seem long, some short.

Some days the party goes along in high spirits, singing and laughing and boisterous. Other days they ride in silence, all of them, as though picking up from the earth itself a sadness which transmits into their hearts and the hearts of their horses.

The seyis rides Azarax but occasionally swaps to the brown horse as Edward Vaudrey struggles to master the doru Karaman, but Vaudrey can never make the leap it requires. In his faltering English, the seyis says to him: forget your hands and legs. Ride him with your heart. Edward Vaudrey looks at him bleakly. 'This is a very sensitive horse,' the seyis says. Edward Vaudrey frowns. 'He has good intuition. He needs to be sure that you know what you want because if you do not know what you want, how can he know what you want?' Edward Vaudrey stares off into the distance. 'This horse, he is called Azarax: his is the Son of Fire. He is a Ghazi horse. He is a pure blood, a Karaman. A Turk. He is very proud, he has high standards, he is like a dervish. A dervish is a holy man. Azarax is like a holy man – pure in his heart. He is not a stone. He does not wish to be owned. He does not understand lies, he expects you to tell him the truth. If you break his trust it is worse than a curse. When you ride him, imagine you are part of him. This is the best way. Then the only way to ride him is with his will and your heart. Do you understand? Imagine you are him and he is you. Let him ride you. Believe him. He is always right. I have never known this horse to be wrong. Do you understand?'

Edward Vaudrey goes stone-kicking away with a face full of lines. He throws his hands in the air. What is this man talking about? It's a horse. He is nothing special; in fact he's an ill-disciplined savage who needs a good hard thrashing. Vaudrey does not trust Azarax, and where there is no trust there is no compassion. So, this horse does not wish to be owned? Well, I own the brute, dammit, he's mine and he's worth a fortune and maybe that's just all he's worth. Take him back to the Queen Dowager's, get into the regiment and then sell him. Sell him to Robert Byerley. He's rich and he's a fool for a fancy horse. He'll buy him.

* * *

Buda to Calais. A thousand miles. The rivers were few: the Leitha, the Raab, the Wein, the Rhine – all with good stone bridges. The streams were the problem. How many thousands of streams did they ford? Big streams, little streams, boggy streams, streams cut deep into the landscape. How many steep banks did they slither down? How many miles of waterlogged tracks leading to them? How many quagmires? How many insecure little wooden bridges spanning these streams have they gingerly crossed, one horse at a time, for fear of breaking through the rotting timber? How many rocky outcrops have they struggled up? How many days of being soaked in the saddle, how many days burned by the sun or dried by the wind? How often did they hear that hoof upon the fern? The strike on the ground? The even beat of the hooves, the music they make? They rode through Austria and Germany, resting at the inns and stables of small villages, then pressed on along disappearing tracks, through vast forests, black forests.

A thousand miles: a thousand miles with a horse and the ultimate goal of the journey is lost to the mind. The ground beneath the horse's hooves yields to its weight: another step along the way; but it is the end of the day that marks the diurnal journey. The passing detail is the journey: everything is noticed; the trees, the peasants working in the fields, the animals drawing carts, the churches and villages, the bells that peal from distant valleys lost from view. Somewhere a dog barks, a cow moos, a horse whinnies, an old man holds up a hand and waves. Strangers stop to talk, a meal is taken by a stream, in a forest, by a lake, in an inn. The horses graze the grasses: they cast their dark eyes to the horizon. They wish to be there. But they are patient and step out, a pace at a time, swiping at the grass-heads, snatching at the wild plums, reaching down for crab apples that drop on the path.

Every dimple in the ground, every hollow, every rut is noticed as the horseman passes by. The sky overhead is hard and clear and the head rings with the sound of birdsong. It is a shared experience: the weather is shared, the feel of sun on the skin, the bite of wind on the face, the misery of incessant rain. A sense of comradeship builds among the travellers and their horses. The man stands close to the horse at the end of the day and the horse moves close to him in the morning. If the man disappears from the horse's sight, the horse will call: he is the known point amongst all the unknown things around him. No other comradeship with a horse is so fine as to travel with one for a thousand miles.

A thousand miles: a thousand miles of heading in the same direction. A compass inhabits the body of a ridden horse, showing him the direction he needs to follow and after a week he will not depart from it. You can toss away your map, hurl away your astrolabe and you will invariably arrive at your goal. Trust the horse. The horse leads. The horse loves to see what lies round the next corner, he loves to see over the next brow, the next hill. He yearns to be in the distance, over there, where the blue of the mountains touches the blue of the sky. Sometimes the horse will cry out loud, in sheer exuberance: he is unfettered, without a boundary, so that he alone comprehends the world and its diversity and finds a place for himself in it. It is good for a horse to see the world at first hand, to share that experience with his rider, and sense the unspoken accomplishment of a land traversed. Then, a division occurs. As the man becomes more exhausted, the horse becomes stronger, and fitter, and glides along with his eyes glittering and neighs at the top of his high, piercing voice at the high-flying world to which he belongs.

He is joy to behold. His head is high, his muscles are honed: his legs are trim, his belly taut: his back is firm and smooth and the gloss on his coat sparkles under the sun. His hard blue hooves beat into the precious earth and he is the King of the World, and upon his proud back is a proud rider. The seyis pats the neck of the horse with a destiny.

17TH OCTOBER 1686

The trees are bronze, the land is wet, the air is wet, the horses' coats have tiny tears of mist attached to each of the lengthening hairs of their coats. The party moves in silence beneath the dripping, fluttering red, yellow and bronze leaves. Their way is strewn in a carpet of majestic colour, the footfalls of the horses soft upon it, the scent cool and peaty. Even the seyis is now wearing a worsted coat, his turban replaced by a jaunty red hat with a feather. When this exchange finally took place, there was a little ceremony involving the horse. Would his horse recognise him wearing the costume of a Spanish Netherlands woodsman?

The riders weave beneath a lattice of beech branches, releasing a slow, steady shower of fluttering yellow leaves. They halt in some woody nightshade enchanter's circle of green. Here they bang the pegs into the ground for their holed and decaying tents. Not a stone's throw away is a hovel, in which a grubby but elfine family hew an existence: a woodcutter's cottage in the depths of the forest. The wife was a spectacle the seyis could hardly believe, with her huge blue eyes, sunshine hair and round bosoms tumbling from beneath her trusses, a belle in the greenwood who smiles and conjures a meal out of nothing for this ravenous group of foreigners. The following morning they offer to pay for their evening's lodgings and simple, yet adequate meal. The money is pushed back into their hands. They ride away.

'Who were those men?'

Long after they have gone, a belle in the greenwood finds a dozen gold sovereigns in a bag of flour. The stuff that transforms lives, the beautiful loan, Christianity and Islam both. Somewhere a Ghazi is smiling. What was that fighting in Vienna and Buda all about? Mahşallah, Ozay! If we had known what I know now, you and I my friend, would have thrown away our weapons and planted cucumbers.

CALAIS. 2nd November 1686

Philip Marchand, purveyor of horses across the English Channel, appears from his hut both the better and the worse for wine, in discoloured breeches and red face, matching hose, a dark blue topcoat with yellow buttoned pocket stitching, lace corselet with wine stain (recent) and a black, greasy-rimmed sugar-loaf hat bearing a peacock feather. Claret-bloomed and jovial with twinkling blue eyes and a rogue's heart, his appearance is a mixture of art and accident. His business philosophy is to note the dress of the customer: the richer the apparel, the higher the price. He meets the party upon their arrival at the gates of the Calais dockyard, to determine what duty they must pay.

It is easy to calculate: the higher quality the horse, the higher its value, thus the higher the duty. 'Tis elementary economics,' he breathes, sitting on a sea-chest, and smiling greasily as he gathers a quill. He stabs it in a sticky-lidded blackened pot and reaches for his port books: 'Ah.. Lord Cutts, Lord Forbes, Lord Mountjoy, Lord Savile... then the duty will pass.' He puts the quill down, folds his pudgy hands on his ample lap, 'from this side anyway, to be gathered on t'other.' Then rising, hand on knee, heavily, he shuffles towards the grey dock and the slimy sea.

'My word, what strange horses, whatever are these? Arabs? Yes, indeed Arabs. From? Buda! Of course, of course. Turkish Arabs from Buda. Ah! The campaign! You were there? The news, yes it arrived on, let me see, the 9th September. Buda back in Christian hands. And the Turks are fled? It is said there was much spoil. Gold? Stones? Or just these... er... Arab... horses?'

Edward Vaudrey clears his throat and signals in self-conscious mumble the presence of Mr. James Fitzjames.

'Saints preserve us! The King's son! Your Most Royal Grace! Your men may take the horses to the stables yonder, and there are lodgings, fastidiously kept and swept, barely a cockroach per yard, by a Breton woman, d'you see? Person of quality – like your Highness. The ship? The ship, the... transport, will be here within the hour... naturally... of course, of course... well... two, perhaps... usually it arrives with the tide, so let us say, well, in fact, well, tomorrow, at, er, nine. Yes. Tomorrow morning. Wine?'

The ship, an inelegant flat-bottomed transport vessel, resembles a squat oak bathtub, with a snub bow, a fat hull and four masts. Men lug provisions aboard: cases of wine and brandy, barrels of salt beef and salt pork are swung aboard from yard arms. This is a merchantman and a transport. For those who own them, the goods are of higher value than the horses. Had the horses not been accompanied by a clutch of gentlemen, they would have suffered short shrift at the hands of Philip Marchand's black-toothed wharfmen.

Entry to the vessel by horse is effected through the loading port, a narrow door set amidships, to the second deck. It's an awkward arrangement, approached by an unrailed duckboard, over which the horses must pass. And along the length of which they gaze into the depths below and baulk, fore-feet spread-eagled. The horses take a few steps back. Whose idiotic idea is this? Are all the horses to be loaded through this absurd hole?

'You have to give them a good thrashing!' shouts Marchand, 'That will set them in. You don't take any nonsense from horses! Good God!'

Lord Cutts steps forward: he's a big man. Someone, somewhere in his lineage, must have had a fling with a wild-boar, leaving the progeny with its indelible stamp: little glittering piggy eyes, rough red skin, coarse, tufty grey hair, and long yellow teeth: 'Spare the whip and bring the Turk,' he growls at Marchand, who backs away, nodding: 'Anything you say, my Lord. Anything.'

The seyis has already spotted the problem. He enters the ship and demands lights. Marchand pulls a face. Apart from a few catastrophes, horses falling off the duckboarding and so forth, a good whipping has usually done the trick, so what is the problem? The seyis re-emerges and demands that the gaps in the duck-boarding be filled. Filled? Cover it so that the horses can't see through. It takes time but boarding is brought. Finally, the seyis takes Azarax and lets him look. He lets him feel the board, see within the ship and then Azarax steps carefully in through the loading port, followed by Lord Cutts' yellow dun. Cutts' horse has a very fine head and a neat muzzle, black mane and tail, black legs and a golden frame. Lord Cutts has been observing the seyis on his doru horse these past few weeks and has been learning to ride like a Turk. The horse is responding.

The Lord Cutts sneers at Marchand. 'Whips, be damned!'

It is not so easy to handle horses on the ship. The seyis' horse has stopped again. He is being asked to step down steep wood-baton planking. His ears are pricked and he has begun to paddle on the decking, pumping his fore feet like a foal. Now would not be a good time to rear. The seyis releases his grip on the rein: now is not the time to hold the horse tight. The grip needs to be released, thereby freeing the animal's head so that tension is lowered, rather than heightened. The horse needs time to see; to adjust. To adjust. The ship stinks. A stench of scours and sea water

222

rises from the bilges. The seyis feels the horse's whiskers touch his hand. He does not speak but stands quite still. One foot forward and the horse feels the plank. Still the seyis does not move. Let the horse breathe. Look around. No: don't offer him food, don't attempt to trick or distract him. Not now. One minute, two minutes and his mind is firm. Head down, Azarax takes the first step into the depths of this creaking, shifting hulk. There is a wistful look in the horse's eyes. He only just fits below the upper deck here. If he throws his head up he'll hit his poll. The seyis reaches up and runs his fingers along the wood of the deck above. It's just here, do you see? It is low. Mind your head.

Lots of noise as the other horses clatter down the planking. Keep them close, but not too close; if one stops, all stop. Down they come, breathy and with eyes rolling. This is not a good place for any horse to be, let alone a bunch of Steppe horses from wide open spaces.

There are tethers, separated by boarding. The horses are now standing beneath the waterline. 'Is this all right? Should they be beneath the waterline?' chomps Lord Cutts.

Mr Marchand, now peering down into the darkness acquaints him with the niceties of balance: twenty horses on deck would be a weight liable to set the ship at an angle, and do horses like to stand at an angle? No sir, so down they must go: horses are, to all intent, ballast, as far as this ship is concerned. Ballast. Nothing more.

The ship creaks. The windlass rope creaks. The block and tackle ropes creak, wind wails across the rigging, sea buffets the black wharves and slipways, and buffets back to the hull with a rhythmic slap. Black-winged gulls cry out. A bell from a distant buoy rings hollowly, across the water.

Down in the darkened depths of the ship, standing with the white-eyed, nervous horses the seyis breathes in a strong smell of tar and seawater, seaweed, and sweat. Directly above his head, on deck, Edward Vaudrey squints up into the November sky, at the high mizzen, the yard arms, the reefed sail, the rigging. The clouds scud at speed behind them and block out the sun. The clouds are stained grey, a cold gripping grey that chills to the bone. The capstan ropes tighten and creak.

A patch of sunlight is chased across the sea by the grey clouds. The wait continues. Two hours pass. What of the promised wind?

A cry rings out across the water, the transport is warped off the quay, a longboat blades her bow to the lee, and the great vessel moves in the water, and she flashes the stud-sail to clear the harbour.

The seyis already feels sick and they have barely left land. He tries the horses with feed: feed, the stabilizer of panic. Feed, the salve of the nervous horse: this is no trick, this is sustenance, this is whisky to the Scotsman, brandy to the Frenchman, slivovitsa to the Serb, Tokai to the Magyar, koumiss to the seyis. The temperature below deck rises. The seyis strips off his clammy topcoat, and, feeling both hot and cold at once, he walks between the horses, whispering them a little calm in the gloomy, claustrophobic, airless, salt and tar-scented, cobwebbed world around them.

A sudden boom and a lurch announce the dropping of the sails; ropes tighten against halyards. The horses' heads flick up. They pull at their tethers. Those that have selected their travelling companions move closer to them and lash out with teeth and feet at the others. 'Yavaş-yavaş ,' the seyis says, running his hand over their backs. Slowly the horses accustom themselves to this writhing world and find the angle best suited to balance the movement of the ship: the lurching, swaying, yawing movement. As the prow rises the horses shift again, but one falls and fights for its footing, starting a chain-reaction panic with the others. The seyis is quickly at its side and slams a board down for it to find its footing, then slackens its tether for it to rise. Softly, softly, he says: yavaş-yavaş. Wide eyes in the darkness, fluted nostrils: it is extraordinary how close the horses huddle to their friends.

Azarax has made a companion of Lord Cutts' yellow dun and they stand side by side with the planking between them, at one moment Azarax's head is across the dun's neck and then in the next moment the dun's head lies across Azarax's. They are a solid pair, though Azarax is the leader. He stands with his eyes glazed, breathing hard in the rising heat: so many horses, such little room, such poor ventilation. The air is putrefyingly foul. The seyis puffs out his cheeks: he bends forward, puts a hand to his mouth and then rushes up the planking to the quarter deck. He just makes the side of the ship before spraying the contents of his belly diagonally down the hull and into the slimy green sea below.

Distant white cliffs have slipped into view as, watery-eyed, he looks out into the grey rolling seascape and, now recovering, coughing, sitting sprawled on the deck, he watches them beat up and down on the horizon with every passing gust. James Fitzjames had pointed at them and spoken with reverence as though this was some kind of magical isle, which no amount of seamanship would allow them to reach. Perhaps that now-you-see-it-now-you-don't, white walled land, would always remain a foggy obscurity amidst the flying spume and grey skies, the creaking timber, the cracking of the great sails. The ship was battling in a brewing storm, but the seyis didn't know this, having never put to sea before. He imagined that

224

the banging and the groaning, the rolling, the being sent hurtling across the deck on his belly, the near-veering into the foaming waters, into the snapping mouths of monsters lurking in its ogre-green depths; the raging clouds and screaming wind, were all part of everyday seamanship. Down in the bilges, the horses are stamping, hock deep in a flotilla of sloshing horse dung and pieces of planking, boxes, items of random clothing. All this, the seyis thought, was an everyday part of sailoring. It is only when he sees the bearded captain on his knees running a rosary though his fingers that he stops to re-assess his views.

The day heaves past in a fury of wind and spume. Though he would prefer to be up aloft looking out to the level horizon, the seyis returns below decks and remains with the horses. Land did not seem so far away: why a mere day's ride, if that, yet the approach is interminable. And it is cold on the upper deck: a damp cold that drives in beneath the skin, deep to the bone. The seyis shivers: never before has he felt cold such as this. Even the horses have reacted. The booming and shuddering of the ship is accompanied by ghostly echoes: eerie wails and groans. Strange fluting sounds, muffled thumps and groans: this dark sea is alive with the ghosts of dead men and dead horses.

Darkness falls in one cold drop: lamps are strung about. Someone shouts that food is ready. Can the seyis eat? He holds his gut and voids bile. Mahşallah, this is a journey through hell. Never again will I do this. When will it end?

The sea churns on. The horses stand with their ears back and heads lowered. They are suffering now. They have ceased eating. Their eyes are dull. Even Azarax's eyes are dull. But slowly, the buffeting dies away and now comes the sound of running water, as though the whole vessel were being filled up from bow to stern by a stream. Laughter breaks out above in a wild, happy explosion. Lord Cutts is shouting. He is King of the Party. Why is he not affected by this heaving hell? It is night. Black, obdurate, moonless, starless night.

The seyis snatches what rest he can beside his silent horse, standing pastern-deep in a sloshing mess of horse-dung, water and vomit. The smell is so overpowering that the seyis' belly has tautened to a constant knot. He straddles the feed trough in front of the horse through which the horse once again picks. The seyis balances precariously with his mouth agape and head thrown back against the wood bulwarking. Surely it would be better to die now? The nightwatch flips the hourglass and strikes the one o'clock bell. Ding-ding. Footsteps clomp overhead: leather on oak. The ropes creak. Sails are raised and lowered and the ship wallows on. Is everyone, except the seyis, feeling well? Ding-ding. Ding-ding. A man shouts from afar. The horses are thirsty, but the water is foul. Lord Cutts' dun thrashes with a forefoot. He's had enough of this. But he's thrashing the fouled water under his belly. More bells. The voice again. The wind has dropped. The seyis looks up into the darkness above his head, dimly lit by dying lamps. Is this night ever going to end?

The water rushes on and the night stumbles by. Hour upon hour. Will the seyis find himself trapped in the bilges with twenty terrorised horses as the sea from above bursts in upon them through the shattered timber? The thought alone brings him out in yet another frozen sweat.

On and on the ship plunges and rises, like a vast slow horse, wallowing in the gluey grey mountains that rise and fall all around. Wind squeals through the ratlines, and then abruptly, the ship swings to port with a lurch and then ceases pitching. Now it glides. The texture of the wind appears to have altered and the pull of the sails brings the ship swiftly through the water.

More voices now, from another direction. The seyis frowns. Where are they coming from? Muffled voices. He ought to go up and see, but knows now is not the time to leave. He must stay with the horses. They are scenting. They have raised their heads. He copies them. Can he smell land? There is a different scent emitting from the water itself. Also a changed atmosphere. A cannon fires from a long way off. What? Are they going to war?

The seyis must look, must see what is happening. On hands and knees he scrabbles up the planking to the second deck and he peers through the windlass ports: land one side, and land the other. They are in an estuary. Seagulls. Low lying land, like a swamp. The sun is rising behind them. They are going west, into this cold and dismal land, in which even the air is wringing wet. And look at this water! It is grey: mud grey. Impenetrable. Lifeless. What of the fish-filled, turquoise Bosphorus now? What of the sun-burnished diamonds in the water: the pale ashlar of the minarets of the Blue Mosque? What of the hot, dry air in the locust trees? What of the dolphins? The crystal Marmara Sea? What has the seyis come to?

A bell strikes seven times.

They are all on deck in the pale light of dawn: Lord Cutts, James Fitzjames, Edward Vaudrey, the Lords Forbes, Savile and Mountjoy. Dark rings shadow their eyes. But there is joy in their faces. They point across the land at distant spires and villages.

A cry rises from below: a voice only the seyis recognises. That high pitched call: where are you?

The seyis turns back down into the gloom. Wait, wait: not long now. The seyis returns to the feed rack and sits, while Azarax sniffs his hands asking: what is this place? Tell me. The seyis smiles and runs a finger across the horse's forehead, rotates it in the whorl between his eyes: making a crescent moon. He traces a finger down his neck. Wait, Azarax. One more hour. Two. There is more light filtering in this black hole now. Is it day yet?

A thump on the keel alarms the horses and they snap back on their tethers. Then another and another. It sounds as though some vast lead-booted creature is trying to clamber aboard. The ship's forward movement is eased. A grating sound emits from the starboard. The seyis listens, as rat lines take the strain of bare feet and reefing sail.

The ship's progress halts entirely. Wood bangs onto stone, and there is the sound of running rope.

A head appears at the top of the planking: Edward Vaudrey, red-cheeked and grinning. He nods once to the seyis, who is slowly emerging from the darkness like the living dead, dark rings under worn-red eyes on his sallow, death-mask face. Vaudrey waves, like a child.

'Welcome to England!'

The seyis frowns. 'England?'

Edward Vaudrey nods and proffers his hand; a positive, friendly gesture. The seyis takes it, weakly, in a clammy, uncertain hold.

'Welcome Mr Seyis, you are most welcome! You and your horses! You are in Deptford, near London.'

It is 4th November 1686.

- 18 -

Byerley's Bid

The loading port drops with a heavy thump onto the stone wharf and the sound of the outside world creeps into the ship, along with the yellow-grey light of a damp November afternoon. Already fidgeting at their tethers, eager to be free of their waterlogged prison, the horses thrash with their forelegs, whinny and cry out. Leather-soled feet stride swiftly across the decking above. Rough men, stock handlers, unshaven 'horse experts' in holed canvas pinafores swagger noisily down the planking into the gloom below. They have done this a thousand times. These men were born with horses, weren't they? Handled them all their lives: there's nothing anyone can tell them about horses. Horses? In getting horses off ships, there's one method and one only. Arm yourself with a good, short stick and at the first sign of any hesitancy, lash out. If the horse refuses again, lash out harder – preferably across the face. Poke them in the ribs. Hit them across the hocks. Bend their tails up. Show them who's boss. Then they're straight up the plank and out, no mistake.

One of the men thrashes a horse before he's even undone his tether. Unsurprisingly, the horse flattens his ears and fires out, both hinds. The sticks rain down: 'You brute!'

The seyis buries his face in his hands and groans. The fragile trust of the herd is destroyed. A horse's nerve is a kite: it may be kept aloft and flying, for ever. But one wrong gust and it is gone, forever. Hind quarters dip, heads toss and panic reigns.

It is not true that a horse will not stand on a fallen man – as the first man to fall on the planking discovers. These are big, fit Turk horses. They may have been at sea but they have not lost their spirit. Uphill is when a horse exhibits power, and the planking is uphill. The outside world lies above and the horses know it. As the horses scramble for the planking, the sticks are wielded more savagely. The seyis seizes a cane as it lashes down. 'No!' he shouts. An elbow from a tattooed man slams into his belly and he's sent scuttling backward and cracks his head against the bulwarking.

'Stay your hand there, damn your eyes!' shouts Lord Cutts from above. The tattooed man's face contorts insolently. He curses and seizes Azarax's tether.

The tattooed man may be a 'horse expert': he may like to think he was born with horses, he may boast and do tricks and have unloaded thousands of horses from the bowels of thousands of transports – but he has never encountered a horse like this before. This is no child's pony: no highly-strung little brown horse frightened of his own shadow. This is not a horse who leaps at the first sound of a rustle in a pile of leaves. This is no half-baked, common hack who backs away at the sight of a whip. This is a horse who has faced the pancerni Cossack in the full fury of battle: this is a horse who has faced cannon and grape shot, musket, lance and sabre: he's not afraid of a man with a stick.

Fire flashes Azarax's his eyes.

The reaction is so fast, so violent, that the man utters not a single sound. What happens is way beyond his lifetime's experience. Even as he is hurled across the floor he is unable to cry out for the shock is so acute.

The seyis rises from the bulwarking, hand on his belly: that thump in the ribs had been hard. Welcome to England. So this is how they do things here, is it? Why, a child who has never seen a horse before would have acted more competently.

Azarax is the last horse to stomp up from the bowels of *The Deptford Garnet*, and he now stands blinking on the King's Wharf, Deptford, swaying on his sea legs, sniffing this brand new world.

He and his seyis gaze about. If the seyis felt sea-sick before, he feels land-sick now. He spits as if to rid the vision of the tattooed man from his mind. He follows the sweep of his horse's gaze: there are no lateen sails here, no golden wharves. No fishing nets draped out like abstract shadows, warming in the sun. Deptford is no Golden Horne with pale minarets and hyaline sky: no silks, no lingering scent of bergamot, no oleanders, no cedars, no fabulously mounted hassa sipahi laughing astride their glossy horses. This is a grey, be-fogged landscape composed of the hulls of half-made ships. The words 'Phineas Pett, Master Shipwright,' are painted on a sign further along the wharf where the 1,500 ton, 100 gun *Royal Sovereign* is having her hull recalked. Waddling, busy-body ship-handlers clutching manifests scuttle along the wharf without looking up, scoundrels and ragamuffins loaf about the capstans and cargoes; plug-chewing matelots load boxes onto smaller vessels lying along the quay; dirty little boys play on oily ropes. The wharf is covered in buckets of pitch, endless piles of boxes of grim-looking vegetables, boxed and salted fish, barrels of brine with floating green hams, bales of cloth, bundles of wood, stacks of repair cord-lumber – oak mostly, and elm – and heaps of shredded canvas being sorted by wrinkled old women in shawls and long, dirty black baggy hessian skirts. And, in wild contrast: squealing children, banners, waving flags, Christian standards, sprinkled Holy Water, kisses, congratulations, music, dancing, beer, wine. The seyis' hand is squeezed along with the rest as he follows his companions through a cheering human gauntlet. His horse is patted and greatly admired, along with the rest; the returning triumphant heroes and their magnificent triumphant horses.

If there had been an ounce of pity in the seyis' heart for the broken man lying in the bowels of the ship, his eyes did not reveal it. A thought drifts through his mind: I know now what I did not know when you were a colt, Azarax. I know now why Ali-aga Izobegović had eyes like a lizard. He had witnessed savagery until it no longer touched him. Something terrible slips into the human heart then. If you live without love, you will die without love. Somewhere, in the mines of Vienna, Azarax, somewhere at the walls of Buda, something terrible slipped into my heart. I feel no compassion for my fellow men. Even this joy leaves me unmoved.

The crowds cheer: 'Look! A Turk!'

Do they know who he is? Does he care? One minute the seyis is in a black hole with a man he could quite calmly stand over and watch his horse kick to near death and the next minute he is surrounded by this jubilant crowd, which could turn on him in an instant and rip him to pieces.

He glances quickly into his horse's eyes. I don't care, Azarax. It is you who are the Sufi. You are the Master. When the pupil is ready the Master will appear. The tattooed man, the pupil, will have learned the one lesson he needed most in the world to be taught and he was lucky: he received it straight from the Master himself. He will remember that for as long as he lives; he will never handle a horse in that way again.

Such innocence. Look at Azarax gazing about, sniffing the air, unafraid, inquisitive. Look at the rigging on the ships, the sea-stroked, sea-weeded wharf steps, the murky river, the hundreds of people, the flags. How are you reacting to this, Azarax? No, it is not war. It is the opposite of war. Give me the breath of a Karaman stallion, the sound of his feet on the ground and the high flying wind. Perhaps we should have gone to Istanbul when the baş imrahor asked. Or maybe I alone should have gone to Istanbul when the baş imrahor asked. It is me who is in the wrong place, not you. What awaits me here, Azarax? Nothing. But what awaits you here, Azarax?

The party's servants chain-gang the saddles along a line and the seyis is handed his. Edward Vaudrey is shouting something. The noise from the cheering crowd is overwhelming. How did these people know they were arriving? How did they know to be here, at this dock? The seyis looks back at the transport. Up in the rigging a flag flies: a strange flag. It was not there yesterday.

**

News of the imminent arrival of King James II's son James Fitzjames and his cortège had been dispatched sometime before. In fact news of James Fitzjames' adventures in the service of the Hapsburg Emperor had been galloped at full speed back to England from the moment he set out for Buda. The King had received a stream of missives from Edward Vaudrey recounting every inch of their journey across Europe; he had received communication from Etheridge in Ratisbon, from Lord Taafe in Hungary. There had been rumours – of all kinds – and then on 7th September, exactly one week after Buda had been stormed, a dusty courier had burst hot-hoofed into London bawling his head off.

'Buda is fell! The Christians is victorious!'

The crowds had gone mad.

On this news the King had immediately ordered that prayers be held, but had decided the service of thanksgiving could not be held until 11th September. They would be held at Bow, in the Chapel Royal and at Westminster Abbey. They would celebrate and give thanks for the wresting of Buda from its century and a half of darkness and for the safe return of the King's son.

James Fitzjames had also sent messages ahead from the Spanish Netherlands to be taken on a merchantman. He had thought of loading on the Rhine and taking the same vessel, along with all the horses. But he recalled the many reports of horses foundering on these long unreliable seas journeys, becoming distempered, holding their heads low and ears loose, running at the nose, filling in the leg, becoming tucked up at the motion of the ship, and, one by one, dying in their dismal quarters. He did not wish that. These Turk horses had a high value. They had been bought at the cost of men's lives and in England horses such as these were at a premium. They could scarcely be had, their breeding was slow and all their foals pledged before they were born. His own grey stallion he could turn to handsome profit and his friend, the impecunious Edward Vaudrey, could do the same. The two yellow duns were to be gifts for Her Majesty.

The seyis stands, confused and exhausted on the harbour front. Everything seemed to be passing in a dream. The tattooed man has emerged from the ship, clutching a hand, red-faced, veins standing out in his neck. He is angry, yelling God knows what, his voice is lost in the roar of the crowd. His appeal to Lord Cutts is cut short. When the man tugs his lordship's sleeve, begging for attention, he is felled by a lordly boot. There is no second chance for the fool.

An armed escort for the King's son arrives: a mounted section from the Queen Dowager's Cuirassiers. With their serious faces, they look like the executioner's cavalcade bound for the scaffold: red coats, sea-green facings, cravats and beaver hats with feathers, muskets and sabres hanging from baldrics. They wait stoically on their nodding bay horses until James Fitzjames' party is mounted. The Queen Dowager's Cuirassiers are a fit-looking lot, well turned-out and trim to the hoof. The seyis approves – except for the breed of their horse, which is uneven – though the horses themselves are reasonable enough and would make excellent third mounts for the servants of an asperless Rumeli sipahi. The men of the Queen Dowager's have noticed the quality of the Turk horses in front of them.

Feet in stirrups, the party ride off, high above out-held hands.

They clip away from the Royal docks and the cheering crowds, away from the flags and the flying hats, past Sayes Court, home of John Evelyn, the diarist.

'Look – over there!' Lord Cutts points to the grimy pall ahead. 'London!'

They are upon it in the half hour and the seyis finds himself riding Azarax over the strangest bridge he has ever seen. These English people have found a bizarre way of spanning a great river. Across it they have built lozenge-shaped footings, which squeeze the water beneath, thus forcing it to run faster, and through these channels, madcap boatmen shoot between the arches with great exclamations of joy. It is both a bridge and a row of houses. It reminds him a little of the Grand Bazaar in Istanbul, having something of its quality, yet this edifice is open to the sky with this raging torrent roaring beneath it. It is possible for the seyis to see in the windows of the bridge's houses as he rides though; into the awnings, the shrouded galleries, the latticed glass. He meets looks of amiable curiosity: he waves; they wave back.

There are stalls selling bolts of cloth and oysters and strange ugly fish, nets and bags, muskets and jackets, old and new, ambergris and oils, murky medicines in suspicious bottles with doubtful corks, wines and beverages, clutches of hens tied by their legs, geese, ducks in wooden cages, bundles of faggots and heaps of shiny wet coal. Everyone is shouting their wares. Hundreds of people crowd on this bridge-street, with horses and traps delivering goods, and children driving pigs and bullocks. Nor has he ever seen so many people smoking pipes. More even than the nargileh houses in Beyazit. This bridge-house or house-bridge extends a good distance because the river is so broad and this appears to be the only crossing. There are also many ferries which plug back and forth across the current, bearing all manner of things: coach and horses, just horses, men and horses, women and cows, just cows – not dissimilar to the small, brown cattle of Anatolia. Though the seyis looks for water buffalo, he spots none.

The horses he sees, though, are ill-conditioned. They are calloused and sore, skin and bone, eyes full of fear. Their riders – or grooms – appear to show little understanding of them. Only occasionally does he see a man well-mounted on a good horse, but even then the horse is small, and ordinary, without style.

The seyis' own stamping, taut stallion attracts instant attention and pointing fingers. Behind him men stop and, hands on hips admire as he goes snorting by. He hears voices whispering 'Turk', and young women – brazen young women, in muddy-bottomed skirts and uncovered heads – point with their stubby pink fingers and whisper, 'Oohh – handsome!'

Stallions are showy creatures and respond to flattery: they prance and dance, this way and that, with plenty of potency, lots of foam, fluted nostrils, ears up, eyes forward, necks arched, chewing their bits. 'Look at my muscles!' they seem to say. 'Look at my hard, black legs! Look at the power in my quarters. I am a sight such as you have never seen, gaze on and admire!'

***

Across the bridge and along the side of a high brick wall, the party swings up to the right and presently the horses clatter beneath a low, wide, limestone arch, flanked on either side by turreted towers, made of brick and stone. Enormous iron gates swing open to reveal a wide grass and cobbled courtyard. Darkness has already descended. Much to the seyis' surprise he sees men lighting lights with long tapers, outside, which dig out the evening shadows from the corners and cast everything in a honeyed glow, which seems needed in so misty a land, though the golden torchlight fails to dispel the clammy dampness, the cold and the strong smell of human ordure and urban grime.

He and Azarax look around, and the seyis surmises that he is in military barracks. He learns later that this vast place covers acre upon acre of ground on the river front, all the way from Charing Cross to Westminster Hall. Elegant flights of steps run down to the Thames. The brick and stone buildings are linked over the London-to-Westminster road by two dressed limestone footbridges.

The Queen Dowager's escort leads the party straight in under the arch and across the cobbles to a long, brick and stone-buttressed building unlike anything the seyis has seen before. The windows are small and latticed, and here and there the walls have been patched with dressed ashlar. A low stone arch in a building opposite is crowned by a crest, embossed in relief, of a rose over a rose. Leafless climbing roses cover walls. The place exudes a sense of peace, stability and permanence.

James Fitzjames dismounts and the party follows suit, the seyis landing lightly on his feet beside Azarax who gazes about, much intrigued by his novel surroundings.

'What place this?' the seyis murmurs, moved by the grandeur around him.

'It is the Palace of Whitehall,' announces Edward Vaudrey, proudly.

The seyis gazes about. He seems not to comprehend. 'The King's House,' Edward Vaudrey explains. Ornamental gardens framed with box hedges in geometrical design stretch out into the darkness. There is a fountain, and beyond it glints the river they have just crossed.

The seyis lays a hand on the horse's neck. Both have been subdued into silence.

'Well, well. In the palace of a King. Your coat has darkened Azarax, even more so than before: in this light, in this place, you look almost black.'

The seyis stifles a yawn. Will they give him a decent bed, he wonders? Edward Vaudrey beckons and he stumbles forward beside his horse. Azarax's head is low. All the horses are quiet. The Buda party is quiet. This boisterous group has suddenly turned into a sober procession. Even Lord Cutts has stopped talking. James Fitzjames, Edward Vaudrey, the Lords Forbes, Mountjoy and Savile all walk in silence beside their horses.

The horses are led into an enormous stable: it has the feel although not the design of the stables in Buda. It lacks the fan vaulting. But it has instead great oak beams, small carved stanchions with gargoyle heads on the individual stables, beautiful filigreed lights, knurled stall ends, there are black iron bars, wooden feed troughs, and long oat straw, plaited around the edges. It's magnificent, but the seyis sees a problem immediately. How can you tell someone in a language you barely know that these horses belong to the wind? Except for the night on the boat, these horses have been travelling in the open air for weeks: they have lived beneath the skies, the sun, the rain and the forest canopy. They are used to birdsong, to a view of the distance, to the men on their backs laughing and arguing, spitting and coughing, cursing. Their home has been among flies and dust and they have endured hail and long black nights in woodlands stirred with the sounds of foxes and wild boar, rabbits and weasels, broken by the shrieks of owls. Sometimes they have stayed in stables on their way but they have sensed these were temporary arrangements, to be abandoned the next morning. The constant walking has made them fit: pure air has filled their lungs. To lock them now, in a stable, and expect them to stay put, to live there, is a tall order. Moreover, they need to be able to see each other, need to be at least within scenting distance. The seyis attempts to put his concerns to Lord Cutts.

'Nonsense!' says he. 'Put them together: whatever for? Just pack them anywhere. Lucky to have a roof I should say.'

The shadows under the seyis' eyes deepen. He hasn't the energy to insist. Let the horses make the point. Azarax is shown a stable by a lad and the seyis leads him in. Where are the others? Out of sight. What does Azarax do? Shouts his head off. And does anyone know why – apart from his seyis?

The stable lad is only ten years old: his expression hangs somewhere between awe and outright terror. He stands on tip-toe ready to make a bolt for it with his hands clapped against the wooden stable walls, staring at the foreign seyis and his mad horse. The seyis ungirths the horse, takes off the saddle, drops the bit carefully out of his mouth and says, 'Azarax,' to the lad, then again, patting the monster: 'Azarax.'

The little boy's eyes widen. What does Azarax mean? It probably means 'This horse eats little boys.' The seyis points to the horse's mouth: 'Eat,' he says. The little boy's eyebrows fill his forehead. He presses himself against the boards. 'You mean he's hungry – for horse food?' The boy bolts for the door and dashes off, returning within the minute with a bucket of black oats. The seyis pulls a face. Oats? Black oats? For this horse? He puts a grain in his mouth and bites: if anything is going to make this horse go insane, it's black oats.

'Is there any arpa? – What's the English word for arpa? Why is it that the one word I need slips my mind the very moment I need it? I shall remember it in the dead of night, when I don't need it. Have you not got something a bit less – explosive? No? You see, these black oats are beautiful, but to this horse, they are like feeding him edible gunpowder. Maybe I am just too tired. Doesn't matter. Put the oats in the trough.'

Azarax's head is up and he is chewing: he definitely approves. He adores black oats. Which horse doesn't? But try riding them after they've had a belly-full. Hay has also been provided. Beautiful stuff: long, hard and green. This is some welcome – but then – this is some horse. And what's happening at the other end of the stable? All the other Turk horses are yelling their heads off. 'Goodness,' shouts Lord Cutts, 'aren't they happy to be here!'

No they are not. They're planning to gang up in the middle of the stable and batter the place to pieces.

What can you do?

Leave it to the horses.

The tallet loft the seyis is shown is as comfortable as a tallet loft can be: bare boards, a tiny window overlooking a stone-tile roof, a table, a candle and a glow of heat emitting from a small fire. There is a billet and blankets with clean linen sheets and even a down pillow: such luxury. A piss-pot, jug, basin, table and chair complete the furnishings. The water in the jug has, the seyis believes, a suspicious scent. He remembers the crystal stream that pours into the stone trough at the medrese in Ali-aga Izobegović's timar.

It is the first time he has been alone for years.

He is exhausted but he has been well fed and has a comfortable bed and his horse is in the safest place he could be, with the best food a horse could have, in a stable and untethered, and the seyis cannot sleep, of course. Sleep is as elusive as that word he had needed earlier: it flies from you if you think about it. Stop thinking about it.

'I am not thinking about it. I am thinking about everything else. What on earth am I doing? Why am I here? I am unable to talk to anyone. They are suspicious of me here. They will make life hard for me. I should have gone to Istanbul. I ignored the signals. Genghis: even the man's name was the same as Ali-aga Izobegović said in the same breath. What was that, if not a sign? I will never find peace. What is Azarax going to do here? Be the horse of the King? I've been down this road before. Barley! that is the English word for arpa. I must remember to ask for barley. Barley. Will I remember the word in the morning?'

It is only when the reveille sounds that his mind is still. His breathing deepens. The distress that has kept him in turmoil all night subsides: a familiar image replaces it. A retreat. A hallowed place.

The mares graze in the heat of the sun. As they swipe at the grasses they swish their tails at the big iridescent blue horseflies. He can hear their teeth chewing the hard stems. They graze without concern, there is nothing for them to fear. The sun is hot, the breeze is buttery, the leaves of the locust trees flicker. Beyond is a hot plain and in the far distance, like a bundle of brown satin, lie the quilted mountains. Between the mares and the mountains, a river glistens. The seyis rises and walks among the mares, running his fingers through their fine tails and manes then he wanders slowly down to the river where two stallions graze on the river bank. 'Bora!' he calls, and a beautiful head flicks up. He waves. 'Malik!' he cries out, and the big slow horse half raises his head then resumes his grazing. The river is clear and runs shallow over the pebbles, little diamonds of light refracting from the high sun. The breeze stirs the reeds on the river bank, a golden oriole calls from the slivova trees. The cicadas ring out and the sun is warm on his back. The two stallions graze quietly. Way in the distance, in the blinding light, is a lone figure, a young girl, yo-yoing wool. She turns her face to him and appears suddenly much closer: she is remarkably beautiful. Her hair is deep auburn and is glossy and fine under her brightly coloured head scarf, edged with tiny cowrie shells. Her teeth are even and white. She smiles and her face illuminates: her high cheek bones sculpt her elegant face: her chin is firm, her eyes a deep, even brown. Her eyebrows are fine; her eyelashes are pure black so that her eyes appear to be lined with kohl and the whites of her eyes are dazzling. She is exquisite.

Her tight, many-buttoned bodice is made of taffeta. Her heavy skirt is fashioned of coarse striped cotton, dyed red and green and held tight to the waist with plaited wool, black and white. She wears naal, fashioned from one single strip of camel hide, bound round and round to make strong, long-lasting sandals. The instep of her small feet and the backs of her hands are a gallery of whorls and wheels, four legged creatures, camels or goats or sheep or all three mixed into one fantastical beast, with stars and a crescent moon crudely daubed in henna upon her golden skin. She turns away and retreats to the distance.

Where is Azarax?

***

Where is Azarax? Azarax is lashing about in his stately stable, kicking the door off its hinges and screaming for his breakfast, that's where Azarax is.

The stable lad who should be feeding him is not going to put a foot near this flashing-eyed, flat-eared, tail-swishing monster who plans to shatter the whole stable to pieces and come bursting out and eat him.

The seyis appears at a run, tucking in his clothes. A seyis rising so late would have had to endure the punishment of the baş imrahor: to stay awake all night, every night, for months watching over the horses and if once he closed his eyes then he might expect to join the decomposing concubines stitched into in their sacks with cannon balls, swaying at the bottom of the Marmara Sea.

The troopers have been teasing these horses. The seyis senses it immediately.

These Turk stallions are strangers in a strange land, out-of-place exotics, and because they are different, they are the object of the taunt. When the seyis appears Azarax calms down, though he still huffs and stomps around the stable floor. One thing is certain about this horse: he has a way of announcing his presence.

The troopers groom their horses, mocking the actions of the seyis: aping his Turkish gestures, acting the fool. There is no jolly welcome here: no hand held out to the stranger, the foreigner feeling his way. No: these are troopers, men in a gang, longing for some good, ugly bullying. They gather strength from their numbers and will pick on the odd man out because he is the odd man out – but if they were on their own and had to face him individually, they wouldn't dare. This man is a Turk, isn't he? The enemy. What's a Turk doing in the Royal Stables?

They leave the seyis to find feed and hay for his horse on his own. Barley? Did he say barley? What's wrong with oats? Oh we see, our oats not good enough for his horse, eh? No there isn't any barley. They lift not a finger to help him.

The Lords Cutts and Mountjoy, Forbes and Savile appear suddenly in high spirits, bursting through the opened stable doors like a ray of sunshine. They greet the seyis happily. He receives pats on the back, his hand is shaken: 'I do not know what we should have done without you!' growls Lord Cutts through his yellow tushes, 'I shall miss you my boy!' He orders that their horses are tacked and, within the hour, all the Lords and grandees and adventurers of the Buda contingent had left, clattering across the cobbles, into the oblivion of a misty November morning. But not one of them had left without palming the seyis a gold coin.

The troopers whistle softly, grooming their horses. Mmm. Maybe they ought to be a bit careful about this one.

Half an hour later the King himself appears, with James Fitzjames and Edward Vaudrey, just as Azarax has calmed himself and now stands as demure as a well-fed calf in a sunny pen.

The King is a tall, slightly built man with watery red-rimmed grey eyes, pasty complexion and ugly, indented lips dipped at the corners of his mouth in the manner of a man who has offended his own soul. He fidgets with his silver-topped cane; he snuffles and clears his throat, pulls at his cloak and keeps looking behind him as though something or someone were stealing up on him. He studies the two yellow duns and declares that they would make admirable carriage horses – a weeping crime, thinks the seyis, for two splendid Turanian saddlebreds. Then his attention turns to the seyis and his doru horse – Edward Vaudrey's bay horse, Azarax himself. The King walks towards the stable in which the stately horse stands and as he reaches the stable door, the horse makes a lunge at him, his ears back, eyes blazing, teeth bared. The King reels, cane flying, cloak beneath his feet, pulling him down and is caught at the last moment by his son James Fitzjames, and saved the ignominy of the stable gutter.

The full force of the attack was arrested by the seyis who had had the presence of mind to stand beside the stable door as the king approached, in the event of just such an occasion as this. Because what the seyis felt about this man, the King, his horse also felt about this man and the only difference was that the horse did not withhold his feelings. The seyis laid a hand on the horse's muzzle and rattled off something sharp in Turkish. The horse desisted from further aggression and backed off yet he continued to mill around his stable, eyes blazing and ears flat, defying the King to take one step toward him. Composing himself as best he could, the King nodded a face-saving 'Upon my word, this is a spirited creature,' before dismissing himself with a waft of a lace handkerchief. In his scuffed white hose, he swaggered through the centre of the stable, flourishing his ebony cane in an attempt to brush off the events of the last few minutes in an extravagant show of pomp.

Curious things bind men together.

No other single act could have ignited comradeship so swiftly. As soon as the King and his retinue are out of sight, the troopers explode into laughter: they burst out guffawing, slapping their knees and holding their bellies. Did you see what he did? Did you? And whereas not half an hour before they had been a surly, hard-bitten mob, unwilling to share the steam off the midden with the seyis, now they are delighted with him and even more so with his lunatic horse. 'Pity he never connected! By Jupiter, that's a handy horse to have about when that King comes courting! Come here, Mr Turk, what's this horse's name then?'

***

Whatever political undercurrent is at work, or why it is that these men appear to dislike their King, the seyis neither knows nor cares. It is none of his concern: his concern is horses and wisely, he confines himself to his subject.

Nor is the seyis aware, during the winter months in which he lives and works with the Queen Dowager's Cuirassiers, that a Royal Warrant is issued conveying instruction for the bestowal of arms on James Fitzjames, his male heirs and descendants, in January 1687. Nor does he know of the proposal of marriage by James Fitzjames to the Duke of Newcastle's daughter.

Nor does he comprehend what Colonel James Fitzjames' investiture is all about, when from a Captain he is elevated to Colonel of the Third Troop of The Queen Dowager's, Lord Lieutenant of Hampshire, Baron of Bosworth, Earl of Teignmouth and Duke of Berwick: all this at the age of seventeen. Nor does Edward Vaudrey's knighthood at Windsor Castle by His Majesty King James II on 28th May 1687 mean anything to him.

The seyis grooms Azarax, he exercises him in the stable compounds, he rides him to the barracks at Hounslow and back, pausing only to contemplate the meaning of his fate, to wonder where and to what it is leading.

***

The winter is long, and the seyis becomes a familiar face about the barracks; the man who is, but who is not, of the regiment; the man who appears to harbour no resentments, and who has a skill with horses that no-one else shares. His calmness pervades all he does: impossible horses are brought to his touch and he returns them tractable, without the use of a raised voice, whip or spur. Even on the troopers, his presence in the barracks has a strange, quietening effect.

The troopers stand with their chins on their arms peering over the low wall to the quarter meadow one day.

'Look at that horse!' Eustace Poyntz, the pot-bellied farrier says, pointing at the seyis riding Azarax. 'Look at him swing his tail. Sign of a happy horse that is, no mistake. Walks like he is floating. Like he is treading on little bags of air. But every sinew in that horse is fit to spring at the next instant. Proud as proud can be, that horse of his. Do you know why? I'll tell you why! That man has never let him down. That's why. He's let him be a horse. Let him be a stallion. Hasn't tried to force him to be what he isn't, like some showy exhibit. No, he's left him alone to be himself. To find himself. To know himself. Proud to be the stallion he is. That horse knows that he always has a friend – not a master – a friend, an ally – someone to trust. Now how many people have horses that trust them? How often have you let your horse down? Even here, in these barracks, our horses don't trust us. But look at him. Look at those horses, they trust him already: they know he is not going to let them down. He makes them feel safe; secure. As if he and they are part of each other. Do you see?'

On another occasion, the troopers give the seyis a tricky black mare to school. He leads her to the quarter meadow and mounts.

'Look!' Eustace Poyntz says to the young troopers: 'Do you see what he's doing now? You look closely. He anticipates her. That's what he's doing. He knows what she's going to do before she does. Look – see? Every single time. There! Look at that! He knew that mare was going to turn there before she did. He was there before her. Then he pushed her into what she was going to do, so that she thought that he thought the same as her. Look, he keeps doing it, all the time! He isn't resisting her, see? And in a very short while she will do what he wants her to do because it will feel like she is thinking it. They will become united, her will and his, who is doing the thinking will merge and very soon, they will think the same. They will be one. They will be one because he will show her what's best for her and she will do it because it is. He's got her in his hand. I'll tell you something about that: that's the first man I seen who understands horses better than they understand themselves. That's his secret. He's a real master, that fellow is.'

***

On 29th May 1687 a fit, self-assured, straight-backed young man breezes into the stables. His hair is tied in a black bow at the nape of his neck and he wears a light brown coat with a turquoise weskit. He is accompanied by Sir Edward Vaudrey.

The fat farrier Eustace Poyntz spots him immediately: 'Oi! Fellahs!' he bawls to the troopers, 'The Captain!' He lays aside the herbs he'd been dispensing and signalling the others to gather round, crowd the young man, squeezing his hand: 'Your Honour,' he says, 'we's been missing you!' The troopers hold out their hands: 'You are welcome Captain, most welcome!'

The young man raises an eyebrow, 'Such touching loyalty, you dreadful rascals,' he says grasping out-held hands, 'I didn't know you cared. Tom, how are you? And Graeme – still the cornet, I see? Master Farrier Mr Poyntz, still killing horses? And how is Mr. Barrett, and you, young Steven? Have they let you loose on lance drill yet?'

The newly-knighted Sir Edward Vaudrey stands aside, bleakly. He had not expected this. This captain lost his commission, didn't he? So why is he so popular? He looks down at his feet. The captain excuses himself from the troopers and walks straight up to the seyis whom he'd noticed as soon as he entered the building.

He holds out a hand: 'And you, I presume, are Mr Seyis, the Turkish groom, of whom we have all heard so much?'

The seyis blinks. He has not looked into eyes as clear as this since Ozay's. His eyes are exactly the same colour. He bows. The Captain appreciates good manners: in all classes of person. He had heard that Eastern manners were particularly delicate.

'Robert Byerley. My pleasure.'

Destiny! That face! The art of physiognomy fascinates the Turkish mind. Character might be read from a face as clearly as bell rings across a valley. Character is laid bare in flesh, scripted, etched, chiselled, cast in the angle of the head, the directness of the look, moulded in the lips and expressed in the set of the mouth. It is written in the cheeks, scarified across the forehead and embossed on the chin as though words were written there describing the man within, in a language that all might read.

What was it the seyis had said to Azarax? When the Master is ready, the pupil appears.

The seyis kisses Captain Byerley on his right cheek, on his left cheek and on his right cheek again. 'Bütün yaşamım şu bir dakika içinde şimdi. – My whole life is within this one single moment.'

'Quite, quite,' says Byerley, taking a step back. Shaking a man's hand is one thing but to be greeted with three kisses from a total stranger quite another. The seyis looks into his eyes: 'Sonunda seni buldum. – Finally I have found you.' And he bows again.

'Well, well,' says Byerley, unsure how to deal with this effusive behaviour: 'Shall we see the horse?'

'Sonunda kader seni çıkardı karşıma. – Finally fate has brought me before you.' With immense courtesy, the seyis gestures for Captain Byerley to follow.

As Byerley and Vaudrey walk behind him through the horse stalls, Vaudrey speaks: 'His Grace the Duke of Berwick, has charged me as equerry to accompany him to the service of His Imperial Highness, the Emperor Leopold, under the command of his Royal Highness the Duke of Lorraine, to the field, in Hungary, in early June.'

Byerley walks with his hands clasped behind his back, his thoughts elsewhere: why did this Turkish groom greet him so effusively? What does he know? Why doesn't Vaudrey just shut up?

'In event of which, I am presented with options,' Vaudrey continues, 'Either to keep the horse and leave it in the care of the Queen Dowager's since my commission as Captain is approved,' he says without so much as glancing at Byerley. He was on sensitive ground, for Byerley had founded this troop, and was its first captain. But Byerley had lost his commission on religious grounds: because he had refused to withdraw his stand on the principle of transubstantiation. Wine does not turn into blood in the cup, as far as Byerley is concerned.

'So,' Vaudrey continues, relieved to have had no reaction from Byerley, 'as you well appreciate, Mr Byerley,' and he emphasises the 'Mister', for he is not going to let Byerley forget that it was he who had been knighted while Byerley remained a mere gentleman; 'as you appreciate, Mr Byerley, I would be expected to find for the horse during my own absence, and my funds – my funds are finite.' He might be a Knight, but he's an impoverished one. 'Nor do I wish to risk the horse in any way in my absence. Although I might have the best groom in London, probably in England, there is nothing to say that some drunken sot of a trooper wouldn't take the horse out and for the price of a few groat one night, smack him up and down the river bank and break a leg, or something. In which case, Mr Byerley, do you see, I would have spent my money on this horse's keep for nothing. My alternative, is um, is um…well…'

The seyis has gone ahead into the stable, popped a bridle over Azarax's head and brought him into the corridor.

The horse stands still, head up, ears forward – a tall, dark bay, almost black, his eyes burning with their accustomed fire. He is all stallion, all presence, strong as a lion and twice as proud, and with his extraordinary groom wearing his red silk chapan and white turban, standing at his side.

Vaudrey smiles delightedly: this little seyis is the finest salesman in London. Vaudrey exercises his toes and bobs up and down: Splendid! Splendid! He decides it prudent not to tell Byerley that he fully intends to bring another collection of such horses back from Hungary – this trade has all the potential of being a quite a money spinner. Fools and horses? The secret of a good deal lies in having another one up the sleeve.

Byerley steps forward to man and horse. He knows in the instant what he is looking at.

'So the opportunity is, well – here. If you don't want him then I shall offer him up to Lord Cutts who brought his own back but wouldn't mind this one too as a charger.'

Byerley walks around the horse. The seyis watches closely. There is no amateur reaction here: gazing in a horses' mouth, picking up his tail, pulling his foreleg forward then dropping it. There is no peering under the flanks, feeling the leg, handling the knees. You see, or you do not see. This man can see. The seyis' face is bright.

'The price?' says Byerley brusquely.

'His price?' stutters Vaudrey. 'Yes, yes, the price. Yes. Yes well, his price is high.'

'Oh? How high?'

Vaudrey stammers out a figure.

'And the groom?' asks Byerley.

'The groom? The groom remains in the barracks.'

'Ah,' Byerley paces the floor.

He wishes, he finally says, to see this Turkish groom ride this horse, the groom that everyone has heard so much about.

The seyis saddles the horse and leads him out to the quarter meadow. The sun is high, it is a late May day. The horse's coat shines, but it is an inner shine that strikes the observer. There are no questions such as: What would you like to see this horse do? The seyis vaults on Azarax and rides. Robert Byerley watches in silence.

This horse is the sky, the clouds, his feet are vapours, he belongs to the air, he scarcely touches the ground, he seems suspended above it. In that moment of suspension, he is a consummate masterpiece of bone and sinew and muscle. One flick of the earth and he is propelled through the air, then feels the ground again as though just to keep in touch; he is weightless. Why would a man sell a creature like this?

Byerley moved from Vaudrey and walked over to Poyntz who was enjoying this spectacle as much as Byerley. 'So tell me, Mr. Poyntz, what are we looking at?'

Poyntz scratches his stubbly chin: 'Well, put it like this Your Honour,' he says, 'it seems, sir, that this horse has never belonged to the man who is supposed to be his owner.'

'You mean Captain Vaudrey.'

'I do, sir.'

'Does the horse not have a name?'

'Indeed he does, sir. A foreign one. I can never remember it.'

'And what manner of a horse is he?'

Poyntz moves from one foot to the other. 'You mind if I go and lean on that rail?' he asks. Byerley gestures: go ahead. Poyntz strides to the rail and gets himself comfortable: 'That's better,' he says.

Poyntz watches the horse, and makes a clicking sound: 'He's a picture to watch, isn't he, sir?'

Robert Byerley gazes on. Now the seyis has moved him to a canter. The symbiosis of horseman and horse. They form one animal, out there, cantering in front of them.

'You are a good horseman, sir,' says Poyntz. 'But look at that!' Byerley gazes on. Mastery is deceptive: it simplifies. What is complex appears elementary, as though a child might do it. Some are fooled; Byerley is not.

'I defy any man to ride that horse like that, sir.'

Byerley slides his eyes to Poyntz. 'Meaning?'

'Meaning there's no bugger in here can even stay on him, sir. There's no one – apart from Mr Seyis. He's a one-man horse, sir – or – he's bewitched.'

'Tush, Poyntz. What nonsense. He's a horse.'

'And he's as savage as a wolf.'

'Is he now?'

'He all but killed the King.'

Byerley looks down at his feet and smothers a smile. He is warming to this horse by the second. He watches as Azarax moves from canter to gallop. The change of gait is so fluid it is impossible to see when it happened. Byerley puts his hand to his mouth as the horse disappears across the quarter meadow and beyond. 'That's another thing, your Honour,' says Poyntz, who has appeared wheezing, behind him: 'He's the quickest thing on legs I've ever seen.'

Byerley returns to stand beside Vaudrey. 'The price?'

Vaudrey clears his throat and nods. 'Yes, yes, as I said.'

'I will pay your price but there is a snag, I fear,' Byerley says, slowly, hands behind his back. Vaudrey is confused. 'A snag? What snag?'

'The groom.'

'The groom?'

'I shall meet your price only if the horse comes with the groom.'

- 19 -

A Dangerous Man

Byerley stands back and regards the Whorl of the Spurs on the horse's rib. It's an unusual whorl, but bears little significance in England. That strange intensity that Byerley had noticed the minute he'd seen the horse still burns in Azarax's eyes. He runs a hand over the horse's shoulder. Has he just spent £1,000 on a neck-breaking lunatic? Or invested in a valuable piece of horseflesh, to be sold on if necessary, or at least used for a few decent stud fees as a little return on his capital?

The seyis invites him to mount.

The troopers of the Queen Dowager's hover round the edges of the quarter meadow. Money has been changing hands among the men. It hasn't escaped Byerley's notice: 'A groat he's on the grass in five minutes' had wafted across to him with the breeze. There's a nice loyal bunch, he'd thought. 'Ten groats says he'll fling him straight over the rails.' They can afford to scoff. He might have been the first Captain of the Queen Dowager's, but he isn't their Captain any more. He was dismissed along with all the other Protestant officers only six months earlier. He's a civilian now and not subject to military authority. He's no friend of Talbot, their new Catholic Colonel. What can he do?

Exhibitionism is not Byerley's forte. He does not like being the centre of attention anywhere and this is perilously close to what might turn into ridicule. 'Go back to work, you idle louts!' he shouts. None of them moves. The seyis makes a tiny noise and Byerley throws him a glance. He's holding the stirrup. Has the groom got money on this as well? The seyis pushes down on the stirrup on the other side of the horse.

Byerley grabs the reins in his left hand, bounces up and he's in the saddle. The seyis stands back. The troopers grip the rail.

This horse is an armchair. He has a long neck, black mane falling to the right. The horse beneath him feels potent, relaxed. Byerley releases the rein. Something tells him that to gather the rein is to make this horse do the opposite of what it would do for his old hunter in Yorkshire. The horse pulls the bit until he is comfortable and awaits instruction. Byerley sits calmly. He has already learned something from watching the seyis. He looks to the corner of the quarter meadow and thinks: over there, at a walk – and the horse responds. Did he touch him with a leg? No. Did he touch the rein? No. How come this horse understands him? It wasn't language, it was pure thought. My God! No wonder he throws people.

The seyis watches as the horse walks away. If a sadness invades his heart then he had anticipated it. He had said something to Byerley that Byerley had not understood at all. He had said: When I first saw you, the moment I longed for and dreaded had come.

No horse can have two masters.

Vaudrey had never been his master and neither had Envir Altinay Paşa. Who is your master now, Azarax?

'To avoid this moment I could have gone to Istanbul, to the baş imrahor. But who am I to go against what is written?' the seyis had pondered.

Byerley reaches the corner of the quarter meadow, turns to his left and points the horse toward the troopers. It's a dead straight line; the horse's head is straight at them. The pace increases, the stride lengthens. A forefoot smacks down, his head goes up and the horse starts to trot: slow, but gathered, like a rocking horse. Masterly in its control. This horse doesn't need reins. Keep at that pace, good boy, you're beautiful. Beautiful. Now back to the walk – and he's there before Byerley completes the thought.

My God: what have I got here?

The horse stops in front of the troopers. 'Well,' says Byerley, 'wish him goodbye, you lot.'

If they hadn't lost so much money on him in those few minutes, their grief at losing Azarax might have been a little more genuine. Byerley's face creases into a smile, the horse turns to the seyis, Byerley takes him back, drops lightly onto the ground and says: 'Bring him to my house in the morning. First thing.' He hands the seyis the reins, pats the horse and walks off in a muck sweat.

* * *

Robert Byerley's house in Great Queen Street near Covent Garden. Late morning. A blazing June day, blisteringly hot, full of birdsong and Robert Byerley hears the clatter of hooves on the cobbles. He pulls a curtain back and peers through the window. Six flanking riders from the Queen Dowager's, the seyis in the middle riding on the bay, have arrived outside his house.

The escort from the barracks is a nice gesture and Byerley had not expected it. He goes out to greet them. Poyntz sits among the horsemen wearing his red livery with its sea-green facings and black beaver hat. They are smartly turned out: a pleasure to see. Byerley looks wistful. 'We's sorry to see him go, your Honour,' Poyntz says, speaking up for them all. 'We shall miss them, sir, both the Turkey man and his horse, sir. I mean your horse, sir. He has brought us good luck, sir. Something about him. There's never been one like him, not in London town anyway. He's a real one-off.'

Byerley holds a hand out to Poyntz. 'Thank you Poyntz.'

A salute and the escort about-turns and rides away. Byerley clicks his tongue: dammit, he was fond of that regiment. Those are my boys. He watches them disappear down the road, sun sparkling on their cuirasses, sabres glinting, feathers bobbing in the beaver hats. Eyes turn from the pavements to watch them go by – yes, that's right, that's the Queen Dowager's. Show them respect. Poyntz turns in his saddle as they round the corner at the bottom of the road and in thoroughly royalist gesture, doffs his hat to his former master. Byerley acknowledges with an upheld hand. Good old Poyntz. Ah well: but now I have this. He bids the seyis good morning, flings open the great doors to an imposing courtyard and the beautiful bay horse steps in.

***

A week or two of riding round London on his new horse and the gossip begins. Two bewigged gentlemen snuff-takers are chatting in the Star and Garter: they say that James Fitzjames, now the Duke of Berwick and Sir Edward Vaudrey have returned to Hungary once more to fight the Turk, so there was not much else that could have happened to the horse other than Byerley buy him. If he had been left in the Royal Stables he would probably have attacked someone – perhaps the King again, since the horse has shown a marked dislike of him – and would have been shot. So for the horse's sake it was a good thing that Byerley had him. What Byerley intends to do with him not even heaven knows. Byerley's hardly a racing man – never exhibited a glimmer of interest.

'What's he want a horse like that for? Hunting?'

'By Gad, sir, that's an expensive mount to go hunting on! Still, then again, money never was much of an obstacle for Robert Byerley. No sir, I think he has something else in mind.'

'Unusual fellow, Byerley. He's not exactly your typical badly-behaved aristocrat, is he? He does not loiter about the coffee houses, he is not to be found drinking port in the afternoon, you will not find him dallying at a party, nor flattering the ladies. He is not to be dug out of a tavern somewhere at three o'clock in the morning. He's a straight-lace, in many ways, though no prude. He is a principled fellow, unusual these days. He was one of the first to raise a troop of horse at his own expense and bring 40 mounted men down from Doncaster to save James II's throne when Monmouth threatened it. You realise it was he and Lord Lumley who started the Queen Dowager's? So it's his regiment, in a way. Quite an irony that both he and old Lumley should be stripped of their commissions by the King they helped save because they weren't Catholic. That must have rankled! He also lost his seat in Parliament, and because he stood up to the King, he lost his job as a Justice of the Peace because he refused to sign the Test Act – they threatened him with prison, but he still refused to sign. Oh yes: Byerley has his principles, of that there is no doubt. We need a few young men like that. He lost what he loved for holding on to what he believed to be right. How many men do you know like that? That takes guts. Got it from his father they say, a hard-boiled old Royalist if ever there was one: Colonel of Foot in 1645, Byerley's Bulldogs they called them. Fought like demons at Naseby and Marston Moor. The young man's grandfather was marched in chains to York by Cromwell and died in prison of wounds he got at Sherborne.

'They are a Royalist family no mistake, and a Protestant one too. I can't see him siding with the King if trouble blows up again. Why should he? James has robbed him of everything he had. And what does that make him, do you suppose? I'll tell you what that makes him: that makes him a dangerous man. He's rich: he's got principles, he's fit, he has estates, land in Yorkshire, houses in London, businesses, is well connected and has friends in high places. The only things he lacks is a beautiful wife and a smart horse and now it seems he's just got one of the two. Now what does that tell you? Has he got something up his sleeve? The Queen Dowager's hasn't seen the last of Byerley, mark my words. When trouble comes – and it's on its way – that regiment is going to need that young fellow again.'

'And have you heard about his groom? The Turkish groom?'

'Well, this is the interesting thing. That groom and that terrifying horse are like two peas in a pod, so to speak. It is as if they are one being: they are always together – you can never go to the Royal Stables and not find the Turk hanging around his horse, grooming him, riding him – sticking close to him. Then along comes Byerley and everyone wondered how the groom would react. But it is as if the groom has just handed the horse over to him. Strange. The Turk even told Poyntz that he has bequeathed the horse to Byerley: now what is that supposed to mean?'

'There is a strange similarity between him and Byerley – not in looks or fortune, of course; it is to do with character. They say that Byerley is the only man who can ride the horse, apart from his groom – that's a peculiar thing, is it not? Anyway, Byerley's taking the groom with him.'

'To Yorkshire?'

'Well no: to Durham. To his house at Middridge. Middridge Grange.'

'I thought he lived in Yorkshire. At Goldsborough.'

'So he does: Middridge is yet another of his houses. Byerley has land and property aplenty. But he'll be back here, I warrant you: you can't keep a good man down, especially when he's mounted on something like that. That horse is the envy of all England. Have you seen him? He's as savage, as self-willed a brute as ever clipped along a country lane, but he's magnificent. He's as glossy as Jacobean oak and if you look into his eyes, they're like opals: burning with fire. Just don't stand in his way, that's all, he'd walk over you without so much as a backward glance. More snuff?'

***

It is said that intelligent people ask questions but this is not true. Any fool can ask questions. What intelligent people do is ask questions and then listen to the answers.

Three days before they set off for Durham, Byerley is in the stable with the horse and the seyis. He grooms one side of Azarax, the seyis the other. Byerley has noted the peculiar mottled pigmentation on the seyis' fingers: how the olive skin on the back of his hand dispersed along his fingers into little islands of pink, not unlike the muzzles of some pink-skinned horses, giving them a delicate, sun-sensitive appearance. It is a strange aberration, Byerley mused as he swept the hay whisp across the horse's shoulder: striking and oddly attractive.

He continued his work and asked a lot of questions about the horse and the seyis responded honestly and fully, as though relieved at last to find someone to talk to, who did not assume that he had just appeared from round the corner, who did not treat him like a serf, who seemed to respect and value his opinions and moreover, who listened to his broken replies. So now Byerley knows that the horse had been foaled in a storm on the Night of Shaban – although he is not sure what this signifies – with the Whorl of the Spurs upon him, meaning he would be safe in battle; that he had been schooled by the seyis; had been in the Privy Stables in Istanbul; that he was a Ghazi horse – whatever that meant – and one-time charger of a high-ranking Ottoman cavalryman. He learns that he had been present both at the Siege of Vienna and the Siege of Buda and yet had not a single mark or scar on him. Byerley had whistled through his teeth on learning that, finding it almost impossible to believe. It was not that he mistrusted the seyis: it was just such a towering story. How many horses survive one campaign, let alone several, let alone unmarked?

Byerley later reflected that the auspicious omens attached to this horse meant nothing to him, despite their significance for the groom, who spoke of them as irrefutable facts. Irrespective of whether Byerley believed it or not, he now knew there was more to this horse than he had at first realised and not for the first time he wondered quite what he'd bought. It was a curiously unsettling sensation to find that he had taken on an animal of such high intrinsic value. Yet he was shrewd enough to realise that, in order for a horse to survive such a life, he must have three things: firstly, inspired and dedicated schooling: secondly, someone very competent looking after him, and thirdly, to be born with an unusual capacity to survive. But as for the rest – the sacred horse business, the luck, the divinity, the mumbo jumbo – it remained mumbo jumbo, as far as he was concerned. What this horse enjoyed was a damn good keeper. That, and an innate ability, which he had in abundance, to fight for his life. Aggression in an animal forced to live a life of danger was the secret of his success.

'So he is schooled to the cannon?'

'Yes, efendi (sir).'

'And to the sabre?'

'No, efendi. He is schooled to the bow.'

'Can you teach me to school him to the sabre?'

The seyis looks away with a pained expression. 'Why do you wish such a thing, efendi?'

Byerley looks at him squarely: we are alike, he and I, he muses: we appreciate honesty. The difference between us is that he is sick of war and I have never seen it.

'There will be war.'

The seyis stops working, and leans against the horse. 'Who will fight it?' he asks quietly: 'And why?'

'It will be a struggle for the throne of England.'

The seyis shakes his head. Does he understand this? Does he want to? Byerley spares him the detail.

'When will it come?' asks the seyis.

'One year: maybe two years.'

The seyis moves away from the horse. 'I could have answered my call,' he says quietly. Byerley is listening. 'Before Buda: I could have gone to Istanbul.'

Byerley waits for him to expand but he does not. He returns to the horse, and runs a hand over his back. 'This horse,' the seyis says in reverent voice: 'There is one way and one way only to fight from the back of this horse.'

Byerley is listening.

'I will not teach you the sabre, efendi. I cannot. But if you ride this horse with your heart and believe that you fight for what is right, then no-one and nothing can stop you.'

* * *

Three days later and two horses trot north to Gray's Inn Road, along York Way, swing right through Camden along Brecknock Road and head for the open fields at Tufnell. On to Highgate, they keep to the east of Hampstead Heath and Byerley keeps a weather eye on any men on horseback standing idly about behind trees. Footpads were always loitering in these places and he was ready for them. Armed with two pistols, a carbine and a sabre, Byerley might not have had the seyis' experience of fighting on horseback, but he looks the part, and it would take a brave man to approach him. The seyis has his bow and quiver strapped across him and looks like the kind of man who would not be afraid to use it. He is riding a roadster which Byerley gave him the money to buy from Lewis's Horse Traders in the Strand. He's a neat little horse with a well set-on neck, small head, short ears and short, close-coupled back. For all that, the horse has a lot of style. Although barely fourteen hands high, he does two paces to the Turk's one but he's a frothy little horse with plenty of energy. He's a gelding, five years old, a walnut bay with apple marks.

Byerley rides Azarax lightly, close to the horse's mind. This is easy for the seyis to spot. Byerley doesn't fiddle with his reins or interfere with the Azarax's judgement. He doesn't kick or pull, jab or shout. Nor does he wear spurs. In short, he treats him as he treats the seyis: with a lot of respect, a lot of give and a willingness to listen.

As is the custom between master and groom, Byerley rides a little ahead of the seyis. Azarax's pace is longer and if he didn't stop every now and then or if the seyis didn't trot his roadster up, they would soon have been standing on opposite ends of the horizon. The seyis has never seen the horse ridden with such ease by another man before. It was a moment tinged with sadness. 'Can you see me Azarax? Do you feel what I think you feel, Azarax? Has the time come? Does life decree that one day, you must always give up the thing you love most, and move on? Why am I still with you now? You have already crossed a threshold, you have already set your foot on a path I cannot follow. How is it that although I have fed you, watered you, protected you, filled my days with thoughts of you – now, after all these long years, you will be taken from me by a man who has everything, leaving me once again with nothing? Why have I been forbidden to own anything in this life, even you? Even after all the love I feel for you? I was born into grime and in grime shall I die. I am the rayah, the common cattle: I am dirt. No matter Azarax: it is not your fault. My heart is always with you. Look after him as you have looked after me. And when you graze the lilac grasses on the plains of eternity, when your long shadow slopes across the rolling seas of time and everyone knows your name, I ask you to remember mine.'

***

The road north is a string of green lanes, oaks trees, villages, churches, cows and villagers and grand houses.

They ride to St Ipollitts, where Byerley dismounts Azarax, suddenly. Waving to the seyis he signals him towards a small, and very ancient church. Intrigued by this peculiar diversion, the seyis obeys, and leaving the horses tethered by the lychgate, follows Byerley within. In the cool interior Byerley points out strange markings on the pillars of this church. These are crosses with lozenge shapes cut around them. He explains that many years ago, men from this place had gone on Crusades through the seyis' country, to fight for possession of Jerusalem. Before they left they had cut these crosses into the stone. If they returned with their horses, they cut a lozenge in the stone, around the cross. He explained that this church was dedicated to a Saint called Hippolytus, Patron Saint of Horses in the Christian world and that this church was therefore, to all horses, sacred.

From the hamlet of Baldock the Roman road stretched ahead for a long way, dead straight and very boggy. After riding all day they crossed a beautiful honey-coloured limestone bridge at Godmanchester, then rode on to Hinchingbroke House, another brick building, belonging to yet another grand paşa, arriving at eight o'clock that night.

The next day they ride yet another straight Roman road, Ermine Street, to Peterborough and then branch west for Burghley House, dazzled by the setting sun of a warm June day. The utter splendour of this house, its immense beauty captures even the eyes of the horses, staring ahead at it as they walk slowly down the long drive.

'This is the greatest house of the Elizabethan times in our land,' says Byerley to his seyis. 'It is over a hundred years old and was built by Queen Bess's Lord Treasurer, my Lord Cecil. It is his descendant with whom we rest this night: Lord Exeter, the fifth Earl.'

The following days take them on through rolling country, the horses scenting the fresh June air, the sides of the tracks lined with hog weeds and mallows, and the seyis runs his fingers, as he passes on his little roadster, through cow parsley and the feathery, tiny little white flowers of the elder. From Ermine Street they take the track to their left and Byerley turns in his saddle and his arm sweeps over the great wooded landscape, as he says: 'Now we shall see fine scenery.'

The track narrows, passing a little willow-lined stream with ducks and coots and to one side stands a remarkably pretty small church, which they find strange that it should stand so alone in this place. 'This church,' Byerley says to the seyis, 'is ancient. It was built in 1470 or thereabouts, and this style is the perpendicular period of architecture. Notice the elegant windows, their proportions.' Indeed the seyis could see and noted a strange resonance with the minarets he knew: a shared lightness of construction, as though the building barely weighed a thing.

The country they now pass through makes for easy riding, the shade of the trees across the lanes is deep and cool, the isolated, churches, elegant and striking with their pale stone dressings, simple towers and low spires.

'And now we shall ride past the house of a man of great stature,' says Byerley, 'a man involved in the greatest intellectual feats of our time, whose processes of thought and trains of enquiry have led to explanations of the strange energies of our world.'

Along a narrow lane they pass, down into a dip running beside a little river on the bank of which, on their right-hand side, stands a big, rectangular house, with small, mullioned windows. The house looks west, catching the sun in the morning on its back and in the evening on its face so that it is light throughout the day. 'Woolsthorpe Manor: simple and stately: a gem of design, a peaceful building: an apt place for Sir Isaac Newton to have been born.'

Four miles further on, Byerley points to a much grander estate, with mature trees, a huge walled garden and fine ancient house: 'My friends the Tollemaches!' he says. 'We shall not stop: we are expected by nightfall elsewhere.'

There are horse-chestnuts and oak trees, beautiful churches in honey-coloured stone with great big windows, windmills and gently sloping hills. Through Croxton Kerrial the land rolls more deeply, solitary trees in meadows; this is pretty country. Huge sweeping beech trees now line the track, which has become more clearly defined of a sudden; it follows deep valleys, dark under the trees, open ground beneath the beeches, 'No wolves!' laughs Byerley. 'See,' he says: 'the fine view! This house is called Belvoir. It is vast. It is the home of his Grace, the Duke of Rutland, who has wished to see this horse. We enter here, there is a steep climb to the house.'

The seyis gazes up at the dazzling new stonework: the long roof and the echoes of castles with which he is familiar: 'This was built in 1654,' says Byerley, 'on the site of an ancient castle built many hundreds of years ago, which is why it still looks like a castle, yet is in reality, a house, a very large and spacious house. We dismount here. You may take the horses yonder to the stables: a groom will help you.'

They spend the following night in a creaking windmill near Sleaford, and the next day they pass the castle in Newark, which had been demolished under the orders of Cromwell. They cross the River Trent and shortly they find themselves riding over the ferny floor of a great oak forest, and then glowing through the trees, they catch sight of Thorseby, the seat of the Earl Manvers, not far from Clumber House. As they ride clear of the trees they see the lake with swans beside a beautiful bridge with three arches. There are water cascades, and water-fowl: swans, ducks and coots beneath the shadowy branches of willows darkening the water margin. The lake is fringed with gorse and ferns and lichen-covered trees touch their leaves on its glossy green surface . To the left is the great house, surrounded by cedars, and beyond is the forest of Sherwood extending as far as the eye can see.

They stop at Welbeck Abbey the next day, to see the Duke with the riding school which was built in 1623 on plans drawn up by Smithson. The school is in a long, fine building, in which the Duke watches as the seyis is made to show off the horse in his many varied riding styles.

They stop off to visit Sir George Hewytt in Shireoaks, a portly man with a churchwarden pipe and who smells of strong spirit. He has a round, bright red face, hooded, wise blue eyes, long straggly grey hair and he coughs and splutters and pats his ample girth. He wears tall soft, brown leather boots with the polish scuffed off so that they appear napped, like the underside of a pelt. As they ride away the following day Byerley confides in the seyis that this portly gentleman will one day be the Colonel of the Queen Dowager's, unless he's much mistaken. Time will tell, time will tell.

They spend the next night in Doncaster, a place full of fond memories for Byerley for here it was that he had raised his troop of horse. Their next night is passed with the Gascoignes in Lotherton Hall and the next with Mr Byerley's mother in Goldsborough Hall, and this is the house of a fine paşa, without doubt.

They stay three days in Goldsborough and finally set out through the Yorkshire market town of Knaresborough, passing by way of the old castle high above the river Nidd. A great forest extends behind them to the south, rising from the river in the valley, and stretching as far as the eye can see. They take the way past Ripon and its spired Minster, its dovecots and flying buttresses reflecting in the water of the river Skell. They spend the following night at Norton Conyers, a pretty, gabled house with an orangery and here they are entertained by the Graham family, whose father, Sir John, had fought with Byerley's own father in the Battle of Marston Moor and who, having received twenty six wounds, rode back to this place and died that night.

The land now becomes bleak and windswept: the Yorkshire Dales to the west, and the Yorkshire Moors to the east. In Kiplin Hall they spend one night with the Calvert family then, rising early for the long final day's push, they ride up to Melsonby, take the Dere Street Roman Road through High Coniscliffe, Houghton le Side, Heighington, past Redworth Hall and, in the late afternoon, they ride the long drive to Middridge Grange. Carpets of blues harebells lie on the deep green, melilotted grass, as the low sun casts long rippling shadows from the horses across the path.

- 20 -

Vanished

Nearly forty years have elapsed since the sound of gunfire and artillery shook the timber, shattered the glass and holed the doors and panelling at Middridge Grange, home of the Byerleys. A generation had grown old who had fought in the Civil Wars, when cannon and musket-shot had hammered into the high paddock walls that surrounded this ancient, gabled house. Then, the shouts of men and the pounding hooves of horses galloping down the drive had driven Byerley's Bulldogs into the trees, where they turned about and fired back into the ranks of light horse that harried them. The Byerley family had paid for that action. His wounded grandfather, humbled in chains, was frog-marched from his home Goldsborough Hall to York. He never returned.

Memories like that are absorbed into the fabric of a place. Middridge Grange is a house that belongs in its setting. It is a house which breathes history, an ancient house built of stone under a stone roof. The windows are mullioned, the glass lattice rattles in a wind. In front of the house stand two yew trees, sentinels to the garden, through which the view from the house extends to Redworth Hall, across the valley. On the east side of the house lie the kitchen gardens and the paddocks: paddocks where a dark bay Turk horse now grazes peacefully under the pale light of a northern sun.

Robert Byerley does not strut around this house like a paşa in his palace: he does not view it as the house of a grandee. He sees it as his home, he wraps it round him, it becomes him, it fits his character. Middridge, with its moulded plaster ceilings, its oak panelling, its creaking corridors, its ghosts, its history, is quiet and harmonious. The place reeks of old timbers and beeswax. Heavy Jacobean furniture dignifies the already dignified rooms. Brass candlesticks and brocaded, wing-back chairs in peach damascene stand either side of the stone fireplace in the drawing room.

The back of the house is squared off by a huge flagstone-floored kitchen, ruled by Mrs Vaizey, a red-faced housekeeper who treats Byerley like an adolescent son, fussing over his food, his clothing, his bedding, his friends, his health, his habits. She regards the seyis with rural reservation.

Byerley shows the seyis to the tallet above the kitchen. It is another bare tallet; with a fire, bed, table, piss-pot, jug, bowl and water. The bed has sheets, there are blankets and the view from the window allows the seyis to look over the small courtyard at the back of the house, where the small stone pillars prop up the roof of a low carriage house. At the bottom of the steps a horse's head greets him: 'This will be the Turk's stable,' Byerley says. 'So that you can be close to him.'

Middridge is a haven. The seyis does what he pleases. The days pass in sunshine, warm winds blowing from the west. The seyis sleeps at night as he has never slept before. The nights are silent except for the owls in the woods, the creaking of the timbers and the bleat of sheep with their manly voices. The horses crop the deep green grass in the paddocks.

The seyis feels the skin on his face change and become smoother. His hands become smooth, and his hair becomes as silky as it was when he was a child. The horse's mane becomes silky: the horse's tail thickens and becomes ever more fine. His coat glistens. 'It must be the water,' the seyis whispers to himself. 'And the purity of the air. The sleep: the peace. The larks in the sky: the buzzards. The owls at night. The excellent food Mrs Vaizey cooks for me. My work is light. I scythe the grass in the sun, I sit under the trees. It is almost like the timar of Ali-aga Izobegović, except that it is cooler and the Ali-aga of this place, smiles.'

The seyis and the horse spend hours in the pastures around Middridge. They walk the lanes, side by side, the horse swiping at the grasses, the seyis getting to know the wild flowers of late August. There are even white harebells here.

The seyis becomes known in the village. The people stop and hand him plums, apples, even pots of honey. Mrs Vaizey's observations travel: 'Changed my mind about him. He's alright. Got the manners of a Prince. Ever so quiet. Never hear a peep. And tidy? His room is a pin. And the stables too – never a blade of straw out of place. He's gentle and he's kind too. Brought me a punnet of loganberries.'

Children run up to him, pat the horse, sit on his back four at a time as he leads them through the village. Once he sat a little three-year-old girl on the stallion's back and her mother had come scurrying out of her house, gripping her flying skirts, flushed in the face and scolding. But the seyis had said quietly and with absolute assurance: 'The child is safer on this horse than she is in your own arms,' and had led her down the street.

Later he had returned and lifted her out of the saddle and put her into her mother's arms whereupon the child burst into tears and asked to be put back on the horse.

'This man is a magician.'

'Bring him to my house as quick as you can. My old mare is poorly.'

***

Summer rolls into autumn, autumn into winter and soon it is the Spring of 1688. It arrives in an explosion of daffodils, of dog's mercury, dandelions and burdock. During the winter, Middridge had been snow-bound: the water frozen, snowdrifts blocked the road to the village. The horse had struggled through the drifts just as he had done in the Balkans and the seyis had turned him out in the day and watched him romp and roll about in the snow in the paddocks, then brought him back in at night and fed him boiled barley and linseed and tossed him the sheaves of hay he had scythed, stooked, tied and stacked the summer before.

The ebullience of spring heralds a hot bumble-bee summer and then the news arrives in the village.

On 26th June 1688, a post rider in Royal livery canters into the village on a dapple grey and proclaims, at the top of his voice, a day of celebration to mark the happy event of the birth of a son to the Queen of England, which took place on 19th June, just seven days earlier.

Such news might have elicited a whoop of joy from a Royal subject.

Byerley is wearing an open shirt, and is sweating alongside his farm staff, pitching sheaves of hay into a heavy-wheeled hay cart drawn by a couple of hefty draft horses. They had gathered a good crop and were working hard, since in the distance thunder clouds loomed and they wanted the hay gathered in before it was ruined.

A man ran from the village across the scythed meadow, straight up to Byerley and gave him the news in six bare words. 'The Queen has had a son!'

Byerley looks at him blankly: 'What?' he asks in disbelief and the man repeats what he has just said. Jabbing his wooden pitch fork into the sheaves on the cart, Byerley shouts for his groom.

The seyis is minding his own business bundling the hay sheaves together and tying them with long stems of cocksfoot grass. 'Fetch the horse!' shouts Byerley and dashes back to the house across the meadows leaving his staff holding sheaves of hay, gaping, open-mouthed, wondering what on earth this news signifies. The seyis does as he is told: he drops the hay and runs back to the paddocks, collects the horse, bridles and saddles him, then leads him round to the front of the house, to the mounting block. Byerley emerges pulling on a jacket, vaults onto Azarax and is about to canter away when he spots the puzzlement on the seyis' face. Placing a hand on his shoulder he says: 'A royal son means a Catholic heir to the English throne. We cannot let it happen,' and gallops away.

The rest of the summer and all the next winter see men coming and going from Middridge, with horses arriving at night and strangers sitting up and talking until dawn. The seyis finds himself stabling hot horses at all hours, feeding and grooming them and the leisurely days he has known, vanish.

In the autumn, more alarming news is galloped to Middridge.

1ST NOVEMBER 1688 A Dutch fleet flying the arms of Nassau and quartered with the English Royal Standard sets sail from the Texel, north of Amsterdam.

3RD NOVEMBER One hundred and fifty vessels, frigates and men-of-war under full canvas sprinkle the Dover horizon.

5TH NOVEMBER The flagship reefs her sails, and plunges her iron anchors into the mud on the sea floor. Prince William of Orange, son-in-law of the King of England, sets foot on English soil in Torbay.

9TH NOVEMBER Prince William marches on Exeter.

17th November Edward Seymour, the most powerful man in South-West England swears allegiance to the Dutch Prince, followed by Lord Bath of Longleat.

21ST NOVEMBER The Prince strikes east.

7TH DECEMBER He stands with his army at the reaches of Hungerford, a sleepy market town in the midst of a sleepy county.
8th December William of Orange states his terms to King James, whose throne he claims with the backing of Parliament.

22ND DECEMBER King James II, his Queen and court, flee England.

23RD DECEMBER Sir John Talbot hands back his Commission as Colonel of the Queen Dowager's, which has since changed its name to the 6th Dragoon Guards. Command of the 6th goes to Sir George Hewytt.

13TH FEBRUARY 1689 William and Mary are declared King and Queen of England.

16TH FEBRUARY Robert Byerley regains his seat in Parliament. He regains his position as a Justice of the Peace.

25TH JUNE 1689
Robert Byerley is re-commissioned as an officer in the Queen Dowager Cuirassiers – the 6th Dragoon Guards – at the rank of Major. With his horse, he will join his unit at Hoylake, where he and horse will embark upon the transport The Invincible for Ireland, under the command of Colonel Sir George Hewytt. He will land in Belfast Lough and from there make his way south to Dundalk with the 6th Dragoons to join the army of the Duke of Schomberg, Commander-in-Chief of William's Forces in Ireland. He will strengthen the security of King William on the English throne and assist in the repulsion of James II.

'Ye Gods! We shall be leaving for Ireland within the month! Get the seyis.' Byerley sweeps his fingers through his hair. 'Tell the blacksmith to check my pistols and snaphanse musket: repair if necessary. And tell him to put an edge on my sabre. Tell the loriner to check the stitching on my baldric. Go on lad, be off with you!' He sits at his desk with a quill dipping in ink, an empty sheet of paper before him, he wishes to write his will. He needs a witness. The seyis will do. Where is he? Can he write?

'Boy! Where's my groom?' The houseboy returns out of breath and slides on the polished drawing room floor. 'He cannot be found, sir.'

'Of course he can be found, he will be with the horses.'

'He is not with the horses, sir.'

'Then check the paddock – the kitchen garden – the meadows – but find him!'

The boy rushes off and Byerley sits down to compose his will. No, no, this won't do, he needs a lawyer. He needs a calm presence. Where's that damn groom?

Byerley walks out of the house into the courtyard where he shouts for the seyis but there is no answer. His horse is looking over the paddock wall, gazing intently at the horizon. Following his line of sight, Byerley tries to see whatever it is the horse is looking at, but finds nothing. Just trees, the moor. He calls out again and still there is no reply. Taking two steps at a time, he runs up the loft steps to the seyis' tallet and bangs on the door. No reply. He opens it. Within, all is as normal, his bed made, clothes on hooks. His bow lies on the table with its quiver of arrows and a small bag. There are no other possessions.

Running back down Byerley enters the kitchen. Mrs Vaizey is plunging dough, making the daily bread. 'Have you seen my groom?'

'He's gone to Middridge, your Honour, to collect some herbs which he said you would be needing for your adventure.'

'Adventure, he called it?' Byerley snorts. Perhaps it would be an adventure to the seyis, who has seen war at first hand, but it isn't to Byerley. The thought sends a chill through his bones. He still hasn't mastered the sabre on horseback and already, the moment when he needs it is upon him.

'Tell him to see me as soon as he comes back.'

Mrs Vaizey continues pushing her fat hands into the squashy ivory ball.

Byerley returns to the library and waits. He can't think how to compose his will. Besides, he has barely a family to leave anything to, only a brother and sister and a mother. No offspring. No doting wife and adoring children.

The hours slip by: the seyis does not return.

Byerley curses.

By ten o'clock his cursing has turned to concern.

The little horse the seyis rode to the village has now been found, but not the seyis. The horse has been taken back to the Grange, and put in the paddock alongside Azarax, who cries out again and again and still looks over the walls to some invisible spot in the darkness. Byerley orders a search for the seyis.

'What, now sir, at this time of night?'

'Yes, now! Find out what my horse is looking at. Search all night. But find the seyis. Search the village, the woods, the fields. Search everywhere!'

He joins the search-party himself. Torches are lit. Lines of men filter through the woods about Middridge in the darkness. Byerley checks the buildings again and again. He checks his room again and again.

By dawn there is no result.

'Go to bed,' Byerley croaks to the men. 'Get some rest. We'll try again later.' Bed for him is a chair in the drawing room and a headful of questions. Where on earth can he be? There is nothing to indicate that he was planning on leaving, on running away. He is not the type. Moreover, he would never leave that horse.

Out in the paddock Azarax cries out, again and again.

Next morning the search resumes. Once again Byerley follows the direction in which the horse is looking. He even mounts Azarax and lets him take him there, but find himself milling about in the middle of a field, the horse sniffing the ground and pawing. All day Byerley rides him, calling out, looking: stopping in the village asking if anyone has seen the groom: Who last saw him? When? Where did he go? One man said he saw him riding Azarax two days earlier. On the heath, beyond Middridge Grange. Just the groom and the horse. He would never forget it.

He said the groom had got off and talked to his horse, very close to his face, he seemed very moved, then he re-mounted and it was then the man noticed the seyis was carrying his bow and arrows. The horse had moved slowly at first, then broke into what the man described as a very great stride, a big walk, from which he skipped into a trot, it was the prettiest thing he'd ever seen a horse do. And then suddenly the horse switched his gait, his head came up and his big powerful hind quarters sprung into the three-beat drum of a canter.

It was a slow, paced canter, said the man.

From paced canter he moved effortlessly into a slow gallop.

From slow gallop he went to half, three quarter, then full.

The horse galloped as he had never seen a horse gallop, the man said. Mud flew behind them.

It was magnificent to watch. The pace was powerful and even.

The wind was buffeting the groom's clothes and the horse's ears were levelled with the wind. The speed was high.

And then, on his own volition it seemed, the horse hit the ground harder. The groom was shouting and yelling. The horse was moving as though the world were spinning beneath his feet.

The horse and the groom were a streak of light in a blur of bracken and moor and heather and sky. The groom was low in the saddle and then the horse pulled on even harder.

His stride had lengthened and it was enormous.

It was as though they belonged to the air. As though they belonged to the air with the pounding touch of the hoof on the face of the earth and the horse was spinning it faster still.

This horse was stretched right out.

Then he went even faster.

It was as if his energy was coming from the sun and the wind and the sky and the rushing floor of the world as he flicked it beneath his flying hooves as though it was a weightless ball. And then, when it seemed impossible and the groom was screaming, the horse went even faster. Then the groom released the reins, drew his bow, turned at the hip and when the horse was stretched out to absolute maximum velocity, he shot three arrows into his last three hoofprints. The man had never seen anything like it in a lifetime.

Then horse and rider were gone. Over the moor's horizon.

Here, these are the arrows, said the man. Three of them. They were in the hoofprints, just as I said.

***

Days pass: a week passes.

Concern turns to loss, loss to guilt. Guilt to recrimination. Where was the little seyis, they whispered. What had Byerley done with him?

In the tallet loft Byerley picks up the seyis' meagre belongings, turns them over in his hands and lays them carefully in a small portmanteau. Sitting on the bed he looks at the contents. All that the seyis owned, barring his bow and arrows, fits into this little bag. Is it possible that the residue of a man's life, all his remaining possessions, can be fitted into one small bag? But the seyis did possess something else: a remarkable soul. More, he possessed another language, the language of horses. He who possesses another language possesses another soul.

Down in the stable the Turk horse cries out. He throws himself around, and when in the paddock, he gallops from one end to the other. 'It is the nature of the horse's voice that is so distressing,' Byerley says quietly to a farmhand: 'I have not heard its like before; the pain in that cry. You can hear the refusal to believe, the rejection of the truth: he will not accept that the seyis is gone. He cries out again and again. It is the most pitiful and distressing sound I have ever heard.'

And the horse will not eat.

As for Byerley, time is running out. He is bound for Hoylake on a fit horse, sabre at the baldric, musket on a sling, pistols in holsters, helmet plumed and cuirass buffed to a polish. Riding a pining horse? Azarax is losing weight, standing head down and dull eyed, or else gadding about pastures, crying out, his voice even penetrating Byerley's sleep.

The horse refuses hay, he refuses water. He refuses boiled barley with linseed. He refuses sugared barley. Nothing will make him eat. And when a meal is put in front of Byerley, he finds himself doing the same thing. He pushes a huge meal from Mrs Vaizey aside; he sits with his head in his hands. She enters the room: 'Come Mr Byerley, sir. You must eat.'

He gets up from the table and walks out into the early evening.

The horse is standing in the paddock, looking into the distance, wholly focussed on it: what is it that he sees?

'I shall have to take a different horse,' Byerley mutters to himself. 'But how can I leave him behind?'

Back in the house Byerley releases a bumble bee buzzing up a window. Mrs Vaizey is laying silver back in a drawer. 'Beg your pardon sir,' she says, 'but it's time to move on now, sir. We don't know where he's gone. It is a mystery. You have to move on now, or else you'll be took ill. Move on. Go and see the horse and tell him the same. You'll see: as long as you suffer, he will.'

Byerley drums a silver knife on the dresser. Yes. We have to live.

He walks swiftly out to the horse in the paddock taking an apple with him. The horse watches him approach and then gazes off again, into the distance.

Byerley puts his hand on the horse, looks in his eye. Come on boy, we've a war to go to. You will be my battle horse and we're going to survive. Your seyis is gone. I do not know where he has gone, but he has gone. Maybe he is dead. Maybe he went back to Istanbul. I don't know what he did. It is a mystery and all the worse for not knowing. Maybe one day he will return. But you are not missing. You are here, with me and we have work to do, so now be quiet and eat this apple.

No response.

Byerley walks back to the house. No good just saying it. He must live it. 'Boy!' he shouts, and the houseboy comes scuttling round a corner and slides into the drawing room across the polished floor. 'Get my uniform out of the cupboard and sponge it. And bring me some tea. And one of Mrs Vaizey's cakes. Now!'

The boy hesitates: 'Which first, sir?'

'The cake.'

Evening. The horse stands at the paddock and gazes over the wall. What is he looking at? Byerley strides purposefully over to him with a handful of cake. He stumbles on a length of hazel wattle on the eastern edge of the paddock, hard beside the wall. He crouches down: there are more, lengths of them, protecting something. Prising the wattle back, he finds trees, young trees – two lines of walnut trees. Who has planted these?

Blessed saints! What a signature! They will be here long after I am gone, still growing. Still Turkish.

The horse approaches from across the paddock; Byerley stands up. He offers the cake in his hand and the horse takes it.

- 21 -

Sea Horses

Byerley feels the horse's hot breath on the back of his hand, his whiskers touch his skin and the horse raises his head, high above him. The horse is bridled and saddled: on his back he wears the shabrac of a Major of the 6th Dragoons. The sabre hangs at his side: the pistols are holstered. The snaphanse musket is scabbarded under a saddle flap, bedroll at the cantle. 'He looks magnificent,' thinks Byerley. 'But is he my horse?'

The four-man escort sent to Middridge by Colonel Sir George Hewytt are ready, their horses tossing their heads, stamping their feet.

Byerley looks into those fiery eyes. 'Are you my horse? Do you accept me? Will you come with me? Will you do everything that your groom told me you could do? Or are you, as Poyntz said, a one-man horse?

'Your groom has gone. Everything I see in you is fine. Your mind is fine, your form is fine. I will be loyal to you, and I ask you to be loyal to me. My life depends upon you.'

As he is about to swing up into the saddle Byerley suddenly sees a tiny glint in the horse's mane. Removing a foot from the stirrup he looks closer. There, plaited into the mane, is a tiny glass *nazar boncugu*, a little blue Evil Eye.

Byerley feels the blood drain from his face. My God, was this there yesterday? Was it there last night? Has it been there all the time?

'Ready when you are Major, sir,' the corporal says.

Five days ride to Hoylake. The horses had scented the sea from a long way back and Azarax had reacted. He had jabbed and jogged, pulled at the rein, snorted and fussed. A stallion acting like this is a difficult creature to hold. The last five miles of the journey had brought Byerley out in a good, hard sweat. And then they had seen Hoylake: the forest of masts, rigging, block-and-tackle; the high-reefed sails, the halyards, shrouds, topping lifts and ratlines, cross trees, trestle trees, bunt-lines and yard arms. The men: red uniforms, blue uniforms, black hats, the coloured hats of infantry officers; the barrels of provisions; the huge fluttering standards, crosses on coloured backgrounds, rampant lions and unicorns, tassles, crowns and glory. Line upon line of men with muskets: boys with muskets.

The hulls of the transports lay along the wharves, wide, square rigged, flat- bottomed.

There they march, some of the soldiers mere boys with musket, flask and ball, the pipes shrilling, drums rat-a-tat-tatting, red-faced men barking orders and lines coming to ragged halts.

Byerley rides on his big Turk at the head of his escort through the soldiers, the provisions and barrels. Not one of these young lads has ever seen a cannon fired, let alone stood in the hot, deafening roar of hundreds of them. They carry swords but most look as though they could not defend themselves against a determined octogenarian with a walking stick.

Byerley regards them coolly, detachedly, as they stand there, fresh-faced in their new but already grubby uniforms, their pink cheeks, clear eyes and floppy blonde hair falling out from beneath absurd, huge brimmed hats making them look even younger. The older men, their sergeants strut amongst them, hands behind their backs, trying to instil manliness, order, discipline. Trying to get them to comprehend the serious nature of this action: this game.

If they only but knew that Byerley was no different from them: Major or otherwise, he was, like them, a virgin soldier.

The horses trot, their ears-pricked, toward the victualling on the docks: boxes and boxes of tools, and boots, and rope; and line upon line of sacks heaped high – sacks of what? Of wheat riddled with weevils.

The docks are a shouting, chain-ganged medley of men and animals, hundreds of carts laden with military issue swords, swords of poor balance, of repair musket stocks, spare barrels, field artillery, spare wheels, axles and piles of holed canvas.

'What in God's name is that?' barks Byerley at a clog-shod man with a ring in a nostril and lank brown hair. He was dressed in an ancient leather doublet and sailors' pinafore, and was pulling at one of the piles of holed canvas.

'It's tents, sir,' replies the man lowering his armful.

'Tents? They're full of holes!'

'I don't know, sir, I'm only loading them, sir.'

'They're rotten, man! Who the hell provisioned these?'

'I don't know sir, I think it was Mr Shales, sir.'

Shales! Byerley slaps his forehead with the flat of his hand. Damn that man! Henry Shales, Commissary to the Camp at Hounslow: how did they let him get his hands on this lot? There wasn't a man more skilled in the art of peculation than he. Shales could take a bottle of excellent claret, drain its contents, fill the bottle with vermilion, cork it afresh then pass it off as quality wine without so much as a whiff of conscience. What a disaster! And a Whig to boot!

A plump, red-faced, bearded man, in red livery with sea-green facings, shouting his fat, bearded head off comes elbowing through the milling soldiers waving his black hat and shouting furiously.

Poyntz arrives at Byerley's leg, sweating, breathing recently-quaffed gin. He gazes up into the Major's face: 'You is welcome sir, in the Scarlets again sir, you is most welcome and congratulations, Major sir,' he says: 'The lads is all here, expecting you sir, over yonder, past the stores. Where is the Turkeyman, sir, the groom? Is he not with you?'

Byerley looks down at Poyntz: 'It's a long story, Poyntz. I'll tell you later.'

Poyntz looks up, and something in those small blue eyes resembles an accusation. Of what? Byerley ignores it and smiles. 'Something strange, Poyntz, which I don't understand. Now, show us where we ought to be.'

Poyntz is not the kind of man who needs to be told twice. He lays a fat hand on Azarax's neck and the horse pricks his ears, casts his head sideways and rubs his cannon-bone with a nostril, indicating: 'I know who you are. I recognise you.'

As Azarax nods his head and chews his bit, even Byerley can feel his bay's forward pull: funny who horses like and who they don't.

'By yon oath!' bawls Poyntz: 'What a brute you are! I forgot how long you was! By God he's all there though, in't he? What a sight! Don't he look grand? I been telling the new lads as the Major is sat upon the peculiarist and most swiftest horse in the whole of these cavalries as is assembled here, Major sir, and they is looking forward to seeing this horse upon my oath, that is true as I is stood here talking to you sir, Major Byerley, sir.'

'Compliments accepted, and mine to you, Mr. Poyntz. Is the regiment mounted?'

'Well...after a fashion, sir.'

'Fashion? After a fashion?'

'Well the new recruits, sir, who is come when Colonel Talbots gets thrown out – I mean resigns, sir, from the Regiment – they was told to brings bays, but Mr Shales says as he will find horses for them, so they leaves theirs at home. But as it is, he bought bays, in the Shires, sir, good horses too, proper bays, but he loaned them to Cheshire farmers in exchange for a few coins, sir, for the harvest, and he pockets the difference and now the farmers is kept the horses so only three parts of our Dragoons is mounted, sir.'

'What?'

'And the Colonel, Sir George, sir, he says if any of us finds Mr Shales, sir, to skin the bugger alive, sir, that's what he says, sir, that's an order. So we been keeping a look-out, your honour, Major sir. Particular as the Colonel says as he will give the man twenty guinea what finds him.'

'Add twenty guineas from me too, Poyntz!'

'Oh right enough, sir; we shall look twice as hard,' declares Poyntz and he knuckles his forehead repeatedly, then counting on his stubby fingers, he struggles to add two twenties together. He does not have enough fingers. He gives up. 'Pray pardon, beg pardon sir, will you come and see the lads sir? They will be ever so honoured, sir, we was praying you would. And the horse, sir: they is dying to see yon horse, sir.'

The sudden rousing tune of the marching song Lilliburlero from Babington's 6th Royal Warwickshires is taken up with gusto by Kirke's 2nd Queen's, Trelawney's 4th King's Own and Hammer's 11th Devonshire, and spreads all along the docks. 'We been singing this one a fair old bit, sir, all the while in fact: the lads they loves this song, sir,' and Poyntz joins in, with his big, excellent voice, as he leads his Major towards the Regiment.

Byerley rides, savouring the scent of sea and the cries of seagulls, behind the waddling form of Poyntz. They pass the burning vats of tar, swearing sailors, lines of men chain-ganging stores aboard, black-toothed matelots gobbing twist, shiftily eyeing the obviously rich and well-appointed Major and his magnificent horse. Past the capstans and ropes and spare masts; past the rigging being sorted by old sea dogs, their faces whorled by the ocean; salt in their blood; men who have sailed from Chesapeake to the Horn, from the Cape of Good Hope to the south China seas; men of mystery and a hundred wives, men of no known tongue and strange, mixed-race features.

The sky is bright, the day cool, a mid-September11 day: the sun reflects off the sea, the water slaps against the quay and the ships ride the long, rolling waves tight on their creaking lines belayed to capstans. Round the corner rides Byerley, pushing through rank upon rank of infantry soldiers parting for him – taking him for a Duke, he looks so grand.

But just look at that horse! Men gasp. What a peculiar-looking animal! Fingers point – 'It must be Byerley!' The word whips round, 'He's the man who defied the King and refused on the Test Act; got tossed out of the Queen's, and now he's back! Huzzah! Look! There's his Turk horse – best horse in the land they say. Fastest thing on legs as man has ever rode!'

'Huzzah! Huzzah!' Byerley grins as he approaches.

'Major Byerley! Three Huzzahs for the Major Byerley! Huzzah! Huzzah! Huzzah!'

Byerley, hand on hip, high on his horse, regards the spectacle with a shake of the head and an indulgent smile. What a crew! Half of them could be dead soon: and they're good men. Good, solid, ordinary men.

Hands touch the sacred horse. The sacred horse takes a step back: flutes his nostrils and snorts, but it's not a warning, it's surprise. Then he mellows and allows the hands to paw him as he gazes over the heads of the new recruits at some minor detail, in the manner of a cat which, if witnessing a cup of tea being poured, gazes at the saucer.

'Never felt anything like this before! Never seen anything like this before...never even heard of horses like this before. Is he really the fastest horse in the world, Major Byerley, sir?'

'You shall see, my lads, in due course, you shall see.'

'Put money on it, sir?'

Byerley clears his throat.

'We'll see. Mr Poyntz, where's the Colonel?'

'On board, sir.'

'Which ship are we?'

'That one, sir: *Invincible*, sir. His Majesty's Ship, *Invincible*. That's the one for you – and Mathew Hylmer, John Cocks and me sir, with our mounts, and twenty of the lads. It is a better vessel, sir – though still a transport – it has six cannon. The others, Lt Colonel Wyndham, Captain Woods, Captain Heveringham and Captain Cornwall and their troops go with the others down there on *The Delight* of Ilford, *The Comb* from Bristol, *The Elizabeth* and *Katherine* – she's two hundred and fifty tons, sir, and *The Sarah* of London, as draws a burthen of one hundred and eighty tons, and *St Jacob* of Ostend, as draws only thirty tons, sir – the transports. We sail by the evening tide, if the wind is still with us.'

***

270

12TH SEPTEMBER 1689

Six ships ride gently to the west on a God-sent sea: a light easterly and a half moon. The ships' lanterns are lit.

The Master walks the quarter deck, his footsteps heavy on the wood, and is joined by Sir George Hewytt.

The receding shore looks dark and black as it slips either side of the ships, their sails billowing in the evening light, the sight splendid and rousing. Byerley leans upon the gunwales and regards the ships in his wake: wide prows butting the water, raising fine, even white walls. For a moment, the countenance of the ships resembles galloping horses: purposeful, expressionless, set to the task they perform. The white sweat, the foam; the flicking turf, the spume and flying sea; yes, the ships are like galloping horses tonight. Their bodies move with the rhythm of the earth, the rhythm of the heavens and the sliding sea; now green, now brown, now black, now blue; it is like galloping across a wet field – the same ring of wind in the ears, eyes watering.

To the north a distant squall casts a dark blue veil of rain pitching at an angle across the sea. Byerley watches as it slides away from them and the Master shakes his head and stares forward. Terns and cormorants fly close to the white crests of the rolling waves.

They sail into the silver sleeve of the half moon, the water sparkling, flashing in many millions of tiny squares. The ship yaws, and for a few moments a flock of storm petrels fly alongside. The whinny of a horse from the decks below sounds out across this watery world of wind and sail, of foam and the running sea.

Byerley gazes down at the backs of the horses on the lower deck, wide bodies and slender necks moving from side to side, men shoving hay into hastily knocked-up mangers; the lads doing their bit, joking, moving between the horses, taking off saddles, cleaning tack, enjoying the experience, the smell of the sea, the spray and gentle roll of the ship. Strange how horses adapt to it so swiftly, shifting their balance to meet the movement.

Byerley gazes out to sea. The sails boom in the wind: a light, fast wind, rippling across the sea.

'A more lovely night you would scarce believe.'

'Indeed,' says Sir George sighing, 'I pray it is not an ill wind.'

Evening moves to night.

In the gloom of the ship, with the horses, away from the high quarter deck and view of the sea, in the confined, hot, low, horse-scented, converted gundecks, the troops play dice, their eyes shining in the semi-light from the musket ports.

Byerley sighs and looks into the ripples of light spangling off the water. He hears the ship's bow casting off the water in a long wake that rides out at an angle to his line of vision, a furling white line, breaking, then smoothing back into the dark, translucent skin that bore it.

Byerley had refused to have the horses swung on board at the harbour master's billing. He had rejected point-blank the captain's offer of ropes and nets. Tempers were smoothed by the diplomatic voice of Colonel Hewytt and his request to let Major Byerley have his way. Byerley told the lads to simply lead the horses onto the ships: it was easy, he said. Do as I do. Then he led that great big snorting stallion straight up the boarding into the loading port, down into the lower decks without so much as a flicker. All he said was 'go quietly' and the horses had responded. Poyntz had followed right behind, neat as a bishop's step.

They'd led over two hundred and fifty horses into six ships that night, without a single casualty. It took a tenth of the time the captains had expected. There was not one squeal, not one complaint, not one backing off or turning sideways, dropping off the quay into the water between hull and harbour wall. Nothing. It was as if the horses all understood.

'My horse must have done it before when he first came to England, I reasoned,' said Byerley, when asked how it was that the horses had been loaded so smoothly, 'And I know who would have led him.'

***

A long way to port, the mountains of North Wales slip below the surface of the sea and are lost in blackness, while to starboard looms a long strip of land. Poyntz gazes at it, puzzled until, cupping his hand against the wind, Byerley shouts to him: 'Isle of Man!'

The sails of the other ships ghost through the darkness, their stern lights flickering, voices echoing across the water, the sound of the bows dipping and rising, the reefs of foam running away behind. A horse whinnies below deck, a curious and unsettling, vulnerable sound. It reminds the men who hear it of their own frailty, that here they stand on wood, on an uncertain sea, that they are off to an unknown land to submit to an unknown destiny. They will either return or they will not.

Byerley had looked up once and seen through the gunwales an island a long way off, and now as he looks again, it seems to have stepped out of the sea right in front of them, solid and dark.

All the men are on their feet, pointing and calling out: 'Ireland!', gazing at the two passing islands, Copeland and Mew, and then pointing to the shadowy line on the northern horizon.

The morning is sparkling and fresh as the ships reef sail and glide into a long bay. Across the water lies another long stretch of land with a stark castle: 'Carrickfergus!' the Master calls to Byerley. 'It's in Protestant hands: Schomberg took it last month!'

Then came the shout. 'Saddle up!'

The six ships move slowly into Belfast Lough with calls of 'the lead if you please!' as lads bridle and saddle their horses, while trying to see the scudding landscape, or any signs of the enemy.

'Sand! Sand and shale! Two fathom!' Abruptly the anchors plunge into the water and the ships swing to their sliding grip. Boats are lowered. Wood pins are beetled from the gunwales and the long landing trestles unshipped from the loading ports and lowered into the water. Two rowing boats moor side by side, and an order runs up: 'Unship!'

The men look at one another, puzzled.

'Get the damned horses off! We got to get out with the tide!'

Byerley looks down. The gangplanks, the trestles, run into the water and stop. How deep is that water?

'Go on! Move!' Poyntz shouts to the men.

The horses will have to jump from the trestles into the sea, then swim ashore.

The water is grey and cold. Poyntz steps forward. 'Out of the way!' he barks, and leads one of the horses reluctantly to the edge of the trestle, where the horse stops, looks and refuses.

Poyntz curses. 'Get a lad in the water down there: the horses want to know how deep it is.'

A lad is pushed forward, long hair blowing about his forehead, tired blue eyes, clutching a musket he does not know how to fire, gazing into water he can't swim. Waves lap the shore a hundred yards distant.

'Can't swim, sir.'

'Get on there damn you!'

Reluctantly the lad walks down the trestle and then jumps into a boat.

'Not the boat, you peasant! In the damned water!'

The boat rocks uncertainly as the lad scrambles back onto the unshipping trestle and looks back at Poyntz for reassurance.

'Well? Jump!' Poyntz shouts as the boy hesitates. As he jumps Poyntz shouts: 'Keep your bandolier...!'

The lad remerges, chest deep and gasping for breath, the coldness of the water having robbed him of breath.

'...dry....' Poyntz finishes limply, shaking his head.

Water laps to the lad's armpits.

'Get out of the light boy, or are you going to catch the horses?'

The horse standing at the head of the gangplank is not encouraged and steps back.

'Hold to!' says Byerley. 'There's only one horse who is going to lead this lot.' Byerley stands beside his horse and vaults up in the saddle. It's a strange combination to sit in a saddle on board a ship – and the horse splays his legs to accommodate the slow pitch and roll. All Byerley will have to do is think, get to the ramp and then hit the water.

'Right you lads!' Poyntz shouts: 'Up you get! And follow the Major! Keep tight behind!'

The bay horse baulks for a minute before believing Byerley. He steps iron-shod onto the slats across the trestle, head down, takes two steps forward and then whoosh!

The splash is huge.

The men burst out laughing.

'Sea horse! Ha!Ha!Ha!'

The horse's head emerges from the spray. His ears are full of water and he shakes his head. His eyes are swimming with brine and now he has to rely on his rider to egg him on. His first reaction is to turn back to the ship but Byerley keeps him at his bit and pushes him forward. As soon as the horse feels his feet in the sand he makes for the shore without any hesitation. The reaction knocks on.

Filled with apprehension and the sense of fun, the lads follow down the trestle, their carbines banging awkwardly at their sides and one after the other, they leap.

'Hold back there! You'll land on the horse in front! Count... one...two...three....jump! You hear?'

One..two..three...splash!....one...two...three... refusal – whoops! Over the side he goes, horse and all, into the water.

The 6th Dragoons assembles wet but in high spirits on the shore. The experience of the leap has not only fired the lads up but their horses too, who now gad about on the sand.

'Mind the buggers don't roll!' shouts Poyntz wading through the last twenty yards of rising tide. 'Don't let them roll, they'll bust their saddles else!'

Watching the antics of the other horses being unshipped from the transports brings howls of delight from the lads as they see Captain Heveringham and Captain Cornwall and their troops leaping off *The Delight* of Ilford, *The Comb* from Bristol, *The Elizabeth and Katherine*.

And they point and hoot as a chestnut on *The Sarah* of London gallops off the trestles straight into the water headfirst like a torpedo then emerges ten yards from where he went in with his rider still in the saddle, floundering and flaying, head up and head shaking. Those not brave enough to ride, try to lead. Gingerly down the trestles they go and then, up go the horses' rears', pitching over backwards and landing upside-down in the water, some of them with their riders in between their legs, giving them a good brain booting as a consequence.

Others try to jump with the horses then find themselves hanging onto reins, dangling off the end of the trestles as the horses pull back, then they step over the edge, and the lad lets go of the reins and that's another in upside down.

'Do what the Major did!' sounds a shout from *The Sarah*. 'Get on and ride! No! Do not lead them! You'll get kicked to death! Ride! Yes! Go on! Get up! Jump! I thought you were huntsmen! You load of lily livers! One...two......three ...Jump!'

Soon the shoreline is filled with men and froth and horses, coughing and laughing. Long boats and cutters are swung off the transports to bring supplies to the shore, where two-wheeler carts are lined up behind an extended camp. At first the lads had thought that the unfamiliar yellow and blue colours with black crosses on the standards were Irish Jacobite and that they were going to have to fight instantly. But the sight of waving hats from the troopers in the camp allayed their fears.

'Germans and Dutchmen. They're on our side; Schomberg's auxiliaries. I hoped they would be here already,' Hewytt says to Byerley as they ride along the beach-head to the camp. 'We'll stay here for two nights before pressing south to Dundalk. Dry the lads off and unwind the horses. By Jove, the Gods were with us on that trip, eh Major Byerley, my friend?' Byerley dismounts and looks back at *The Invincible*, running in her trestles, her sails dropping. Yes, the Gods were with us.

Or someone else was.

And he feels for the little blue bead in the horse's mane.

It's still there.

- 22 -

Dundalk

The horses are plaited to sea-green, manes and tails, their hooves oiled, groomed to a twinkle, saddles tallowed and polished. All metals are worked with grease, clean and shining, hats brushed, scabbards polished, boots buffed. Stirrups bright, gloss on frogging, pistols heads and musket stocks polished to catch the sun, such as there is. The drizzle does not assist in these matters.

'Regiment fit for inspection, sir.'

Colonel Sir George Hewytt rides his bay ahead of Byerley on his Turk. Hewytt's horse looks compact and small by comparison although he is by no means a small horse; more of a spare horse, an English hunter, a hobby type, from an Irish background somewhere, white blaze and very steady. 'Me and my old nag are more or less the same creature,' he once admitted fondly to Byerley over a glass of port. 'Bred him at home. In Shireoaks, from my old mare and an Irish stallion who was standing at Temple Cross for three whole weeks. Dare say there were a few of us took advantage of that horse and a damn good sort he was too. Threw a sovereign or two the stallion man's way I should wager. Still: no regrets. Solid old beast, a leg on each corner. Do you see the way he jumped off the trestles? Ha! Afraid of nothing, this old jade, you mark my words, eh? What, Byerley?'

'Schooled to the cannon, is he sir?'

'Schooled to the cannon? Schooled to the cannon? Good God man, 'course he's schooled to the cannon. He's a hunter ain't he? Schooled to the cannon! Not like your blasted foreigner. I expect the minute you show yours a pistol he'll clear the field quick as a jacksnipe, eh what?'

Byerley raises his eyebrows. 'He might not be the only one, sir. Ashamed to say that I have not seen a pistol fired myself.'

The Colonel's kettledrummer strikes up the beat. The bugler sounds the walk. Magnificent in their red and sea-green, with their back, breast and pott, fine black hats with feathers for the officers, long broadswords, pair of pistols and snaphanse musket, the 6th Dragoons set off, their bay horses of a colour if not a type. Plenty start with a bang, a few out of gait, even a buck or two, but on the whole, good. Hundreds of hooves strike the wet ground.

They ride to the jingling of the harness, stirrups and scabbards shining. With bright faces and clean kit, eager and ready for action, the regiment advances in all its splendid and dazzling glory, its huge standards unfurled, waving above line after line of horse and straight-backed rider. They move easily with the saddle, glued to the horses' backs – during their time at the Barracks, these lads have learned how to ride. There is no shouting; no whips: only the sense of command and the unity of man and mount.

The lads in the regiment had watched the transports drop sail shortly after they had unshipped and they now gaze across the water to Schomberg's ships riding at anchor in a tossing sea by the black wharves and slips of Carrickfergus. It is good to ride along the shore in the cool breeze, in the knowledge that behind them lies the baggage wagon and in front a landscape that has been cleared of enemy. Although they had been warned to be sharp-eyed and always alert to the danger of ambush, their ride along the sea is quiet, enjoyable both for man and horse. Large rocks in the water loom like monsters' backs: a balmy breeze moves the deep green grass, waves lap the shore, waders and oystercatchers fly up, cormorants dry their wings on the edge of a solar sea.

Cheered through Belfast, they ride over the river Lagan, and into open country, lush with rose-bay willow-herb and tall hogweed. Gigantic colonies of briar bearing huge, shiny blackberries, entice passers-by to bend down and swipe a mouthful – offer it to their horses even – and ride on, purple-lipped. Pigeons coo from nearby copses, jays and magpies fly low and screech. The land they pass through, except for the birdsong, is silent. They ride past tiny houses, single storey and thatched with wheat straw, as they travel through Lisburn and Hillsborough, Bainbridge and Newry, with the Mountains of Mourne to their left and Dundalk ahead.

They'd spotted smoke from a long way back. The smoke, the smell, the sound – of gunfire. Colonel Hewytt had ordered them to be prepared to receive the enemy. But as they'd pressed on, the gunfire had become less sporadic, more systematic.

'It's only practice!' shouts Hewytt, 'Tell the men to stand down! Old Schomberg's doing a bit of training. Only hope he isn't firing our way! Tell your man to go ride to point.'

'Poyntz!'

Poyntz canters up on a coloured horse that looks as though its last job was pulling a circus tender, or even performing in the centre ring.

'Good grief!' says Byerley as he approaches. 'What kind of animal is that?' Even Byerley's stallion stares at it with surprise.

'Oh sir, it's one of Mr Shales', sir. As I was saying he got one or two – as was plough horses or something – and me – I was told to leave mine at home because.....'

'Never mind: go ahead and find out what the din is.'

'Aye, aye, sir.'

Poyntz's flapping coat and fat backside on his fat backsided feather-foot go gallumping off under a stand of elms and disappear over the grey, lichen-rocked brink.

The column moves on in the light drizzle. A grim little cottage, somewhere between a home and a hovel, slides by: its occupants gone, the one and only cart broken, overturned, the stone and dirt walls of its small yard smashed, its single glass window shattered. There is the carcase of a donkey, half-gorged by foxes and crows, now crawling with maggots. The young lads with their pistols and carbines, their swords and dreams of gallantry, turn away and some retch as the sticky stench hits them. The scorched-earth tactics of war: destroy everything in the way of the advancing enemy.

Presently Poyntz returns on his bit-fighting, head-tossing, sweating, wound-up, hairy-heeled gypsy performer.

'It's them, sir.'

'It's who?' snaps Colonel Hewytt.

'I think it's the General, sir. Down on the flats, hard by the sea shore, sir. I think.'

'Which General? What do you mean, you think?'

'Well, it's hard to tell, sir. There are that many standards I do not recognise, but they are foreign, whether it is our General Schomberg – or their General whoever he is, sir.'

***

Dundalk – seaport, borough, market and post town – lies in the barony of Upper Dundalk County Louth, Province of Leinster, fifty miles north of Dublin, ten and a bit from Newry on the post road to Belfast. The Duke of Schomberg's forces are camped on the edge of the tidal, mud-banked estuarine river of Castletown. It's a stand off between the Catholic forces of King James II, reinforced and provisioned by the French King Louis XIV, and the Protestant forces of William of Orange. A stalemate.

The 6th Dragoon Guards ride into this hell. Colonel Hewytt gazes about in horror. 'My God!' he exclaims to Byerley, 'what have we come to?' There is no colour here other than the grey-brown taupe of mud and disease. Enter this place and die. Schomberg's forces have been here one month and already half of them have died from the bloody flux: dysentery. Azarax whickers softly and thrashes a foot in the mud.

The arriving soldiers look on in revulsion: are we to camp in this place? Such tents as they have are pitched on the wet ground. The pegs won't hold and the tents collapse. The men complain. By the end of the first night, none have slept and already ten have gone down with dysentery.

The horses are tethered out in lines in the mud. There is no food. Azarax is not going to stick for this: he has always had food. Byerley wades through the mud to the lines and the horse sees him coming. Holding his head high the horse peers down the length of his nose and Byerley feels the full weight of his mistrust. You cannot cheat a horse and hope to get away with it: and this horse's trust hangs on a fine line. His groom has gone, no-one knows where. Except, perhaps, the horse. Globs of muddy water blind the horse's eyelashes: blobs of muddy water hang in his mane. The little bead is dull. The horse's feet are sunk beyond the pastern in mud: his legs are muddy, his back is muddy. Even is face is muddy. The horses in the lines are squealing and fighting. They snatch at each other's necks. They nuzzle for roots in the mud. Azarax gazes down at Byerley.

'Poyntz!' Byerley shouts.

Poyntz appears from under the awning of a muddy tent.

'6th Dragoons to the saddle!'

'...yes, sir...'

A bugle sounds: shivering lads appear from all across the camp, bringing wet saddles, wet saddle blankets. 'Do what you can to clean the horses up,' Byerley shouts 'and saddle up!'

'The Colonel, sir? Is he...?'

'The Colonel is sick, Poyntz. I am assuming command.'

The 6th Dragoon mount their hungry, muddy horses. Byerley points a finger toward the Mountains of Mourne. 'There – we're going over there. These horses need feed.'

A dismal column of dismal men, Azarax at their head. 'Does he trust me now? Does he know what I am doing?' wonders Byerley.

Byerley rides through the drizzle, frozen to the bone. The column passes cottages, barns, a tiny village, but there is no food in these places. Bilberry on the mountain gives the horses something to chew on. 'Let them graze. The more they graze, the further they can take us. Send riders out to Carlingford and Killelagh, Armillan and Newtown.'

Byerley stands beside Azarax, watching him bite into the bilberry and the thin mountain grasses. Good job this horse has been living on the edge of a Yorkshire moor for the past two years: at least this terrain was familiar. Some of the other horses are picking about, selecting a bit here and a bit there. Azarax has always been an excellent feeder. He knew what it was like to live in places where grass was at a premium. He did not waste time and energy looking for it. He stood still and mowed. And when he'd stripped the nearest patch, he'd move again, conserving as much energy as possible, on to the next bit and do the same again. It would be easy to put weight on this horse once the Spring came.

A trooper shouts. 'Someone coming!'

Byerley looks up: it is a galloper from the camp, with an order to return. Byerley ignores him. Give the horses plenty of time. We'll return here tomorrow and the next day and the next. Keep them out of that camp as much as possible – and you too. Come with me and stay alive: remain in that camp and die.

The troop mounts up two hours later and returns to camp in the dark.

Byerley orders the same routine for the next three weeks and in doing so, keeps morale high, keeps the horses alive, keeps his men away from disease as much as he can and, importantly, he builds a bond with a big Turk stallion.

December brings bitter winds but still Byerley takes the 6th out every day. On the evening of 30th December, he returns and is summoned to the Commander in Chief, the Duke of Schomberg's quarters. And the Duke of Schomberg's quarters are little better than anyone else's.

Byerley enters. He has lost weight. But his eyes are still shining and Schomberg notices.

'You have been taking your men out every day, I see.'

Byerley doesn't deny it.

'Who gave permission for this?'

Byerley clears his throat. 'I did, sir.'

Schomberg regards him with surprise and grunts: 'At least that's honest.'

'Colonel Sir George Hewytt's ill, sir. I have assumed command until he is better.'

'On whose authority and by which expedient?'

Byerley looks down into the mud at his feet. He would like to have said, 'On the authority of wishing to remain alive and the expedience of a little common sense', but holds his tongue.

Schomberg then hands him a parchment with a wax seal.

'George Hewytt is dead,' he says bluntly. 'You are now in command of the 6th Dragoon Guards. Congratulations Colonel Byerley.'

Byerley steps out of the tent in much the same mood as he stepped in. He might be Colonel but men continue to die. The camp is rife with disease. Provisions are not reaching them. There are no slips: no wharves. Men flounder in the mud with half-carcases of half-rotten beef, dragging them through mud to be washed in muddy sea water before cooking them, partially, on small fires and consuming them, along with sand, mud and seawater, and the detritus the men themselves produce. Holes cannot be dug. To dig a hole it is make a place for water to gather. The camp seethes in excreta. The tents are full of holes, there are no ground sheets, no bunks, billets or beds – not even blankets. Men's uniforms drop from their bodies, and they drink the health of the devil in usquebagh.

The sick are carried by the sick to boats, rowed by the sick, hauled onto ships by the sick and sailed to Belfast by the sick where a great hospital for the sick is prepared. One such ship was found, heaped with dead bodies, and exuding the stench of death, without a living man on board.

Sickness numbs the human soul. Eternity edges closer. That distant shore of which all mankind is afraid, is but a short step. The earth does not mourn her losses. She does not mourn the passing of her creatures. She does not stir.

JANUARY 1690

Intelligence reaches the Duke of Schomberg that the Jacobite troops have broken camp and headed south. The Duke sighs with relief, and runs a hand though his thinning hair. 'Thanks be to God.' He calls for his Colonels: 'Gentlemen,' says he, 'we shall head north, to Newry and Loughrickland, to dry ground. To camp anew. To await the arrival of King William, fresh forces and fresh provisions from England.'

Three days later, Byerley rides the way they came, at the head of the 6th Dragoons, already weary of a war that has dragged on for four months, in which eight thousand Williamite troops have died before a man has drawn sabre from scabbard.

Newry, Loughbrickland and dry ground: there is fodder for horses, and the promise of Spring. 'Now you will have time to recover,' Byerley tells his men as he rides through their lines. 'Feed up yourselves and your horses and then, when the King comes, we shall head south in greater numbers and we will thunder our chargers into the Jacobites' maw.'

- 23 -

A Horse Race

King William III, The Prince of Orange – King Billy as he becomes known – boards his yacht *Mary* at Hoylake and is escorted by Sir Cloudesley Shovell's squadron of 280 transports and six men-of-war to Ireland.

On 14th June 1690, the green hills of Ireland rise from the sea following a stormy crossing, and in the afternoon Sir Cloudesley Shovell's fleet drops anchor off the Carrickfergus shore in Belfast Lough, already cluttered with Schomberg's fleet, listlessly riding the tide. The Rear Admiral's cutter is ordered to the King's yacht, from which the King alights and is rowed to the Old Quay beneath the shadow of the castle keep.

Set about with Royal standards, huge kettle drums, fifes, the rat-a-tat-tat of regimental drummers and the hautboys' piping, the King marches south. Line upon line they file down the road to Lisburn; cavalry and infantry, flying standards, squealing pipes, dazzle, pomp and glory. If a man had lacked conviction, this sight renews his spirit: it revives his confidence in his cause and his King.

This dark King with his steady eye and certain manner is so complete a contrast to the wavering, indecisive James II that he is cheered from Belfast to Loughbrickland.

Only half of his soldiers are British. The Duke of Ormonde commands the Life Guards; the Earl of Oxford, the Blues. Sir John Lanier leads the 1st Dragoon Guards. Beaumont and Hastings command their regiments of foot. Kirke's Lambs shoulder muskets and the 6th Dragoons have Colonel Byerley at their head, riding high upon his Turk, Portland and Ginckel bring regiments in yellow and blue uniforms from Holland, Solmes heads the finest infantry in Europe. The Prince of Hesse brings mercenaries, the Duke of Wirtemberg commands the Danes, Brandenberg brings Germans; there are also Finns. Mitchelbourne, Wolseley and Cunningham lead the Protestant forces from Ulster: 800 Derrymen, 4,500 Inniskilleners with two companies from Bandon in Cork.

The King halts at Hillsborough.

The day is hot. Intelligence is brought continually to the King, whose scouts are active well ahead of his army.

A strange story reaches his ears. One which amuses him. The Governor of the Castle at Hillsborough entertained him on the first evening with the tale.

'It is about three Colonels, their mounts and a public house, called the *Flying Horse*. Fights had broken out in the ranks following news of a challenge that had been made between three of your young Colonels in March earlier that year, 1690, following a terrible winter, when so many of their men had died. Enjoying the early Spring sunshine, the three Colonels had planned to resurrect a local race to compete for King James II's Plate in the lanes of County Down.

'News of this challenge had been spread about by a red-bearded farrier called Poyntz who, while eavesdropping at a dinner shared by these gentlemen, learned over port that the race had been proposed and promptly stepped away into the night and spread the news like fire in the city. Unbeknown to the gentlemen, by dawn the troops had already made a book, and a certain Mr. William Hill, resident in these parts, had encouraged it by the placement of heavy bets on the outcome of this race. It was to be a three-horse race, run from the *Flying Horse* tavern on 16th March 1690. Such was the enthusiasm that had been whipped up about the potential winnings in this encounter that some men had bet their entire purse. The astute Mr. Hill was willing to risk his own fortunes against it, believing that where enough troops were involved then he would walk away at least not out of pocket.

'On the appointed day, the three Colonels met at the *Flying Horse* tavern at eleven o'clock sharp, and put their steeds to the test.

'Much money had been laid upon the Turk of Colonel Byerley, his troopers believing it to be the favourite. One look at the opposition convinced them of their decision. His challengers were Colonel Heyford on his Barb and Colonel Gus Hamilton of the 20th Lancashire Fusiliers, on a borrowed Cob. Rules had been set: there was to be no unhorsing, no swords or clubs, no whipping of the other contestants or missiles hurled at them from the crowd and the race was to be run clean on a circuit which the three contestants had paced beforehand. The race was to be started with three horses in line at the report of a pistol.

'At the appointed time, many troopers had slipped away from their regiments and appeared, without leave, in front of the *Flying Horse* tavern, careless of what their officers might say, each backing his own Colonel. With generous offers of advice about how to ride and win a horse race, matters in which every trooper now seemed to be master, the Colonels were cheered to position amongst fights and scuffles which broke out in the ranks. They crowded the track and the spectators had to be pushed back at the end of a pike by a man called Poyntz, who apparently had laid all his earnings on his Colonel's horse, dubbed for the day, the Byerley Turk.

'The three horses were ridden to the appointed place, and good specimens they were too, although Colonel Hamilton's Cob was not quite of the same mettle as the two that opposed him. The handling of the horses could not have been more different, since whereas Colonel Heyford was generous with the whip and Colonel Hamilton with the spur, Colonel Byerley rode without either, although he had entered the enclosure – a ring of scoundrels standing at the beginning of the course – white as a mainsail, as his horse reared and plunged and laid his ears flat and bared his teeth. Whoever was near him had to scuttle away as fast as he could lest he be kicked over the heads of his comrades or lose his fingers to the flashing tushes. In truth the horse was as savage a brute as ever set hoof in Ireland but magnificent to look on. When he appeared, many of the opposing troopers hedged their bets, which threw a look of deep concern into Mr Hill's eyes. But then he had calculated his position nicely and did not aim to find himself the loser, whatever the outcome of this venture.

'A pistol had been raised, a shout to ready themselves had gone up, the horses held tight to the bit – very tight to the bit – the pistol fired and two of the horses loosed into a fine turn of speed, while the last, the one carrying the greatest purse, was left standing on his hind legs waving his feet in the air, with Colonel Byerley on his back muttering his prayers – much to the horror of the 6th Dragoon troopers, who could see their money rapidly disappearing before their eyes. These fellows now rushed at him to get the horse off. Poyntz was there first and, slapping the horse across the quarters with a flat of a sword, put the Turk into such a frenzy that he took off very nearly without his rider and in the opposite direction.

'Much shouting and cursing and hurling of hats onto the ground followed, while Colonel Byerley wrestled the animal about, pointed him at the tails of the two disappearing contenders now half a league ahead and went thundering off down the track to shouts and howls and yells and curses and men falling to their knees, hands clasped together, wringing out prayers not heard since the time of Elizabeth I, not in these shores at least. Down the lane the horses sped, to cries of woe from troopers of the 6th Dragoons and to the high delight of the Fusiliers and Royal Dragoons and although they agreed to a man later that Colonel Byerley's Turk did, in fact, have the edge on speed, he was such a long way behind Heyford's Barb and Hamilton's Cob as for the race to appear over for him. On and on they sped, the horses' nostrils fully extended, their limbs thrashing sod and air, along the Flying Horse road, turning the corner, up the hill and back toward the public house. The cheering became louder and louder as Colonel Byerley's Turk squeezed the gap, at last narrowing the distance between himself and Hamilton's Cob.

'With the end of the race looming it still appeared that no magic on earth could secure Colonel Byerley the King's Plate, and yet on he galloped, gaining lost ground by the stride. On and on the horses thundered and then witnesses beheld a most remarkable thing.

'It was as if Byerley's Turk took wing. The ground seemed to fly beneath his feet as though he weighed not a pound. His legs flicked out in front of him and on his back the wind tore at the Colonel's clothes, at his hair, at his face which by now was dark with mud from the horses galloping in front.

'Suddenly the great Turk horse went hurtling past Colonel Hamilton's Cob and with the end of the race in sight, he was narrowing the gap on Colonel Heyford's Barb with every stride.

'Not a hundred paces lay between them and the end of the course and soon they were galloping neck and neck. Then another kind of energy seemed to fill the limbs of the Turk: as if some magical power overcame him; as if some wondrous elixir coursed in his veins. He shot past the Barb and took the finishing line with a length to spare. The 6th Dragoons went insane with joy.

'Thus Colonel Byerley galloped to glory and took the King James's Plate to the frenzied euphoria of his men while Colonel Heyford came in a strong second on his Barb and Colonel Hamilton third, on his Cob. As the horses slowed to a walk the 6th Dragoons surrounded their Colonel with shouts of delight and much throwing of hats in the air, yelling and patting the horse who now walked as quiet as a kitten up to the doors of the tavern, with barely a trickle of sweat on him and it was agreed by one and all that the horse was fit to run the race again.

'It was interesting to note, Your Majesty, that Colonel Byerley's horse was already well known in the barracks in Hounslow and indeed in Whitehall Palace stables, having been brought there as a spoil of war from Buda by Sir Edward Vaudrey and the Duke of Berwick. Both these men now stand ranged against us in the ranks of King James II. Apparently the horse was, even in England, regarded as a mascot. But now that has been surpassed a hundredfold. There is nothing these men will not do for this horse: he is, in short, the darling of the greater part of the English army. His fame travels before him.

'It was excellent sport, despite the fights that followed, the insults thrown about and the black looks that Colonels Heyford and Hamilton received from their men which might well have proved disastrous for regimental cohesion. All anger was allayed by the generosity of the Colonel of the 6th Dragoons who, being a man of considerable substance, bought all there was to be drunk in the public house and dispensed it lavishly, to winners and losers alike. Then, standing in his stirrups and holding a frothing pint of good ale in his hand, he cried: 'Long Live King Billy!' knocked it back in a draught and trotted the horse back to camp, where, it is said, he spent the next two hours communing with the animal, as though he were talking to a man, calling him his Treasure over and over again.'

So amused was King William, and so glad that the race had been run in the right spirit, despite the odd broken head, black eye and lost tooth – and that his men had, on the whole, acted properly, commiserating over their losses and rejoicing in their winnings – that he decided to inaugurate a Plate himself. Thus it was that the races at Downroyal were the only ones in the world in which two contesting Monarchs (who were to fight one another not a week later) inaugurated their own respective King's Plates.

- 24 -

The Boyne

Byerley dismounts from his sweating horse in Tullyallen, a hamlet set above the fertile, green valley of the Boyne. It is late afternoon. He pulls off his feathered, beaver hat. His hair has matted to his head in the heat, the thick worsted red coat he wears is soaked. The march south from Ulster has been fast, and most of the horses are galled. Flies and midges have harried them all the way. The sun has burned their faces and the backs of their hands. There has been constant tacking up and untacking; the sweaty shabracs have not been given time to dry, the ill-fitting saddles, the broken reins, loose shoes, lame horses, difficult horses, mares in season with stallions near-by – the everyday occurrences of massed men on massed horse – have cost time and tempers. God knows what the seyis would have had to say. When they stop at night, the horses have had to be fed, watered, checked. Injured horses attended to: lame horses set with the baggage train. Then the sick men: men with dysentery, men with wounds – caused by fighting within the regiment: absurd jealousies, petty arguments – are patched up; the putting up of tents and lighting fires – usually in the rain – finding firewood, shortage of food – all this has conspired to shorten the men's dwindling patience.

Byerley leans against his horse's sweating shoulder and lets out a long, exhausted sigh. The burden of being Colonel of the regiment is trying enough, without his apprehension of the days ahead. His nights have been sleepless. This will be his first military engagement and the thought overwhelms him. He had felt sick with nerves before the race three months earlier, but that was nothing compared with this. He cannot put out of his mind the grim fact that these might be the last hours of his life. He has found it hard to rest, even in the depths of night.

Down in the valley lies the old ruined Abbey of Mellifont, not far from the river Boyne. Byerley has been summoned to muster with the King at six o'clock that evening to review orders for battle. Review orders for his death? Is he now to be collaborator in his own demise?

The stark reality of the prospect makes him feel weak. He leans over and holds his knees. His fear tells in his arms: he could barely lift a sabre now, not to save his life. Every man going into battle for the first time knows this moment: this dark hour. Byerley stands up, stretches – and feels no better.

* * *

The sensitive soul suffers in both these armies, the army of King William and the army of King James: to be deadwood between the ears is best. The man whose head touches pillow – wood, earth, stone, steel or the limb of a comrade – and flutters into instant sleep will thrive better than he who lies awake, tense to the tiniest sound, thrashing through the night, mind wrestling with the monsters of tomorrow or beating off the dragons of yesterday, unable to find repose.

Poyntz heard not a sound as the last of the cannon drew in, well past midnight. He failed to hear the oxen, the owls, the bats or the shouts and curses of men running the cannon up on their limbers, the unshackling of the oxen, then the horses – taking them to the lines, feeding and watering them – and then, eventually, the men themselves, dropping heavily onto the bare earth and instantly falling asleep.

Poyntz heard nothing.

He had seen the fires of the Jacobite camp through the trees, earlier. He had heard their music – before he crawled under a wagon, near the stallion, to sleep. He loved that music: it reminded him of his mother and a childhood in County Kildare, though he had never breathed a word of that earlier life. He saw, in his mind's eye, the flashing eyes and the flying skirts, the drumming fingers, the rocking fiddle bow and the happy young beings – his mother and father – carousing late into the night. He prefers it to the music of his own side: the pipes and Lilliburlero, the beating drums of his late night comrades. His heart is torn, but what can a simple farrier do?

So he'd rolled over and fallen asleep, dead to the world, dead to the snorting horses, the pawing horses, dead to the stallion's loud call right in the depths of night which had penetrated his dream and given it shape, set it on some entirely eccentric tangent. Nor was he aware that his Colonel, Byerley, in his own tent, lay tossing and turning, lying one minute this side, next minute the other.

Byerley had risen later in the night and stalked out, exhausted and exasperated. He looked out over the profound hush of the sleeping camps, up into the glittering stars and marvelled at the stillness and at the thought that tomorrow, this would all be broken, that this night might be his last. He walked to his horse, whose eyes glistened with the reflected light of the stars and who greeted him with a whicker. He put a hand on the horse's neck and ran his fingers through its mane and, finding the little blue bead still plaited into it, held it between his thumb and forefinger and in unspoken words, prayed that the seyis would watch over them. He found more hard feed and placed it in front of the horse and all the time the horse stood with his ears pricked, looking across the valley as though he too knew that tomorrow destinies would once more be decided.

* * *

'There is no bridge,' blusters General Douglas, 'there is a ford, an oblique ford, exposed at low tide – the river being tidal, affected by sea currents, to the mid-ford that is, what they call the Old Bridge – which is not a bridge. Lower down, toward Drogheda, towards the sea, past the ford, the river runs deeper. It has a tricky, curling current. There are reeds and a rocky outcrop, awkwardly positioned: too high and exposed to mount cannon and yet not wide enough to shelter large numbers of men. The north banks slope in two levels down to the river and opposite, about a quarter of a mile south from the river, runs a level scarp, behind which it is hard to say what might be hidden. Yet, all-told, the lie of the land is to our advantage.'

'James's troop numbers?' King William asks, hoping for a simpler answer.

'Twenty six thousand men.'

'All armed?'

'No, no. The infantry – many of them – bear only scythes.'

'His strengths?'

'Cavalry, decidedly – led (to all intents and purposes) by Sarsfield. Otherwise he has titular heads. French. Not popular with the Irish patriots.'

'Weaknesses?'

'James II himself. No stratagem in him. Spurns advice and tosses aside opportunity. A confused chain of command.'

'Mmmm.' King William taps the map with a forefinger. 'Sarsfield sounds a challenge. Who is he?'

'Descended paternally from Anglo-Irish stock, mother a daughter of Rory O'Moore. Fought at the Battle of Sedgemoor, knocked from his horse and took a beating himself. Sarfield's very loyal to the Jacobite cause. Assisted Tyrconnel – Talbot – late Colonel of the Queen Dowagers, now 6th Dragoon Guards, which our eminent Colonel Byerley presently heads. Sarsfield helped Talbot to remodel the Irish army, commanded James II's Irish troops in England in 1688; returned to Ireland the following year. The men love him. A true Irish patriot. A good man, much honoured. Underrated by James. Well-bred and well-mannered. A gentleman.'

'Hmm.' The King purses his lips, stands and paces with his hands behind his back. 'Then we shall have to divert him.'

TUESDAY 1ST JULY 1690, 4 A.M.

A misty dawn in the Boyne Valley. The river is smooth, disturbed only by the flop of a lazy salmon and a sudden flight of mallard. A heron stabs the water and coots pick their way through the reeds. The water is dark, the tide is running and the great lamp of the sun rises slowly behind Drogheda.

Companies of William's men jog, bandoliers rattling, through the mist; mustering to troop, regiment, battalion. Then, a soft mumble. Through the mist, men line up, hats off:
'Our Father, which art in Heaven,
Hallowed be thy name,
Thy Kingdom come,
Thy Will be done....'

***

A stream that runs into the Boyne in the valley is filled with minnows. Byerley takes Azarax down to it after prayers to let him drink and crop some of the sweet grasses at the water's margin. When the horse has drunk he stands very close to Byerley, then in a deliberate movement, swings to his right and lays his head on Byerley's shoulder. It is a conscious action and Byerley had not expected it. A dribble of water spills from the horse's lips but he stays quite still, with his head on his master's shoulder, breathing softly. Taken aback by the closeness of the act, Byerley responds by running a hand along the length of Azarax's face but the weight of the horse's head and the gesture makes him feel as though the horse is

291

transmitting a message, as if to say: It is alright. Emotion tugs suddenly in Byerley's chest: does the horse sense his fear? The moment is profound, gentle, surprising. Like a wild bird landing, inexplicably on his finger: it feels portentous. Is it sympathy? Is he about to die? Today? Does the horse know something he does not? The horse raises his head and looks at him, squarely, then glances back at the horse lines.

An enormous iridescent dragonfly alights that moment on a gunnera leaf and both he and the horse see it at once. Beneath it, the minnows continue their play in the shallows.

Byerley bends down and, cupping his hands in the cold, clear water, lifts some and pours it over the horse's muzzle and the horse stands still, seeming to enjoy its refreshing coldness. Then, as if a spell had suddenly broken, the moment passes, Azarax turns and Byerley walks him back up the hill to the horse lines, where Poyntz is feeding them oats and barley.

He takes the horse back to his tether and watches as he eats, head down. His horse's gesture stays in his mind and though tempted to touch him, to run a hand across his back, he knows that now is not the time: the moment has passed. But what a moment! The horse is eating and has his 'leave-me-alone' look in his eye. It takes a horseman to spot it and Byerley spots it. Noli me tangere. Do not touch me. The horseman observes the lore and offers him the distance he wants. An unconscious blessing passes and the horse relaxes his ears. Strange how he knew. Byerley only just knew himself. Something right on the limits of the conscious mind and yet the horse picked it up as though he had shouted it. 'It is the inner voice they hear,' Byerley remembers the seyis explaining. 'Ride him with your heart and if you believe that you are right, nothing can stop you.' Something has been resolved. Byerley feels better and straightens his back. If he can fight on foot with a sabre, then he can surely sabre-fight on the back of a stallion.

5 A.M.

The regiment is mounted and the soft early morning sun is pushing the mist out of the hollows in the valley. The line of the river emerges as the mist evaporates. It is a crystal day. Byerley sits firm on his solid bay stallion at the head of his regiment. Azarax looks magnificent: Byerley looks good on him – every inch the Colonel on his battle charger. The lads are proud of their Colonel: he's a good looking fellow, just over twenty nine years old, broad-shouldered, brown-eyed and wearing a very old but highly polished baldric bearing a Civil war sword. He carries two pistols and a snaphanse, his cuirass reflects the sun, he has highly polished boots and an ostrich-feather hat showing a green sprig. All the lads in the regiment wear green sprigs in their hats: in fact every man on the north side of the river has a sprig of green in his hat, just as every man on the other side has a white cockade in his. There's not a distinguishable uniform between the two sides: to lose your hat is to lose your head: the only way either side can be told apart are by these signs on the hats.

If the Colonel is tired he isn't showing it now. If fear of death fills his mind, not a flicker of it shows on his face.

Six battalions of infantry troops pass along the bank below the 6th Dragoons, marching to the beat of the drum and to the Dutch fifes. They are a splendid sight, the fresh morning sun glinting off their muskets, uniforms of red with blue facings, yellows and pale blues, black hats and furred caps and coped crowns. The command is taken by General Douglas and Meinhart, Count Schomberg – the Duke of Schomberg's son, who had also been in Buda and who also rides a Turk.

There are twenty-four squadrons of horse, with Byerley's 6th Dragoons taking first position.

Up goes the shout, the young Colonel moves not a muscle, leaving it to the horse. His powerful Turk eases forward, those big, flat, black knees rising high at the head of his regiment of 250 horse. A subtle command flicks the entire regiment to the canter and now it's the turn of the infantry to look up at the 6th Dragoons dropping down at an angle from the heights toward Slane. Colours flying, standards high, scarlets and sea-green, matched bays (Poyntz and his skewbald disguised in the middle somewhere), manes and tails plaited, helmets and cuirasses gleaming; the chink of steel against steel, jingling spurs and harnesses, they feel the ground tremble as the hooves thunder down.

Down, down toward the tributary river Mattock, up and across to the Boyne, which curves away from the bridge a little past Oldbridge, in a southerly direction. On the far side of the river, standards are seen shadowing them: a huge Jacobite force of 17,000 men sent to meet small outflanking force led by Byerley.

Intelligence has the Williamites to understand they will meet a plain where they can sweep up to Duleek, behind and to the south of the Jacobite front lines. There are no illusions about what they will meet. The Irish foot may not be well armed but they will be determined: these are not pressed men.

And the cavalry? The Irish cavalry is the stuff of legends. They have every chance of gaining the advantage. There are veterans in that cavalry: clever men on canny horses. It's going to take the Williamites all their skill and every inch of their courage to meet them.

293

The 6th lopes on, now high above the Boyne, above the valley through which it runs, the other side of Dowth.

Behind them they leave the Dutch cavalries and the Enniskilliners. This band of horsemen, this Protestant gönüllü, this uniformless unit of men on unmatched horse, with their servants to the rear and their women behind them, are a wild sight. 'Like Tartars,' the Count Schomberg had observed. They reminded him of Buda. 'No doubt they offer the same mercy. No doubt they have the same skills. I should not care to face them.'

Suddenly there is a crackle of musket fire; shot sputters in the mud at their feet and cannonballs fly over their heads.

'Down to your left, three hundreds yards to left, where the swans are lifting – the ford! Rossnaree!'

Leaping into the water – which is deeper than they had thought – Azarax bounds, belly-deep, through the river keeping his head high. He is responding magnificently; the depth of the water did not bother him, the gunfire hadn't alarmed him, he'd not flinched, unlike many of the others behind him. Some had taken fright in the river and reared, others whinnied and halted, then fought their riders and tried to gallop back. In mid-stream a hail of fire divides the regiment. A cry goes up. 'Enemy horse!'

Byerley leaps out of the water onto the far bank followed quickly by two troops of horse. Ahead, through the trees, he can see the left wing of Sir Neil O'Neil's foot, and skirmishing cavalry drawn up in good order, though at a distance.

'Have at them!' shouts Byerley. Heels to the horse and away goes the stallion. In a shower of flying mud, with pounding hooves and bunching haunches, his horse is a streak of light. Sabre drawn and yelling at the top of his voice, presuming his troops are following, Byerley rides out, widening the distance between himself and his own men by the stride. All he hears is the roaring of wind in his ears, the even breath of his horse, the rising and falling mane, the pounding of blood and hoof and the sight of the steel at his arm's length, steady at its target, closing, closing. He hears only his own voice shouting in his head.

The skirmishers pour out from the trees, in a headlong face-to-face, sabre-to-sabre charge. A shot is fired, whistling past Byerley, then another and another. Lowering his sabre for a split second, Byerley pulls a pistol and, cocking it on his cuirass on the way up, he discharges a shot and finds his mark. Away goes the pistol and up comes the sabre, plunging straight into the midst of five approaching skirmishers. He is like a demon on a horse out of hell. His troop is a full hundred yards behind.

Azarax bunches down on his haunches, seizing a man in his teeth and he spins as Byerley's sabre strikes: two men fall in the instant, one screaming at the horse's feet, his shoulder crushed by massive front teeth, the other sabred through. The three other skirmishers falter but Byerley's horse is immediately upon them: controlled, those teeth again, glaring eyes and flat ears – this is a war horse. One man's hand is crushed on the hilt of his sword; another swing from Byerley and the fourth goes down. By now the first of his troop have caught up and another wave of skirmishers dash into view. Musket and pistol fire crackles. 'Have at them!' Have at them!' Byerley shouts.

Sabres clash and hack as Byerley wheels the great horse about. A shot rings out and a ball rips through Byerley's collar. Six Jacobites gallop toward him, pistols steadied and Byerley spins the horse once more. Forward the stallion gallops again, toward the skirmishers, followed to his rear by Captain Cornelius Woods who is plastered with the mud flicked up by the flying hooves in front of him. Both men are yelling at the tops of their lungs, sabres bloodied and closing like devils on their flat-eared, wild-eyed horses. A clang of steel: that Civil War sabre is heavy and knocks the sword straight out of the skirmisher's hand. A holler sounds out from the troop as they join their Colonel. Galloping at their head on his sweating horse, he leads them straight at a massed body of skirmishers, into the deafening crack of pistol shot. The blinding shower of spent powder peppers Byerley's face as they hit the skirmishers as one fast and furious body.

Musket fire exploding from banks and ditches drives Byerley's troop back. Re-mustering with the main body of the regiment, they canter to Schomberg and Douglas' advancing position and report large numbers of Irish cavalry drawn up to the left. The skirmishers have melted back, through paths thick with briar, into the trees.

Gallopers are sent for reinforcement, while the squadrons swing to the left, away from the trees to the plain beyond, on the other side of which the Irish horse regiments are drawing up in smart order.

But Schomberg's advancing force suddenly halts.

'Quagmire! Quagmire!'

Scouts are sent to check the ground. They report back: impassable. The horses won't make it. The two forces face each other across the treacherous bog. Horses' blood up, men's blood up, Byerley's blood up – it is a stalemate.

'Damnation and curses! Poyntz!'

Poyntz gallops up on his rotund skewbald. 'Find us a way through this damned bog!'

'Sir!'

From the distance comes the sound of drums. The drums cease, replaced by crackle of musket fire and the shouts of thousands of men.

'Hurry Poyntz!'

Poyntz flounders about in the trees, his fat garron refusing to put his foot into the quagmire. Byerley watches from afar. So that's why the cunning old devil's riding that disreputable beast: the horse knows the ground. Byerley can't suppress a shard of admiration. Crafty old fox.

After five minutes, Poyntz reports back.

'It's alright Poyntz,' Byerley says quietly: 'I could see. Return to the ranks.'

Byerley paces the edge of the bog on his horse, impatiently.

Count Schomberg canters up, reins his horse hard and moves in the saddle. The two Turkish horses respond to one another, nostril to nostril, the deep-throated whicker, then a nose to a knee: a gesture of recognition. Both Schomberg and Byerley notice. 'Is that a Buda horse, Colonel?'

'He is indeed, Sir.'

'Ha! So is this one. By God they know it too! Anyway, look, we've done it.'

'Sir?' Byerley asks, puzzled.

Count Schomberg points. 'Lauzan. We've drawn him off William's front.'

Byerley gazes out over the long bog: thousands of horsemen milling about.

'See!'

'And now we shall have to sit it out.'

'Damn frustrating though, isn't it, Sir?'

'Yes, but it serves its purpose. William has already struck with his main force at the Irish centre. James fell for the gambit.'

'Chess?'

'Precisely.'

'We've locked up his best pieces.'

To their left, across the River Boyne, the action has intensified judging by the sounds of men thrashing in water, the roar of cannon, the screams and constant barrages of pistol and musket shot.

The mounted lads in the regiment behind Byerley mill around on flighty horses: 'Can't we go and do something sir, I mean, our lads are being cut to pieces sir, can't we get stuck in?'

'Stay where you are!'

The sounds of battle come in waves now: at first loud and then soft as a breeze, it squeezes and expands upon the ether. For Byerley's men, the wait goes on: a few pot shots crackle across the bog but the range is beyond musket fire. And there's no artillery.

Suddenly the Irish cavalry on the far side of the bog break off.

'To the right and find another way and cut them off on the south!' Count Schomberg shouts the instant he spots their withdrawal. 'Leave the infantry stand here!'

The unit swings as a body and rides hard along the edges of the trees, past the bog, to Roughgrange Ravine. This gully had been dismissed before as unrideable. Now they must try. Down the horses plunge, slithering on the scree. Once more Azarax is well ahead of the others: he's not sitting back on his hocks with his head in the air, thrashing his forefeet about like most of the other horses, he's jinking, slithering down it Is there nothing this horse does not know? He bounds up the steep far bank and charges square on into the retreating Irish infantry, who are heavily protected by their own cavalry. It's a bitter fight and the Irish cavalry turn and guard their infantry with flashing sabres, musket shot and lowered lance. Byerley lunges at a well-dressed man on a big Irish horse: their sabres meet in mid-air and they hack, lunge and parry at one another. But their match is equal and the fight exhausts both men. They retreat, sabres lowered, all their strength gone. They catch each other's eye and salute, gentlemen to the bone. There is a flicker of admiration, respect: another day, perhaps, and then may the best man win – or, let us drink together, when all this is over – and the Irish horseman canters elegantly away.

A bugle sounds.

'Their colours are not struck, sir. Give them chase, sir?'

A head is shaken. 'No. The day is ours.'

The lads in the 6th Dragoons wave their weapons joyfully above their heads. 'Huzzah!'

A bloodied Irish cavalryman rides heavily by, sweating, exhausted and bleeding, upon a sweating, exhausted, limping horse.

One of the lads raises a carbine.

'Put that weapon down, boy!' shouts Byerley angrily. The lone horseman gazes at Byerley, nods, and rides on. 'Let that man ride off with his honour or you shall lose yours.'

The lads fall silent and watch him go.

'Men died here today,' says Byerley. 'Better men than us. We count ourselves lucky we are not amongst them.' He scabbards his sabre.

'Poyntz!'

The fat man on the garron canters up: his hat has disappeared and his nicotine- coloured hair is standing on end. His face – where visible beneath the mud – is burned scarlet by the sun, his horse and uniform are soaked in sweat and are glistening. He is a fright to behold. Byerley's face cracks and he bursts out into a hacking guffaw: 'By God Poyntz, you must have scared them to death!'

'Sir?' replies the bewildered Poyntz, reining his fidgeting garron.

'Nothing, Poyntz, nothing. Tell the lads to muster. We need a head count.' Most of them are mustered already, standing around their Colonel in a wide circle several horses deep. They are silent. Byerley suddenly becomes conscious they are all staring at him and his horse.

'What's the matter with you lot?' he barks, feeling uncomfortable under such concentrated gaze.

'Three cheers for the Colonel and his horse!' shouts one of the lads. 'Huzzah! Huzzah! Huzzah!'

Azarax's ears are pricked and he paws the ground with a forefoot. And what a sight he is, muscled, sweating, those huge eyes gleaming. At least he knows how to take a compliment. He's loving this. He tosses his head and shakes, sticks his nose in the air and blows a good, strong, snotty snort.

'Huzzah! Huzzah! Huzzah!'

'What have we done to deserve this?'

Captain Cornelius Woods offers an explanation: 'We're going to stick with you and that horse of yours, sir, wherever you go! You're like a damned whirlwind!'

'What?'

'Remind me not to get into a fight with you when your horse is around!'

'What? What?'

'Never seen anything like it!'

Byerley pats the horse's sweating neck with gusto. It was true; this horse fought as well, didn't he? Like a tiger! This horse saved my life! Emotion catches in his throat.

'It's thanks to you!' Byerley shouts back, his voice breaking. 'Well done, lads!'

The troopers sit on their horses, gazing at the Turk horse and the young Colonel on his back. They're going to follow him anywhere. Even if it is just out of curiosity.

'Head count, Lads, who's with us?'

The 6th Dragoons line up, each man in set formation, behind this man and this horse, beside that man on his left and that horse on his right. The gaps reveal the losses.

'Twelve men missing, sir!'

'Find them. Report to camp. Bury the dead. We shall hold prayers.'

1st July 1690. Night

Byerley stands alone in the horse lines listening to his men singing in the camp away to his right. Smoke billows about. The sky is pricked by a wash of stars. The river runs black and silent in the valley. Orderlies pick their way through the darkness carrying stretchers. Small points of light smoulder on the bank opposite. Oxen draw cannon away from emplacements over the brow of the hill toward Drogheda. The smell of death and saltpetre hangs in the air.

    Beside the Colonel, the big bay Turk crops thick, high summer grass. Byerley doesn't need to speak. He doesn't need to say a single word. The horse's ears are pricked. His big eyes are shining. He knows.

    He knows.

- 25 -

King Amongst Horses

FINGLAS, NORTH DUBLIN. 5th July 1690, Evening

Byerley swirls brandy around his goblet. He stands in what has become the officer's mess-tent in Finglas. Captain Cornelius Woods is pouring himself another glass. They had marched down with the army from the Boyne three days earlier, following the battle, surprised that King William had not wished to chase James II's forces and rout them completely. Woods breaks the silence.

'Well?' he asks. 'Did we win or didn't we?'

Byerley takes a sip. He looks over the blue range of the Wicklow Mountains to the south. 'What do you think?'

'I don't think we did, that's what I think.'

Byerley rolls the brandy round his tongue.

'I mean did you see the way they retreated? It was magnificent. Their cavalry closed in around their infantry, protecting them as savagely as a wolf her young: it was absolutely superb.'

Byerley purses his lips: good brandy.

'And I heard they pushed back our lot time and time again. Even the Enniskilliners. I don't know if we would have made a lot of difference frankly, what with Sarsfield and the rest of their lot loose. We might well have been sent scuttling.'

'Tush, tush, Cornelius. That's treasonable stuff.'

'Yes, but my hat, they are a force to be reckoned with, no mistake.'

Byerley looks into the amber liquid in the glass: 'I fear we are here for the duration. We are about to be led a merry dance.'

Woods refills his glass. 'I heard Vaudrey was killed. Did you know? And Berwick had his horse shot from under him. Our lads trampled all over him without knowing it was him – he was lucky to get away.'

'And poor old Schomberg. The Count took it badly. The old man was magnificent.'

A moment of quiet again. Byerley sits on an upturned grenade case.

'That horse of yours is astounding, Colonel,' says Woods.

Byerley holds out his glass and Cornelius Woods recharges it.

'We thought you'd had it. On your own like that.'

'I had no idea.'

'You're quite a swordsman.'

Byerley raises his eyebrows. 'If only you knew,' he thinks.

'Here's to your health Colonel and that of your extraordinary horse,' says the young Cornelius Woods, with a gleam in his eye.

Goblets touch.

'And now I hear that King James himself has fled to France, and left his army altogether!'

Byerley nods slowly. 'They're better off without him.'

'That's a strange state of affairs, isn't it?'

Byerley looks at the young captain, his fresh face and far-away blue eyes. There's not a lot of difference between their ages, yet somehow Byerley feels a lot older and wiser. But Cornelius Woods has a lot of spirit. He's a good fellow to have on your side. 'They will have trouble in their camp. Their chain of command never was very good, even with James at their head. Especially with James at their head. Now they have his son, the impetuous Duke of Berwick, and Sarsfield and the French Commanders James has insisted should lead the army. I can see all that leading to confusion.'

Cornelius Woods is pensive. 'No doubt we shall find out. What's our next move?'

'Limerick. We march tomorrow. Via Castlemartin.'

***

Byerley mounts his big stallion at seven the following morning. The horse is in bright fettle. That little Evil Eye bead is still in his mane. The night had brought a tremendous storm and the camp had been awash. 'You snored loud enough to shame the thunder,' says Poyntz, handing Byerley his gloves. 'I could hear you from where I was myself, sir.'

Byerley looks down at his impudent farrier from his high horse, not knowing what to make of that remark. True enough though: he'd slept better than he had for years.

'First blood, Colonel sir, if you don't mind my saying. You and this horse is a fine match. You shan't go wrong now. '

Byerley's head moves a fraction: a shadow of a smile: that was a compliment. He has felt a huge lift in respect from the lads as well. The little tell-tale gestures: the glint in the eye, smiles, salutes, bows. Admiration glowing in their faces, the anxiousness to talk to him, befriend him, pat the holy horse, take him a whang of bread: 'Mind the bugger doesn't eat you though, he's as wild as a bear!' 'And don't go and visit that horse if you've got the drink in you or he'll boot your head off!'

Poyntz slaps the horse's glossy neck. 'You and this horse was a sight to behold back there sir, that's the honest truth, Colonel, sir.'

Byerley pulls on his gloves. 'Get on your gypsy garron, Sergeant.'

A moment's surprise. 'Sergeant?'

'Yes, Sergeant Poyntz. Now you can really shout at the lads.'

Poyntz stares at him with his mouth open.

Byerley nods once and the horse takes a step forward. As he moves away, Byerley adds: 'And don't let it go to your head, Poyntz. It's only because we lost Brooks at the Boyne.'

* * *

Two nights in Crumlin and then on to Castlemartin to camp there. The town has a beautiful bridge and an ancient abbey. It feels like a retreat, a sacred site.

'The question is,' muses Byerley as they cross the bridge, 'did it feel sacred in the first place, as though it were somehow special, and set apart, which is why they built the abbey here, or did they build the abbey and then the years of religious devotion have made it sacred?'

Azarax sniffs the air and looks about as they walk past, as though he too had picked up on the compelling stillness. The place is not big and soon they find their way to the Royal Standard and Arms of Nassau fluttering on a wooden pole in a light breeze. A Dutch guard challenges Byerley, then leads him and his horse to a low building where Azarax is stabled beside a grey: 'This is Sorrel, the King's horse,' the guard says baldly. Byerley dismounts, the guard unsaddles the horse and points Byerley to the main house.

The army has been divided: five regiments of cavalry and twelve of infantry under the command of General Douglas have been sent off to Athlone. Officers left in charge of regiments, battalions and even troops find themselves invited to ride or to dine with the King. Byerley had attracted attention in another way. His show of dash at the Boyne had not gone unnoticed. Not only had Riffel and Lanier spotted it but Count Schomberg as well, and King William had been curious to find out more. Accordingly, while in Castlemartin, the King had summoned Byerley to dine and ordered – by way of his equerry – that the Colonel's horse should be stabled with his own, since he was anxious to have a close look at this Turk, recalling that he had won the King's Plate and now appeared to have cut quite a figure in the army.

The high summer days were long, so they had dined outdoors, and after dinner the King had asked for the horse to be brought for him to look over.

Taking scent from a small, tight yellow rosebud in his hand, the King steps past as Byerley holds the horse.

The King, King William III, King Billy, the Prince of Orange, is of smaller stature than Byerley. He has a slightly-built frame, olive skin, a mop of straight black hair, a good profile, with a slightly hooked nose: he has a strong chin and brown, deeply intelligent eyes. He is a man devoid of pomposity. He has the fine, long fingers of a philosopher, set on long-palmed hands. It is almost impossible to believe that this slender man was struck on the right shoulder by a cannon ball, was nearly drowned in the river Boyne when his horse floundered and threw him, then remounted and wielded a sabre for nineteen straight hours with his left hand. This alone commanded the immense respect of his men. Moreover his soldiers revered him because he lived as they live, he did not order fancy food nor special wines, he ate and drank what his soldiers ate and drank, he needed no props to bolster his innate authority, no fawning flunkeys to flannel a withering ego, no regal artefacts to massage his sense of self-importance. He is the kind of man, Byerley imagines, who takes his pleasures from intellectual rather than carnal sources. He does not move his eyebrows when he speaks and he speaks plainly.

'A Turk.'

'Indeed, sir.'

'There are a number of Orientals in the English cavalry, I have noticed.' Byerley clears his throat, 'Sir.'

'My own dragoons have brought some.'

'I have noticed, sir.'

'From both sieges. Vienna and Buda. Quite a number came to our states following Vienna. They made quick trade, I believe.'

'Some were brought to England, from Hamburg by ship, sir, by a German officer. A Brandenburger, I understand.'

'This is an unusual one. Longer in the back than most.'

'I know little of his type, sir. Through his Turkish groom, an excellent fellow who came with him, knew his breeding. Called him a Kairman, or some such thing.'

The King looks into the distance, 'Kairman?' The blue hills deepen in the sinking summer night and the King is pensive, rolling this familiar sounding name around in his head: it's not quite right. 'And your Turkish groom? What became of your Turkish groom?'

Byerley clears his throat again. 'He disappeared, sir. It was a great mystery.'

'Ah.'

'But the horse himself, I bought him from Captain Edward Vaudrey, later knighted by King James, who was killed at the Boyne. He was in King James' camp, sir. A Catholic.'

The King raises an eyebrow. 'Hm. That is an irony.'

'Indeed, sir.'

'How did he die?'

'On horse, sir.'

'On a slower horse, I'll wager – what an irony!'

'I am only too aware of it, sir: the positions might so easily have been reversed.'

'It is a story worthy of a Greek tragedy.'

'So it is, sir.'

'And what will you do with the horse?'

'When I return to England? Retire him, I imagine, sir.'

'What? Not race him – you won once, I am informed.'

Byerley smiles self-consciously. 'I am not a gambler, sir. I have no real interest in the sport.'

'Will you not breed from him?'

'Perhaps, sir.'

'It would be a pity not to: blood like this would benefit the horse-flesh I have seen in England. Put some heat into them.'

'Indeed, sir.'

The horse looks off: he's scented something. A mare probably, and he is about to embarrass everyone. Byerley hangs on, taking a tighter grip higher up the halter rope. The stallion lets out a deep, throaty whicker. His eyes roll and he pulls forward, lifting Byerley off his feet. The King tightens his lip: a smile? 'Hmm. Strength and spirit.'

'Absolutely, sir.'

'A fine combination, if you can control it.'

'Yes, sir, he is a quite a handful.'

The King sniffs the rose: he can well believe it. 'What do you know of his origins?'

'His groom told me that he had once been in the stables of the Ottoman King – their Sultan, sir.'

'Indeed?'

'And then he was at Whitehall Palace, sir, under King James.'

'Well, well.'

'And now here, with you, sir – he is – a horse amongst Kings.'

The King walks round Azarax, examining the point of his shoulder, his wither, the set of his tail: straight hocks, flat knees – nothing escapes his notice.

The horse whickers again and raises his head.

The King's expression darkens. 'No sir, Colonel Byerley. This is not a horse among Kings, no sir, you are mistaken.'

Byerley looks at his feet, his pride crushed. It had been an absurdly presumptuous thing to say. Why had he said it? He must retract somehow. His mind races to find some charming, apposite remark with which to excuse such a blunder.

The King continues his inspection of the horse in silence leaving Byerley gazing at his feet, neck reddening, lips pursed.

Having been round him twice, still sniffing the yellow rose, the King stops opposite Byerley and glancing between man and horse says: 'No sir, this is not a horse amongst Kings. No, sir. This sir, is a King amongst horses.'

8TH JULY – 7TH AUGUST 1690

Houses are stripped and burned; crops destroyed; livestock is driven from the land. Protestants fleeing the Catholics, hoping for a better reception from the Williamite forces, rush up to them in hope of food and protection, but are often musket-butted to the ground as the army moves on.

The Williamites pass Roscrea, County Tipperary, a fortress town. Another one. Cromwell had garrisoned this Castle in 1660, knowledge of which raised the spectre of a ghost for Byerley. He loathed the name of Cromwell as much as the Irish Jacobites he now rode against. This war was becoming more complex by the minute. Had he really come this far, now to be siding with Cromwell? The man who had battered his grandfather half to death on Sherborn field then dragged him in chains to York?

Byerley chews the inside of his cheek. His father had fought for these Stuart Kings, these latter-day Jacobites and had paid the price that

Cromwell exacted: 'a delinquent', the Parliamentarians had called him and they fined him for supporting the Royalist cause. And now this? He, Robert, his father's son and heir, was following in the footsteps of the man his father – and grandfather – detested, who nearly ruined their fortune. He is waging a war against the very dynasty his father and grandfather struggled to protect.

He pinches the corners of his eyes with thumb and forefinger. These thoughts won't bear that kind of analysis. He must think on other things.

Riding on, gazing through the ears of his great horse, Byerley looks across Azarax's glossy black mane on his long hard neck. He feels beneath him, the power, the potency of muscle and bone. But what, exactly, is he riding to?

More grand houses, Moncha Abbey, St Anne's, and, in time, he enters a tree-lined landscape after the long, dreary bog outside Kildare. Lame horses and sore backs. With stiff legs, the soldiers get off to walk their tired horses past little thatched homesteads in little thatched villages, looted in the wake of one army, then burned in the bow-wave of the next.

Bigger mountains lie ahead: Nenagh Castle and several more abbeys. Naked mountains rise to the left, the Silvermine Mountains, and beyond still, the Slievefelim Mountains, Ballenagh Castle and Castleconnell.

William unfurls the Royal Standards before the walls of the castle of King John, Limerick, on August 7th 1690.

A horse gazes up at the stone walls with his big dark eyes. To his left, runs the river Shannon: or is it the Danube?

Roaring water and black rocks, wild geese flying up the river, swans and seagulls. The water is murky, the current fast.

Vienna! Buda!

Green hills lie beyond, green and beautiful.

Here today: antiquity, peace and pride. Tomorrow the reins will be loosened on the red-nostrilled horses of war.

The Siege of Limerick grinds on. Despite cannon shot, grape shot, gunpowder, lost lives, heroes and madmen; despite neighing horses, flashes of muskets at night and the constant barrage of a siege – Limerick will not be broken.

King William returns to England, leaving orders for his Commander-in-Chief, Baron Godart van Reede de Ginckel, to stand down the army and resume hostilities the following Spring.

The hooves of 184 horses shuffle through the mud in Mountmellick in central Ireland as the 6th Dragoons are led to their appointed winter quarters by their Colonel on his bay horse.

It is a thin, cheerless winter, but Colonel Byerley makes the best of the respite by having broken saddlery repaired, by having the war-ravaged horses fed and rested, by having their feet trimmed. Poyntz applies his skills as a farrier to those horses that require it. Yet their days are harried by reparees, Irish skirmishers, and Byerley finds himself echoing the behaviour of the man whose name he detests above all, Oliver Cromwell. Now he fears, he must even seem like him.

An event takes place to lighten his heart.

He calls for Poyntz, one Monday afternoon.

Poyntz obliges, appearing more-or less-sober. 'Sir,' he says, removing his hat: 'you wishes to see me?'

'Come in Poyntz.'

Poyntz steps into a panelled room sweetly scented with burning fruitwood. Checking the bottom of his boots, he stands in front of the large desk behind which Byerley has now seated himself. Clearing his throat he asks: 'You are well and in good health, Mr Poyntz?'

'Oh yes thank you, Your Honour. And the horses, too sir.'

'Excellent. I am pleased to hear it.'

'Thank you sir, thank you sir, it is great warmth to me that you cares about the well being of myself, sir.'

'And the horses...'

'Oh yes, sir. And the horses, sir.'

Byerley looks at him, his beard straggled as ever, hair a wild mop, great brawny chest, hard blue eyes, strong, hard hands. Short thick legs, short thick neck and powerful arms. Poyntz is a man of immense personal strength, yet there remains in him a core of tenderness, hard to detect upon first encounter but definitely present in this imperishable soul. Byerley had witnessed it in his handling of injured horses. He is a master of his trade, of that there is little doubt.

'And how does Mountmellick suit you, Poyntz?'

'Grand, sir, grand. Home from home, sir.'

Byerley nods.

'So you are content here, Poyntz?'

'Oh yes, sir, yes sir. Very content sir.' The fire crackles. The wind buffets the leafless branches of the trees outside.

'And what do you make of the horseflesh about these parts?'

'Oh, they're a bit of a mix sir, bit of a mix.'

'Mmm,' says the Colonel leaning back in his chair. A long pause follows.

'Would you not agree, Poyntz,' he continues, now sitting upright, 'that the indiscriminate breeding of horses is a bad thing?'

Poyntz wrings his hat in his hands, shuffles his feet and responds: 'Oh utterly, sir. The worst. The most terriblest thing, sir. Indiscrimerate breeding is the worst, sir.'

'Would you not say,' continues the Colonel rising, 'that to find some local mare and cover her with some arbitrary stallion would be a good way to weaken the fabric of a herd of horse, let us say?'

'Certain to be sir. I can't not think of anythink more worser. Unless of course – the stallion is superior, sir.'

'Quite' says Byerley reflectively.

'You know what they say, sir?' offers Poyntz.

'No Poyntz, what do they say?'

'They say the mare is a sack sir. You puts gold in and you takes gold out. That's what they say, sir.'

Byerley looks at him and then looks away. There is something extraordinarily coarse about that remark. He opens a drawer of the desk, takes out a piece of folded parchment and places it on the desk in front of him, levelling a signet-ringed little finger at it. 'Do you recognise this, Poyntz?'

Poyntz takes a step forward, looks at the folded piece of paper and says: 'No, sir.'

Byerley sits.

Presently he unfolds the piece of paper and reads: 'Pedigree. This day of our Lord, 17th November 1690... does this sound familiar, Poyntz?'

Poyntz scratches his neck and pulls a face, a reddening face.

'Allow me to continue,' says Byerley reading:

Pedigree
This day of our Lord, 17th November 1690.

Be it known unto all men that the said horse
described as the Turkey Stallion,
Treasure of the regiment of the 6th Dragoon Guards,
being free of all impediments and charges,
whose Illustrious Pedigree extendeth
Across all the horses of Araby and of Barbary and of Turkey

and of The Dominions of the State of The Grand Signiour,
of The Ottoman Empire,
Henceforth be set apart from all other horses,
Being the Rarest and Fastest, most Bold and
Courageous Horse in the Kingdoms,
Of England and Ireland and France
Hath this day, Of the 17th inst.
Covered the Mare of Mr. Caron O'Connor
for a fee of Five Shillings and Sixpence, payable immediately.
Failure of the mare to hold to service non-negotiable.
Signed,
Master Farrier to the 6th Dragoons Guards.
Eustace Poyntz, Sergeant.'

Byerley lowers the letter, keeping as well as he can, an even face, as Poyntz gazes through the dark glass to the towers beyond. His head has just emptied.

'Pray,' asks the Colonel, 'who wrote this – pedigree?'

Poyntz wrings his hat in his hands. Points of sweat have erupted across his forehead: 'It isn't much, sir... on account of the man Caron O'Connor sir, with the hobby... said it was with your permission sir... he's clever with horses sir, spotted your Turk immediate, sir... he said you said... he wishes only to improve the blood in his hobby stock sir, they are for work sir... he is a person of quality, sir...like yourself Your Honour...it was only the once, sir.'

Byerley drops another letter on the desk and another and another. A bead of sweat trickles down Poyntz's right temple. 'It will do the local breeds some good sir, you knows that yourself sir...they needs...some... some fresh blood...sir....'

Byerley allows him to dig his hole himself. When Poyntz finishes stammering and conjuring wild reasons, as magicians conjure doves, sweat pouring off his face, the Colonel rises, and stepping toward his farrier, places a hand on his shoulder. 'I admire your acumen, Mr. Poyntz.'

Poyntz looks at him in bewilderment. He wonders where and what his acumen is.

'Indeed, as means of earning an income, it is polity.'

'Oh yes, indeed, sir,' says Poyntz brightening, 'Yes sir!'

'That makes, let me see, one, two... three... four mares covered at a sum of five shillings and sixpence a mare – a very good price Mr Poyntz – which adds up to a little over a guinea. Which you now owe me,' the Colonel says, sitting upon the desk, facing Poyntz.

Poyntz's jaw drops. The Colonel folds his arms.

'He is my horse, Mr. Poyntz, after all. Not yours.'

'But... '

Byerley awaits the excuses: 'the... the... the scribe sir, he was an expense sir....it was he who writed the pedigree sir... not me, sir... he's a hard man, sir... I mean... I have spent a large... sum... of it already, sir.'

Byerley leans forward. 'Then you better go and talk to him, Poyntz,' he says, 'and now you may leave.'

Poyntz shuffles through the door. Byerley listens for the groan beyond.

The Colonel stands up, smiling. It was opportunistically shrewd of Poyntz to do such a thing, although any future transactions will be conducted by the Colonel and not by his farrier. Undoubtedly Mr O'Connor will have some good, hot Turk blood in his breeding stock from now on, so long as his mare was sound, and knowing Poyntz she will have been. He puts the pedigrees back in the desk drawer, pours himself an Irish whiskey, sits down and gazes through the window at the grey world outside. How the seyis would have appreciated this moment! To think that his horse, Azarax, had come so far, been through so much, and handed a little of himself on. Yes, when Byerley gets back to England he will do as the King suggests. He will put his horse to stud. Though not for fees. Byerley feels there is something ugly about that. And what about Poyntz and the guinea? Good heavens, I hope I am not that much of a swine. He can keep it.

***

Spring 1691 brings a new wind and a new rally to arms.

Byerley's 6th Dragoons find themselves among forty squadrons of cavalry and dragoons which, in addition to thirty battalions of infantry, are assembled under Baron Von Ginckel.

'Refreshed after your winter quartering Colonel?' barks Wynne through his white whiskers one splendid May morning. He steadies his horse with his gnarled old hands.

'Indeed sir,' replies the Colonel. He's getting as bad as Poyntz: lies, white lies. This war has wearied him.

'Fit for a round more?'

'I should say so, sir.' Byerley gazes down at his horse's mane. Telling untruths does not come easily to him.

'And your men?'

'Thinner in number but stronger in mind and body, sir.'

'I hear you were severe with reparees?'

'We had our share of engagements.'

'And how is your horse?'

Byerley pats his neck. 'As stout as they come, sir.'

'And what do you think will be the outcome this year, Colonel Byerley?'

'There's a rumour about, that will embitter the Irish and French relationship.'

'Oh? What's that?'

'The new French General, the Marquis de St Ruhe, whom they call St Ruth, spread it about that James Stuart would ennoble any gentlemen in Ireland if he appeared at Limerick on horseback.' Byerley explains moving in his saddle: 'So off every catholic with half an acre and a horse to ride went to Limerick – expecting to return home with an Earldom or Dukedom or knighthood at least and the French Marquis de Ruhe greeted them warmly. He then set his troops amongst them, threw them from their horses and sent them packing back home, on foot and titleless.'

'Ye Gods!'

'The Irish and French had been short of horses at the time but this added five thousand to their ranks. The Marquis has gained himself horses but few friends in Ireland. The meanest Irishman is fine enough bred to prefer an honest enemy to a dishonest friend.'

'Ha! I have heard this St Ruth is a butcher into the bargain. Undoubtedly we shall face him!'

'Undoubtedly,' says Byerley without enthusiasm. The little bead in the horse's mane has gone. Does this signify anything?

But how is his horse? He's in excellent form. He has improved in condition over the winter, albeit there have been some hard days out chasing reparees. But he's as savage as ever, still lays his ears flat, still glares at anyone he takes an instant dislike to and there's plenty of those. His encounters with the mares has increased his already lofty opinion of himself. If he was a handful to manage before, he is a keg of living gunpowder now. Whenever he got loose over the winter, he refused to be caught, staying just beyond arm's reach and even if two or three or ten or twenty troopers tried to corner him as he galloped round Mountmellick neighing and whinnying, he threatened them with flattened ears and bared his teeth and lashed out with both hind and forefeet until none in their right minds had dared approach. When they threw their hands up and walked off, then later, at Azarax's convenience, he was to be seen wandering slowly back to his stables, as mild and pleasant as a country padre, gazing at this and looking at that and sighing and yawning as though nothing had taken place and the time taken up by half the 6th Dragoons in trying to catch him had been just a game.

And now he stamps his hard black feet, tosses his head, lashes his tail – he's right at the front of the regiment, which is where he wants to be. Breath billows from his nostrils, muscles ripple: if this horse could talk he'd tell everyone here to go to hell and he'd fix the whole damn Irish problem all by himself. Byerley canters him down the line of the 6th Dragoons assembled in force for the first time since last October and the lads cheer and shout as he thunders by. 'Huzzah for the Byerley Turk!' And they bang their cuirasses and rattle their sabres. 'Huzzah for the Turk!'

'The men is mounted and ready to go, sir!' shouts Poyntz.

The Colonel canters back to the standards. The horse spins, an arm goes up: 'Sound the advance!'

Aughrim

'Baron Godart van Reede de Ginckel. What a mouthful!' says Poyntz riding at the Colonel's back, chewing on a ham bone.

'Put the bone down, you disgusting man,' Cornelius Woods snorts indignantly. 'And do not speak of your senior officers like that or you shall find yourself flogged.'

'Never meant no harm sir, but it is a bit of a mouthful isn't it? Is he a nice man, sir?'

'Don't be insolent, damn you! Get back to the ranks!'

Poyntz jettisons his bone, wipes his hands on his scarlet coat and fingers about at the meat daggings in his teeth, sucking at them noisily and continues riding beside the Captain.

'I mean you must have to admit, Captain', he says, losing the thread of his own conversation, 'that Colonel's horse is a very fine mover.'

'Poyntz! You disobedient swine, I ordered you back to the ranks!'

'See, lovely straight action,' says Poyntz blithely, continuing with his observations of the various qualities of Colonel Byerley's Turk: 'No daisy cutting with him, no swinging his legs about like a drunken sailor, sir.'

'Poyntz. Are you deaf? Did you hear me?'

'And look at his hocks, sir,' says Poyntz strapping along on his garron with all the grace of a sack in a barrow: 'Look at him clear the ground level. Why, there's not a horse like him in all the others – if you casts your eye along the line: most of them is cow-hocked or bandy-legged.'

Poyntz is a shocking fellow in almost every respect: he is disobedient, tardy, ill-disciplined, has never mastered the military art at all, he has the vaguest of inklings about chains of command and what orders constitute and on top of this his turn-out is always lamentable. He's the kind of man that, if dressed in the finest silks, with powdered periwig, satin weskit, white hose, buckled shoes and gold-frogged jacket – he would still manage to look as though he'd just been pulled through a hedge backwards. Yet there remained something likeable about him, though quite what it is, Cornelius Woods finds it hard to fathom. He is one of those people with whom it is impossible to lose one's temper.

Cornelius sighs. Is it really worth the candle? Poyntz is never going to understand. Abandoning any attempt to discipline him, he follows Poyntz's grubby outstretched finger and looks along the horses to his left and right, then returns his attention to the Colonel's horse, who seems to be watching them with a backward glance, as though perceiving that he is under discussion. 'That's a strange thing, Poyntz, do you not think?'

'What is, sir?'

'Horses seem to know when you are taking about them.'

'There's nothing strange about it, sir. They speaks our language.'

'Do they, Mr Poyntz?' Cornelius remarks flatly, looking away. On top of everything, this man really does speak some appalling tosh.

'Oh indeed, sir.'

Cornelius rides along smoothly beside Poyntz who, on his exchequer garron, is a full hand beneath him.

'And what did your horse say to you this morning, Poyntz?'

'Oh, I don't mean as they can speak our language, sir, to talk it, sir,' he wheezes, hand upon his chest, 'I mean as they can understand it, sir.'

'I see,' says the young Captain, who rides on pensively for a few strides. 'So if I say that I am going to shoot the horse in front in the backside with my pistol, he should run away, shouldn't he. Since he understands our language?'

'If you shoots the Colonel's horse in the backside with a pistol sir, it's not the horse as is going to be running away sir, no sir, it isn't.'

Cornelius looks at him sharply.

'And it's not me that shall get the flogging neither, sir.'

AUGHRIM. 12TH JULY 1691

The 6th Dragoons have fallen in behind Levison and Ruvigny. The troops are spread across miles of rolling, hedge-lined ground. They are lined up on the North Pass in sight of the crumbling Aughrim Castle on the edge of the village. St Ruth commands the high ground, three quarters of a mile or so, to their left.

'Right now you lads, you watch Colonel Byerley and his horse. That's all you've got to do. Understand? Listen to the drums and watch the Colonel. That's a lucky horse he's on, you all knows that. Stick with him and you'll live. Just follow everything he does!' Poyntz trots his horse back to position behind Captain Woods and sits still.

The afternoon had been hot and calm: one of those hot summery afternoons, when all was still, lethargic and sleepy.

Then suddenly, all hell breaks loose. At the head of the regiment Byerley straddles his horse: his hands are shaking and his mouth is dry. The lads behind all have their eyes on him. The responsibility is immense. One wrong move and the whole lot could be killed. Byerley clenches his jaw: he does not show fear.

Azarax is extremely alert, watching everything. Though the crackle and smoke of musket shot is already filling the air and explosions have sent vast columns of dirt flying skywards and spirals of black clouds across the land in front of them, yet the horse is remarkably calm. Most of the other horses are rolling their eyes and chewing their bits, they are already white with sweat, they thrash with their forelegs and paddle their feet and rear and some even try to make their escape. But Byerley's great Turk stands his ground, solid as a rock, eyes to the fore, ears pricked: sniffing, scenting, sensing. Byerley pats his neck: I envy you your sheer nerve. This going to be a terrible day. St Ruth has a reputation for savagery; we beat him at Athlone but he's well dug in here. He's chosen an excellent position, and he's well armed. Will our luck hold? Please God, let me survive just one more time, I pray. I never did get round to writing that will. Our Father, which art in heaven, Hallowed be thy name, Thy Kingdom come...protect these good men that stand here, with me, this day...

What is it about this day that reminds Byerley of the Boyne? The place is completely different. It is late afternoon, not early morning. There is no glorious river here – is there? There is a river, a small river – but not beautiful like the Boyne. Azarax suddenly tosses his head and cavorts sideways to his left, clearing twenty yards. Byerley lets out a shout, more out of shock than anything else: the whole regiment behind follows suit, 184 horses executing a sudden twenty yards full-pass. A cannon ball rips through the air, grazes the ground and goes skimming off at horse height right where Byerley had just been standing.

The horse knew it was coming! He saw it!

Half the damn regiment would have been wiped out.

315

Byerley gulps.

'Huzzah!' comes from the lads behind.

Byerley's hands are shaking uncontrollably. This horse just saved all our lives!

'Huzzah!'

If any other horse had done that, Byerley would have walloped him for disobedience, but this horse? He knew it was coming. Trust the horse; the horse knows. Trust the horse.

Azarax's muscles are taut as sprung steel. Byerley can feel them. Every sinew in this horse is tingling. His muscles are tightly bunched, set to leap. There is a deep intuition at work, some peculiar inner power, a sixth sense. Trust the horse, trust the horse....

What did Poyntz say? This horse hasn't got any friends, that's what he said. 'He used to have a friend and now he doesn't.' What an absurd thing to say! 'Not like the other horses,' Poyntz had said. All the other horses had a friend: some other horse they wished to be beside. All the lads knew it: some horses ride in column and some don't. Not unless their friend is beside them. It is important to the horses so it is important to the lads and the lads are aiming to survive. They'd only go into combat beside the horse their own horse likes: his friend. Never mind the man. Otherwise there is no surviving. But Byerley's own horse has no friends. What is he supposed to think? Poyntz had said a peculiar thing: he said the horse once had a friend. Once had a friend. A horse just like him. He was sure of it, he said. Once Azarax knew a horse whom he trusted and although he's looked, there's never been another to match – that's what Poyntz had said. How the hell would Poyntz know a thing like that? But wait: come to think of it, when he met Count Meinhart Schomberg's Turk at the Boyne, his own horse had reacted to him, hadn't he? As though he recognised him. By heaven, so he did!

'Steady to the cannon! Firing left! Move to the right!'

Before he had finished saying it, his horse has shifted. Just a matter of yards. Another cannon ball comes screeching through the air and skims the ground, then goes screaming off through what would otherwise have been a body of horse.

The lads cheer again. Byerley's gut writhes. If he had ever been told that his life would depend upon the wit of a horse, he would have laughed it to scorn. If I survive this day I swear on my father's grave that I shall never be parted from this horse, come what may.

Woods moves his horse up besides him. 'Any drums, sir?'

'No; wait, we'll wait. I hope to God we hear them.'

'Watch the Colonel you lads!' Poyntz shouts, 'Steady to the horse,

316

lads. Steady to the horse.'

Cannon balls slam into the ground or skim over it. The lads are watching the Colonel's horse, swerving when he swerves. Moving when he moves.

Is it the horse or is it the Colonel?

Boom!

The infantry on their left encounter a deep bog. They will never be able to cross. Byerley does not claim to be a master tactician but any fool could see that St Ruth is in an invincible position. He has Kilcommadan Ridge, musketeers and then the bog – and what is St Ruth planning to do? Entice them straight into it and then scythe them down like nettles.

Things might go wrong yet. Aughrim Castle – what remains of it – is stacked with musketeers. What a deadly gauntlet! If Byerley's Dragoons have to charge, then not a single one of them will emerge alive. This country is bogged snare. The hedges are lined with musketeers – gone are the times when standing men shoot at standing men. Now they hide behind trees and in dykes and fire from cover at the men on horse. Usually they fire first at the bigger target: the horse. Then the man.

Azarax takes a step to his right. A bullet whizzes by: he shifted before it reached him. He even seems to sense the bullets. Horses usually can't see things that are thrown at them: projectiles that approach them at speed. He must have been schooled to it. Or learned it on his own. What a creature! There's no horse in the cavalry like this. Quick as a viper and twice as cunning, Poyntz had said. His ears are pricked and he's listening all the time, watching and flinching, waiting, taut. 'Ride him with your heart and if you believe you are right then no-one and nothing can stop you.'

The firing from the castle increases and a cry rises from the infantry. They're in the bog. God have mercy on their souls! Why did they wade into that trap? All that Byerley can hear are the cries of men and a barrage of musket fire. Towering columns of saltpetred smoke rise to their left.

Then come the drums: a huge sound. Ginckel has imported native drummers from Indonesia with vast drums that can be heard over and above the cannon. Each regiment had been taught a particular rhythm to listen out for, to hear its order. It is a strange and unearthly sound: the beating deep, dense. Byerley listens. That's the left going off: La Forest and Holzapfl's horse. And Foulks. And la Melionmière. The sound of musket fire is deafening even from the great distance away that the 6th now stands, and waits. The frustration of this battle is the not knowing: their own forces cannot be seen behind a rise in the land.

The drums beat again: an enormous deep sound, deeper than

cannon: the men feel it in their chests and listen hard to the rhythm.

The beat tells them: 'Form at two abreast!'

Compton's Blues are to lead Ruvigny's and Byerley's Dragoons.

Byerley shouts to Woods, Woods to Poyntz. 'Follow the Colonel's horse lads!'

Now into the bloody tunnel.

Musket shot, cannon shot, thundering hooves and shouts; the cacophony of war. The lads follow their Colonel, watching the plunging quarters of the bay. He's quick. The lads are riding tight with jingling harness and rattling scabbards.

'Pistols and sabres!'

The Castle ruins appear amid blinding gunshot and walls of smoke. Galloping horses disappear into clouds of smoke.

'Have at them!'

Their Colonel's voice, the voice they heard at the Boyne and Athlone, that had rung out in Mountmellick and Ballymore, rings out again and with a roar they thunder into the flame and smoke of musket and cannon.

The Jacobites, firing at will at every horse, had not anticipated the fury of the Captain, nor of the sergeant, nor of the lads, nor of the horse, nor of the Colonel of the 6th Dragoons bearing down upon them. Into a wall of lead the lads charge, their Colonel at their head, his men following his every move. They hack, cut, slash and fire and the fight rages at the walls of a castle that, until then, time had passed by.

From behind the ivy clad stone walls and remaining battlements, musketeers fire and when out of lead, they rip buttons off their tunics and fire those and when the buttons are gone, they come out swinging their muskets. Pistol meets sword, musket butt meets sabre, meets jaw. A man on the ground swinging a musket by its barrel is little match for a man on a galloping horse and in the frenzy, lives, hopes and dreams are ripped away. Young men in scarlet lie prostrate upon the grass dying for a cause most never understood.

The battle storms on until darkness descends and the fighting slowly dies away. Bloodied, exhausted men drop to their knees, hands in the air. 'Quarter!' they shout, 'Spare us! Quarter!' The firing ceases. The 6th rein in their exhausted horses and Colonel Byerley, upon his bay, summons the bugler.

'Disengage!'

The battle seems to have lasted only minutes: it has been hours.

No-one can speak.

'Round up the French and Irish survivors,' Byerley orders Poyntz, with a mouth as dry as a powder pan. 'And take their standards!' Some of the lads dismount and along with the remaining infantry, some scramble up the walls and take down the Irish and French standards.

Byerley canters up to the French commander, who offers the hilt of his sabre, with a salute. Remaining on his sweating horse, Byerley takes the sabre, holds it to his forehead, salutes the French Commander and his officers and men – those left alive. Sheathing his own sabre Byerley enquires: 'How many of you survive?'

The Frenchman orders his survivors on the battlements to lay down their weapons and step forward.

Byerley counts thirteen officers and forty troop. 'My God,' he breathes. 'Out of how many?'

'There were over two hundred of us.'

Byerley canters back to his men now assembled in ragged columns behind Cornelius Woods a hundred yards away from the castle. Woods relays a report that has just arrived by galloper. 'St Ruth is dead, sir, decapitated by chain-shot. They lost forty four standards. Over seven thousand men were lost here today. They say our own losses stand at some six hundred.'

'And our lads? What are the losses in the 6th?'

'Nineteen, sir.'

Byerley gazes at his regiment, intact but for nineteen young men. How the hell did so many survive? 'Well done, lads,' he says.

'Hip, hip, huzzah!' they cry, 'Hip, hip, huzzah!'

Byerley smiles. His face is blackened, as is everyone's, with spent powder. Pale rings rim his eyes where the sweat has run.

The lads roar. 'Huzzah for the Colonel! Huzzah for the Colonel's horse!'

Byerley salutes.

'Find our dead, lads. We shall honour them,' he says, and gazes around and sees as though for the first time, the carnage: the prostrate bodies of men and horses, the fire and smouldering corpses, the blasted trees and broken hedges, the blood and shattered limbs, one hanging incongruously from the ivy. Men pick their way through the smoke and the dead, looking for the living. The air itself feels shocked, as though stunned by the impact of what has just taken place. No birds sing. The only sounds are the cries and groans from injured men, and from the horses, pitiful neighing.

Byerley dismounts, runs a hand down his horse's shoulder. Lines of sweat follow the bridle leather on the horse's face and Azarax turns and rubs his head on Byerley's shoulder. It is a partnership, a real, firm partnership. Byerley smoothes a hand over the horse's velvet nostrils. And he knows he doesn't even have to look. There won't be a mark on him: not a mark.

Keeping his muzzle close to Byerley's face, the horse blows a hot breath into his face, rubs his head on Byerley's shoulder again, then bends his neck and crops the trodden grass at his feet.

Such a horse!

- 27 -

Surrender

Even in the deepest country where they had been ordered to 'mop up' any remaining pockets of resistance, they had heard the guns boom in Limerick. Day after day they had sounded, and by the night the sky had been lit with brilliant flashes, flickering constantly, followed by the crackle, roar and thunder of the guns. Each night, from their camp, the 6th Dragoons watched the sky in silence, thinking of those within the city, wondering how it was that anyone could possibly survive.

'By yon oath, that Baron von Ginckel is a warrior,' Poyntz had muttered peeling a potato: 'I never credited a man could pour so much hate at a people.'

'What is worse Poyntz,' Byerley had asked looking into the flashing sky: 'to end it swiftly or to have it drag on?'

'You've got me there, sir. But there's no pity in the man, is there?'

'There's not much pity in war, I fear, Poyntz.'

Even from miles away, they could see that the town had caught fire several times and munitions had exploded. Rumours of the extraordinary valour of the people of Limerick reached their ears, and both sides longed for the day when it would all end.

At last, on the 23rd September 1691, the people of Limerick and their defenders ran out of ammunition. The assurances of support and fresh provisions that had been promised from France, never came. Drums beat from within the town.

The surrender came and the war was over.

At the end of the fighting in Ireland the 6th Dragoons remained there for another long month and while they waited, they had begun to hear the stories of terror, of anger and rampaging violence of men in the regiments, court-martials and hangings, floggings and summary executions.

During that last month, Byerley gave orders for his lads to mount every day and ride away from Limerick, to exercise the horses and keep clear of the pillaging that was rampant in the camp. Many troopers had not been paid and theft had become commonplace. He took the lads along the Shannon, to the sea, and camped away from the towns, only returning as duty bade him, when he had to attend military dinners and conferences.

Those last weeks in Ireland were been trying. When it is time to leave, it is time to leave and delay is irksome and hard to bear.

The lads had watched the remnant Irish army, the Wild Geese, march to the ships that would take them to France. They'd marched with their fifes playing and their drums bearing: men on crutches, men with bandaged heads and shattered limbs, with lost teeth and powder-scorched faces, with missing fingers and hands shattered by cannon blast.

Even those toothless, broken old men, who had done nothing except load musket upon musket for better shots than them to fire – even they retained that unmistakeable spark of defiance in their eyes.

But when those ships dropped their sails in Cork, the wives and children of the men on board ran into the sea trying to join them, and clung on as the overloaded ships moved to deeper water. Many could not be taken aboard and drowned beneath the waves and the lads of the 6th Dragoons had watched on, powerless to help.

HOYLAKE, CHESHIRE, ENGLAND. 23rd November 1691

The mood of the 6th Dragoons is not what he had expected. Byerley had presumed that the lads would be boisterous and difficult to handle, happy to be back in England and full of merriment and mischief. Yet they are not. They are quiet and reflective, as indeed is he. They unloaded their horses quietly, as though the little Turkish groom had been there amongst them, and the horses had been led from the bowels of the transports to the docks without incident. Byerley had not wished to see them jump the horses out again, into the water and then swim ashore.

The stone wharf at Hoylake had been a welcome sight. They'd led the horses from the ships straight into columns, without command or order, then waited until they were all assembled on the quay before leading them to the long lines of militia stables, occupied by the horses of all the other regiments, and had found places for them.

Quietly they'd fed them, then stayed with them as they ate, grooming. Many of the lads had looked tearful. Byerley even seen one or two of them throw their arms across their horses, heads bowed.

The horses had survived too. A shared terror forges bonds. Byerley's Turk had been led to a stall and, when the lads had finished grooming their own, two or three of them had come to help whisp him over, or lean on the stall ends, saying nothing, running hay stems round their fingers, looking blankly down into the ground.

Later on Byerley had even seen Poyntz sitting on a granite capstan gazing back out over the sea, as though longing to be back in Ireland. As though he had left a piece of himself there. His frosted breath had filled the air around him and though it was damp and dark and cold, Poyntz had remained there, watching the seagulls at the cold day's end, looking at the ships, listening to the shouted orders from the Masters, seeing the sailors reef sail, watching the ropes being coiled, fishing nets being laid out on the quay. He had looked acutely lonely. Presently the Colonel had walked to him and asked him if he was unwell.

'No, sir,' Poyntz replied, standing immediately, 'no sir, I am not unwell. I am... well... I don't know what I am, sir.' Byerley gazed over the moving black sea. 'Two years we been over there, sir, two years and two months. 'Tis a wonderful country to my reckoning, sir. The people have a lot of spine.'

Byerley stood with his hands behind his back, regarding the lines of the Fair Wind, the transport that had returned them, and he cleared his throat. He said nothing, straightened his back, breathed the salty air and the hardening winter wind. He'd shivered suddenly and said, 'Come on Poyntz, I'll stand you a drink.'

Poyntz's eyes had brightened and he'd looked up at the Colonel with such surprise on his face that Byerley had been taken aback. 'What is it?' he'd asked suddenly, frowning.

'Nothing,' says Poyntz, ''tis only that, I mean, and you a gentleman sir, and me just a....just a...farrier, sir.'

Byerley had seemed genuinely stunned. And then he said: 'And the best farrier in the cavalry. I said I shall stand you a drink, did I not? Are you refusing?'

'Oh, Lord, no sir, not me!'

- 28 -

Foyal et Loyal

The clatter of hooves beats along the muddy road towards the barracks. It is a sullen, drab, damp winter's evening on Hounslow Heath. A group of weary, heavily-armed horsemen in ragged uniforms are returning to base.

The horses had squealed as they reached the barracks. Their heads went up, their nostrils moved to the familiar scents and their ears twitched to the sounds as they approached their home. Byerley's Turk had begun neighing and whickering four miles before they reached Hounslow.

'They don't forget where home is, do they Poyntz?' Byerley had shouted.

'No sir,' Poyntz had replied, bellowing, 'if you were to take that horse to within a mile or two of the place he was foaled I warrant he would remember it just as clear, even after all these years and after all he has been through.'

They clatter into the quad in darkness, form up into two lines in front of their Colonel and wait for the order to dismount.

It's a cold, grim night. The lads' fingers are frozen, their feet are frozen, their legs ache.

'Stand the men down,' Byerley says quietly to Cornelius Woods, who passes the order on to Poyntz who bawls out the order at the top of his voice. The men dismount and lead their travel-weary, war-weary horses into their stalls. And if the lads have forgotten which stall was which, the horses have not.

Off comes the tack. In goes the feed.

As Colonel, Byerley is not expected to feed or untack his own horse but he's not a man to stand on ceremony: he's shared too much, too intimately, too long with these lads to be frightened of losing his authority

324

through a lapse of protocol. He has felt what they have felt, seen what they have seen, eaten what they have eaten, been sick when they were sick, rejoiced when they rejoiced, felt lonely when they felt lonely. He's big enough to forgo petty niceties.

Besides, there is something else.

It is only when a man tends his own horse that the horse really responds. A horse respects the hand that feeds him: he remembers the hand that grooms him. The closer the contact, the tighter the bond. And Byerley knows it. He also knows another thing: if you deliver to a horse what he deserves, then he will deliver to you. Withhold it and so will he.

HOUNSLOW. November 1691–March 1692

Daily visits from various grandees from all over England become a common event in the barracks, and the lads find themselves giving conducted tours, showing them the lines of horse and then taking them to visit the Byerley Turk, whose reputation has spread throughout the kingdom and of whom they are immensely proud. King of all Horses, they call him, Protector of the Regiment, The Horse with the Sixth Sense. The horse who sees cannon ball and senses musket shot about to bear down on him. The horse who is afraid of nothing and no-one, who marks his man and who once made a lunge for King James himself. He's a charm, a mascot, an augury: it is even counted as good luck if he walks across your path, good luck if you see him drinking. A fortune will be yours if he gazes upon you with his black fiery eyes.

One Sunday, a great yellow coach with a coat of arms emblazoned across its doors, bangs into the barracks on the heel of four matched black Barbs. The coachman is dressed in black serge with yellow facings and a new hat. A new type of hat. A beaver hat curled on three sides: the cocked hat.

A page springs from the back of the coach, pulls down the steps, and a heavily embroidered sleeve, a gloved hand, and silver-topped cane, emerge from the coach; then a leg, with costly hose and a garter – and there is the man himself, in yellow finery, with gold and embroidered turquoise, in a floral design. The man takes snuff, peers down his powdered face, with beauty spot on the right cheek, and advances, asking: 'Pray, The Colonel?'

Poyntz who had been pretending to work in the courtyard, has already disappeared indoors upon the man's appearance and informed the

Colonel. 'A person of quality, sir,' he says with much agitation, 'is alighted from a great yellow coach, with arms.'

'Oh?' says Byerley, clasping his hands behind his head, 'Who?' Rising leisurely to his feet, he pulls on his coat and strolls out into spring sunshine. The man in all his finery is a Duke whom Byerley recognises at once. He greets him cordially, although without ostentation. He is, after all, the Colonel here, and in charge, so whether this man is a Duke of not, Byerley holds the higher position here.

'I have come to see your horse,' says the Duke, 'this Arab of yours. The one of which people speak so highly.'

'My pleasure,' says Byerley, 'but Your Grace must understand that he is not in his smartest turn-out this moment. We have been exercising this morning and he is sweated up.'

'Oh, it matters not, my dear sir. It's the horse himself I am curious to see, I care not if he sweated. Where do we find him?'

Byerley gestures to the stables, to which Poyntz is now running.

Byerley walks slowly beside the Duke.

'You were at the Boyne, Colonel?'

'The Boyne, Limerick, Athlone, Mountmellick, Aughrim and Limerick again. And the final surrender.'

'With your regiment?'

'Of course.'

'I hear you are rather soft on them.'

Byerley is surprised by the remark and not a little stung. 'We enjoy good discipline in this regiment, Your Grace.'

'You do not flog them.'

Byerley clears his throat and says softly: 'There is no need: besides no punishment ever bettered man or beast.'

The Duke enters the stable, where now most of the lads are busy whisping sweating horses. The Duke wrinkles his nose, fumbling for his smelling salts. 'So which is he?' the Duke asks.

'He is here, Your Grace,' says Byerley, pointing to a stall not six yards away, in which Poyntz now stands, whisp in hand, smoothing the bay's back.

'Ah yes, I see. Yes, yes, indeed. Yes, he is quite different, is he not, from the run. Yes, yes I see. Fine these Arabs, are they not?'

'He's a Turk, Your Grace, not an Arab.'

'Yes, yes, they are one and the same.'

'They are of completely different root – the Turks...'

The Duke, not listening, takes a step towards the horse, making appreciative noises, whereupon the horse lays his ears flat and raises a hind leg. Taking a stand between himself and the horse in order to save what might become a catastrophe, Poyntz is rewarded by a: 'Get out of my way, wretch!' from the Duke.

'Lead him out here!' the Duke snaps at Poyntz, who throws a look to the Colonel, but fails to catch his eye. Poyntz unslips the halter rope from the log and as the Duke and Colonel make way, he backs the horse from the stall into the central divide, between the stalls.

All the lads in the stable are now watching the horse and the Duke, the Colonel and Mr Poyntz, to see what becomes of this.

'Walk him away from me!' the Duke barks at Poyntz, who dutifully walks the horse between the stalls. 'Turn him and trot him back!'

With a blank expression, Poyntz does as he is commanded.

'Excellent!' says the Duke as the horse trots up, straight to the action, head up – although his ears are back and his eyes on fire.

'Byerley!' he says, 'By Jove, he is all I have been told! He is well described. He needs no further inspection. I shall have him.'

The horse curls his nostrils and takes a step forward. Poyntz hangs on to the rope at a steep angle.

Byerley moves. 'I – beg pardon? You wish what, Your Grace?'

'I shall have him from you. Three thousand guineas. A very fair price. Yet I believe him to be worth it.'

A gasp comes from the lads, astounded by the sum.

Byerley looks at the Duke without uttering a sound. It is Poyntz, holding fast to the straining horse, who speaks: 'The horse ain't for sale,' he grunts under the strain, flatly.

The Duke turns to him slowly, reddening beneath his powder, and with one brutal gesture strikes him hard across the face with his cane, and shouts 'Do not presume to address me!'

Poyntz lets go of the horse and staggers back, reeling from the strike, a hand to his face. The horse rears, Byerley lunges for the halter rope and shouts angrily: 'Do not strike my men!' Signalling to a lad to help Poyntz and another to hold the horse, Byerley steps up to the Duke face to face, grabs his coat facings and beads him with a blood-red eye: 'You heard Poyntz correctly. This horse is not for sale!'

The Duke raises his cane to strike Byerley but the Colonel stops it in its flight, seizes it, snaps it across his knee, tosses it in a gutter and says grimly, through gritted teeth: 'Out!'

The Duke stands rooted to the spot. His breath catches in his throat. His face is blotched, his lips pale, he makes as if to speak, changes his mind, and gathering himself together, storms from the stables as the lads erupt: 'Huzzah! Huzzah! Huzzah!' banging their dandy brushes on the stalls and then upping with:

> *Hard on the tail of the Colonel's horse*
> *And we, his fighting men, sir*
> *And ride with him through the gates of hell?*
> *There and back again, sir!*

'The Duke won't forget that, sir,' says Poyntz, dabbing the welt on the side of his face, 'He'll be back.'

'No, he won't,' replies Byerley. 'He might be a Duke and he might be rich, but,' he says, turning to the lads, 'he hasn't got the guts. And I don't care for his money. I don't care if he offered me ten million guineas. The value of this horse is way beyond what a man like that could even dream of!'

Bang go the dandy brushes: wallop, wallop, wallop... bang, bang, bang...

> *Did you ever see such a fighting horse?*
> *To gallop straight at a gun, sir.*
> *And follow his tail to the ends of the earth?*
> *And to the far side of the sun, sir!*

5TH MAY 1692

Byerley orders Poyntz to muster the lads in the stables.

It's a clear, May morning. At ten o'clock sharp the Colonel enters, lithe, crisp, fit, as ever without periwig, hair swept back and held in a bow at the nape of his neck. He looks good these days. He's put flesh back on his bones – all the lads have. He enters with a casual salute. 'Gather round,' he says.

'And how are you all?' he asks, 'how are your horses? Any lingering injuries? Have you all seen your mothers and fathers and wives and sweethearts? Have you visited your treacherous uncles in America? Australia?' This brings a good hoot of laughter, since there are lads in this regiment whose fathers had fought with Monmouth at the Battle of Sedgemoor in 1685. Many of them had been hanged as traitors, and the rest sold into slavery and exported to the Caribbean and the new colonies of America and Australia.

Byerley steps to the Turk: 'Has he attacked any painted Dukes lately? Torn any Kings' heads off?'

Good rich belly laughs. That's a standing joke in this barrack, especially since quite a few of them have felt the kind of pressure this horse is able to exert with those long yellow teeth of his.

Presently orderlies appear pushing a couple of big wooden crates on a four- wheeled dilly. They lift them off and set them down on the floor of the stables and the Colonel tells the lads to open them up.

Within are pewter tankards, a pint measure apiece, one for each lad with his name engraved on it, the date and the names of the battles they fought in. Such a gift and to the whole regiment! How much did this cost? Poyntz winks at them: he's a canny man the Colonel: he'd have made a good bargain, but never mind, he's a gentleman and he's rich and when you have that combination in a Colonel and one that thinks about his men, then you have a regiment. Those lads who can't read are handed their tankards by those who can, and their names are read out to them at the end of grubby pointing fingers, and they all admire them, turn them round and round in their hands, re-living the battles, remembering whose horse did what, and how the colonel was always at their head: 'Follow the tail of the Colonel's horse!'

A brewer's dray draws up presently: a shout outside, beaming faces and no shortage of hands to lug the barrels to the stable, to find a place to set them, spile them and bang in the tap and it's small beer all round, a bit clouded but what's that to a bunch of thirsty lads with new tankards to fill, and who cares if it's only ten in the morning?

Even the Colonel drinks with them, now leaning on a stall end by his horse.

'You are splendid men!' he shouts, holding up his tankard. 'And I am the proudest man in the army to have had the privilege of serving with you!'

Loud cheers. Plenty of banging on wood. Wolf whistles.

'We have all ridden to the gates of hell and back and we left some of our comrades behind. So here's to them. To those who did not return!' And he holds his tankard high.

They drink. 'To those who did not return!'

'And here's to you: to the lads of 6th Dragoons!'

'The 6th Dragoons!' they shout, holding up their new tankards, clanking them together, then they guzzle back their muddy ale, wipe the froth off their mouths and line up for the next. As soon as the tankards are recharged, the Colonel holds up his hand and says:

'Lads! I am resigning my commission.'

For a minute nobody seems to hear. They have misheard.

'Beg, pardon, sir?'

So he says it again.

'I am off to Parliament. I wish to ensure that lads like you never go short in war again: that your provisions are good, timely, of quality and delivered to the place they should be. That none of you will suffer without tents in pouring rain again, nor live in swamps in the winter, and watch your friends die through the incompetence of the provisioners.'

And though the lads understand his reasoning, and hear what he says, they shake their heads. They look around, devastated, their tankards dangled loosely in their hands. There could be no more crushing blow. Some stand by their horses, throw their arms over their necks and look away.

'And what about the horse, sir? The Turk, your Treasure?'

'I shall be taking him with me.'

'But, who will protect the regiment when he is gone?'

'I have thought about that,' Byerley replies quietly. 'Be patient. Wait and see. You will find that the horse and his Turkish groom will look over you always. Byerley's Turk will be with this regiment for all time. He will protect you: you will see. I would not leave you without that.'

Slapping twenty guineas on the groom's table, Byerley says: 'That's for Shales!' Then adds another twenty and says: 'Sir George Hewytt promised you that and would have paid had he lived. Divide it amongst yourselves.'

'They got Shales, sir?'

'No: I shall get him and anyone else like him. Through Parliament and the Courts.'

He offers them a final toast, salutes, then turning to one man who is gazing up at him in utter disbelief, he adds: 'Poyntz: good old Poyntz, the finest farrier in England. I shall miss you.' He wrings his hand. 'I shall miss you all. Have my horse tacked up by nine tomorrow morning sharp, please Poyntz.'

- 29 -

Beyond the Distance

The regiment watch their Colonel mount the great horse in the quad for the last time. They are unaccustomed to seeing him out of uniform, and Byerley looks quite different in his hazel brown top coat with its great horse pockets, turquoise weskit and white stock, his fawn riding breeches and shining black-top boots, his heavy Civil War sword hanging from its glossy baldric, his Colonel's insignia embossed upon it in silver. Colonel Robert Byerley is a fine sight. A handsome man and such a handsome horse: Azarax, Byerley's Treasure, is almost black now; his coat has darkened to deep Jacobean oak. The stallion is tall, dignified, sure of himself, those large eyes burning, the big black feet smacking into the hard ground.

Byerley holds up a hand; he can't speak at this moment, so he doesn't try. Too much has happened in his shared life with these young men before him to be able to express what is running through his mind.

He hesitates and keeps looking at the gate. The sound of an approaching wagon brings a welcome diversion to the intensity of the moment. He regains his composure as the wagon draws in.

The driver greets Byerley. 'Good morning sir! I trust I am in time!'

'You are in excellent time, Mr. Wickett. My thanks to you.'

'Where would you like it?'

Poyntz, his face full of lines, his deep blue eyes brilliant behind their tangled, ginger eyebrows, mouth open, hands spread in front of him, looks to his Colonel. 'Show the gentleman the stable, Mr. Poyntz,' Byerley says abruptly, wheeling the great Turk. 'I would not go without honouring my promise.'

And without another word, he turns the horse to the gates and canters away.

The lads cheer and shout and wave him off as he rides out of the quad, past the fields, past the tents and barracks, past the high wall that marks the end of the exercise rings – they cheer until he disappears from sight in the woods and stone buildings of Hounslow. It has been a moment divided between watching their Colonel leave and their curiosity about the wagon now rumbling across the quad toward the stables. Yet the lads stand watching the empty space where their Colonel had been for several minutes, in silence, not quite believing that he has gone, expecting him to return, as though this were some kind of dress rehearsal. The young bugler kicks a stone. Before he has a chance to give voice to his thoughts, Poyntz calls out: 'Come on you lot!' And beckons them to the stables. 'Give us a hand here!'

Mr. Wickett halts the wagon horse at the stable door, jumps down from his seat, enters the stable, stands for a moment with his hands on his hips staring at the empty wall at the end of the stable and then says to Poyntz who has entered by the same door. 'It was on this wall he wanted it. Are you ready?'

Within ten minutes the work is complete.

On the empty wall now hangs an oil painting: The Byerley Turk and his Groom.

NINE YEARS LATER. 15th June 1701

Byerley throws his arm over the horse's neck.

He is standing with his Treasure in the field in front of Goldsborough Hall, the house he chose over Middridge following his retirement from the army, nine years earlier in 1692.

The horse has done little work since he came to Yorkshire. He has been casually at stud, as Byerley puts it, since Byerley is not interested in the fees, finding it a rather louche way of earning money, and so has allowed his Treasure to cover mares free of charge. It has been his lack of interest in money (having plenty of his own), that has kept the horse at Goldsborough, rather than have him running around the country in the company of a stallion man, clocking up fees in every shire.

The horse has enjoyed a pleasant retirement, and in his advancing years his nature has finally mellowed to become quiet and tractable. Gone is all the aggression, all the ear flattening, the teeth baring, the kicking, the bucking and the roaring. Gone is all the fury and the wild eyes, the screaming at the top of his voice, the dashing gallops across open spaces, the thrashing of feet, the stamping of hooves, the lashing tail, the tossing mane, the instant judgments of people who approach, the threatening glares and vented hostilities.

Now he stands, peacefully, ears pricked, though his eyes remain filled with their power, still brilliant, still reflecting light as no other eyes can. He still stands tall and dignified: is magnificent to behold. He still commands his position as the most famous horse in all England.

At dinner parties stories are woven about him: children are told stories about him, even Byerley's own children – of which now he has several – listen to stories about him, as they snuggle down on their pillows, their father sitting beside them in the candlelight; telling marvellous tales of the great horse and his magical powers: how he fights the goblins in Sherwood Forest, chases the sprites from the Yorkshire Moors, leaps from cliff tops and saves his rider from being turned into a toad as he gallops him away from the witches and the warlocks that stir deadly potions in their smouldering cauldrons in the ivy-clad caves along the river Nidd.

In the local village tavern, wizened old men with calloused hands sit in the nicotine-yellow tap room and, puffing on church-warden pipes and over frothing pints of ale, they tell again the story that has been told up and down the country of Colonel Byerley at the Battle of the Boyne, how he charged the enemy single-handed far ahead of his men and how the horse too fought with fury as the Colonel slashed with his sabre. They even name the tavern after him and call it The Bay Horse.

In summer the stately Turk attends fetes and harvest festivals, gives rides to little children, is patted by all who come near: 'Isn't he a lovely, gentle old horse?' they say. 'Never once seen him bite. Wouldn't hurt a flea. Kick? This horse? Never. No. This horse has never been a biter, you can tell. Wouldn't know what a kick was. No, he as soft as butter, a lovely old gentleman.' And they pat him and give him apples and slices of bread with jam.

As Member of Parliament for Knaresborough, Robert Byerley divides his time between his home and his constituency, to which he rides two or three times a week, three miles distant from Goldsborough Hall.

There comes a time when Byerley looks at the old horse and perceives that his face has thinned, that the flesh that used to lie thick and taut across his bones has flattened. His gaskin and stifle muscles have lost their tone and the great crest of his neck has dipped and his mane, once so dense and glossy, is brittle and dry. His head, which once appeared so fine set upon his hard, crested neck, now seems big and out of proportion.

In winter his coat grows dense and curly and takes a long time to shed in the summer and magpies hang on his cheeks and pluck the long hairs beneath his chin, for their nests. Younger horses bully him and push him around: mares flatten their ears at him and level their heads. Byerley orders that he is given paddocks of his own, that he may be left alone, to graze in peace and remain untroubled.

The horse spends his time aloof in his paddocks then, resting one hind leg at a time, eyes closed and ears back as though recalling, in his fading memory, and in his silence, all the events of his days.

When Byerley approaches, the old horse wakes with a start and suddenly some of the vigour of his youth seems to reappear, to rise again. Momentarily, he is the alert, formidable stallion he was when Byerley first saw him, when he was in his prime. Yet swiftly the moment passes and the old horse stretches out his old, thin neck and sniffs Byerley's hand. And his owner smiles and looks into his horse's ageing face and reflects on his own mortality; knowing that somehow he and this horse share a bond deeper than words can express; that there exists a link between him, this horse, his seyis and some arcane sense he can only grasp at the very cusp of his own consciousness. Yet it is there, it is there.

The old horse's orbital fossa has sunk in his head, grey hairs crowd his muzzle and at night, he walks stiffly to his stable and picks at this feed with decreasing interest. Not a day goes by when Byerley does not spend an hour in his company, yet as the years move on so the old horse seems to withdraw, as though aware that time, for him, is running out.

16TH MARCH 1703

It is night. Winter lingers late this year. There is the scent of a lambing snow in the air. The old horse gazes out in the darkness, over the stable door. He hears the vixens in the woods; somewhere an owl hoots, a strange single call, echoing through the darkness. The great limbs of the leafless trees move slowly across the dark sky: the wind stirs the church bell which tolls softly and irregularly. The night is deep.

The candlelights in the Hall have long been extinguished and the very place itself seems to sleep. The horse is the only one alert in this quiet, winter world.

He looks into the far distance, and up into the stars, which appear and disappear behind the slowly moving clouds. His ears are pricked, his chin trembles and his eyes, always so bright, have become milky: a film has passed over them.

A bolt on a door slides and a light falls across the courtyard in front of the Hall. A figure emerges from within, holding a swinging oil lamp above his head, and peers into the darkness.

Feet trudge across the gravel towards the stable and though at first the horse flutes his nostrils in alarm, presently he relaxes and watches the figure loom closer, swinging the lantern through the shadows.

The old horse whickers softly; a warm, gentle, throaty note, a welcome sound, of recognition, comradeship, friendship. Brotherhood.

Byerley holds out his hand and feels the whiskers on his fingers, the soft muzzle in the palm of his hand.

He enters the brick stable block, hangs the light on a hook, opens the great Turk's stable door, and stands beside him. He runs the back of his hand down the old horse's cheek. 'I thought I heard you calling,' he whispers, though the horse had not made a sound.

He moves his hand down the horse's long neck and gazes into the dark eye which now looks back out into the night.

'Where is it you go when you look far away like this?' His hand smoothes the soft coat, warm beneath the mane.

'What is it you see?' He follows his line of vision as he has done hundreds of times before, yet as always he perceives nothing. The horse's eyes remained fixed on the distance.

Byerley moves around the horse, covered now with blankets, creased over his wither. He undoes the buckles on the surcingle, straightens the blankets, feels for warmth beneath them, folds them in a vee over the withers, lays them back, and buckles the surcingle again.

'Do you remember your little Turkish groom?' he whispers to him. 'How he used to do this?'

'Remember how he worked around you? How he was always looking at you, picking specks off your coat, wiping the corners of your eyes?' An image of the seyis fills his mind: the serious, small, open-featured, honest face; the turban, the long red chapan; the look of concern that often lit his eyes; the slender, brown, outstretched arm, the mottled fingers.

Byerley moves to the horse's head and listens to him breathing. The horse swings his head slowly to him, sniffs his hands, then turns away and once more faces the darkness and gazes out into the night. Byerley moves closer. The wind has dropped. The night becomes absolutely silent.

A moment passes and then the horse withdraws from the stable door, and very gently lays his head on Byerley's shoulder. This gesture surprises Byerley as much as it had the first time. And he finds himself reacting in the same way, though this time, he senses something he has not sensed before: something deeper. He runs a hand along the horse's face: 'Do you remember that day at the Boyne? The minnows in the little stream? How clear the water was? How you and I looked into it? Do you remember the dragonfly landing on the leaf?'

The horse stands still as though listening, as though he hears what

Byerley is thinking. He sighs and releases more weight onto his shoulder. Byerley runs both hands slowly down either side of the horse's face.

'Do you remember the mist lifting off the river? What a beautiful dawn it was? Do you remember the greenness of the leaves of the trees and the moorhens in the reeds? The way the swans rose at Rossnaree?' Byerley crimps his chin, recalling the moment for himself, when his courage was about to fail him and, had the horse not done what he is doing now, he did not think he would have survived. A light catches the corner of his eye: 'Do you remember the scent of the sea at Limerick? The colour of the sky?'

The old horse moves his weight but keeps his head on his shoulder as Byerley runs a hand down the length of his face. 'Do you remember how the cathedral rose from the ground at Kildare with the great stone tower beside it? The river Shannon and the wild geese on the water? The scent of the grass and wild flowers when first we got to Aughrim?

'Do you remember your homeland? What was it like there? Were there great trees and hot plains? Were there rivers and rolling fields of rye?'

'Remember how you used to flatten your ears? Lash your tail? Stamp your feet?' Byerley clears his throat. 'How everyone backed away? How you terrified them? You remember? Now I know why: why you were so aggressive: so hard to handle. Such a stallion. It was how you stayed alive. How else could you have survived so much? Remember how you jinked at the cannon balls, listened out for the musket shot? Someone, somewhere, when you were young, taught you how to do that, didn't they? They gave you the finest schooling a horse has ever had. And look what it made you!' Byerley runs the back of his hand beneath the horse's jaw, on the soft, black hair.

The horse raises his head from his shoulder and stands still, in the darkness, breathing evenly. Byerley reaches out and putting one hand over his neck, with the other hand he smoothes his great jaw.

'How often have you been tethered to a cannon? Or lashed to a limber? Tied to a shard of wood in some burned-out house, at the end of a battle? What must you have thought then, of the world of men? You have lived your life through the demands of men and their ambitions and greed and desires, so that your own world became narrowed and confined, a world you could only enter at the end of a length of rope or the control of a bit.

'Was there a time, when you were young, when it was not like that? Was there? When your little groom let you be what you are? Allowed you to feel the wind, to know the stars, to hear the crickets and frogs and the vixens in the wood?'

The old horse sighs. He lowers his head and his eyes glaze further. The oil lamp throws a deep yellow glow across the stable. The horse's breath billows in the gloom.

His eyes are closing.

'My Treasure,' Byerley whispers.

Snow has begun to fall and the world outside is still and muffled.

The horse is tired.

In the scent of the straw and the quiet of the night, he lies down.

He tucks his fore legs beneath him and sighs.

Byerley kneels.

He smoothes a hand along the horse's neck and listens to him breathing. 'Did I ever tell you that my heart leapt when I first saw you?

'Did I ever tell you that when I first touched you, I felt a frisson, a charge that ran from you into my fingers and I put my hand on your rib and felt your heart beating with mine?'

The horse rolls onto his side and lays his head down in the straw. A voice calls his name.

Byerley bends over him and lays a hand on his shoulder. 'Invincible Turk!' he whispers, 'My Treasure.'

The horse tries to raise his head but he is too tired.

A hand touches his skin and he hears the voice breathe again, his name. Another voice, from afar.

'Such a horse!'

Byerley runs his hands over the fine coat.

What was it the seyis had said? Byerley had once asked him what happens when a man dies.

'He goes to Paradise,' he had said.

And a horse?

Byerley looks down at the great body under his hand.

He is already there.

Byerley knows it: he can see it. Azarax is galloping through the grasses, the lilac grasses, this very minute. The grass streaks beneath his glossy body. He plunges and gallops through the grasses to the distance, to a pebbly river where there is a horse just like him and then another emerges from beside the trees. Beyond, Byerley can see a little girl waiting in the full glare of the sun. The horse calls out and gallops up to her in the distance, that place beyond the distance he had looked into and known all the days that he lived.

The Byerley Turk died in his stable on March 16th 1703. Byerley buried him not a stone's throw from where he died. On his grave, he planted a tree.

EPILOGUE

In 1697 Soliman Chia, baş imrahor, Master of Horse of the Ottoman Sultan in Istanbul, was succeeded by his 37-year-old protégé, a man who had previously worked as a groom in the Privy Stables, and who had fought at the Siege of Vienna and at the Siege of Buda. Captured by Christian forces, he had escaped and returned to the Privy Stables in Istanbul in 1690, where he worked as a groom until the death of Soliman Chia. He was said to have taken horse breeding in the Ottoman Empire to new heights. He was killed in the second Siege of Belgrade in 1717 at the age of 57.

In 1791, James Weatherby, nephew of the first James Weatherby, first Secretary of the Jockey Club, founded in the Star and Garter Coffee House in London, published the first General Stud-book. In this, he laid down the commonly-accepted principle that the lineage of all thoroughbred racehorses could be traced to three foundations sires: The Godolphin Barb in 1729, The Darley Arabian in 1706, and the Byerley Turk, in 1686.

END NOTES

CHAPTER ONE

THE TURK HORSE

Turk horses imported into Britain are often incorrectly described as Arabs. The Horse Breeds of the Ottoman Empire listed below represent only some of the major breeds of horse found in Turkey of which there still are (although in ever-decreasing numbers) a great many sub-breeds, and sub-divisions. The Ottoman Empire produced fabulous horses of great variety, of which Arabs formed one part, but the vast majority of military horses used by the Ottoman Turks were of Turkik origin. They were distinguished from Arab horses in the C17th by the Duke of Newcastle in his book *Méthode et Invention Nouvelle et Dresser Les Chevaux*, in which he clearly describes the Turk as standing 'high, though of unequal shape, being remarkably beautiful, active, with plenty of power...' and distinct from an Arab. Miles (see Bibliography) states that 'The Byerley Turk was a Toorkman horse.'

The Ghazis, who had Eastern Turkik roots, had a powerful influence on the whole Ottoman Empire, and the Ghazis rode their own Turkik, Steppe-bred horses. Everything else they regarded as inferior.

HORSE BREEDS OF THE OTTOMAN EMPIRE

Anatolian Ancient breed: exceptionally hardy, good endurance qualities. Possess a high percentage of Turkoman and Armenian blood.

Ayvacik Midillian No data.

Canik Historically assumed to have been bred around Trabzon (Trebizond) on the Pontic Coast (Black Sea).

Çukurova Cilician horse, thought to have been imported by Solomon. Height 1.50-1.54m and 400-500kg, said to be larger than the Anatolian. Old Çukurova type. Breed almost wiped out following WWI.

Gemlik West coast, around Bursa.

Germiyan Ancient Turkish breed, preceding the Karaman (Sumer, p.27)

Karaman Most widely-distributed Ottoman horse, described as a Turk, having Turkoman blood. Bred all over the Ottoman Empire, from Europe, the Balkans, to Eastern Anatolia, their traditional homeland. They were much favoured in timariot systems. 1.50–1.60m. (Sumer).

Karaçabey Refined during the 18th century.

Kapadokya Ancient Turkish breed, thought to be one of the precursors of what is termed an Arab horse.

Kastamonu No detailed data available.

Kurdish Thought to have been Arab-sized, ie. 14-15 hands.

Malakan Composite of Bityug (heavy trotter) and other native Russian breeds, (also influenced by Steppe horses). From North Eastern Turkey, now probably extinct. (FAO: Food and Agriculture Organisation, Rome)

Rumeli Karaman/Germiyan breed.

Uzunyayla Akhal Tekke/ Turkoman strain, usually bay.

QUOTE FROM: *An Early History of Horsemanship*, Professor A. Azzaroli, 1985
'This story may be closed with the Arab. Strictly speaking, this breed is outside the limits originally intended, because its history begins in the late Middle Ages, but this is one of the most ancient and noble breeds that have survived and it would be unfair not to mention it.

The Arabs started breeding horses rather late and in Mahomet's time they still had a very small number of them. The Arab of course belongs to the oriental, hot-blooded group, but its real fatherland is not Arabia but Turkestan, and the race was bred and fixed in its present character in Egypt, by people who had come from central Asia.-The Turkish origin of this breed is also attested by its name:- the Arabic word to designate any horse in general is 'faras' or 'husan', but a horse of noble blood is called, with a Turkish word, 'atik.'

The history of the Arab was reconstructed-by Jankovich as follows.-Breeding of noble horses on a large scale was started in Egypt by a man of Turkish origin, Sultan El Nasser El Mansour, who reigned for fifty years, from 1291 to 1341. He spent enormous sums purchasing horses of noble breeds, breeding them, organising races and all sorts of games. His love did not end with horses;-he liked camels (dromedaries) as well, particularly racing breeds.-At the time of his death his stables numbered 4500 horses and 5000 camels. El Nasser strove to extend love for horses among his subjects and took particular care in breeding, but discarded the horses from Barka, favoured by his father, and imported horses that were called Arabs.-The name however was inaccurate, owing to a rather free use of geographical terms in the chronicles of his time:-because the horses imported by El Nasser were bred in Syria by two nomadic tribes, the Beni Fadl and the Muhanna, who had come to the Middle East from Turkestan about three centuries earlier.

Being primarily interested in breeding problems, El Nasser established regular stud books.-They are now extremely interesting documents as they give evidence that the most valued Arab strains, the Baya, the Siglawi, the Hamdani, the Habdan, all also collectively called Kehailan, descend from El Nasser's studs.'

HORSE COLOURS

Al Red, expected to be untalented.

Demirkir Iron-coloured, sometimes with white and brown. Considered sacred.

Doru Between red and bay. Good for tough missions.
Kir Grey, also good for tough missions.
Kula Between red and light brown: thought to be unlucky.
Yağiz Between black and red, considered naughty.

THE HORSEMAN ARCHERS
The Turkish clans of Western Siberia, notably the Kipchaks, owned in excess of two million horses. (Sumer, p.10) Of the Uigar Turkik clan, there was a contemporary saying that: 'the number of horses only God knows.' p.11.)

THE GHAZIS
The Ghazis were an elite group of chivalric warriors who took a sacred oath which bound them to an overlord. They obeyed a futuwwa, a mystical code which developed in the tenth and eleventh centuries and which was adopted by guilds and corporations in the Islamic world. Most Ghazis were Turks. They came from the east and not from the south. The horses they brought with them were Eastern, and not southern horses: the Ghazi horses were the early Turkomen horses that became the root stock of horses that were bred for and by the great Ottoman Military machine.

CHAPTER TWO

Janissaries From the 1400s the Janissaries formed a crack regiment of infantry, originally staffed by youths conscripted from Christian families in the Balkans, under a system known as devsirme. Discipline for Janissaries was strict. Paul Rycaut – author and diplomat, English Consul in Turkey (1667-1678) recorded: '...wine is drunk on pain of death; the camps are quiet and orderly, no abuses are committed on the people by the March of their army; all is bought and paid with money...there are no Complaints by mothers of the Rape of Virgin-daughters, no Violence or robberies offered on the inhabitants; all which order tends to the success of the armies, and Enlargement of their Empire'.

CHAPTER THREE

The Topkapi. The Royal Privy Stables were one of the most important institutions of the Ottoman government.
During the 16th and 17th centuries, quartered in billets above the horses in the Privy Stables were the Sultan's seyises or grooms (26 in number), saddlers, farriers, wagoners, water carriers (for horses), muleteers, cameleteers, and donkey drovers.

Over 300 saddlers and 300 farriers were employed directly by the palace. In all 3341 officials, grooms, saddlers, horse masters, trainers and horse doctors were engaged by the Sublime Porte.

Baş imrahor The Royal grooms, the seyises, were maintained under the scrutinizing eye of the baş imrahor, who was responsible for the selection of the best quality horses and brought them from all across the Empire for hunting, for training, for horse games, which included cirit, top, çevgan; and for war. His staff managed the great state studs.

Ottoman attitude to horses Ogier Ghiselin de Busbecq, the Flemish Ambassador to the Ottoman Empire for the Holy Roman Emperor wrote: 'There is no animal accustomed to humans like Turkish horses. They recognise their masters and the grooms that look after them, immediately. When they train their horses, they treat them gently. When I travelled through the Pontus region and Bithynia into Cappadocia, I saw the peasants giving close attention to their horses. They treated them playfully; they took their horses into their homes, nearly invited them to dinner, caressed and loved them. They love their colts like their children. There are necklaces around their necks, which are written with charms against the Evil Eye. People are afraid of the Evil Eye. Those who look after animals also treat them gently. They win their hearts. They do not hit them with sticks when they lose their tempers. As a result, the horses are friendly to humans. There is a vast difference between the way in which we treat our horses and the Turks treat theirs. Our grooms believe that if they do not shout at their horses and hit them that they will do nothing. Because of this when the grooms enter the stable the horses are trembling already with fear, hating them. The Turks like to train them so that they will kneel down on a single command to let their masters mount easily. The horses are trained so that they pick up a stick or rug, lifting it above their heads, giving them to their masters. Silver rings are attached to the noses of talented horses as a token of their training. I saw horses that remain motionless if their rider falls.'

The sipahi A feudal cavalryman who had been granted a timar, a piece of land, in return for military service rendered to the Sultan.
By far the greatest number of horses that went to war bred by the timarli sipahi. In return for holding this land and enjoying its fruits, in the event of war, a timarli sipahi had to supply horses and men, and the richer he was, the more he was expected to supply. The hassa sipahi were the richest and were expected to supply large numbers of horses and men. No timarli nor hassa sipahi owned the land they occupied: it was land upon which the incumbent lived and from which he drew his income, and upon which the rayah the country people, the common cattle as they were called, worked. All sipahi trained their own horses and would not have

ventured onto the battlefield on a horse that was either unschooled or did not know the sound of gunfire.

THE LORE OF WHORLS

Whorls of Positive Influence
The Whorl of The Prophet, or The Prophet's Thumb Print, on the sides of the horse's neck. The master will live and die a good Muslim.
The Line of the Sultan, along the length of the neck following the windpipe. The horse has the power to avert bad luck.
The Whorl of The Spurs,on the flank. If inclined upward, means safety in battle; if inclined downward, riches.
The Whorl of The Breast: the rider's tent will be filled with booty.
The Whorl of The Girth: the tribe's herds and flocks will increase.
Whorl between the Ears, or the crown-piece of the bridle, denotes swiftness in races.

Whorls of Negative Influence
The Whorl above the Eyebrow: the master will die of a blow to the head.
The Whorl of the Coffin, close to the withers with a downward inclination toward the shoulders: the rider will die in this horse's saddle.
The Whorl of Lamentations, found on the cheeks: debts and ruin, labours will not bear fruit.
The Whorl of Theft, is found on the fetlocks. The horse will be stolen.
The Whorl on one side of the Tail, brings trouble, misery and famine.
The Whorl on the inside of the buttocks means that wives, children and livestock will all be lost.

Sipahi and Cavalry Regiments By the mid-1600 an elite professional dragoon was drawn from the nobility – the hassa – in the direct pay of the Sultan. Talented horses that were brought to Istanbul from the Provinces were gifted to members of the hassa, who were frequently related to the Sultan.
The hassa horses wore diamonds, rubies and emeralds. Their reins were made from silk-embroidered nappa leather; their saddles from the softest hide, their shabracs of felt embroidered in silver and gold, and the martingales were tassled with gold, inlaid with precious stones and silk lined so as not to mark the horse. The Turks did not have dress armour; they went to war in all their finery. Examples of it may be viewed in the Topkapi Palace in Istanbul; also in Vienna and Krakow.

Chanfrons Chanfrons are protective face plates that were used for horses during 15th–17th centuries. Both the Askeri Museum in Istanbul and the Stibberts Museum in Florence hold large collections of chanfrons. These items have survived intact because they are made of copper and plated in gold. Each chanfron was made to fit an individual horse. All of the chanfrons in the Askeri Museum in Istanbul were made to fit horses with either straight faces or with slightly convex faces. There appear to be none made to fit horses with the spoon, or dished faces characteristic of Arab horses. Chanfrons to fit spoon- or dished-faced horses may be found in the Stibberts Museum in Florence, which houses collections of Mameluke armour from Egypt. This would be consistent with the use of Arab horses. The chanfrons in Stibberts were made to fit faces considerably smaller than the Ottoman chanfrons in Istanbul, which measure from 58 cm to 71 cm, so they would fit horses ranging from 15.3 hh to 17.2 hh.

CHAPTER 4

At Meydan The At Meydan arena can still be seen today in front of Sultan Ahmed, The Blue Mosque, in Istanbul. It was originally built as a arena for chariot racing in Roman times. Today the Column of Theodosius remains, the Obelisk and the Spiral Column. The four horses of the quadriga, overlooked this arena from Roman times until the 12th century, when they were plundered by Crusaders, taken to Venice and set on the portico of St. Mark's Cathedral. (They are now in a museum and replicas stand on St Mark's).

CHAPTER 6

Topkapi stables The original stables consisted of seventeen separate buildings along the outer palace walls and along the shore of the Marmara. They housed more than a thousand horses, reserved for state occasions and pastured in the meadows of Kagithane on the Golden Horne.

Horse tack treasury was kept in great chests eight foot long and four foot wide in the case of the baş imrahor. This was kept outside the palace at his HQ in Vefa near Saraçhane.

The Turk horses went to battle in all their finery and their finery was dazzling. Wonderful examples of Ottoman armoury can be seen at the Topkapi Museum (Armoury) and Askeri Musee in Istanbul.

Sultan's entourage Eye witness account of the Sultan and his bodyguard leaving Istanbul on October 10th 1682. (With thanks to the Bodleian Library their permission to reproduce this).

'..a sight so expos'd to view the greatest riches of the Empire, consisting in Jewels of inestimable value, Horses, Clothes and furniture, The magnificence whereof is not to be expressed in writing, unless it was possible to shew you Horses Furniture [harness] covered over with Diamonds, Rubies and Emeralds; and the Horses themselves more remarkable than their furniture: they proceeded in order: First, A Body of horsemen Armed Cap-a-pe with their bows, Quivers, swords and lances; Next the Bashaws, each with his retinue of led horses, handsome pages with Coats of Mail richly drest: And next, all the Caddees, or Justices, with Turbants at least a yard in diameter, with their attendants: After them proceeded the Chiaufs of the Viziers who bring people to justices before him, with prodigious long turbants, but not so big as the Caddees, and with them their followers: To them succeeded the Emirs, or Kindred of Mahomet, all with Green Heads to distinguish them: next came the Vizier's chia (Nor Secretary) with a vast and rich retinue of led Horses, pages and Agas; next came the Great treasurer, or Defterdar, with a greater [number of] Attendants of like nature; then appeared a great number of Horses richly trapped, and led by very fine pages, and followed by many persons of quality, Attendants on the Two, which immediately succeeded on most stately Horses, with rich furniture, being the Mosaip, or Favourite, (who married the Grand Signiours Daughter) and Kara Kiah, the greatest officer in the Empire, next the Vizier, called Chamcham, who were attended by a vast number of pages, on foot and on Horseback; Then past the two Cadalesches or Lord Chief Justices, then the Vizier's Guard covered with the skins of Lyons, Bears, Tygers and Leopards and every one differently habited: next came the Six Horse-Tails; carried before the Vizier by Eighteen Men, on poles of ten yards long; then Fifty of the Vizier's Pages on foot on each side the way, between whom Rode Himself, and the Mufty: After him all his Agas and great Officers of his Household, with a number of pages; Next several of the Grand Signiours, Eunuchs; and after them a Kizler Aga or black Eunuch, with Attendants equal to the Viziers; He was succeeded by bawling Holy Men; Lean, ill favoured, praying all the way for the Signiour's Life, and the Propogation of their Law: These were followed by two of the greatest camels to be found in the Empire; the first of which carried the Cloathes of Mahomet, which he wore in his Life time: the latter carried the Alcoran as it was delivered by Mahomet to his Successors: which Beasts, when they die, the Turks perswade themselves go to heaven. After the camels, and before the Grand Signiour, Rode Soliman Chia (Friend of our Nation) Master of the Horse to the Grand Signiour, and his Favourite, but mortal enemy to the Vizier; after him rode the Grand Signiour on a Milk White Horse, covered with unvaluable jewels, attended by pages drest alike with caps of Masly-Gold; their Habit Cloth of Gold; reaching down below their knees, girded with a girdle of three inches broad, covered as thick with diamonds and other jewels as they could be fet togther. After these rode the Prince in a plain habit, and on an ordinary Horse, followed by about four hundred, all the Grand Signiors Pages, Armed with Caps and Coats of Mail, Gauntlets, Swords and targets, each with a Quiver of Gilt arrows on his right side and bow on his left; the Case of which and the Quiver of some, was set with diamonds and other jewels; they wore a loose flying garment of Satin, some Green, some Scarlet, some Blew, some Yellow, and all-colours, which mix'd, made a delicate show; between every Ten or Twelve rode Two White Eunuchs, the Turks being as jealous of their young Men as of their Women. After these the Officers of the Grand Signiours Household, in the midst of whom, his coaches and wagons, with loaded mules, camels etc. The rear was brought up by about five thousand Sipahees or Horsemen each carrying in his hand a Pike Advanced, with a Bandera of several Colours flying, which made the sight delightful; with which it concluded, having lasted Five or Six hours.'

(Dated: Constantinople October 10th, 1682).

A Letter from an Eminent Merchant in Constantinople to a Friend in London, giving an exact Relation of the Great and Glorious Cavalcade of Sultan Mohamet the Fourth, present Emperour of The Turks, as he marched out of Constantinople, for the invasion of Christendom, and the Siege of Vienna *(Bodleian Library)*.

Gyor Occupying a powerful strategic position over Ottoman Hungary, Győr was a fortress held by the Hapsburg Imperial forces. It was to be the principal focus of the Turkish attack.

Hunting Mehmed IV's hunting expeditions were notorious. He hunted all his life on a massive scale, some of his expeditions involving fifteen judicial districts, the services of 30,000 men and in one case the deaths of 30 people.

Kara Mustafa He was reputed to have flayed captured Christians alive and sent their stuffed hides, or what was left of them as a prize to the Sultan. It is possible that he wished to carve out a realm of his own in the west. (see Dimitri Cantemir)

CHAPTER 9

The Size of Ottoman Force These can only be estimated. Armed troops arrived from all over the Ottoman Empire and we have only eye witness accounts and estimates of numbers. However, some of these appear to concur. In any event, they represent a vast body of fighting men.

Most figures are sourced from the diaries of Caprara and Kunitz: the latter remained in Turkish captivity after Caprara was released. Other figures have come from F. le Bèque and Ferdinand Stöller (see Bibliography).

240,000 warriors made up of:

8,000 Egyptians, 37,000 Janisseries, 30,000 Istanbul Sipahi, 24,000 Tartars, 6,000 Wallachians, 6,000 Moldavians, 129,000 Timarli

The figure frequently quoted (I believe incorrectly) is 150,000 Ottoman warriors.

Stallion fights Also described by John Evelyn as taking place in England during the seventeenth century. He witnessed one and was appalled by the spectacle. Stallion fights still take place in some countries of the former Ottoman Empire.

The medicine This refers to methods of parasite control known at this time. Walnut, wormwood, garlic and often pomegranate compounds were fed to the horses at the waxing of the moon – which ties up interestingly with endo-parasitic migrations.

CHAPTER 10

Felting Turkish miniature paintings reveal that many horses were 'felted', which is a tradition peculiar to Turkoman horses and is still practiced today. It was copied by the Arabs.

Tetanus A major killer of horses in battles at this time.

CHAPTER 11

Polish hussaria The most spectacular cavalryman in the western world.
They wore helmets, 'wings', arm and leg armour, panther skins; and each was armed with two sabres, two pistols, a battlehammer and a 19-foot lance.

Jan Sobieksi's attack was planned for 11 September. (I. Parvev - see bibliography).
Among the volunteers at the Siege of Vienna was the future King of England, George I (1714-1727).

CHAPTER 12

Glacis A wide, sloping paved scarp, running toward the town from the outer curtain walls, allowing for unobstructed firing at invaders in the event of their breaching the **ravelins: the zigzag, thick outer walls.**

Casualties at Siege of Vienna The number of Ottomans killed by 7pm are estimated as 10,000 (I. Parvev). The total number of Ottomans killed during the lifting of the Siege of Vienna was thought to be 40,000. The Christians lost 2 (T. Barker).

Returning horses A lot of loose Turk horses were found outside the walls of Vienna the following morning. Horses have a strong homing instinct, even to a temporary home, and when their security is threatened, they will bolt for it.

CHAPTER 14

British Volunteers are known to have fought at the Siege of Buda from June–September 1686. They included:
Jacob Richards (an engineer, sent by James II to report back the Imperial war machine); **James Fitz-James** (later Duke of Berwick); **Edward Vaudrey**; Captain **Frederick Fife** of the Scots Army (who passed through Ratisbon – today's Regensburg – in May 1686); **Lord Savile** (wounded by musket shot 13th July 1686); **Lily Christian** (a military engineer who was present at the sieges of Neuhausel, Caschaw, Polak and Buda. In 1688 he entered the service of William of Orange, and fought at the Battle of the Boyne and the Sieges of Limerick).
Many of those who survived the Seige of Buda were likely to have brought horses home.

Cutts' horses 'Fighting Lord Cutts' as he was called, was reputed to have been the man to raise the Hapsburg standard over Buda when it fell. According to Lord Raby's letters to Ormonde he also took horses home from Buda.

ROBERT BYERLEY'S PRESENCE IN BUDA

Although I searched diligently, I could find no source nor any reference at all to Robert Byerley's ever having been in Buda, nor of his having left England to join any expeditionary force, either in 1683 at the Siege of Vienna, or in 1686 at the Siege of Buda. The reference quoted most frequently which assumes Byerley was at these campaigns, is C.M. Prior's *The Royal Studs of the Sixteenth and Seventeenth Centuries,* (Horse and Hound Publications, 1935), which states on page 83 that:

"the **Lister Turk** was brought to England about 1687*, by the young Duke of Berwick, who had joined Charles of Lorraine's forces in wresting Buda from the invaders. It is quite probable that the Byerley Turk came from the same siege, as his owner was at that date a freelance** as regards the army, being only the Captain of a small irregular force of his own raising in the North, which was not incorporated into the Sixth Dragoon Guards (The Carabiniers) till 1688…"

* 1687: The Siege of Buda took place from June to September 1686. The Duke of

348

Berwick arrived back in England on 4th November of the same year. (Reresby).
**Byerley was not a freelance in the army. He was commissioned in Whitehall following a call to arms by King James II to oppose the Monmouth insurrection in June 1685. Byerley raised a troop of 40 horsemen in Doncaster and marched them to London, where they became part of the Queen Dowager Cuirassiers. This was not an expeditionary force and it did not travel overseas. Byerley remained as Captain of the QDC until he lost his commission in the purges of James II in February 1686. Edward Vaudrey, on his return from Buda was given his place, since Vaudrey was a Catholic and Byerley, a Protestant, was out of favour.

When King James fled the country in 1688 Byerley returned to the QDC, and left for Ireland in 1689 taking his horse with him. In 1692 the 6th Dragoons was named The Carabiniers by King William III, in recognition of loyal service following two years' campaigning in Ireland.

It is probable that Edward Vaudrey returned the horse to England with James Fitzjames (later Duke of Berwick) and that he then sold the horse to Byerley, since Vaudrey was impoverished and had to flee the country. He would have already known Byerley as he had been given Byerley's commission following the purges. Vaudrey was mortally wounded at the Battle of the Boyne, whereas Byerley went through the entire two year Irish campaign unwounded. However he suffered from the bloody flux in 1689, as did the Colonel of the regiment, Sir George Hewytt, who subsequently died of the disease and as a consequence of this Byerley became Colonel of the regiment in December of that year.

CHAPTER 17

England to Buda Edward Vaudrey had travelled to Strasbourg by water, made the crossing to Ulm on horse then continued their journey to Vienna, then on to Györ in May and June earlier that year. A return journey on the same route would have been possible. Boats were drawn along the Danube and Rhine by teams of horses and sail. He arrived on 31st June. The Siege of Buda began on 18th June 1686. C.M. Prior's dates for the import of both the Lister Turk and Byerley Turk from Buda in *Early Records of the Thoroughbred Horse*, and *The Royal Studs* are, in my view, incorrect.

Evelyn's diaries. In his diaries of 1683 John Evelyn reported on the presence of three horses 'which trotted likes does' which he, and others, including King Charles II, had watched one day in London. These had been brought to England by a German from Hamburg by ship, and were assumed to have been taken from the Turks at the Siege of Vienna. There were four horses in the original consignment, but one of them had died at sea. It has been conjectured that the Byerley Turk was one of these, but there is no evidence to prove it.

Philip Marchant Philip Marchant was an early horse-transporter ferrying horses across the Channel from England to France and vice versa (Dover Ports Books. PRO: ref: E 190/661/4).

Horse handling René Descartes' proposition that animals were machine-like in their responses destroyed western horsemanship for centuries. The belief that animals had no souls, promulgated by the Catholic Church, also led to a system of brutal handling, of which the east – in this case Turkey – was largely free. Travellers to the Ottoman Empire at the time commented upon it. They were astonished not only by the quality of the horses, but by the gentleness of their handling and the responsiveness of the horses to their handlers.

CHAPTER 18

Turk horses The following Turk horses are known to have been in England in or around the time (excluding those brought from Buda by the Irish and English volunteers).
c.1670 **Darcy Yellow Turk**: James, Lord Darcy of Navan, Sedbury Hall, Richmond, Yorkshire.
c.1675 **Darcy White Turk**: James, Lord Darcy of Navan also called the **Sedbury Turk**
c.1681 **Shaftesbury Turk**: Anthony Ashley Cooper, first Earl of Shaftesbury near Newmarket, Suffolk.
c.1686 **Helmsley Turk**: Thomas, 3rd Lord Fairfax Helmsely Stud, Yorkshire; known to be covering in 1685.
c.1687 **Lister's (Gray) Turk**: Matthew Lister, or **Stradling Turk**; Burwell Place, Louth, Lincolnshire.

Byerley as Member of Parliament
Durham:1685-87
Knaresborough: 1695-1713
(He was on active duty in Ireland between September 1689 and November 1691).

CHAPTER 19

Lilliburlero The words to *Lilliburlero* were written by Lord Wharton, who was to become Robert Byerley's father-in-law in 1692. The music was composed by Purcell.

Missing groom This account is consistent with local legend which has it that a foreign man brought a beautiful horse to Middridge, that Byerley took the horse and the man disappeared and Byerley was accused of killing him.

Walnut trees I was told by the present owners of Middridge Grange that local legend has it that the two lines of ancient, gnarled walnut trees at Middridge were grown from seed collected at Buda and walnuts grown in Budapest, as described earlier in this story.

CHAPTER 20

Robert Byerley promoted to Colonel
'December 7th: Duke of Schomberg to the King, in favour of Mr Bayerlay, whose Colonel, Colonel Huatt, died at Chester. Baylerlay is lieutenant-Colonel of the regiment now fit for Colonel.'
(Calendar of State Papers, Domestic Series, William and Mary. 13th February 1689-April 1690. PRO).

CHAPTER 22

Downroyal Races
The Downroyal Races are one of the oldest in Ireland, possibly second only to the Curragh. The races were formed, under the Royal Charter of James II, by the Down Royal Horse Breeders' Corporation who were charged with "encouraging the breed in the County of Down". The race course was instated by Colonel Vere Essex Cromwell in 1685, however, the first recorded race was not until March 1689.
According to A. Wilson (see Bibliography), the first plate recorded was won by Colonel Hayford's Barb (Matthew Hayford was Colonel of 1st Royal Dragoons) over Major Hamilton's Cob (There are three Hamiltons associated with the Williamite forces: Col Gus Hamilton of 20th Lancashire Fusiliers, Col George Hamilton of George Hamilton's Foot, and Col Hamilton also of Hamilton's Foot) and Captain Byerley's Turk in March 1690. This however needs to be re-examined since it cannot be correct. Byerley was not a captain at the time; he was a colonel. I have taken advantage of this area of doubt to place the Byerley Turk as winner, as the eminent historian C.M. Prior (see Bibliography) claims he was. My licence is, however, artistic rather than factual.
At that time, races were usually run between two or three gentlemen on their own mounts between two points, and the one involving the Byerley Turk was run from

the Flying Horse Crossroads, outside Downpatrick (which road name still exists) – which adds credence to Wilson's account.

When William III landed in Ireland he stayed at Hillsborough Fortress in June 1690 (from approximately 18th–25th) and learned that though the race had been incorporated by Royal Charter, the Horse Breeders' Corporation had no subsidy or grant. He duly authorised a grant of £100.00 per annum out of Royal Revenues to provide "that which is known as the King's Plate."

Thus, both King James II and King William III can be claimed as patrons of the Downroyal Racecourse.

CHAPTER 23

The Williamite Order of Battle at the Boyne, records Bierly (sic) commanding his section of cavalry with Lanier and Riffel.

CHAPTER 24

Date of the Battle of the Boyne Due to the change to the Gregorian calendar now used by most of the world (which corrected an error that had accumulated over hundreds of years), the recording of dates for this period can be confusing, and some people may date the Battle of the Boyne as 12th July.

CHAPTER 25

Aughrim casualties Aughrim was a far bloodier conflict than the Boyne with more men was lost at Aughrim on each side than at the whole battle of the Boyne.

CHAPTER 26

The 14,000-strong Garrison in Limerick was given the option of remaining in Ireland or taking permanent exile in France.

11,000 left Ireland with Sarsfield for France.

The ships of Chateau Renault anchored in the Shannon and took the Irish troops to France – the first of the Wild Geese.

Following the Treaty of Limerick, October 21st 1691, Penal laws were imposed. The aim of these laws was to reduce Irish Catholics to 'insignificant status, fit for nothing but to hew wood and draw water.'

Irish catholics were denied the right to:
All forms of education (including sending children abroad for an education).
Service in the military.
A career in any of the professional vocations.
Civic responsibilities (including voting and holding public office).
Attend Catholic services (catholic priests were exiled and if they returned to
Ireland, they were hanged, drawn and quartered).
Purchase land.
Own a horse valued at £16 or more. If a Protestant wished to buy a horse
owned by a Catholic, the owner was legally bound to sell to him. Some
owners shot their horses rather than sell them.

CHAPTER 27

I have tracked down five paintings of the Byerley Turk, four of which are attributed
to the artist John Wootton; there may be more. Of these, I understand that only
one is believed to have been painted from life. This used to hang in The Durdans,
a stately home in Epsom, but it is no longer there. The other paintings are clearly
inspired by it. A replica of it hangs in the Officer's Mess of the Royal Scots
Dragoon Guards at Bad Fallingbostel in Germany, wrongly ascribed as having an
'Indian' groom with the horse. A similar, though more beautiful life-sized painting,
hangs in the K Club's Byerley Turk Restaurant in Straffan, County Kildare. The
attitude of the grooms in each painting is the same, the position of their hands the
same, the way the horse stands, the same. The backgrounds differ.
Interestingly, another of John Wootton's painting of the Black Byerley Turk was
probably again copied from one of these and the hands of the groom occupy the
same position as in the original and the stance of the horse is the same.
It is, however, unlikely that Wootton ever painted the Byerley Turk from life.

Arline Meyer makes an interesting observation: 'Apart from attention paid to
colouring and individual markings, Wootton made little distinction between
the Bloody Shouldered, The Hampton Court Chestnut, The Godolphin and
other famous Arabians, repeating instead the standardised silhouette which he
had contrived to represent the ideal Arabian form.' Despite the fact that Turk
and Arab horses were frequently confused, a viewing of Wootton's painting in
Wimpole House of the 'Three Arabians' is recommended.

CHAPTER 28

Byerley's wife   There is a strange story attached to Mary Wharton, Robert Byerley's cousin, who later became Byerley's wife.

While out shopping with her aunt in London one day, the young Mary Wharton, daughter of Lord Wharton, was kidnapped by three conspirators, who knew of her personal fortune of some £50,000 (equivalent today of around £5m). Their plan was to force her into marriage with the impoverished the Honourable James Campbell, 4th son of the 9th Earl of Argyll, who would then have rights to her fortune and income, which he had agreed to divide in part with his fellow conspirators. She was to be held by Sir John Johnston, Bt., until the marriage was formalised. A great hue and cry went out across London following her abduction, and a large reward was put up of £50 for information leading to her discovery. Unhappily for Sir John Johnston, his landlady betrayed him, the girl was found, Sir John Johnston was taken to Newgate, and an Act of Parliament passed on 4th December 1691, annulling any marriage that was alleged to have taken place between Mary Wharton and the Hon. James Campbell (who, in the meantime, had fled back to Scotland). Sir John Johnston was committed to be hanged at Tyburn.

Mary married her cousin Robert Byerley three months later on 15th March 1692.

Byerley in Parliament   Byerley was as good as his word and spent the rest of his life hounding down corruption in both military and Parliamentary affairs. In fact he was so zealous that he won the reputation of being 'the most despised man in the House.' In his later Parliamentary career, Byerley was to pursue Whig mishandling of money in state hands with relentless efficiency and he brought to book all those found guilty of peculation in any form. He set high standards and had he not died when he did – at the age of 54 in 1714 – he would surely have been knighted for his life's work.

Glossary

TURKISH WORDS

Ağa Title of an official, and a courteous address.
Asper or **akçe** Small silver coin, unit of Ottoman currency.
Bey Military title; governor of a sançak.
Beylerbey Governor of an eyalet.
Çavuş Guard/guide, or in some cases a courier.
Çebelu Light cavalry, commanded by the Toprkli
Çirit Popular Turkish equestrian sport involving small lances, played in arenas and on open meadow land. Part of equestrian military training. It was banned in the nineteenth century.
Divan Council
Eyalet Province
Ghazi Early Islamic Holy Warrior, bound to a strict code of chivalric conduct.
Gönüllü Volunteer feudal aspirant, noted for feats of outstanding courage and skill-at-arms on horseback.
Han Inn or caravanserai
Hassa Aristocrat, the nobility
Hirasi Huge state-run horse breeding farms set up all across the Ottoman Empire. In Rumelia alone there were nineteen supplying a vast number of Turk horses for the war effort. Some of these continued to exist long after the Ottoman occupation of the Balkans and Eastern Europe had ended.
Imam Prayer leader
Kadi Judge
Kanuni Secular law issued by the Ottoman Sultan, based upon his Divine Right; or the Sultan's prerogative in matters not covered by the şeriat (the Ottoman Islamic code of law).
Kapikulu Slave of the Porte, literally: a soldier.
Medrese Theological school, sometimes very small.
Menzil-hane Victualling depot: food and military stores, set up all over the Empire.
Müfti Head of jurisprudence – a kind of elevated judge.
Müsellem Breeders of horses and other livestock.
Padishah The Ottoman Sultan
Paşa A peer equivalent: a Lord.
Racking The horse's gait between trot and canter, both legs of one side being lifted almost at once, and all four feet being off the ground together at moments.' Today, very few western horses do it. (OED, Oxford, Clarendon Press)
Sançak Sub-Province or county of an eyalet.

Sançakbey Governor of a sançak

Sejan The triple horsetail standard of Genjhis Khan– three horsetails suspended from a horizontal pole was later adopted by the Ottoman Turks, revealing their links with their horsemen-archer ancestors. The Turks called the sejan a tugh. Six horsetails denoted the Sultan, three the Vizier.

Sipahi Timariot cavalryman and a state cavalryman in the pay of the Sultan.

Tayçi Specialised colt-rearing farms of very high standard.

Timar Land held in trust for military service. Privately run, on condition that at times of war the owner supplied men at arms and horses.

The seyis worked on someone else's timar, being too poor to have his own. His two horses – over which he held responsibility not ownership – would have been a surrender of that timar to the Sultan in return for military service where the timar holder himself was unable to fight, usually on account of old age or illness

Toprakli Heavy cavalry, the 'officer class' of the timarli sipahi, commanded by the Sultan.

Yayla Summer pasture.

Ziamet A timar providing an annual income of over 20,000 aspers.

1689
12th September, shipped from Hoylake.
13th September, unloaded in Belfast Lough.
18th September, the march south.
23rd September, arrival in Dundalk.
30th December, the march to Lisburn.

1690
27th February, start of march to Downpatrick.
15th March, the race at Flying Horse Road.
17th June, to Hillsborough to meet William III, who had
    landed in Carrickfergus on 14th June.
25th June, the march south.
1st July, Battle of the Boyne (due to the change to the Gregorian
    calendar which corrected an error that had accummulated over
    hundreds of years, the recording of dates for this period can be
    confusing and some people may date the Battle of the Boyne as
    12 July)
2nd July, James I flees to France.
5th July, Muster at Finglas, Dublin.
9th July, marches west in pursuit of Jacobite army.
8th August, start of First Siege of Limerick.
Mid-August, Byerley engaged with reparees.
27th August, Siege of Limerick is lifted, Byerley winters in
    Mountmellick.

1691
June, Second Siege of Athlone (there were two sieges of Athlone
but   Byerley was only present with his horse at the second).
12th July, Battle of Aughrim.
17th July, start of the march to Limerick.
July-August, Second Siege of Limerick.
14th August, death of Tyrnconnell.
28th August, Jacobite forces surrender.
3rd October, Treaty of Limerick. The Wild Geese sail to France.
7th November, the march to Dublin.
19th November, shipped back to Hoylake.

Bibliography

Abbot, G.F. *Under the Turk in Constantinople*. A Record of Sir John Finch's Embassy, 1674-1681. London. Macmillan, 1920.

Alderson, M. *Pers Comm. Letters from King William III to Lord Carmarthen (Danby)*. Verified by the British Museum. Private collection of manuscripts.

Alexander, D. (ed), *Furusiyya*, D. King Abdulazziz Library, 2002.

Articles of Galway, Exactly Printed from the Letters-Patent: wherein They are Ratified and Exemplified by their Majesties under the General Seal of England, Published by Authority, Dublin. Printed by Andrew Crook, Assignee of Benj Tooke, Printer of Their Majesties on Ormonde Key, 1692. The Joly Pamphlets 1692-1791.

Andrić, Ivo. *Bridge Over the Drina*, George Allen & Unwin, London, 1959.

Andrić, Ivo. *The Damned Yard*, Dereta, Belgrade, 2000.

Azzaroli, A. *An Early History of Horsemanship*, E.J. Brill, Leiden, 1985.

Babinger, F: *Encyclopaedia of Islam*, E.J. Brill, Leiden, 1987.

Baldock, C. *Diary of the Golden Hinde*.

Balaman, A. *Halkbiliminde Özgün Konu: At Kültürü*. Folklor ve Etnoğrafya Araştirmalari (FEA) Istanbul, 1985.

Barber, N. *Lords of the Golden Horn*, Macmillan, 1973.

Bargrave, R. *The Travel Diary of Robert Bargrave, Levant Merchant, 1647-1656*. Long Riders' Guild Press, 2005.

Barker, T. *Double Eagle and Crescent: Vienna's Second Turkish Siege and Its Historical Setting*; State University of New York Press, 1966.

Başbuğ, H. *Aşiretlerimizde At Kültürü*, Istanbul, 1986.

Başbuğ, H. *Aşiretlerimizde At Kültürü, Türk Dünyasi Araştirmalari Vakfi*, Istanbul, 1986.

Batu, S. *Turk Atlari ve At Yetişirme Bilgisi, Zootekni Enstitüsi Doçenti*, Ankara, 1938.

Baudier de Languedoc, M. *History of the Imperial Estate of The Grand Seigneurs*. Tr. Edward Grimeston, 1635.

Baykal, B.S. *Peçevi Ibrahim Efendi*, Kültür ve Turizm Bakanliği, Ankara, 1981.

Bayrak, *Panorama of Turkey*. Galeri Mintatür, Istanbul, undated.

Bearman, B.J. et al, *Encylopaedia of Islam*, new ed., Brill Academic, Leiden, 2000

Beaston's Political Index, vol. ii.

Beck, B.H. *From the Rising of the Sun: English Images of the Ottoman Empire to 1715*. Peter Lang, New York. 1987.

Berenger, J. *History of the Hapsburg Empire*. Longman, 1977.

Berenger, Richard. *The History and Art of Horsemanship*, T Davies and T. Cardell, London, 1771.

Berjeau, Philibert Charles. *The Horses of Antiquity, Middle Ages and Renaissance*, Dulau and Co, London 1864

Bevan, B. *James, Duke of Monmouth*, Robert Hale, 1973.

Blundeville, *The Foure Chiefest Offices belonging to Horsemanship*, Imprinted at London by Wyllyam Seres dwelling at the west ends of Paules Church, at the signe of the Hedgehogge. To the Righte Honourable and his Singular Good Lorde, the Lorde Robert Dudley, Erle of Leycester, Baron of Denbighe... etc. 1580.

Bökönyi, S. Mecklenburg Collection Part 1: Data on Iron Age Horses of Central Europe and Eastern Europe. Peabody Museum. 1968

Boyer, Abel. *The History of King William III*, 2nd Edition, 1702, Vol 1.

Bramston's Diary (Camd. Soc.).

Brocquiére, Bertrand de la. Bertrandon de la Brocquiére in Denizaşiri Seyahati, çev. Ilhan Arda, sunuş: Semavi Eyice, ed. Ch. Schefer, Istanbul, 2000.

Browning, A. *Memoirs of Sir John Reresby*, The Complete Text and a Selection from his letters, Second Edition, London, Royal Historical Society 1991.

Bruce, S.D. *The Thoroughbred Horse*. His origin, how to breed and select him, etc. 'Turf, Field & Farm', New York, 1892.

Bryant, A. *Samuel Pepys, The Years of Peril*. Cambridge University Press, 1947.

Brzezinski, R. *Polish Armies 1569-1696*, Osprey 2003.

Bunyan, J. *Pilgrim's Progress*, Oxford University Press, 1998.

Bury, A. *The Best of Wootton*, The British Racehorse, XI, 1959.

Calendar of State Papers, Domestic Series, James II, Vol. II, Jan 1686-May 1687, HMSO, 1964.

Calendar of State Papers, Domestic Series, William and Mary. 13th February 1689-April 1690. PRO. Also, National Library Ireland, Dublin. HMSO. 1895.

Calvert, M. *History of Knaresborough*. Printed and Published by W. Parr. 1844.

Cannon, R. *Records of The 1st Life Guards and 6th Dragoon Guards*. Longman and Orme. 1840.

Cannon, R. *Historical Record of the Sixth Regiment of Dragoon Guards or the Carabineers*, containing an account of the formation of the regiment in 1685 and of its subsequent services to 1839. Longman Orme. 1839.

Cantemir, Dimitri. *The History of the Growth and Decay of the Othman Empire*, London, 1734.

Carsten, F.L. Ed. *The New Cambridge Modern History*, Volume V, The Ascendancy of France 1648-1688, Cambridge University Press 1961.

Childs, J. *Armies and Warfare in Europe, 1648-1702*. Manchester University Press, 1982.

Childs, J. *The Army, James II and the Glorious Revolution*, Manchester University Press. 1980.

Childs, J. *The British Army of William III, 1689-1702*, Manchester U. P., 1987.

Chishull, Edmund. *Travels in Turkey and back to England*, London, 1747.

Christians, P.R. *A Short Relation of the most Remarkable Transactions in several parts of Europe between the Christians and Turks*; including an exact diary of the siege of Buda. London, 1685.

Crist T. (ed) *Charles II to Lord Taaffe: Letters in Exile*, Rampant Lions Press, Cambridge 1974.

Cruickshanks, E, Handley, S & Hayton, D.W. *The House of Commons, 1690-1715*, Cambridge University Press. 2002.

D'Alton, Rev. E.A. *History of Ireland from the Earliest Times to the Present Day*: Half Vol: 1649-1782. Gresham Publishing, London.

Dalton, C. (ed.) FRGS, *English Army Lists and Commission Registers 1661-1714*, Edited and Annotated, Vol III; 1689-1694, Eyre and Spottiswoode, 1896.

Dankoff, R and Elsie, R. *Evliya Çelebi in Albania and Adjacent Regions* (Kosovo, Montenegro, Ohrid) Brill, Leiden, 2000.

Dankoff, R (transl.), *The Intimate Life of an Ottoman Statesman: Melek Ahmed Pasha (1588-1662)* State University of New York Press, 1991.

Daumas, General E. *The Horses of the Sahara*, University of Texas Press, 1968.

Doğru, Halime, Osmanli Imparatorluğu'nda Yaya-Müsellem-Tayci Teşkilati (XV.Ve XVI. Yüzilda Sultananönü Sancaği), Istanbul: Eren Y. 1990.

Du Pasquier, R. *Unveiling Islam*, Islamic Texts Society, 2002.

Durham Protestations or The Returns made to the House of Commons in 1641/2 for the Maintenance of the Protestant religion for the County Palatine of Durham for the Borough of Berwick-upon-Tweed and the Parish of Morpeth. Published by Andrews and Co, Grafton St, London, 1922. Edited by Herbert Maxwell Wood.

Egerton, Judy: *British Sporting and Animal Paintings, 1655-1867*, London 1978.

Erskine's Journal Vol XIV. 1683-1687. Edited from the original manuscript by Walter MacLeod, Edinburgh, 1843.

Evelyn, John. *The Diary of John Evelyn*, O.U.P. 1983.

Fanshaw, Mrs: *A True and wonderful account of a cure of the King's Evil* by Mrs Fanshaw, Sister to His Grace, the Duke of Monmouth. Printed for Ben Harris.

Fiennes, Celia. *The Journeys of Celia Fiennes*, Long Riders Guild Press. 2003.

Finch, A.G. Vol 2, Historical Manuscripts Commission, London, 1922.

Flood, J.M. *The Sieges of Limerick 1690-91*. A Narrative based on Contemporary Sources Limerick Leader Ltd, Printers. Limerick, January 1944.

Ford, Lord Grey. *The Secret History of the Rye House Plot and of the Monmouth Rebellion*, London, Printed for Andrew Millar, in the Strand. MDCLXXXV (1685).

Fortescue, Sir John. *History of the British Army*. Naval and Military Press, 2004

Foster, J. (ed) *Pedigrees Recorded at the Visitations of the County Palatine of Durham*, 1887.

Foster, Joseph. *Alumni Oronienses*. The Members of the University of Oxford 1500-1714, Alphabetically Arranged, Revised and Annotated by Joseph Foster. Parker and Co, Oxford

Foster, R.F. *Modern Ireland 1600-1972*, Allen Lane. 1988.

Gilbey, W. *Animal Painters of England, from the Year 1650*, London 1900

Giovanni Benaglia's Diary 1683. British Library.

Haralambos, K.M. *The Byerley Turk*, Three Centuries of the Tail Male Racing Lines. Kenilworth Press Ltd, 1990.

Helm, P.J. *Jeffreys*. Robert Hale, London, 1966.

Henning, B.D. *The Commons*, 1660-1690. Secker and Warburg, London, 1983.

Henty, G.A. *Orange and Green. A Tale of the Boyne and Limerick*. Preston Speed Publications, Pennsylvania, 2001.

Heper, M. *Historical Dictionary of Turkey*, 2nd edition: Scarecrow Press Inc. Maryland and London, 2002.

Historical Records of the British Army, prepared for publication under the direction of the Adjutant General. The 6th Regiment of Dragoon Guards or Carabineers. No author given, London, 1836.

Hurmuzaki,V. *Documente privitoré la istoria românilor*, Bucharest, 1885.

International League for the Protection of Horses: The Green Books. International Training. 1997-2000, (unpublished: reference only).

Jacobs, Richard. *Journal of the Siege and taking of Buda under the conduct of the Duke of Lorraine and his Electoral Highness the Duke of Bavaria. Anno Domini 1686*, Published by His Majesty's Command. Printed for Mr Gilliflower at the Black Spread Eagle in Westminster Hall, and J.Partridge at the Post House at Charing Cross, 1687.

James, J. *Debt of Honour*, The Story of the International League for the Protection of Horses, Macmillan, 1994

James, J, *Saddletramp* - From Ottoman Hills to Offa's Dyke, Pelham 1989: reprinted by Equine Travel Classics: The Long Riders' Guild Press, 2004

James, J. *Vagabond* - Through Eastern Europe on Horseback, Pelham, 1992, reprinted by Equine Travel Classics, The Long Riders' Guild Press, 2004.

Jones, G.F. Trevallyn, *Saw-Pit Wharton*. The Political Career from 1640 to 1691 of Philip, fourth Lord Wharton, Sydney University Press, 1967.

Kendall, G. *Notes on the Life of John Wootton*, with a list of Engravings and Pictures, Walpole Society, 1932-3.

Kinross, J. *The Boyne and Aughrim*, The Windrush Press, Gloucestershire, 1997.

Kinross, Lord. *The Ottoman Centuries*, Harper Collins, 1977.

Kluczycki Franciszek, *Pisma Do Wieku I Spraw Jana Sobieskiego*. Krakow, Nakladem Akagemi Krackow, 1881.

Koca, S. *The State Tradition and Organization among Ancient Turks*, The Turks, Vol.1, 2002.

Kostenko, L.T. *The Horses and Camels of Central Asia*. Simla. 1883.

Kropf, Lajos. *Historical Archive*, Municipal Szabó Ervin Library, Budapest, 1986.

Lachs, P.S: *The Diplomatic Corps under Charles II and James II*. Rutgers University Press, New Jersey. 1965.

Lawrence, John. *The Battle of Sedgemoor*, The Sedgemoor Preservation Society. Pamphlet. 1975.

L'Estrange, R. *The Reconquest of Buda in 1686*. A Relation by an Unknown Englishman.

L'Estrange, R. *Historical Description of the Glorious Conquest of the City of Buda*, London, 1686.

Lewis, S.A. *Topographical Dictionary of Ireland*, 1837. Gilbert and Rivington, Printers, St John's Square.

Le Bruyn, Corneille. *A Voyage to the Levant*, Translated into English by WJ, 1702.

Lenihan, P, (ed.) *Conquest and Resistance, War in Seventeenth Century Ireland*. Brill, 2001.

Loch, S. *The Royal Horse of Europe*, J.A Allen & Co Ltd., 1986.

Maguire, W.A. (ed). *Kings in Conflict*. The Revolutionary War in Ireland and Its Aftermath. 1689-1750. Blackstaff Press, Belfast. 1990.

MacLysaght. E. *Irish Life in the Seventeenth Century*, Talbot Press, Dublin.

Macaulay, Lord T.B. *The History of England*. Penguin Books, 1977.

Mansûr, Abdullah. *The Land of Uz*, Macmillan, London. 1911.

Malcolm, N. *Bosnia: A Short History*. Macmillan. 1994.

Marshall, J.D. (ed). *The Autobiography of William Stout of Lancaster, 1665-1752*, Barnes & Noble, New York, 1967.

McCracken, M. *The Spahis*. Hamish Hamilton, London, 1953.

McKay, D. *Prince Eugene of Savoy*, Thames and Hudson, London, 1977.

Meyer. A: *John Wootton, 1682-1764* Landscapes and Sporting Art in Early Georgian England. The Iveagh Bequest, Kenwood, Greater London Council, 1984.

Miles, W.J. and Lupton, J.I. *Modern Practical Farriery*. A Complete Guide to All That Relates to the Horse, Its History, Varieties, Uses etc. William Mackenzie, London, Glasgow and Edinburgh, 1868.

Millar, Sir Oliver *The Tudor, Stuart, and early Georgian Pictures in the Collection of Her Majesty the Queen*, 1963.

Millar, *The Life of James Fitz-James, Duke of Berwick*, Marshal, Duke and Peer of France, General of his Most Christian Majesty's Armies: London, Printed and sold for A Millar, at Buchanan's Head, over against St. Clement's Church, in the Strand.

Moody, T., Martin F.X., Byrne. F.J. *A New History of Ireland*. III. Early Modern Ireland. 1534-1691. Oxford University Press.

Murphey, R. *Ottoman Warfare 1500-1700*, Routledge, 1999.

Murtagh H and O'Dwyer M (eds) *Athlone Besieged*, eyewitness and other contemporary accounts of the sieges of Athlone in 1690 and 1691. Including Dean Story, Charles O'Kelly Jacobite Colonel, Robert Stearne, Williamite captain; Mort O'Brien, Jacobite officer; John Stevens, Jacobite Captain. Temple Printing Ltd, Old Athlone Society, 1991.

Newman, P.R. *Royalist Officers in England and Wales, 1642-1660*, A biographical Dictionary. Garland Publishing, New York and London, 1981.

Nicolle, D. *The Janissaries*, Osprey, 1995.

Nicolle, D. *Armies of the Ottoman Turks 1300-1774*, Osprey 1983.

O'Hart, J. *Irish Landed Gentry when Cromwell came to Ireland*. James Duffy, 1887

Ottoman Diplomacy in Hungary, letters from the Pashas of Buda, Alumni Cantabrigiensis.

Paget, Guy. *John Wootton, Father of English Sporting Painting, 1685-1765*, Apollo, 1944.

Pallis, A. *In the Days of the Janissaries*, Hutchinson, London, 1951.

Parkes, J. *Travel in England in the Seventeenth Century*, O.U.P., 1925.

Parkinson, E., *The City of Down from its Earliest Days*. Erskine Mayne, Belfast, 1928.

Parvev, Ivan. *Habsburgs and Ottomans Between Vienna and Belgrade (1683-1739)*, East European Monographs, Boulder, Columbia University Press, 1995.

Petrie, Sir Charles. (Bart.) *The Duke of Berwick and his Son*, Some Unpublished Papers. Eyre and Spottiswoode, London, 1951.

Pinkerton (ed.) *Travels of Sir John Chardin*, 1671.

Prior, C.M. *The Royal Studs of the Sixteenth and Seventeenth Centuries*. Horse and Hound Publications, 1935

Prior, C.M. *Early Records of the Thoroughbred Horse*. The Sportsman's Office, London, 1924.

PRO, Kew. *Dover Port Books*

Reresby, Sir John. *Memoirs of Sir John Reresby*, The Complete Text and a Selection from his letters, Edited with an introduction by Andrew Browning, Second Edition, London, Royal Historical Society, 1991.

Reese, M.M. *The Royal Office of Master of the Horse*. Threshold Books, 1976.

Relation of the Battle of the Boyne in Ireland, printed on April 11th 1700 for Thomas Cockerill, Poultrey. (Newspaper cutting.)

Richards, Jakab. *A Journal of the Siege and Taking of Buda by the Imperial Army* (under the conduct of the Duke of Lorrain and his Electoral Highness the Duke of Bavaria) [Transl. Erno Simonyi], M. Gilliflower & J. Partridge, London, 1687.

Richardson, Charles. *The English Turf: A Record of Horses and Courses*, Methuen, London, 1901.

Ridgeway, Sir William. *The Origin and Influence of the Thoroughbred Horse* with numerous illustrations, Cambridge University, 1905.

Rink, B. *The Centaur Legacy*, Long Riders' Guild Press, 2005.

Roberts, G. *Life, Progress and Revelations of James, Duke of Monmouth*.

Robertson, J.B. *Origin of the Thoroughbred*. Article in the Lonsdale Library on Flat Racing

Robertson, J.B. *The Origin & History of the British Thoroughbred Horse* - The Principles of Heredity applied to the Racehorse.

Rycaut, P. *The History of the Present State of the Ottoman Empire*, containing maxims of the Turkish Polity and Their Military Discipline, London, 1682.

Shaw, S. *History of the Ottoman Empire and Modern Turkey*, Volume 1: Empire of the Ghazis: The rise and Decline of the Ottoman Empire 1280-1808, Cambridge, London, New York and Melbourne, 1976.

Shirliyev, C. *The Divine Akhal Tekke Horse*, Türkmen Atlari, Dönlet birleşigi, Aşqabat, 2003.

Simms, J.G. *Jacobite Ireland 1685-1691*. Routledge and Kegan Paul, London, 1969.

Spielman, John. P. *Leopold I of Austria*. Thames and Hudson, London, 1977.

Sponenburg, Phillip. *Equine Color Genetics*, Iowa State University. 1996.

Stawell, J. *The Burford and Bibury Racecourses: a History*. (Pamphlet). Hindsight of Burford, 2000.

Steele, Sir Richard. *Memoirs of the life of the Most Noble Thomas late Marquess of Wharton*; With his speeches in Parliament both in England and Ireland. Printed for J Roberts in Warwickshire, 1715.

Stöller F. *Neue Quellen zur Geschichte des Türkernahres 1683*, 1933.

Stoye, J. *Marsigli's Europe, 1680-1730*, The Life and Times of Luigi Ferdinando Marsigli, Soldier and Virtuoso, Yale University Press, New Haven, 1994.

Stoye, J. *The Siege of Vienna*, Berlinn Press, Edinburgh, 2000.

Sumer, F. *Türkler'de Atcilik ve Binicilik, Türk Dünyasi Araştimalari*. Istanbul. 1893.

Surtees, Robert. *The History and Antiquities of the County Palatine of Durham*, John Nichols and Son, 1823.

Taaffe, Earl of Carlingford. *Taaffe's letters from the Imperial Camp to his brother the Lord Carlingford*, Being an Account of the Most Considerable Actions both before and at the Raising of the Siege of Vienna: With an Addition of two other Letters from a Young English Nobleman, a Voluntier in the Imperial Army, 1684

Tekeli, S. (ed). *Military Museum Collections*, Askeri Musee, Military Museum and Cultural Centre, Istanbul

The Turkish History, The Second Volume, Beginning from Mahomet III and Continued to the Present Year 1687. Sixth Edition. London, Printed for Robert Clavell, at the Peacock at the west-end of St. Paul's. 1687

Thompson, E.M. (ed.) *Letters of Humphrey Prideaux to John Ells*, Camden Society, 1875

Thorpe, P. *Full and True Account of the Remarkable Actions* and things that have happened in Northern Ireland since 15th November 1689 and the 7th inst. and The Seizure of the Commissary Shales, London, for Richard Baldwin in the Old Bailey, 1689.

Upton, R. *Newmarket and Arabia*, An Examination of the Descent of Racers and Coursers, Garnet Publishing, 2001.

Upton, R. *Travels in the Arabian Desert* C.K. Paul & Co., London, 1881.

Van Strien, C.D. *British Travellers in Holland during the Stuart Period*, E.J.Brill, Leiden, 1993.

Várkoni, A. *Vienna, Buda, Constantinople* Reprint from the New Hungarian Quarterly. Budapest. 1984.

Velkov, A., Radushev, E. *Ottoman Garrison on the Middle Danube*, Budapest, 1966.

Venn, J. and Venn J.A. *Alumni Cantabrigienses*, A biographical List of all known students, Graduates and Holders of Office at the University of Cambridge, from the earliest times to 1900, Cambridge, 1922.

Vernam, G. *Man on Horseback*, Harper and Row, New York, 1964

Vesey-Fitzgerald, (ed). *The Book of the Horse*, Nicholson and Watson 1946.

Walton, C. *History of the British Standing Army 1660-1700*, Harrison & Sons, London, 1894.

Wanklyn, C. *Lyme Regis, A Retrospect*. Humphries Publications, 1922.

Wentworth, Lady J.A.D. *Thoroughbred Racing Stock and it's Ancestors*, George Allen and Unwin, 1960.

Wilson, A. *St Patrick's Town*, Downpatrick Public Library.

Winstone, H.V.F. *Lady Anne Blunt, A Biography,* Barzan Publishing, 2003.

Wharton, T. *Memoirs of the Life of Thomas, Marquess of Wharton,* 1715.

Youatt, William. *The Horse: with a Treatise on Draught,* and copious index, Baldwin and Cradock, London, 1831.

You may also like to read:

Over the Farmer's Gate £12
Roger Evans
What is it really like being a farmer today? Roger Evans, active dairy
and poultry farmer for the last 45 years, tells it like it is, candidly and
with wonderful humour.

Hoof-beats through my Heart – *a life shared with horses* £7.99
David Edelsten
'Horses have been the signposts at crucial turnings in my life', writes
Edelsten in this compelling memoir of a diverse equestrian life.

And Miles to Go Before I Sleep – *a British Vet in Kenya* £8.99
Hugh Cran
A lively account of working as a vet in Kenya today, at the sharp end.

My Animals and Other Family – *a rural childhood 1937–1956* £16.99
Phyllida Barstow
'Phyllida and her siblings enjoyed a freedom that contrasts so sharply
with the lives of today's overprotected children.' – *BBC Countryfile*

The Racingman's Bedside Book £18.95
A winning anthology of the turf, including memorable pieces by
Evelyn Waugh, Philip Larkin and Jeffrey Bernard.

Available from Merlin Unwin Books, 7 Corve Street, Ludlow SY8 1DB
To order: Tel. 01584 877456 or www.merlinunwin.co.uk

About the author

Born in Kenya in 1949, educated at the Royal Agricultural College, Cirencester and University of Wales, Jeremy James spent most of his early life working with horses and cattle in Africa and the Middle East.

In 1987, he wrote his first book, *Saddletramp* which described his journey on horseback from Turkey to Wales. In 1990, he rode on horseback through the collapse of communism in Eastern Europe and wrote *Vagabond*. In the early 1990s he was Turkish correspondent for several broadsheets and magazines, and in 1992 was commissioned by the International League for the Protection of Horses to write their story in *Debt of Honour*. This work initially involved his dealing with Lipizzaner horses in the Balkan conflict and his subsequent management of Hergela Vucijak – the Bosnian State Stud.

During the late 1990s he worked as Senior Consultant for the ILPH on the campaign opposed to the long distance transport of live horses for slaughter, which brought him into contact with many of the disappearing horse breeds of Eurasia.

Jeremy lives in Ludlow, Shropshire, where he now writes full-time for his living.

Jacket photograph by Caroline Norris: the racehorse is *Definite Article*, acknowledged by Weatherby's as a direct descendant of the Byerley Turk. He is now a much sought-after stud at Yeomanstown & Morristown Lattin Stud, Co. Kildare, Ireland and one of his most famous progeny, at the time of writing this book, is *Vinnie Roe*, four times winner of the Irish St. Leger and second in the Melbourne Cup.

Background painting: *Fight over Turkish Standard* by Jozef Brandt, courtesy of National Museum, Krakow.

Jacket Design: Merlin Unwin